Social Movements and Organization Theory

Although the fields of organization theory and social movement theory have long been viewed as belonging to different worlds, recent events have intervened, reminding us that organizations are becoming more movement-like – more volatile and politicized – while movements are more likely to borrow strategies from organizations. Organization theory and social movement theory are two of the most vibrant areas within the social sciences. This collection of original essays and studies both calls for a closer connection between these fields and demonstrates the value of this interchange. Two introductory, programmatic essays by leading scholars in the two fields are followed by nine studies that directly illustrate the benefits of this type of cross-pollination and two closing essays. The studies variously examine the processes by which movements become organized and the role of movement processes within and among organizations. The topics covered range from globalization and transnational social movement organizations to community recycling programs.

Gerald F. Davis is Sparks/Whirlpool Corporation Research Professor and Chair of the Department of Management and Organizations at the University of Michigan Business School and Professor of Sociology at the University of Michigan. His work has appeared in a wide range of journals.

Doug McAdam is Director of the Center for Advanced Study in the Behavioral Sciences and Professor of Sociology at Stanford University. Among his best-known works are *Political Process and the Development of Black Insurgency, 1930–1970* (new edition 1999), and *Freedom Summer* (1988), which was awarded the 1990 C. Wright Mills Award.

W. Richard Scott is Professor Emeritus of Sociology at Stanford University. His most recent books are *Institutions and Organizations* (2nd edition 2001) and *Organizations: Rational, Natural, and Open Systems* (5th edition 2003).

Mayer N. Zald is Professor Emeritus of Sociology, Social Work and Business Administration at the University of Michigan. His books include *Organizational Change: The Political Economy of the YMCA* (1970) and *Comparative Perspectives on Social Movements* (1996, edited with Doug McAdam and John D. McCarthy).

Cambridge Studies in Contentious Politics

Editors

Jack A. Goldstone   *George Mason University*

Doug McAdam   *Stanford University and Center for Advanced Study in the Behavioral Sciences*

Sidney Tarrow   *Cornell University*

Charles Tilly   *Columbia University*

Elisabeth J. Wood   *Yale University*

Ronald Aminzade et al., *Silence and Voice in the Study of Contentious Politics*

Charles D. Brockett, *Political Movements and Violence in Central America*

Jack A. Goldstone, editor, *States, Parties, and Social Movements*

Doug McAdam, Sidney Tarrow, and Charles Tilly, *Dynamics of Contention*

Charles Tilly, *The Politics of Collective Violence*

Charles Tilly, *Contention and Democracy in Europe, 1650–2000*

Deborah Yashar, *Contesting Citizenship in Latin America: The Rise of Indigenous Movements and the Postliberal Challenge*

Social Movements and Organization Theory

Edited by

GERALD F. DAVIS

University of Michigan

DOUG McADAM

Stanford University

W. RICHARD SCOTT

Stanford University

MAYER N. ZALD

University of Michigan

CAMBRIDGE
UNIVERSITY PRESS

CAMBRIDGE UNIVERSITY PRESS
Cambridge, New York, Melbourne, Madrid, Cape Town, Singapore, São Paulo

Cambridge University Press
40 West 20th Street, New York, NY 10011-4211, USA

www.cambridge.org
Information on this title: www.cambridge.org/9780521839495

First published 2005

Printed in the United States of America

A catalog record for this publication is available from the British Library.

Library of Congress Cataloging in Publication Data

Social movements and organization theory / edited by Gerald Davis ... [et al.].
    p.   cm. – (Cambridge studies in contentious politics)
Includes bibliographical references and index.
ISBN 0-521-83949-1 (alk. paper) – ISBN 0-521-54836-5 (pbk. : alk. paper)
1. Social movements.   2. Political sociology.   3. Organization – Research.
I. Davis, Gerald Fredrick, 1961–.   II. Series.
HM881.S6293   2005
303.48′4 – dc22   2004051186

ISBN-13   978-0-521-83949-5 hardback
ISBN-10   0-521-83949-1 hardback

ISBN-13   978-0-521-54836-6 paperback
ISBN-10   0-521-54836-5 paperback

Contents

Contents

Contributors

Elizabeth A. Armstrong, Indiana University
John L. Campbell, Dartmouth College and Copenhagen Business School
Elisabeth S. Clemens, University of Chicago
W. E. Douglas Creed, University of Rhode Island
Gerald F. Davis, University of Michigan
Dong-Il Jung, Cornell University
Michael Lounsbury, Cornell University
Doug McAdam, Stanford University
John D. McCarthy, Pennsylvania State University
Calvin Morrill, University of California at Irvine
Hayagreeva Rao, Northwestern University
Marc Schneiberg, Reed College
W. Richard Scott, Stanford University
Maureen A. Scully, University of Massachusetts Boston
Jackie Smith, SUNY-Stony Brook
Sarah A. Soule, University of Arizona
David Strang, Cornell University
Timothy J. Vogus, Vanderbilt University
Mayer N. Zald, University of Michigan

Preface

Until very recently social scientists who studied complex or formal organizations and social scientists who studied collective action and social movements had little to do with each other and seemed to have little in common. Students of complex organizations such as corporations, government agencies, and the larger nonprofit organizations studied organizations that were large and had relatively clear boundaries, bureaucratic and formal procedures, and fairly well defined authority structures. By contrast, social movements and collective action were characterized as more spontaneous, fluid, and unorganized. To the extent that organizations played any role in social movements, they were thought to be small, ephemeral, and resource poor. Moreover, leaders of movements and collective action depended upon charisma and rhetoric, not formal-legal authority, to induce participation in their followers.

On both sides some early theorists and studies suggested that the sharp division of the fields of study overdrew the differences. Robert Michels's study of political parties (1962 [1911]) showed how parties that originated in social movements developed formal organization and authority structures that resembled those found in bureaucracies. Michels's "iron law of oligarchy" may have been overstated, but it nicely captured the transformation of what had been participatory and less bureaucratic organizations into formal organizations with hierarchic and self-reproducing authority structures. Social movements and collective action events that endure for any length of time are likely to develop some formal mechanisms for coordinating action and develop social movement organizations that are amenable to organizational analysis.

On the other side, at least since the development of the human relations approach to organizational behavior, sociologists and social psychologists have studied the extent to which a focus upon the formal structure of organizations ignores the informal processes that structure member interaction, and out of which informal leaders, coalitions, and conflict relationships develop. In short, internally formal organizations would seem to exhibit emergent features and mobilization processes very similar to those we see in social movement groups. Similarly, in their external relations, formal organizations also would seem to mirror their movement counterparts, participating, as they do, in fluid relationships with other organizations, joining in coalitions, and engaging in political action to affect state policy. Thus, they engage in political and mobilization processes that resemble those studied by social movement scholars. Still, until very recently, few scholars have bridged these areas of study.

Developments in the wider society and in scholarship have made it clear that the time is ripe to break down the barriers between these two fields. This volume and the conferences that preceded it represent our attempt both to create a network of movement and organization scholars and to show the advantages of applying social movement metaphors, concepts, and theories to things organizational and the utility of using theories and concepts developed in organizational study to inform research on social movements and collective action. After a theoretically oriented pair of introductory chapters that stake out the terrain, this book seeks to show concrete research consequences exemplifying the kind of crossover we have argued for. One purpose of the book is to show how concepts developed in one of the domains (organization theory or social movement theory) are useful for the other. For example, theorists of organizations have contemplated alternative structures for organizations with many subunits that are geographically dispersed, and when and why they work as they do. Chapters on social movement "franchising" (by McCarthy) and on transnational social movement organizations (by Smith) document how these concepts help illuminate relatively new organizational forms in the social movement sector. Conversely, social movement scholars have described movement/countermovement dynamics during struggles over policy, which provides an enlightening framework for analyzing the struggles among the "shareholder rights movement" and more-or-less organized corporate elites over state-level corporate law (in the chapter by Vogus and Davis).

These chapters continue a tradition initiated by the article by Zald and Berger (1978) on movements within organizations. But the years since this paper was published have seen great advances in theory and methods in both organizational studies and social movement studies. Social network analysis and dynamic statistical methods, for instance, have greatly expanded the empirical sophistication and rigor of both areas and have enabled more subtle (and testable) cross-level theorizing. Thus, although we have argued that the current period is especially characterized by examples of crossover, the theory and research we present are useful to explain phenomena from earlier times. The authors of the chapters have been particularly attentive to highlighting the added value of the combined approach.

Organization of the Book

We organize the book into five main sections. The introductory section lays out the case for convergence by showing the value of a common field-level approach and the centrality of social mechanisms for constructing cross-domain theory. The next section, "Political and Mobilization Context," highlights the multilevel nature of movement activity and describes how political contests play out in nested systems. The prototypical study of social movements involves struggles between "elites" with privileged access to state power and "challengers" with limited access to formalized channels for political change. Yet within the United States, and in a global economy, states are nested within higher-level jurisdictions, and themselves contain important political subdivisions, and there may be multiple authorities responsible for particular issues. The four chapters in this section use a diffusion framework to examine struggles at the level of the American states and document how elites, challengers, and state authorities in one locale are embedded in larger systems that shape structural and political outcomes. State laws, for instance, are deeply influenced by what laws in other states look like and what is happening at the federal level; to examine states in isolation misses the multilevel dynamics that shape movement outcomes.

Section III, "Social Movement Organizations: Form and Structure," uses theory about nontraditional organizational forms – franchise organizations and transnational firms – to examine dispersed multiunit social movement organizations. While the prototypical social movement organization might be envisioned as the homespun formalization of a singular grassroots movement, contemporary movement organizations often seem to have absorbed the organizational logic of the corporate sector, in which economies of scale and the efficiencies available through contracting out have shaped the kinds of organizational structures observed. Most movement activities, from recruitment and fund raising to lobbying legislators, can be contracted out, and thus a "movement organization" may be little more than a part-time staffer with a fax machine – much like the "hollow corporations" enabled by the elaboration of a specialized business services sector (Davis and McAdam 2000). But the same technologies enable the development of both corporations and movement organizations with a much wider geographic reach, and the chapters in this section theorize the parallels in organization forms adopted by franchised movement organizations (such as Mothers Against Drunk Driving) and transnational social movement organizations.

The following section, "Movements Penetrating Organizations," picks up the theme of organizations as polities harboring internal social movements. With the articulation of firms as analogs of nation-states, employing "citizens" that possess rights, the application of the techniques of social movements to organizational change followed directly. Social movements do not stop at the factory gate: they have their impacts in the office and on the shop floor, in the expectations and demands of those who work in organizations, and in the policies adopted by firms. Movements likewise take place within organizations, as small-scale mobilizations aimed at challenging the status quo parallel their society-wide counterparts. Moreover, the generic tactics of change-oriented collective action turn out to be tools that can be appropriated for top-down as well as grassroots change within organizations. The chapters in this section describe how movements in the larger world influence organizations and how internal social movements arise from above or below, and how they have their effect.

The fifth and final section contains two concluding essays. The first places the convergence of the study of organizations and movements into larger historical shifts in social organization and social theory and suggests areas for future research, while the second assesses what the studies reported in the book say about the value of and prospects for joining the study of social movements and organization theory.

Acknowledgments

Our attempt to bridge the organization/social movement divide goes back more than a decade. McCarthy, McAdam, and Zald, along with Woody

Powell and Neil Fligstein, wrote a short proposal for a conference in 1989. A few years later Zald asked ICOS (the Interdisciplinary Committee on Organizational Studies at Michigan) for funding for a conference on this topic. It was turned down. Davis and McAdam got together at the Center for Advanced Study in the Behavioral Sciences in 1998 and wrote a paper (2000) that showed how the two fields complemented each other. Later, after McAdam took a position at Stanford, he and Dick Scott began to work through the commonalities and differences in emphases of the fields. In 2000 Davis and Zald received funding from ICOS to hold two conferences on organizations and movements at Michigan in 2001 and 2002.

The first gathering was a "get acquainted" conference. A group of scholars were invited who were known to have some interests in the intersect. Some of them had been most active in the study of social movements and came out of a resource mobilization and political process theory background. Others came out of an organizational studies background, especially in neoinstitutional theory and in population ecology. They varied in whether they were more "micro" or "macro" and in their methodological commitments. The conference was loose in its structure; some sessions were devoted to idea sharing, while others were devoted to rough paper outlines.

The second conference, held in May 2002, included most of the participants in the first conference and several others especially recruited because they were doing exciting work in areas not well represented at the first gathering. This volume includes revised versions of the papers presented at the second conference as well as two others commissioned to effect an overall integration of the selections. At the risk of being immodest, we think the volume fulfills its "agenda-setting" mission and amply demonstrates the great benefits to be gained from ongoing collaboration between organization and social movement scholars. Let the conversation continue.

We close with several heartfelt acknowledgments. We begin, appropriately, with our enormous debt to ICOS. Quite simply, without its financial and institutional support, this project would not have been possible. But beyond its crucial role in this effort, ICOS provides a home for interdisciplinary and interschool collaboration about organizational studies possibly unmatched at any university in the country. Besides ICOS, we also received substantial financial support from the University of Michigan Business School, from the Horace H. Rackham School of Graduate Studies, from the Office of the Vice President for Research at Michigan, and, finally, from the economic sociology program of the Social Science Research Council. We are grateful to all of these sponsors. We are also greatly indebted to Pat Preston for expert editing and Mary Sinkewiz for superb coordination of the manuscript through its long gestation.

Gerald. F. Davis
Doug McAdam
W. Richard Scott
Mayer N. Zald

Creating a Common Framework

A ssume for the moment that you are convinced that these two fields of scholarship – the study of social movements and organization theory – can be usefully brought to bear on each other; that theories, concepts, and problems raised in one of the areas can be usefully used to focus on issues that are less prominently featured in the other area. How does one do that? Are there intellectual strategies for synthesizing and integrating somewhat disparate fields? One strategy, which no one in this volume attempts, would be to subsume both objects of analysis, organizations and social movements, within a larger or more abstract theory or framework of analysis. For instance, one could show how both social movements and organizations can be analyzed in the language of a general theory of action or of social systems. Another approach, which is in fact adopted by most of the authors of the chapters in Sections II to V, is to begin with a fairly concrete problem or issue in one or the other of the domains, and to seek guidance for understanding in the literature of the other or related domains.

To take one example, in Chapter 10 David Strang and Dong-Il Jung ask the question of how they can account for the adoption of innovations related to the movement for Total Quality Management (TQM) in a large corporation. They want to understand how and why employee attitudes develop in the way that they do; why there is so much cynicism or skepticism; why there is so little institutionalization of TQM practices. They find that thinking about the adoption of these practices as part of an elite-sponsored social movement within the organization and nested in a larger social movement in modern industry gives them substantial purchase on the issue. To take another example of applying a concept or mode of thinking from one area to another, John D. McCarthy (Chapter 7) employs the concept of "franchising" – well developed in the organizational study of

1

the replication of units of corporations such as McDonald's or Marriott Hotels – to think about the reproduction of chapters or local social movement organizations (SMOs) based on national movement models or templates. McCarthy uses the spread of chapters of Mothers Against Drunk Driving across the United States to illustrate the perspective.

A third intellectual approach is to systematically survey some of the main developments and concepts in each area and ask two related questions: how much commonality is there in some of the major theories or approaches as they have developed in recent times, and how can the differences in the fields be usefully imported to their neighbor? The two essays in Section I attempt to answer these questions.

"Organizations and Movements," by Doug McAdam and W. Richard Scott, and "Where Do We Stand? Common Mechanisms in Organizations and Social Movement Research," by John L. Campbell, are overviews of the convergences and divergences of the two fields of studies. McAdam and Scott note that organizational studies and social movements have been two of the most active and creative areas of scholarship during the past few decades but, with some exceptions, have moved in different directions. Organizational studies focused on formal units governed by institutionalized authority; social movements on emergent processes aimed at challenging and destabilizing established organizations and/or institutions. They note that in recent times a number of commonalities have emerged. For instance, both fields have begun to emphasize analyses of the context of organizations and social movements. In the case of organizational studies, analyses have shifted to institutional logics and the institutional fields in which organizations are embedded. In the case of social movements, the dominant focus has been on the role of the broader political environment in shaping the emergence and development of movements. Building on their understanding of the developing commonalities, Scott and McAdam construct a conceptual framework that allows scholars to view the two bodies of work not as competing but as complementary. The utility of the framework is demonstrated by a reexamination (by Scott) of changes in the U.S. health care sector and (by McAdam) of the phases of the U.S. civil rights revolution.

John Campbell takes a somewhat different tack on the question of the overlap of the fields. This chapter shows that in important respects these two literatures have already developed striking similarities. Many of the similarities have to do with how organization theorists and social movement theorists study social change. First, much organization theory is concerned with

2

explaining how organizational practices evolve in path-dependent ways. Similarly, social movement scholars discuss how the already existing repertoires and tool kits inherited from the past contribute to the evolution of movement structures and strategies. Second, the social movements literature stresses the importance of issue framing as critical to movement success. Recently, organizational analysis does too. Third, organizational theorists have sought to explain how different practices diffuse within organizational populations. Social movement scholars have adopted a diffusion approach to map, for example, how social movements develop and disseminate programs and strategies through networks of activists. Fourth, organization theory suggests that the regulatory, normative, and cognitive dimensions of institutions affect how organizations develop. Thus, organizations are embedded in institutions. Research has also demonstrated that cognitive structures limit the range of practices that social movement activists can imagine; normative structures limit what is considered appropriate movement practice; and regulatory structures limit the range of practices that movements pursue. Fifth, the social movements literature has been concerned with how states spark, repress, and channel movement activity in one direction or another. Organizational theorists have made similar arguments about organizational change. For instance, different types of political arrangements (liberal, statist, corporatist) affect how business is organized just as they affect how social movements are structured. Finally, much organizational theory is devoted to identifying the conditions under which different organizational forms, such as decentralized networks or centralized hierarchies, emerge. The same is true for social movement theory, which specifies the conditions under which social movements become centralized or decentralized. The point is, Campbell argues, these two literatures have already developed serendipitously along parallel tracks that, if fully appreciated and exploited, could provide the basis for mutually beneficial cross-fertilization.

1

Organizations and Movements

Doug McAdam and W. Richard Scott

Introduction

There is little question that two of the most active and creative arenas of scholarly activity in the social sciences during the past four decades have been organizational studies (OS) and social movement analysis (SM). Both have been intellectually lively and vigorous in spite of the fact that scholars in both camps began their projects during the early 1960s on relatively barren soil. Students of OS took up their labors alongside the remnants of scientific management, their human relations critics, and scattered studies of bureaucratic behavior. SM scholars were surrounded by earlier empirical work on rumors, panics, crowds, and mobs together with a "smorgasbord" of theoretical perspectives, including the collective behavior, mass society, and relative deprivation approaches (McAdam, McCarthy, and Zald 1988: 695). In both situations, prior work provided scant theoretical coherence and little basis for optimism. Moreover, in this early period no connection existed or, indeed, seemed possible between the two fields since the former concentrated on instrumental, organized behavior while the latter's focus was on "spontaneous, unorganized, and unstructured phenomena" (Morris 2000: 445).

OS began to gain traction with the recognition of the importance of the wider environment, first material resource and technical features, then political, and, more recently, institutional and cultural forces. Open systems conceptions breathed new life into a field too long wedded to concerns of internal administrative design, leadership, and work group cohesion. SM studies also began to revive because of increased recognition of the environment – not just as contexts breeding alienation or a sense of deprivation, but as the source of resources, including movement members and allies – as a locus of opportunities as well as constraints. In addition, SM scholars increasingly came to recognize the importance of organizations and organizing processes. Resources must be mobilized and momentum maintained for movements to be successful, and both tasks require instrumental activities and coordination of effort: in short, organization.

Since the onset of the modern period, then, both fields have flourished and there has been some interchange and learning. The learning to date, however, has been largely uni-directional. SM scholars have been able to productively borrow and adapt organizational ideas to their own uses; OS scholars have been far less opportunistic in taking advantage of movement ideas. (We detail this imbalance below.) Recent developments in each field, to our eyes, suggest a pattern of complementary strengths and weaknesses. If this is the case, then increased interaction of the two sets of scholars, with heightened collaboration and diffusion/adaption of ideas and methods, should be especially beneficial.

Today, as we ease into a new century, we see signs of increased interest and interaction among participants in the two fields. We seek to encourage this interchange and to help insure that the ideas flow in both directions. Both of us believe that the most interesting problems and greatest advances in the sciences often take place at the intersection of established fields of study.

In section I of this chapter, we outline in broad strokes the development of the two areas, paying particular attention to weaknesses in one field that might be redressed by insights from the other, and we begin to sketcha general analytic framework that draws on recent work from both fields of study. In section II, we pursue the development of concepts designed to move from an organization or movement focus to an organizational field approach and from a static to a more dynamic examination of change processes linking movements and organizations.

In section III, we illustrate the power and generality – and, inevitably, no doubt point up the limitations – of our schema by applying it to two "cases" on which each of us has previously worked. The first case involves contention over changes in health care delivery and financing during the period 1945–95, a situation that Scott and colleagues have studied (Scott, Ruef, Mendel, and Caronna 2000). The second case involves contention over civil rights during the period 1946–70, a set of developments that McAdam has examined (McAdam 1982–1999). Both cases occurred in the same country, the United States, and in the same general historical period, but beyond that they differ in many ways, as our analysis attempts to make clear. If the framework can be helpful in examining these varied situations, it is likely to find applications to other times and places.

Two Bodies of Work

No attempt will be made to provide detailed overviews of what have become two substantial, diverse literatures. Rather, our brief review is intended to identify broad trends as well as lacunae or weaknesses in each area that might be addressed by strengths and insights in the other. We conclude this section by noting some recent signs of convergence.

Social Movements

Beginning in the mid-1960s, a group of young scholars, including Gamson, Tilly, and Zald, began to formulate more explicit organizational and political arguments to account for social unrest, converting the earlier focus on "collective behavior" to one on "collective action," "social movements," and, even, "social movement organizations" (Gamson 1968, 1975; Tilly and Rule 1965; Zald and Ash 1966). Some of this work usefully built on a theoretical perspective spearheaded by the early OS scholar Philip Selznick (1948, 1952), that employed an institutional perspective to examine the ways in which tensions between value commitments and survival concerns shaped the development of an organization (e.g., Zald and Denton 1963). SM scholars reframed the view of protest and reform activities from one of irrational behavior – a flailing out against an unjust universe – to one involving instrumental action. Rather than stressing common grievances, SM theorists focused attention on mechanisms of mobilization and opportunities to seek redress. While sharing broad similarities, two somewhat divergent approaches gradually emerged.

Zald and colleagues, in crafting their *resource mobilization* perspective, privileged organizational structures and processes (Zald and McCarthy 1987). Drawing on developments in OS, these theorists stressed that movements, if they are to be sustained for any length of time, require some form of organization: leadership, administrative structure, incentives for participation, and a means for acquiring resources and support. Embracing an open systems perspective, the importance of the organization's relation to its environment – social, economic, political – was underscored. Following the early lead of Michels, analysts were sensitive to the contradictory and complex relation between organizing and bureaucratizing processes and retaining ideological commitments (McCarthy and Zald 1977). More so than in mainstream OS, this work stressed the central role of power and politics, both within the organization and in its relation to the environment (Gamson 1975; Zald and Berger 1978).

A complementary *political process* perspective was pursued by Tilly and his associates. Though probably best known for its stress on shifting "political opportunities" (and constraints), this "external" focus on the political environment was always joined with an "internal" analysis of the "critical role of various grassroots settings – work and neighborhood, in particular – in facilitating and structuring collective action" (McAdam, McCarthy, and Zald 1996: 4). In many situations, the seedbed of collective action is to be found in preexisting social arrangements that provide social capital critical to the success of early mobilizing processes when warmed by the sunlight of environmental opportunities that allow members to exploit their capital (Tilly 1978; Tilly, Tilly, and Tilly 1975).

Organizational Studies

Foundational work by Simon (1945) and March and Simon (1958) provided important building blocks in identifying the structures and processes that undergird "rational" decision making, supporting the systematic collective pursuit of specified goals. The differences between organizations and other, "nonrational," collectivities were stressed. This seminal micro *administrative behavior* approach was soon joined by a number of more macro perspectives emphasizing the relation of the organization to its environment. An early and still widely employed modern, macro perspective on organizations, *contingency theory*, emerged in the mid-1960s as a guide for research on the adaptation of organizations to their environments (Lawrence and Lorsch 1967; Thompson 1967). Organizations that were better able to match their structural features to the distinctive demands of their environments were expected to be more successful. Contingency theory continued to focus on those organizational features and processes that were thought to be most distinctive to organizations, allowing them to serve as rationally constructed collective instruments for goal attainment.

Within a decade, however, a number of alternative theoretical perspectives were developed – we focus on developments at the macro level – that shifted attention to less rational, more "natural" political and cultural conceptions of organizations. The *organizational ecology* perspective, applied primarily at the population level of analysis, resembled contingency theory in its focus on the material resource environment. However, emphasis shifted to organizational survival, rather than efficiency or effectiveness, with analysts expressing skepticism regarding any straightforward linkage between performance and persistence (Aldrich 1979; Hannan and Freeman 1977). *Resource dependence* (Pfeffer and Salancik 1978) and *conflict theory* (Collins 1975; Clegg and Dunkerley 1977) directly challenged rationality-based conceptions of organizational design and operation, arguing instead the central role played by power. Resource dependence theorists directed attention to the political implications of asymmetric exchange processes while conflict theorists resurrected and refurbished Marxist arguments viewing organizations as fundamentally structures of dominance and exploitation. *Neoinstitutional theory* (Meyer and Rowan 1977; DiMaggio and Powell 1983) emerged during the same period, calling attention to the role of wider cultural and normative frameworks in giving rise to and in sustaining organizations. These theorists asserted that organizations are evaluated in terms of their "social fitness" as well as their performance: legitimacy and accountability are as important as, if not more so than, reliability and efficiency.

In sum, OS experienced a highly creative period during the past four decades, which witnessed the development and testing of several somewhat conflicting, somewhat complementary theoretical perspectives. Rational system models were joined and challenged by political and cultural models; but all embraced open systems assumptions (Scott 2003). The general trend in theoretical frameworks and research designs has been both up and out: "up" to encompass wider levels of analysis and "out" to incorporate more facets of the environment.

Complementary Strengths and Weaknesses

Even this brief review begins to showcase some of the obvious strengths of past theoretical work in the two areas and to suggest important differences. (See Table 1.1.) First, many SM theorists had the perspicacity to embrace OS concepts and arguments fairly early and adapt them for use in their own theories. But, in doing so, they retained their distinctive focus on social process. They have given particular attention to such phenomena as the mobilization of people and resources, the construction and reconstruction of purposes and identities, the building of alliances, and the crafting of ideologies and cultural frames to support and sustain collective action. By contrast, OS scholars have devoted more attention to structure, including both informal and formal – but with increasing attention to the latter – within

Table 1.1. *Complementary Strengths and Weaknesses*

Organizational Studies	Social Movements
Structure	Process
Established organizations	Emergent organizations
Organization field	Movement-centric
Institutionalized authority	Transgressive contention
Localized regimes (sectors)	Societal regimes

as well as among organizations. While there are important exceptions that feature process approaches – for example, case studies such as those of Selznick (1949), Blau (1955), and Barley (1986); change-oriented analyses such as those by Fligstein (1990), Pettigrew and Whipp (1991), and Van de Ven et al. (1999); and ecological and evolutionary studies such as Hannan and Freeman (1989), Baum and Singh (1994), and Aldrich (1999) – the vast majority of OS works up to the present focus on structure. More so than their SM counterparts, OS scholars have emphasized organizations over organizing, structure over process.

A closely related difference pertains to the origins of organizations. Only very recently have OS students concerned themselves with the creation of organizations – with entrepreneurship and organizational "genetics" (see Aldrich 1999; Suchman forthcoming; Thornton 1999). SM scholars, in contrast, have spent much time and effort attempting to discern the conditions under which new (movement) organizations arise and do or do not succeed in gaining sufficient mass and momentum to survive and flourish.

A third difference pertains to the scope or level of analysis employed by the two sets of scholars. Although there are important exceptions, most SM scholars have been relentlessly movement-centric in their research designs, focusing either on a single movement organization – for example, the Knights of Labor (Voss 1993) – or on organizations of the same type (an organizational population), such as chapters of Mothers Against Drunk Driving (McCarthy et al. 1988). Even though McCarthy and Zald (1977) were quick to appropriate the concept of *industry* (or organizational field) from OS, they and others have generally employed it to examine the effects of other, alternative and rival, movements on a focal movement organization and population rather than consider the industry or field itself as the subject of analysis. Exceptions to this generalization include McAdam's (1982–1999) study of the civil rights movement, which included an examination of the major movement organizations and their sources of resistance and support, and Clemens's (1996) analysis of the alternative forms utilized by groups active in the American labor movement during the period 1880–1920.

While OS scholars have conducted many studies of individual organizations and organizational populations, they also in recent years have expanded their concern to the industry or organizational field level. In this respect, the concept of *organizational field* developed by OS students represents a valuable new analytic lens. As defined by DiMaggio and Powell (1983: 148), a field refers to

those organizations that, in the aggregate, constitute a recognized area of institutional life: key suppliers, resource and product consumers, regulatory agencies, and other organizations that produce similar services and products.

(See also Scott and Meyer 1983; Scott 1994a.) The concept of field identifies an arena – a system of actors, actions, and relations – whose participants take one another into account as they carry out interrelated activities. Rather than focusing on a single organization or movement, or even a single type of organization or movement (population), it allows us to view these actors in context. Representative studies include DiMaggio's (1991) analysis of the high culture field of art museums, Fligstein's (1990) study of the transformation of corporate forms in the United States during the twentieth century, and Dezalay and Garth's (1996) examination of the emergence of an institutional framework for transnational commercial arbitration.

A fourth difference pertains to the treatment of power in the two literatures. SM scholars have from the outset emphasized the crucial role of power and politics in social life. These studies are replete with discussions of activists, bloodshed, conflicts, contentious uprisings, challenges to authority, polarization, rallies, repression, riots, sit-ins, strikes, and tactics. For their part, thanks to the enduring legacy of Max Weber and Karl Marx, OS scholars also recognize that organizations are systems of domination, so that issues of centralized decision making and control loom large. However, with only a few exceptions – for example, scholars such as Clegg and Dunkerley (1980), Perrow (1986), and Pfeffer (1981; 1992) – OS students have opted for the Weberian rather than the Marxist framing. Their subject has been institutionalized power: power coded into structural designs and bolstered by widely shared cultural norms and ideologies. They have attended less to the ways in which power in and among organizations operates in unintended or unconventional ways to challenge or change existing structures.

In general, the benign frameworks of administration and management – of authority, technology, and rational design – or those of institutionalists – of taken-for-granted beliefs, normative systems, and entrenched routines – have trumped naked power and politics in OS.

Thus, while both camps attend to power, they focus on different aspects of power, on different moments of power processes. SM scholars have tended to limit their purview to what McAdam, Tarrow, and Tilly (2001) term "transgressive contention" – change efforts that require the conscious mobilization of marginalized or disenfranchised elements. By contrast, OS students have largely restricted their attention to "prescribed politics" (McAdam 1999), involving the activation and reproduction of institutionalized authority.

One final difference between the two scholarly areas can be identified. While SM students have focused on incipient or nascent power to the neglect of established power, they somewhat paradoxically have concentrated on collective action aimed at influencing official governmental policies and systems – the authoritative structures of public order – to the neglect of more localized and specialized regimes. Their preferred subjects of study have been broad, society-wide movements aimed at affecting politics with a capital "P." OS students have been more willing to examine the operation of governance activities and structures that are targeted to specific sectors of the polity involving more delimited policies and players, such as professional and trade associations. Wholey and Sanchez (1991: 743) develop a closely related distinction, differentiating between "social" and "economic" regulation. Social regulation pertains to governmental policies that "cut across industries," affecting all workers, the environment, civil rights. Economic regulation tends to be "industry specific, focusing on market structure and firm conduct within markets." SM theorists have focused their studies on movements aimed at influencing social regulatory policies; OS scholars have emphasized forces and factors affecting economic regulation. We view this distinction as congruent with our own but slightly narrower, since its exclusive concern is governmental policies. We, of course, attend to governmental policies, but also to the actions of what Selznick (1969) has termed "private governments": organizations and associations that are empowered to exercise governance functions in specified arenas – for example, professional or trade associations.

In sum, OS and SM arrived on the scene at about the same time, but have tended to go their own ways, rather like twins separated at birth. As

11

summarized in Table 1.1, OS has concentrated on stability, SM on change; OS on existing forms, SM on emerging forms; OS on prescribed politics, SM on contentious politics; OS on sector-specific, SM on society-wide systems. Finally, OS has been more hospitable to employing field-level approaches while SM has favored movement-centric models aimed at affecting national policies.

Looking Forward

Our objective in this review is not to diminish past efforts or to take sides but, drawing on the strengths of each camp, to discern promising directions for future work. Learning from the SM scholars, we are convinced that future approaches will benefit from embracing a process framework. Studies of structure need to be augmented by greater attention to structuration. Learning from OS scholars, we believe that the organizational field level represents a particularly promising vantage point from which to view organization change. If treated longitudinally, the field level is particularly hospitable to the study of dynamic systems. As the boundaries of single organizations (including movements) and organizational populations become more blurred and permeable, as new forms arise and as new linkages are forged between existing forms, a field-level conception becomes indispensable to tracing the complexities of contemporary changes.

Rather than choosing between the other two dimensions – established versus emergent power and society-wide versus sector-specific arenas – we prefer to propose a framework that encompasses both. If we cross-classify them, we can characterize in broad strokes the fundamental division of labor that has developed between OS and SM scholars. (See Figure 1.1.) Generally speaking, OS analysts have concentrated their energies in quadrant 1: the study of established organizational forms operating in specialized sectors or arenas, such as education or the automobile industry. For their part, SM scholars have focused primarily on quadrant 4: the study of emergent and challenging social movement organizations targeting society-wide concerns, such as women's or worker's rights. What of the two remaining quadrants? Quadrant 2, established society-wide governance structures, would seem to be more the realm of general and political sociologists, although SM theorists must take these systems into account, as context, since they provide the background of opportunity and constraint for any social

Scope of Inquiry

		Sector-specific	*Society-wide*
Organizational Focus	*Established Organizations*	1. Organization studies e.g., education, health care	2. Industrial and postindustrial studies e.g., corporate networks
	Emergent Organizations	3. New industries e.g., biotechnology	4. Social movements e.g., civil rights, womens' rights

Figure 1.1 Division of Labor: Focus and Scope

movement. Quadrant 3, emergent industries, has received relatively little attention until recently but is currently a growth area in OS and economic sociology, as detailed below.

This division of labor appears to be serviceable enough although, on reflection, it can be seen to be too tidy and overly simplified. First, societal sectors and broader societies are not airtight containers, but interdependent and interpenetrated. A social movement originating in a specialized arena – for example, consumer safety concerns in the automobile industry – can be generalized as consumer rights and diffuse into other specialized sectors as well as national debates. Second, all the quadrants are composed of both established and emergent organizational forms, although their numbers and influence will vary greatly over time. The so-called established arenas – whether entire societies or sectors such as health care services – can undergo fundamental change, as prevailing conventions are questioned and entrenched interests challenged. In such situations, attending to the structure and actions of both established and emergent players is critical to understanding subsequent processes and outcomes. Relatedly, it is wrong to concentrate on either contentious or prescribed politics as if they were mutually exclusive. Transgressive contention occurs in established organizational settings, as Zald and Berger (1978) have insisted. And social movement organizations clearly confront and themselves utilize prescribed politics. In short, OM scholars need to be more attuned to the suppressed or emergent forces at work while OS scholars, for their part, need to be sensitive to the actions and reactions of established organizations as well as to the increasing institutionalization of power within SM organizations. And, of equal importance, may there not be other types of power processes, currently overlooked or understudied, that would be illuminated if the lenses of SM and OS scholars were employed in combination?

Returning to Figure 1.1, and focusing on those quadrants that do not represent the natural territories of either SM or OS scholars, there has been promising recent work in both quadrants 2 and 3. A number of scholars have drawn freely on both organizational and movement ideas to consider organizational change at the societal level (quadrant 2). Important studies by Fligstein (1990), Davis and colleagues (Davis and Greve 1997; Davis and Robbins 2005), and Palmer and colleagues (Palmer, Jennings and Zhou 1993; Palmer and Barber 2001), among others, depict changes over time in the structural forms and strategies pursued by major American corporations as a consequence of contests between owners and various breeds of managers, the networks in which they embedded, and shifting norms and cognitive models. These studies all focus on the largest U.S. corporations, treating them as a single, society-wide organizational field. As for quadrant 3, a growing number of organizational scholars – primarily evolutionary and institutional sociologists – have examined the multiple forces at work – technological, economic, political, institutional – in creating and sustaining a new type of product or a new industry. (See Aldrich and Fiol 1994; Powell 1999; Suchman, forthcoming; Van de Ven et al. 1999.) All of this work recognizes the importance of both established and challenging actors with their contending interests, as well as established and challenging ideas and norms that inform, motivate, and constrain action.

We applaud this work and can learn from it, but our primary interest is in strengthening research in the more conventional areas of OS and SM – quadrants 1 and 4. It is our hope, then, that these two research arenas can be combined – or, at least, brought into closer juxtaposition enabling more productive intercourse between the two fields. Our aim is to begin to craft a broader and stronger foundation for describing and explaining organizationally mediated social change processes in modern societies.

Constructing a Framework

To illustrate and advance a growing convergence between OS and SM scholarship, we draw on our own recent writings, which, we believe, exhibit surprising and promising synergies and parallels. We begin with the framework proposed by Scott and colleagues, then turn to review a parallel

14

effort by McAdam, McCarthy, and Zald. The two schemas were developed at about the same time, but were independently conceived.

In an attempt to develop a framework to guide the comparative and longitudinal study of institutional change in U.S. health care systems, Scott and colleagues (Scott et al. 2000) differentiated among three components of institutions:

- *Institutional Actors* – (both individual and collective) that "create (produce) and embody and enact (reproduce) the logics of the field" (p. 172)

Actors serve both as *agents*, who are capable of exercising power to affect and alter events and rule systems, and as *carriers*, who embody and reflect existing norms and beliefs.

- *Institutional Logics* – the "belief systems and associated practices that predominate in an organizational field" (p. 170)

As Friedland and Alford (1991, p. 248) note, institutional logics provide the "organizing principles" supplying practice guidelines for field participants. It is possible and useful to identify dominant logics that reflect the consensus of powerful actors as well as secondary and/or repressed logics representing other, subordinated or emergent interests.

- *Governance Structures* – "all those arrangements by which field-level power and authority are exercised involving, variously, formal and informal systems, public and private auspices, regulative and normative mechanisms" (Scott et al. 2000: 173)

"Jurisdiction has not only a culture, but also a social structure," as Abbott (1988:59) has pointed out. Some of the most interesting recent work in political sociology has explored the wide variety of governance structures at work at the level of societal sectors or organizational fields. (See, e.g., Streeck and Schmitter 1985; Campbell, Hollingsworth, and Lindberg 1991.)

Scott and colleagues view institutions as being comprised of these components, and, as we detail below, gathered data on each as a way of assessing change processes linking institutional arrangements and organizational systems. Unbeknown to them, SM scholars had constructed earlier a remarkably comparable framework to guide comparative research on social movements. McAdam, McCarthy, and Zald (1996: 2) identified three broad factors as important in examining "the emergence and development of social movements/revolutions":

- *Mobilizing Structures* – the "forms of organization (informal as well as formal), available to insurgents" (p. 2)

The structures include all those "meso-level groups, organizations, and informal networks that comprise the collective building blocks of social movements" (p. 3).

- *Political Opportunities* – the "structure of political opportunities and constraints confronting the movement" (p. 2)

This concept points to the clear linkage between "institutionalized politics," which define the structure of opportunities and constraints, and social movements that arise to challenge and reform existing systems.

- *Framing Processes* – the "collective processes of interpretation, attribution, and social construction that mediate between opportunity and action" (p. 2)

Symbolic elements mediate between structural parameters and the social actors, as actors collectively interpret their situation and devise remedies and proposed lines of action.

We detect a strong affinity between these two conceptual schemas. Scott and associates' concept of institutional actors corresponds closely to McAdam and colleagues' notion of mobilizing structures. Note, however, that the concept of institutional actors tends to privilege established actors whereas the concept of mobilizing structure favors emergent actors. Scott and associates were developing lenses to examine changes in a highly institutionalized field, while McAdam and associates were crafting frameworks to assist them in explaining the emergence of new forms challenging the existing order. The concept of institutional logics connects to that of framing processes. Both refer to ideas and belief systems, and recognize the role they play in providing direction, motivation, meaning, and coherence. However, the former tends to emphasize the power of dominant ideologies and shared cognitive frameworks whereas the latter stresses challenging ideologies and conflicting beliefs and values. The strategic framing of ideas and frame-alignment processes are particularly salient to groups that are suppressed or challenge dominant logics (Snow et al. 1986).

The concept of governance structures relates to that of political opportunities. In examining governance structures, OS scholars, including Scott and colleagues, tend to emphasize the constraints and supports provided by existing arrangements. By contrast SM theorists stress the presence of opportunities afforded by weaknesses, contradictions, or inattention by governing authorities (McAdam 1996; Tarrow 1996; Tilly 1978). In fewer words, OS institutionalists stress "structures" while SM scholars stress "structural holes" (with connotations broader than those associated with the related work of Burt [1992]).

Collecting these ideas – both the areas of convergence and divergence – we commence the construction of a common framework by provisionally stressing the following seven analytic conventions:

1. Following OS insights, we replace the individual organization or social movement with the *organization field* as the fundamental unit of analysis.

2. As the starting point for the analysis of any episode of field-level change, the analyst is urged to identify the relevant period of interest and to define the composition of the field in terms of three classes of *actors*:

   • *Dominants* – those individuals, groups, and organizations around whose actions and interests the field tends to revolve

   • *Challengers* – those individuals, groups, and organizations seeking to challenge the advantaged position of dominants or fundamental structural-procedural features of the field

   • *Governance units* – those organizational units that exercise field-level power and authority. Governance units can be field-specific or components of broader political systems relevant to the field's development. Equal attention should be accorded the strengths and weaknesses, the constraints and the opportunities associated with these units.

3. All fields exist within a wider social *environment* containing:

   • *External actors* – those individuals, groups, and organizations that, at the outset of the episode under study, are not recognized to be participants in the focal field, but in some manner influence the course of action

   • *External governance units* – the authority and power structures operating at broader societal levels, providing opportunities and constraints affecting field-level action

4. Social actors are constituted by and their behavior guided by diverse *institutional logics* – including values, norms, and beliefs regarding

means-ends relations. Logics may be *primary* – the ideas guiding and legitimating the actions of dominant actors – or *secondary* – the ideas associated with emerging or suppressed actors. Events occurring in fields and their environments are differentially interpreted by actors holding divergent logics, providing contrasting frames of reference. The extent of *alignment* among these frames signifies possible sources of support or opposition.

Although it is derived primarily from OS, we are nonetheless convinced that this basic tool kit of concepts has broad relevance for OS and SM analysts alike who seek to describe periods of significant conflict and change within whatever field they are studying. What these concepts cannot explain, however, are the origins of such periods. For that, we need more dynamic, process-oriented, concepts. Borrowing from recent conceptual work in SM (McAdam 1999b; McAdam, Tarrow, and Tilly 2001), we offer the following, additional concepts:

5. Under ordinary circumstances, we believe that fields tend toward stability. This is not to reinvoke the disembodied notion of "social equilibrium" from traditional structural functional analysis. The stability we have in mind is rather the hard fought and fragile state of affairs that Zysman (1994) terms an "institutional settlement" – an agreement negotiated primarily by the efforts of field dominants (and their internal and external allies) to preserve a status quo that generally serves their interests. Given this presumption, we think most periods of significant field contention/change begin with *destabilizing events or processes* that often have their origins outside the narrow confines of the field. (This is likely to be truer in the case of social regulatory than economic regulatory fields, the latter being characterized by destabilizing market pressures and ecological dynamics that the former are generally spared.)

6. But it is generally not the destabilizing events/processes themselves that set periods of field contention and change in motion. Rather it is a process of *reactive mobilization* defined by the following set of three highly contingent *mobilizing mechanisms* that mediate between change pressures and a significant episode of field contention. Reflecting the contingent nature of these mechanisms, we pose each in terms of a question:

   • *attribution of threat or opportunity* – do field actors respond to potentially destabilizing events/processes by interpreting those events as representing new threats or opportunities to or for the realization of their interests?

- *social appropriation* – having successfully fashioned a new more threatening (or opportunistic) understanding of the field or its environment, are the authors of this view able to establish it as the dominant institutional logic of the group in question?
- *new actors and innovative action* – once insinuated as the institutional logic of a given group, do these new attributions of threat or opportunity lead to the emergence of new types of actors and/or to innovative action with the potential to destabilize the *field* all the more?

7. If the answer to all three questions turns out to be "yes," then we can expect that field dominants and challengers alike will begin to act and interact in innovative and increasingly contentious ways. The end result is likely to be a significant *shift in the strategic alignment* that had previously structured and stabilized the field, leading to a new *institutional settlement*.

Armed with this mix of more static structural and more dynamic change-oriented concepts, we are ready to revisit our two cases with an eye to assessing the utility of this synthetic framework for encompassing what otherwise might seem to be quite disparate cases.

Two Cases

Case One: The Emergence, Institutionalization, and Restructuring of the Health Care Field

Scott and colleagues (Scott et al. 2000) conducted an empirical study of changes occurring in the health care delivery system serving one large metropolitan area in the United States, the San Francisco Bay area, concentrating their data collection on the period 1945–95. While the geographic region was selected for convenience, the sector and time period were chosen to represent an instance of profound institutional change. The question of interest was: how did it happen that a sector long noted for its unique and stable institutional arrangements became destabilized and moved in directions more isomorphic with other service industries? We recognized that although we could limit our examination of changes in the delivery system to one localized area, to account for these changes we would need to attend to structures and forces operating at wider, state and national, levels. Three phases (or eras) were identified to highlight important changes in actors, logics, and governance structures.

1. Origins: Early Decades of the Twentieth Century to 1964: Era of Professional Dominance

Dominant Actors and Governance Structures   The early history of the structuration of the health care field is largely one of success of the "professional project" pursued by allopathic physicians: MDs. This history has been recounted in detail by Freidson (1970a) and Starr (1982), among others. Early in the twentieth century, physicians were able, with the help of the Carnegie Foundation, to set their own house in order by standardizing training requirements and restricting access to physicians meeting minimal standards. Securing legitimation via licensure by state bodies, which they controlled, physicians acted to successfully exclude or restrict the opportunities available to alternative types of practitioners. Other heath care professionals, such as nurses, pharmacists, and various types of ancillary therapists, quickly learned the advantages of cooperating with physicians to develop their skills and define their spheres of operation in ways compatible with and subordinate to physicians (Freidson 1970b).

To secure and advance their interests, physicians created (in 1846) what became arguably the most successful and powerful professional association in history (*Yale Law Journal* 1954). The American Medical Association (AMA), organized to operate at county, state, and national levels, was for the first half of the twentieth century the primary de facto governance structure of health care overseeing its development in the United States.

In addition to their success in mounting internal reforms and overcoming the challenges mounted by other types of providers, physicians also were effective during this period in controlling the number of physicians, the conditions of their work, and the nature of financial systems. Physicians strengthened their guild by controlling the size and quality of training programs and overseeing licensing systems, thus restricting competition. Insisting on the overriding value of the physician-patient relation, physicians successfully resisted organizational authority, denouncing medical groups as "the corporate practice of medicine" (Starr 1982). In the same fashion they were able to maintain their access to but independence from the only major organizational form that had emerged for the delivery of complex services – the community hospital – by creating professional staff structures that were autonomous from administrative hospital structures (White 1982). And, throughout this period, physicians successfully retained their independence from financial structures by insisting on direct fee-for-service payments or insurance plans that provide indemnity or service benefits (Starr 1982).

Hence, the situation found at the time when our study commenced (1945) can be characterized as a highly stable institutional settlement involving the following principal features:

Field Actors
- *Physicians* become the dominant actors.
  (Earlier challengers, such as homopathic physicians, osteopaths, chiropractors, are successfully suppressed or contained.)
- "Voluntary," non-profit community *hospitals* are the major organizational form for the delivery of complex services.
- The *AMA* is the primary governance body, allied with state-level licensure agencies.

External Actors
- *Employers and labor unions* are increasingly involved in providing employees with health care insurance coverage, but are not active in directly attempting to control health care prices or delivery systems.
- The *federal government* remains largely on the periphery of health care delivery, several proposals for national health insurance having been defeated. After the end of World War II, however, it becomes increasingly active in providing infrastructural support: for basic medical research, hospital facility construction, and physician training (see below).

Institutional Logics
- Physicians espouse the sanctity of the *doctor-patient relation* as the logic by which they resist organizational and financial controls, and insist on the overriding value of *quality of care*, which is the doctor's prerogative to define.
- A *"voluntary ethos"* legitimates the dominance of nonprofit, community-based health care systems.

Destabilizing Events and Processes   With the advantages of hindsight, it is possible to identify several important processes and events occurring late in the first era that paved the way for disruptive change. Scott and colleagues (2000) emphasize that the unitary front provided by physicians that supplied the foundation for the power of the AMA began to erode. They document the dramatic rise of medical specialties – by 1960, half of practitioners were specialists – together with their corresponding associations, and a parallel decline in AMA membership. Starr (1982) points to another developing source of fragmentation: the growing size and significance of medical schools, teaching hospitals, and allied institutions meant that an increasing proportion of physicians was no longer engaged in independent, community practice. A third force that worked over time to weaken the market power of physicians was the passage, in 1963, of the Health Professions Education Act that provided public funds to create new medical schools and expand existing ones. This act, and subsequent amendments and renewals aimed at shaping the geographical and specialty distribution of doctors, increased the ratio of active physicians from just under 120 per 100,000 in 1970 to over 206 in 1990 (Scott et al. 2000: 140; see also Thompson 1981). This legislation, along with increases in public funding for research and facilities, provided early warning signs of a new institutional logic that had begun to surface indicating that "there was a *public* interest in both the quality and availability of medical care" (Scott et al. 2000: 189).

Two other developments, one within the health care field, the other a broader societal-level change, provided fuel for major restructuring of this arena. The endogenous development was the gradual, but continuous, increase in the costs of health care – increases that, from the early 1950s, regularly exceeded the consumer price index. The broader trend was demographic: the aging of the American population resulting in a higher demand for health care services.

2. Era of Federal Involvement: 1965–1982

Shift in Strategic Alignment   Wider political developments during the mid-1960s challenged professional prerogatives that had long held sway. Following the assassination of President Kennedy, a liberal, democratic majority took power in 1964, controlling both the Executive Office and the Congress. Following many failed attempts in previous decades, legislation was successfully passed in 1965 under the leadership of President Lyndon Johnson to provide governmental financing for health care services for the elderly and the indigent. How did these ideas gain support? Why did they succeed in the 1960s rather than earlier? A liberal administration and Congress were vital, but it appears that the *framing* of the issues was also of great importance. Among social movement theorists, Snow has emphasized the importance of framing processes in efforts to mobilize ideological support. (See Snow and Benford 1988; Snow et al. 1986.) The 1960s witnessed

the mobilization of formerly suppressed interests on a broad scale resulting in the "rights revolution" in the United States (see Case Two), and it
is hence not surprising that parties engaged in heath care reform couched
their concerns in terms of securing every individual's "right" to health care.

With the launching of the Medicare Program, the federal government
overnight became the single largest purchaser of health services. Medicare
was strongly supported by the growing ranks of elderly Americans through
their increasingly effective lobbies – in particular, the American Association of Retired Persons – who were just beginning to discover their political
clout. Popular support was readily marshaled since "the aged could be pre-
sumed both needy and deserving" (Starr 1982: 368). A companion program,
Medicaid, to be administered by the states, broadened coverage for the indigent. In combination, this landmark legislation gave dramatic expression
to the new institutional logic of providing "equal access to care" for all
citizens.

Reactive Mobilization   Although organized medicine and its allies were not
sufficiently strong to derail the liberal juggernaut, their collective political
power was sufficient to allow them to exclude governmental influence from
physicians' clinical decision making and from the setting of hospital and
physician charges. Wanting to secure the cooperation of doctors and hospitals, the framers of the legislation practiced the "politics of accommodation"
and created numerous "buffers between the providers of healthcare and the
federal bureaucracy" (Starr 1982: 374–5).

Attribution of Threat-Opportunity   Although they feared the worst, hospitals and physicians suddenly found themselves in a beneficent environment
in which they were able to determine what services were required and to
set "usual and customary" fees for reimbursement from financial intermedi-
aries, who remained both distant and respectful. The enlarged patient pool
coupled with the security of public reimbursement encouraged a variety of
entrepreneurial health care professionals to develop more elaborate delivery systems. Medical groups – important foundation blocks for subsequent
organizational forms – began to increase rapidly, and a variety of more specialized forms began to appear and multiply (see below). An opportunistic
framing of the new situation confronting physicians was associated with the
emergence of new actors and innovative actions.

Health care professionals exploited these perceived opportunities with
such energy as to threaten the long-term viability of the new public programs. The relaxation of financial constraints on demand resulted in a rapid
escalation of health care services and costs and, because public monies were

now involved, provoked a perceived crisis in public finance. Political actors, in turn, reacted to the crisis by rapidly constructing a range of new administrative agencies to exercise regulative oversight, treating health care services more or less as a public utility. Scott and colleagues (2000) document that, in the Bay area, the number of health-related regulatory bodies increased from fewer than ten in 1945 to nearly a hundred in 1975 (p. 198). *Effects on Health Care Delivery Organizations* Following decades of "dynamics without change" (Alford 1975), the health care field had entered into a period of creative turbulence. As one important indicator of such change, Scott and colleagues systematically charted foundings and failures occurring, between 1945 and 1995, in five organizational populations providing health care services in the San Francisco Bay area. The five populations selected were: hospitals, home health agencies (HHAs), health maintenance organizations (HMOs), renal disease centers (RDCs), and integrated health care systems (IHSs). At any given time, there exists only a limited repertory of organization forms – cognitive models and the associated relational structures and operational strategies – in a given organizational field (Greenwood and Hinings 1993; Clemens 1996). Hospitals represent the most traditional organizational form while the other populations reflect newer templates. HHAs involve a reinvention of an earlier organizational model – visiting nursing associations – while RDCs reflect a growing tendency for specialized units within hospitals to be reconstituted as self-standing organizations. IHSs capture the opposite impulse of independent health care units to band together, through horizontal and vertical mergers as well as via alliances, forming broadly differentiated systems. HMOs, the most novel form, will be discussed below.

An important indicator of institutional change, we argue, involves changes over time in the relative numbers of organizations exhibiting a given form. Although the organizations studied are not identical in the work performed, they are in a broad sense all competitors, supplying acute patient services. Our data reveal that, prior to 1965, hospitals were virtually the only type of organizational provider of health care services. Their numbers peaked in the Bay area in 1965 and have slowly but steadily declined since that date. After 1965, all of the other, more specialized forms exhibit significant increases, from two- to five-fold (Scott et al. 2000: chap. 3).

New Actors and Innovative Action Between the beginning and end of the second half of the twentieth century, then, a number of "new" (reinvented, modified, hybrid) health care delivery forms appeared on the scene, each associated with relatively innovative health care practices. None of these,

24

however, was the direct result of social-movement-type mobilization processes. Some, like the RDC, were the product of entrepreneurial efforts, particularly by physicians, who recognized the profit-making possibilities of renal dialysis facilities and took advantage of Medicare provisions extending coverage to its chronically ill patients (Rettig and Levinsky 1991). Others, like the HHA, revitalized an earlier health care delivery form and took advantage of new technologies and emerging institutional logics emphasizing the advantages of home-based over institutional care. Medicare funding was also instrumental to the development and growth of this form. Thus, it is important to recognize that mobilization activities occur at other than the grassroots level. Each of the new service delivery forms – HMOs, HHAs, RDCs, IHSs – developed a federation or association to represent and advance its interests. Such associations function, to varying degrees, both as governance structures and as advocacy agents.

Taking stock, we find a dramatically changed cast of actors and governance structures and altered logics evident during this second era:

Field Actors
- *Physicians* remain central actors, but are increasingly involved in some type of organizational unit, such as medical centers or medical groups.
- *Hospitals* remain important delivery sites, but are increasingly challenged by the appearance of more *specialized forms*.
- The *AMA* and related professional associations increasingly share governance functions with public actors and with new associations of specialized provider organizations.
- *Public officials and agencies*, at both the federal and state levels, multiply and actively participate in health care governance, including financing, quality assurance, planning, and cost containment.

External Actors
- *Employers and labor unions* continue to provide employees with health care insurance coverage, and, while they are rarely involved in directly negotiating costs and services, call for greater efforts by public officials to regulate costs.
- *Policy experts, politicians, and public officials* are less apt to believe that health care issues can be left in the hands of health care professionals, and more likely to regard health care as an area requiring public controls.

25

Institutional Logics
- While the logic of *health care quality* continues to be of central importance, it is now joined by a new logic stressing the importance of *equity of access* for all citizens.

Destabilizing Events and Processes   Scott and colleagues (2000) identified several forces at work affecting the direction of change into the subsequent period. One of these involved a revision in the locus and type of training of health care managers. Until mid-century, hospitals were administered primarily by lay administrators, by which time training programs had developed in numerous schools of public health. Beginning in the 1960s, however, an increasing number of public health programs offered degrees in business administration, several business schools developed special public health or hospital administration programs, and other business schools offered joint programs with schools of public health. The generic aspects of management, rather than the specialized health attributes of health care organizations, began to be emphasized, and a stream of professional managers entered the field.

Quite early, during the 1950s and early 1960s, a collection of academic economists had begun to question the value of regulation – of price, firm entry, or exit – as a tool of governmental intervention in the economy. The intellectual critique, supported by accompanying research on a number of key industries, began to spread to public policy circles during the early 1970s. By 1975, deregulation had developed into the "new religion in this town: . . . much of Washington was doing it or professing to do it" (Derthick and Quirk 1985: 29). During this period, the cause was championed by individuals as diverse as Senator Edward Kennedy, on the grounds that it protected consumer interests, and President Gerald Ford, because it served business interests, free enterprise, and reduced governmental interference.

Deregulation connected to and gained momentum from the development of a broad-based consumer movement during the 1960s. This movement entered the health care arena during the late 1960s to challenge the notion that "the doctor knows best" and to insist that health maintenance and improvement were not the responsibility of the provider but the consumer. Health care was increasingly viewed as similar to other personal services. An even broader challenge questioned the physicians' claim to an exclusive base of knowledge pertaining to health and healing when, during the late 1960s, an interest in and tolerance for "alternative" providers emerged and grew among the public (Scott et al. 2000: 210–15).

3. Era of Managers and Markets: 1983 to the Present

A New Institutional Logic   This third era was marked primarily by the ascendance of a new logic – improving health care efficiency – together with the development of new organizational forms and governance mechanisms designed to achieve it. Economists cast doubt on the efficacy of many medical procedures, but more generally, insisted that economic criteria and calculations were as applicable to health care as to other areas: whatever benefits were forthcoming had to be weighed against the costs and alternatives forgone (Fuchs 1974). Since these costs were rapidly escalating, politicians and the wider public were receptive to these arguments.

Following the new policy fashion, economic advisers and political leaders called for the replacement of "regulatory and administrative agencies with private markets operating under suitably designed incentives" (Melhado 1988: 41). The approach was determined suitable for a wide variety of arenas, and, notably, health care was not treated as an exception, as in past decades. Early attempts targeted consumers, focusing on various cost-sharing mechanisms, such as copayments, that increased costs to consumers. Later programs were aimed at providers, rewarding them for providing early and less care rather than late and more care. An important new instrument for this purpose was the HMO form of health care delivery.

The HMO was the brainchild of one reform-minded physician, Paul Ellwood, who advocated the model in the late 1960s for its preventive (health-maintenance) features. However, its success was rather due to its ability to restructure physicians' incentives, rewarding them for rationing services. This feature endeared it to the health policy designers of the Nixon administration, who embraced the model in the battle to reduce health care costs (Brown 1983). However, its rapid adoption and diffusion did not occur until the early 1980s.

HMOs represented the most novel form of health delivery to emerge in the second half of the twentieth century. Embodying an older model of pre-paid group practice, HMOs grafted on the insurance function so that the providers within these forms were more directly exposed to financial risk. Two functions formerly insulated from one another, housed in separate organizations, were brought under the same roof. We have here an instance of *bricolage*, the cobbling together of pieces of familiar forms and routines to embody new logics and support new modes of action (Clemens 1996; Haveman and Rao forthcoming; Stark 1996). Such hybrid creations are particularly likely to appear in organizational fields during times of

27

rapid change. They combine the strengths of the old and familiar with the advantages of the novel and unusual. By employing a recognizable structural vocabulary and action schemas so that change is perceived to be incremental rather than discontinuous, they enable more radical changes than would otherwise be possible.

Insurance functions (health plans) were joined with varying combinations of providers – a medical group, collections of groups, networks of independent physicians, physician-hospital partnerships – giving rise to a dizzying variety of subforms: staff model HMOs (with full-time salaried physicians), independent practice associations (networks of independent physicians paid on a capitated or fee-for-service basis), preferred provider organizations, and point-of-service organizations, among others (see Edmunds et al.1997). Competition among these provider systems on the basis of price, quality, and consumer amenities meant that entrepreneurial and managerial skills were much in demand. Indeed, informed observers, such as Robinson (1999: 213), regarded the contemporary scene as one involving "continued innovation in forms of organization, ownership, contract, finance, and governance."

Finally, throughout the period of the study, ownership arrangements have undergone change. Public ownership of health care facilities showed a marked decline among all types of care organizations. Among the private providers, the most traditional forms such as hospitals have tended to remain nonprofit, while most of the newer forms are primarily for-profit. An increasing number of health care organizations are owned by and operated as subunits of corporations. The first health services firm appeared among the 1000 largest American firms in 1975. By 1995, there were more than thirty such firms with a combined value of over nine billion dollars (Scott et al. 2000: 231).

Taking stock of these developments, we find, in summary:

Field Actors
- *Physicians* remain central actors in care delivery, but now exercise much less influence in policy and design decisions.
- *Hospitals* continue their decline in influence and in numbers. Most are no longer independent but are components of IHSs.
- A variety of new types of *managed care organizations* have entered the arena and by the mid-1990s account for most acute care services.
- The *AMA and other professional associations* share governance functions with *public* and *corporate* actors.

- *Professional managers* have increased power and are much more active in the design and coordination of professional activities.

External Actors
- *Employers* are playing a more active role in health care governance, often entering into coalitions to negotiate plans and oversee performance.
- Policy experts, especially *economists, politicians, and public officials*, regularly and actively participate in the governance of health care affairs.
- *Corporations* increasingly own and manage health care delivery organizations.

Institutional Logics
- While the logic of *health care quality* is espoused, the logic of *equal access* has become much less salient. A significant proportion of the population lacks adequate health insurance.
- *Efficiency and cost-containment* have become important new values and the use of *market mechanisms* and *competitive pressures* is the favored governance mechanism.

Destabilizing Processes: Reactive Mobilization In the early years of the twenty-first century, we seem far from attaining stability in the health care field. The initial governance structure, dominated by an occupational association, has not disappeared but now must share power and legitimacy with other professional and trade associations, public agencies, corporate organizations, and market processes. Consumer movements have been revived, but now, in addition to promoting a "patients' bill of rights" seek increased discretion for physicians to make medical decisions unconstrained by either big government or big business – a "doctors' bill of rights." "Patients over profits" is a rallying cry heard as often as "reducing bureaucratic interference." Many reimbursement programs, including Medicare and Medicaid, fail to fully cover the costs of care with the consequence that hospitals and other organizational providers are forced to cut back on staffing and services. Faced with such constraints, nursing groups have more frequently resorted to protest strikes, and some physicians are actively exploring unionization. The population continues to age, and new technologies boost demands and costs. A shrinking proportion of U.S. firms provide health care benefits to their employees, and 44 million Americans currently lack health insurance. The health care field is undergoing profound change, but no stable settlement is in sight.

*Case Two: The Emergence, Development, and Institutionalization
of the "Rights Revolution"*

McAdam has written extensively about the origins and subsequent development of the civil rights period of the African-American freedom struggle (McAdam 1982, 1983, 1988, 1998, 1999b). Here we want to revisit that history but through the lens of the synthetic framework sketched above. If the framework has merit, it should add texture and new emphases to the movement-centric account offered in the earlier work. There are really four phases to this history, the first three of which are familiar to movement scholars. Reflecting much more the emphases of OS than SM, the fourth phase largely has been glossed in movement accounts of the civil rights struggle. We take these phases in chronological order.

1. Origins: 1946–1955   This period presents the sharpest contrast between our two cases. While the earliest phase of the health care case involved the destabilization of an established field or fields, heightened conflict over race in the immediate postwar period occurred in the absence of any well-defined "social regulatory" field with respect to racial issues. Instead, the onset of the latter conflict marked the beginning of a process that would eventually give rise to a number of established fields. Despite this difference, however, we think the analytic framework sketched above enables us to understand the origins of both of these cases. Reflecting the dynamic change elements inherent in the origins of contention, our analysis of the initial phase of the civil rights case is structured around the final three elements of our synthetic framework.

Destabilizing Events or Processes   Until recently, the consensual account of the rise of the civil rights movement focused almost exclusively on domestic change processes thought to be responsible for ending the federal "hands off" policy with respect to Southern race relations. That tacit policy held for nearly seventy-five years, from the withdrawal of federal forces from the South in 1877 until the civil rights reforms of the Truman presidency. Among the domestic change processes argued to have undermined the federal/Southern "understanding" on race are the marked decline in the cotton economy (especially after 1930), the massive northward migration of blacks set in motion by the decline of "King Cotton," and the growing political/electoral significance that attached to the black vote as a result of the migration (McAdam 1999b [1982]; Sitkoff 1978; Wilson 1973).

Without discounting the importance of these domestic factors, a spate of recent works on race and the Cold War has offered a very different account of the origins of the civil rights struggle (Dudziak 1988, 2000; Layton 2000; McAdam 1998, 1999; Plummer 1996; Skrentny 1998). The strong claim advanced by these authors is that the key to understanding the developing conflict lies not in the domestic context so much as the new pressures and considerations thrust upon the United States and the White House in particular by the onset of the Cold War. Writing in 1944, Gunnar Myrdal (1970: 35) described these "new pressures and considerations" with eloquent prescience.

The Negro Problem . . . has also acquired tremendous international implications, and this is another and decisive reason why the white North is prevented from compromising with the white South regarding the Negro. . . . Statesmen will have to take cognizance of the changed geopolitical situation of the nation and carry out important adaptations of the American way of life to new necessities. A main adaptation is bound to be the redefinition of the Negro's status in American democracy.

In short, the Cold War exposed the United States to withering international criticism of its racial policies, prompting Truman and other federal officials to embrace limited civil rights reforms for their foreign policy, rather than domestic political, value.

Reactive Mobilization   Although substantively quite limited, the embrace of civil rights reform by certain federal officials following World War II signaled such a clear break with the previous policy regime that it was almost immediately defined as significant by the established parties to the conflict. In turn, this emerging definition of the situation set in motion *reactive mobilization* efforts by *dominants* and *challengers* alike. These efforts featured all three mobilization mechanisms noted previously. For their part, Southern segregationists – led by their representatives in Congress – saw in the new reform efforts a clear *threat* to their political power and to "the Southern way of life" more generally. To counter this threat, segregationists *appropriated* a host of established organizations (e.g., church and civic organizations) and created new forms (e.g., the States' Rights Party, Mississippi's State Sovereignty Commissions, the White Citizen Council) as vehicles for mounting *innovative action* designed to preserve the social, political, and economic status quo. These actions included the "Dixiecrat Revolt" of 1948 (in which South Carolina's Democratic senator, Strom Thurmond, ran against his party's incumbent in the 1948 presidential race), resurgent Klan activity in the mid-fifties, and the flood of anti-integration statutes passed by Southern state legislatures in the wake of the 1954 Supreme Court's decision in the Brown case.

Civil rights forces also mobilized during this period, seeing in Truman's efforts and the philosophy of the Warren Court an unprecedented *opportunity* to challenge Jim Crow on a number of fronts. A host of established organizations, such as the National Council of Churches and the YWCA, embraced integration in the postwar period. Existing civil rights groups – especially the NAACP – experienced dramatic growth in membership in the same period (Anglin 1949; Wolters 1970). Finally, new groups emerged to press the fight through more *innovative action*. These groups included the Congress of Racial Equality (CORE) in 1942, the NAACP (National Association for the Advancement of Colored People) Legal Defense and Education Fund in 1946, and, following the stunning success of the Montgomery bus boycott (1955–6), Martin Luther King's Southern Christian Leadership Conference in 1957.

With respect to Montgomery and King, however, it is worth noting that this account marks the temporal beginnings of renewed racial contention in the United States nearly ten years before the mass movement phase of the struggle. The broader analytic framework sketched above helps place Montgomery and King in context by alerting us to the important role played by established *dominants* (e.g., Southern elected officials), *challengers* (e.g., the NAACP), and, most importantly in this case, *external governance units* (e.g., the Supreme Court, Truman) in setting the conflict in motion. Montgomery then represents a crucial escalation of the conflict – one that signals the onset of phase two of the struggle – but not its point of origin. Indeed, rather than Montgomery making the movement, the reverse is actually true. It was the prior onset of the *national* conflict that granted the *local* struggle in Montgomery so much significance. Without its embedding in the existing national episode, it is not at all clear that Montgomery would have had the impact it did, or perhaps that it would have happened at all.

Shift in Strategic Alignments This period also saw a significant restructuring of the strategic relationships that had previously sustained the federal-Southern "understanding" with respect to race. The key rupture in these years occurred within the Democratic Party, as Dixiecrats reacted with alarm and open revolt to the reform policies pursued by Truman and the liberal/labor wing of the party. The emerging division between these two crucial components of the New Deal coalition thoroughly destabilized electoral politics in the early Cold War period (and beyond) and in so doing decisively shaped the direct action strategies of civil rights forces.

2. Heyday: 1956–1965 If Montgomery did not actually trigger the episode of interest here, it certainly represented a significant escalation and qualitative shift in the nature and locus of the struggle. The rise of the mass movement served to shift much of the action out of Washington and into the streets and statehouses of the South. Emergent *challengers* pioneered or adapted sit-ins, mass marches, and other forms of public protest and civil disobedience to supplement the legal and institutionalized political battles that had characterized the earlier period. The result was extraordinarily high levels of sustained contention – both institutionalized and non-institutionalized – and further deterioration in the *alignment* of the northern and southern wings of the Democratic Party.

The period also marks the clear emergence of a civil rights *field*, the evolution of which would powerfully shape the conflict well into the late 1960s. The field was a fluid conflict or action arena comprised of at least five major sets of actors: movement and countermovement groups, federal officials, Southern officials, and the national media. The gradual mastery and exploitation, by movement forces, of a recurring strategic dynamic involving these five actors account for much of the action – and resultant policy victories – that we associate with the period. The dynamic can be described simply. Lacking sufficient power to defeat Southern officials in a local struggle, movement groups sought to broaden the conflict by inducing countermovement forces to engage in dramatic disruptions of public order which, in turn, compelled media attention, generated public outcry in the North, and forced otherwise reluctant federal officials to intervene in ways generally supportive of movement aims.

The central new population of actors within this field was the *social movement industry* (SMI) comprised of the major civil rights organizations active during the period. Dubbed the "Big Five" by movement analysts, this well-defined aggregation of collective actors proved highly effective as a source of concerted movement action during the movement's heyday. The strength of this SMI owed, in part, to profitable *resource linkages* established during the period between the groups and liberal Northern foundations, church groups, and individual donors. These highly functional linkages did, however, create a serious *resource dependency* that would come back to haunt several of the key organizations as they embraced more radical goals and tactics after 1965.

3. "Black Power" and the Decline of the Movement: 1966–1970 The mass movement phase of the civil rights struggle wound down during the latter half of the 1960s. The decline of the movement resulted from six principal factors.

1. At the broadest level, the international pressures that had prompted the federal government to embrace civil rights reform in the Cold War era eased considerably in the late 1960s. President Nixon's historic overture to China and simultaneous embrace of *détente* with the Soviet Union marked the beginning of an extended Cold War hiatus. This, coupled with the rise of Vietnam as America's dominant issue – internationally and domestically – robbed civil rights forces of the public attention and criticism that had helped leverage policy gains in the early 1960s (McAdam 1999b [1982]; Skrentny 1998).

2. Then too, those gains – reflected in the effective dismantling of Jim Crow – also contributed to the decline of the movement, both by removing the symbols of American racism that had fueled criticism, and by forcing the movement to confront forms of institutional inequality that would prove far more difficult to attack.

3. In confronting these more difficult targets, the strong consensus with regard to goals (integration, voting rights) and tactics (nonviolent direct action) that had characterized the *social movement industry* during the movement's heyday collapsed, ushering in a period of divisive conflict and change in SMO relations. The *institutional logic* of civil rights clashed with that of *black power*, effectively ending the prospects for organizational coalition that had made the movement such a formidable and unified force in the early sixties (McAdam 1999b [1982]: chap. 8).

4. The embrace of more radical goals, tactics, and rhetoric by two of the Big Five – the Congress of Racial Equality (CORE) and the Student Non-violent Coordinating Committee (SNCC) – exposed both to the dangers of external *resource dependence*, leading to the wholesale withdrawal of liberal financial support. Neither group was able to offset this loss with stronger resource ties to the black community, thus depriving the movement of much of the tactical energy and innovation that had fueled action campaigns in the early sixties. With King's assassination in 1968, the direct-action wing of the Big Five was completely gone (Haines 1988; McAdam 1999b [1982]: chap. 8).

5. When combined with the Northern riots of the period, the movement's growing militancy prompted state officials at all levels to take increasingly repressive action against insurgent groups, further weakening the organizational structure of the movement.

6. This repressive impulse was further strengthened by Nixon's strident embrace of a "law and order" rhetoric during his presidential campaign. More importantly, Nixon's successful "Southern strategy" left him with no electoral debt to African-Americans and deprived moderate civil rights leaders of the kind of White House access they had enjoyed since Roosevelt.

The irony in all this is that even as the mass movement was declining in the late 1960s, at least two *social regulatory fields* embodying the central goals of the civil rights phase of the struggle were beginning to take shape in the United States. However, the full institutionalization of the rights revolution would have to wait until the 1970s.

4. The Institutionalization of the Rights Revolution: 1971–1980 Reflecting the preoccupation of movement scholars with periods of non-institutionalized contention, research on the civil rights struggle all but ignores the years after 1970. But as John Skrentny's work (1996, 2002) showed, this ignorance comes at considerable cost. What is lost is any real understanding of the institutionalization of the "rights revolution" after 1970. This "march through the institutions" worked through two processes. The first was the rapid expansion of social regulatory fields embodying many of the central aims of the civil rights movement. The second was the powerful impact that the policy and more amorphous cultural changes we associate with the "rights revolution" had on other established fields during this later period.

Creation/Expansion of Social Regulatory Fields There exist two highly elaborated social regulatory fields with clear origins in the civil rights struggle. These we will term the *employment opportunity field* (EMOF) and the *educational opportunity field* (EDOF). Even a cursory history of both fields is beyond the scope of this article. To illustrate our perspective, we focus only on the evolution of the EMOF. It is a fiction to say that either of these fields was created after 1970. Both existed, at least in embryonic form, much earlier than this. The EMOF dates back to at least 1941 when President Franklin Roosevelt, acting under pressure from the March on Washington movement, issued his one and only civil rights measure, creating a Fair Employment Practices Commission to investigate charges of discrimination in wartime defense industries. Truman nominally expanded the field during his term by creating a fair employment board within the Civil Service Commission (1948) and a Committee on Government Contract Compliance

(1951). None of these agencies, however, had any real reach to them or was backed by effective enforcement mechanisms.

The same deficiencies were evident in regard to the major institutional expansions of the field mandated by the civil rights legislation passed during the 1960s. So in 1964 Congress established the Equal Employment Opportunity Commission (EEOC) to enforce Title VII of that year's Civil Rights Act. A year later President Lyndon Johnson issued an executive order creating the Office of Federal Contract Compliance (OFCC), designed to monitor equal employment in a sector – government contracts – not under the jurisdiction of the EEOC. But for all the laudable intentions and impressive bureaucratic machinery that attached to the EEOC and the OFCC, the regulatory reach of the field remained minimal. "Of the first 15,000 [EEOC] complaints received, 6,040 were earmarked for investigation, and 3,319 investigations were completed. At the level of conciliation, only 110 were actually completed" (Skrentny 1996: 123). Through 1968 the OFCC had yet to cancel a single federal employment contract as a result of employment discrimination (Skrentny 1996: 134).

The real expansion of the field took place in the early 1970s through an initiative – the so-called Philadelphia Plan – offered by the Nixon administration. Skrentny (1996: 177) captured the irony in this: "Perhaps the greatest irony of all in the story of affirmative action is that this controversial model of justice owes its most advanced and explicit race-based formulation to a Republican president who based much of his campaign on appealing to the racially conservative South." Proposed and enacted late in 1969, the plan effectively replaced the "color blind" logic of earlier regulatory efforts with an explicit embrace of "affirmative action," conceived as targeted percentages of minorities to be hired. Nixon's motives for supporting the plan make for a fascinating story (Skrentny 1996: chap. 7). Even more interesting is the story of how a Republican-backed plan that was initially opposed by liberal Democrats came over time to be repudiated by the right – including Nixon himself – and embraced by liberals as the very symbol of racial justice. But these stories are beyond the scope of this article.

The crucial point for us has to do with the impact this fundamental shift in *institutional logic* had on the structure, operation, and reach of the EMOF. Whereas "color blind" approaches to employment regulation had put the onus to evaluate and challenge questionable hiring/firing practices on the *employee* (or job applicant), affirmative action required *employers* to meet explicit hiring targets. Though controversial from the start, this shift in the locus of regulation nonetheless granted *institutional legitimacy* to the *social logic* of affirmative action, prompting organizational actors in many institutional spheres to modify the structure and practice of their work settings.

Destabilizing Effects on Established Fields   The Philadelphia Plan applied only to firms negotiating government contracts. But its implementation and the legitimacy it granted the regulatory logic of affirmative action set in motion destabilizing change processes that would eventually reach into countless other organizational fields. As a field, American higher education was in no way subject to the plan. Yet over time, most American colleges and universities came to embrace some version of affirmative action and to modify their organizational structures and practices accordingly (Bowen and Bok 1999). The history of major league sports in the United States over the past quarter-century reflects a similar pattern. Lauren Edelman's work (1992; Edelman and Suchman 1997) shows how these field- or industry-level pressures play out in the individual firm, with organizational actors seeking to interpret and implement recent legislation or legal trends in light of field-level competitive pressures. Even the previous case of health care betrays both a direct and an indirect impact of the institutionalized "rights revolution." The direct effect is clear: large health-care employers also came to embrace some version of affirmative action in their hiring and firing practices. Less directly, but more consequentially, the rights revolution afforded consumer rights and patient rights advocates both a *frame* for their claims-making activities and a broader political/cultural credibility that strengthened their hand against field *dominants*.

This is by no means a full accounting of the emergence and subsequent development of the civil rights case. Having been given short shrift by movement scholars, the first and fourth periods in particular demand more systematic attention. But we do think this account is suggestive of the increased empirical leverage to be gained by wedding the perspectives and concepts of OS and SM. By doing so – even in this thumbnail fashion – we have highlighted the crucial conflict and change processes that bookend the mass movement phase of the struggle. Montgomery and the later sit-ins did not so much initiate the struggle as broaden it while introducing a host of new *challengers* to the action field. Nor did the struggle end with Martin Luther King's death or any of the other events that movement scholars have seen as marking the temporal close of the case. Indeed, one of those events – Nixon's ascension to the White House – helped, as we have shown, to usher in a dramatic expansion in a key civil rights regulatory field and a related period of unprecedented disruption to other established fields as organizational actors everywhere sought to react to the *social logic* of the "rights revolution."

Concluding Comments

We believe important benefits will be reaped by SM and OS scholars who embrace a broader framework which encompasses structures and processes, established and emergent organizations, institutionalized authority, and transgressive contention, and who attend to the connections between local or specialized fields and broader societal systems. Social change exhibits varied moments and is transported by many carriers. It may result in the transformation of existing organizations or the creation of new or hybrid forms. It is advanced by institutionalized processes as well as by tumultuous battles. Settlements are realized but they in turn give rise to different struggles among contending interests and logics.

We think that our own past work is strengthened and improved by utilizing the broader framework. Scott and colleagues' original study (2000) of the transformation of health care systems highlighted changing logics and organizational populations, including the construction of new forms, but accorded too little attention to the ways in which the differing governing structures gave rise to different modes and bases of reactive mobilization. In reviewing the Bay area case with the aid of the conceptual framework, it becomes apparent that each era, defined by distinctive governance structures and logics, created different political opportunities for excluded or disadvantaged groups. The era of professional dominance was marked by the mobilizing efforts of various competing occupational groups as they attempted to challenge the growing hegemony of physicians. Most of these efforts resulted in failure or in the challenging groups settling for a subordinate role and/or a restricted sphere of operation. It was not until later eras, after the unity of physicians had eroded, that alternative providers achieved some success.

During the era of federal involvement, as the federal government suddenly became a central player in the field, it was the physicians' turn to mobilize, finding new ways to defend and advance their interests. Entrepreneurial physicians took advantage of guaranteed payments to identify profitable areas of practice. New, specialized health care organizations were created, and older, more traditional forms such as hospitals, became financial casualties. Political actors and public officials in turn reacted to rapidly escalating health care costs by constructing rate-review and other regulatory apparatus.

With the advent of the era of managerial and market competition, other kinds of reactive mobilization have emerged. Consumer groups have become more active, pressuring legislatures to protect patients' interests and doctors' prerogatives in making medical decisions. At local levels, a variety of community groups have mobilized to protest the closing of or, to the extent they are able, prevent the loss of hospitals and their vital services, including urgent and emergency care units. As the nation returns to deficit financing and Medicare deficits loom, there seems little doubt but that health care politics will return again to the top of the political agenda.

The expanded analytic framework significantly alters our understanding of the civil rights movement as well. Indeed, the framework mandates a fundamental reconceptualization of the basic object of study. Instead of viewing the civil rights movement as the phenomenon of interest, we are compelled to see the movement as but one (albeit a singularly important one) of a number of challengers contesting the legal and normative understanding of race and racial practices in the United States. This shift in focus requires that we also extend the temporal boundaries of our analysis of civil rights contention back at least to the end of World War II and forward through the 1970s.

By 1980, a new legal and institutional system of racial practices was largely in place. This new institutional settlement, hammered into place by dominant actors, provides the frameworks within which these actors exercise legitimate power and carry on the principal business of the field in routinized ways. But they also provide the conditions that give rise to political opportunities, allowing new actors to mobilize around under-served interests as they seek to challenge existing arrangements and to propose new and different institutional settlements. Both our fields remain subject to these dynamic processes.

More generally, in retrospect, the OS theorists (Scott and colleagues) accorded too much attention to established organizations and not enough to mobilization, both generative and reactive. And the SM theorist (McAdam) focused excessively on the transgressive phases of contention in examining the civil rights movements. But change occurs in many ways: the march that begins in the streets may transmigrate and begin to move through the institutions – legislatures, courts, agencies and firms. Mobilizing for struggle and negotiating settlements are two moments within the same process and need to be viewed in relation to each other to be fully understood. When seen in their broader context, it becomes clear that no movement ever manages to "succeed" – to fulfill all the hopes of those who labored to instigate institutional change. Goals are transformed as they are translated, and today's "victories" give rise to tomorrow's disappointments, provocations, and – eventually – to new reform efforts.

2

Where Do We Stand?

COMMON MECHANISMS IN
ORGANIZATIONS AND SOCIAL
MOVEMENTS RESEARCH

John L. Campbell

The premise of this volume is that both organizations and social movements are forms of coordinated collective action and, therefore, ought to
be conducive to similar forms of analysis (Perrow 2000: 472–4; Zald and
Berger 1978). Furthermore, the editors and contributors suspect that if students of organizations and social movements paid closer attention to each
other's work, then opportunities for creative conceptual and theoretical
cross-fertilization might occur, and our understanding of both organizations and movements might improve. To date, researchers in these fields
have made limited progress in this direction.

A few organization theorists have used social movement theory to
generate new hypotheses for organizational analysis and provide insights
into the development of organizational forms (e.g., Davis and McAdam
2000; Davis and Thompson 1994; Lounsbury 2001; Rao et al. 2000). But
they acknowledge that social movement theory still has been employed
only intermittently to explain these and other organizational phenomena
(Swaminathan and Wade 2001). Social movement theorists have been somewhat more ambitious in capitalizing on organizational analysis to explain
how social movements emerge and develop (e.g., Clemens 1993, 1997:
chap. 2). In particular, the resource mobilization tradition drew on organizational analysis to argue in part that social movement organizations, like
many types of organizations, tend toward bureaucratization, professionalization, and conglomeration, and that these organizations often adjust
their goals in order to better fit their resource environments and survive

Thanks go to Michael Allen, Denise Anthony, Elizabeth Armstrong, Frank Baumgartner, Jerry
Davis, Joel Levine, Marc Schneiberg, Dick Scott, and Mayer Zald for comments on a previous
draft of the chapter.

(Kriesi 1996; McCarthy and Zald 1973, 1977; Zald and Ash 1966). Another more recent example of the application of organization theory to social movements is the effort to apply population ecology models to the evolution of social movements (Minkoff 1993, 1997). Nevertheless, as contributors to this volume agree, much also remains to be done to integrate the insights of organization theory into the analysis of social movements, particularly with the emergence of new theories of organizations such as neoinstitutionalism, which rejects rational actor models, views institutions as independent variables, embraces cognitive and cultural explanations, and maintains an interest in supra-individual units of analysis (Powell and DiMaggio 1991: 8).

Scholars might be willing to take the call for integration more seriously if they appreciated, as this chapter does, that the organizations and social movements literatures *already* have developed striking similarities. Given the extent of these similarities, blending the insights from these literatures is not an especially radical or difficult analytic move. To be sure, scholars who have utilized the insights of one field to shed light on the other occasionally acknowledge that these literatures have things in common. But they typically do this in a narrow or ad hoc fashion, focusing at most on only a few characteristics shared by both literatures (e.g., Strang and Soule 1998). Certainly there is much to be learned from the intense scrutiny of one or two commonalities. What is missing, however, is a broad and more systematic mapping of the common ground shared by these fields. This chapter provides one such mapping and indicates just how close together scholars in these fields stand. It shows that the organizations and social movements literatures have developed serendipitously along parallel paths and, as a result, share insights regarding several important issues. In particular, there are strong similarities in terms of the mechanisms by which organizations and social movements develop and change. This chapter articulates the nature of some of these mechanisms, recognizing how important the identification and elaboration of mechanisms is for both organizations and social movements research (Davis and McAdam 2000: 216; McAdam et al. 1999: 160).

By *mechanism* I mean simply the *processes* that account for causal relationships among variables. Mechanisms are the nuts, bolts, cogs, and wheels that link causes with effects (Elster 1989: 3). The specification of causal mechanisms involves more than just establishing correlations among variables. The identification of a correlation may demonstrate that a relationship exists between variables, but unless we understand the underlying mechanism that caused it, we will not know why the relationship exists (Hedström and Swedberg 1998). Mechanisms, then, are the workhorses of explanation (McAdam et al. 2001: 30). So, for example, if we determine that the rapid escalation of protests in a population of social movement organizations is associated with a change in the political environment, we may have revealed an interesting correlation between changing political institutions and the diffusion of social movement activism, but we still do not know why this relationship obtains. Among other things, we do not know how movement organizations recognize that the environment has changed in their favor. This requires that we specify through additional empirical research the causal mechanisms that are responsible, such as a political learning process whereby the first movement organizations to protest successfully in the new environment spread word of their achievement to other organizations that subsequently follow suit, thus triggering the rapid diffusion of protest throughout the movement population (Minkoff 1997b).

My purpose here goes beyond helping to integrate the analyses of organizations and social movements. The advancement of social theory, particularly theories of institutional change, depends in part on our ability to identify mechanisms of social change that apply broadly to different realms of society. After all, one of the goals of science is to develop theories that are generalizable. Although no social mechanism is likely to operate in every situation, some mechanisms may operate in several situations, so their specification enables us to generalize beyond atheoretical descriptions of a single case but without necessarily making claims about universal laws (Elster 1998; McAdam et al. 2001: chap. 1; Merton 1967; Stinchcombe 1998). By identifying change mechanisms that already operate in two distinct realms, such as those involving organizations and those involving social movements, we may in fact be identifying mechanisms that operate even more widely. If so, then by identifying these mechanisms we will also contribute to the development of social theory more generally.

Scholars have suggested several general types of social mechanisms (e.g., Elster 1989; Hedström and Swedberg 1998). For example, Doug McAdam and his colleagues (2001: 25–6) identified three that are particularly relevant to the study of organizations and social movements, and that are used by others in this volume (e.g., Vogus and Davis). First, there are *environmental* mechanisms, that is, external factors that affect actors' capacities to engage in change. Second, there are *cognitive* mechanisms that alter how actors perceive their identities, interests, and possibilities for change. Finally, there are *relational* mechanisms that affect the connections among actors and their networks in ways that enable them to cause change.

I begin by discussing mechanisms associated with the state and political opportunity structures – examples of environmental mechanisms. Second, I examine a cognitive mechanism – framing. Third, I investigate three more cognitive mechanisms, diffusion, translation, and bricolage, which are mechanisms that offer particularly important insights about the processes of evolutionary and path-dependent change. These processes have received much attention in both the organizations and movements literatures. Fourth, I address network mobilizing structures and leadership under the rubric of relational mechanisms. I conclude with some more general thoughts on social mechanisms. Along the way I also suggest some opportunities for cross-fertilization between the organizations and social movements literatures as well as a few instances where they suffer from common deficiencies and blind spots. Because the literatures in both of these fields are vast, I concentrate primarily on the recent trends in each. Specifically, I examine the political process approach to social movements (e.g., McAdam et al. 1996) and the neoinstitutionalist approach in organizational analysis (e.g., Powell and DiMaggio 1991).

Environmental Mechanisms: Political Opportunity Structures

Political process models have become a cornerstone of social movements research. Key to this approach is the idea that movements confront a *political opportunity structure*, a set of formal and informal political conditions that encourage, discourage, channel, and otherwise affect movement activity. Political opportunity structures are said to constrain the range of options available to movements as well as to trigger movement activity in the first place (McAdam et al. 1996: 3). Important dimensions of the political opportunity structure include the degree to which formal political institutions are open or closed to challengers of the status quo; the degree to which political elites are organized in stable or unstable coalitions and alignments; the degree to which movements have allies within the political elite; and the degree to which political authorities are willing to use repression against challengers (McAdam 1996; Tarrow 1996). The conventional view of opportunity structures has been criticized for being too narrow, such as by neglecting how opportunity structures may be gendered so that a change in gender relations may create new movement opportunities (McCammon et al. 2001). Nevertheless, for the sake of brevity, I focus here only on how political institutions, as traditionally viewed in the movements literature, influence how movements and organizations mobilize for action. Political institutions are environmental mechanisms insofar as they constrain actors from pursuing some courses of action and enable them to pursue others.

Movement scholars have shown that political opportunity structures affect the *strategy*, organizational *structure*, and ultimate *success* of social movements. For instance, during the 1970s and 1980s the French movement against commercial nuclear power confronted a closed, insulated, and centralized set of political institutions that afforded activists little access to policymaking arenas, such as nuclear power plant licensing hearings or the courts, where they might have prevented new plants from being built or brought into service. As a result, they resorted to mass demonstrations and civil disobedience, luring tens of thousands of demonstrators into sometimes violent confrontations with police. They also entered electoral politics where they forged an antinuclear alliance with the Socialist Party. Nevertheless, they managed only to temporarily slow the development of France's nuclear power industry precisely because policymaking was so impermeable to opposition. In West Germany, things turned out somewhat better for the movement. Because West Germany was a federated state, political institutions were more decentralized and porous, so in addition to mobilizing through electoral politics and helping to organize a successful Green Party, German antinuclear activists used the courts to delay or stop licensing and construction of several new plants. In Sweden, where policymaking typically involves inclusive public discussions of important policy issues, activists worked closely with allies in one of the main political parties to convince the government to hold a national referendum on the future of nuclear power, which passed and required the phasing out of all commercial nuclear plants by 2010. Finally, in the United States, with its two-party, winner-take-all electoral system, party politics were out of the question. Instead, antinuclear forces tried to work through legal channels by creating formal professional organizations, such as the Union of Concerned Scientists, which was staffed by nuclear engineers, physicists, and other technocrats, and which lobbied Congress and regulatory officials. But when their success seemed limited due to government stonewalling, activists formed more radical and informal networks of organizations and turned to nonviolent civil disobedience. Eventually, both approaches contributed to a de facto moratorium on new nuclear orders after 1978 (Campbell 1988: chaps. 5, 8; Kitschelt 1986; Nelkin and Pollak 1981). In sum, the political opportunities associated with state institutions constrained the options available to activists, affected their strategies for seeking change and the organizational forms through which they chose to pursue it, channeled their efforts toward different arenas for protest and dialogue, and exerted significant effects on movement outcomes.

As this example illustrates, much of the work looking at the effects of political opportunity structures on social movements has been cast in a comparative, cross-national framework (Kriesi 1996; Rucht 1996). The same is true for some of the literature on the development of organizations. For instance, researchers have shown that the Italian economy developed an organizational structure based on small- and medium-sized firms in part because several Christian Democratic governments, whose electoral strength resides among the petty bourgeoisie, provided tax breaks, subsidies, and other incentives that deliberately encouraged the creation and maintenance of small businesses (Weiss 1988). Political elites also intentionally facilitated the organization of regional industrial districts where networks of these firms shared research and development, accounting, marketing, and various other services in a strategic effort to enhance their collective international competitiveness – a strategy that was relatively successful in the 1970s and 1980s insofar as it encouraged an approach to manufacturing based on principles of flexible specialization (Best 1990: chaps. 7–8; Piore and Sabel 1984: chap. 9). In contrast, much of the malaise experienced by the U.S. economy during the same period has been attributed to the dominance of comparatively large, bureaucratic, and inflexible business organizations that pursued a mass production strategy. These types of organizations grew in response to a very different set of political opportunities, including the unique American character of property rights law, that facilitated their development (Best 1990; Fligstein 1990; Hollingsworth 1991). Other countries offered very different political opportunities – sometimes intentionally, sometimes unintentionally – and, therefore, generated very different organizational structures, strategies, and records of success (e.g., Chandler and Daems 1980; Doremus et al. 1998; Guillén 1994; Hamilton and Biggart 1988).

Of course, political opportunity structures are not static. Students of both social movements and organizations have recognized that as these structures change, so do the movements and organizations that are embedded within them. Sidney Tarrow (1996) argued that, in order to understand the dynamics by which movements change over time, we must recognize that they are often linked to state building episodes. Recent work on Third World revolutions confirms that protest cycles often correspond to state building and other shifts in political opportunity structures. Misagh Parsa (2000) showed that changes in political opportunity structures, notably variation in levels of state repression, often caused the ebb and flow of outbursts of revolutionary activity in Iran, Nicaragua, and the Philippines (Parsa 2000; see also Tilly 1978: chap. 4; Della Porta 1996). Verta Taylor (1989) found that the U.S. women's movement was dormant and in abeyance until the political climate changed. Similarly, organization theorists have shown that as states redefine business regulations and civil rights law, firms overhaul their organizational structures and governance systems in order to better fit the new regulatory environment (Davis and Thompson 1994; Dobbin et al. 1993; Edelman 1990; Fligstein 1990). Shifts in how states define property rights also have triggered organizational and governance transformations at the level of economic sectors and national economies (Campbell and Lindberg 1990; North 1981; Streeck 1997).

There are also interesting parallels in how the social movements and organizations literatures view the dynamics underlying political opportunity structures. For instance, both literatures understand that the motivation for change can come from at least two directions. On the one hand, both recognize that change in political opportunity structures may be driven by *political authorities* in ways that transform the structure, strategy, and success of groups in society. As noted above, sometimes this is deliberate, such as when the Italian Christian Democrats moved to cultivate vibrant small- and medium-sized businesses. Other times it is not. The U.S. Congress passed the Celler-Kefauver Act in 1950 to limit the size of vertically integrated business firms, but inadvertently created a legal environment that led to the growth of a new organizational form – the highly diversified conglomerate (Fligstein 1990). Similarly, political elites have manipulated the opportunities available to social movements in ways that reduce the level of social protest, co-opt movement leaders, or otherwise undercut activism. The West German government cracked down on social movement activism in the 1970s with increased levels of police repression in order to better control terrorism. So did the Italian government in the 1950s to control leftist groups of all sorts as part of the government's campaign to repress the labor movement and rebuild the economy with low-wage labor (Della Porta 1996).

On the other hand, *societal groups* may provide the impetus for changing political opportunity structures, either as a means to some greater end, or as an essential goal in itself. Dairy farmers successfully pressed the U.S. Congress to pass the Capper-Volstead Act in 1922, which permitted them to organize producer cooperatives, a new organizational form in the industry, and successfully counteract the power of milk distributors (Young 1991).

Corporate shareholders managed to alter the law on proxy voting during the 1980s so as to transform corporate governance in ways that counteracted the power of corporate managers (Davis and Thompson 1994). Social movements also often seek to change their political opportunity structures, such as when the U.S. civil rights movement succeeded in opening new opportunities for itself by winning passage of the Voting Rights Act in 1965 – a legislative milestone that dramatically altered both the structure and the strategy of the movement (Piven and Cloward 1979: chap.4).

Two points require further elaboration. First, there is a remarkable similarity in how researchers in both of the fields of organizations and social movements specify political opportunity structures. In the organizations literature, for instance, Frank Dobbin (1994) wrote about how variation in the degree to which political institutions were open or closed, centralized or decentralized, and strong or weak contributed to the development of different organizational arrangements in the French, British, and U.S. railroad industries (see also Campbell and Lindberg 1990; Lindberg and Campbell 1991). Precisely the same distinctions are prevalent in the movements literature (e.g., Gamson and Meyer 1996: 281; Kriesi 1996). Second, the causal effects of political opportunity structures are cast in two different ways in these literatures. On the one hand, political opportunity structures *motivate* actors by creating grievances or other incentives for them to seek change, as occurred when the government stimulated the creation of small firms in Italy, and when the discriminatory policies of the United States government fueled the civil rights movement. On the other hand, political opportunity structures also *constrain* the range of strategic actions from which actors are most likely to choose as they pursue change. This was evident in the channeling of nuclear power protest to different arenas in different countries depending on the prevailing political institutional arrangements. It was also evident in antitrust and other forms of property rights law that limited the range of organizational forms that businesses could adopt in the United States.

Cognitive Mechanisms: Framing

Social movement scholars have argued that in order to be successful, activists must frame issues in ways that resonate with the ideologies, identities, and cultural understandings of supporters and others who might be drawn to their cause (Snow and Benford 1992; Snow et al. 1986). *Frames* are metaphors, symbols, and cognitive cues that cast issues in a particular light and suggest possible ways to respond to these issues. Framing involves the strategic creation and manipulation of shared understandings and interpretations of the world, its problems, and viable courses of action. Framing is a cognitive mechanism of social change insofar as it affects how actors perceive their interests, identities, and possibilities for change. Hence, frames mediate between opportunity structures and action because they provide the means with which people can interpret the political opportunities before them and, thus, decide how best to pursue their objectives (McAdam et al. 1996, 1999; Zald 1996). So, for instance, some researchers have argued that leaders of the U.S. civil rights movement framed their efforts in the broad language of equal rights in part because it resonated with traditional American political rhetoric – a rhetoric that was shared by the black middle class, the movement's main constituency, as well as white sympathizers. This sort of rights discourse is typical of movements in the United States, but not in other countries, whose basic political rhetoric is different (Tarrow 1994:129; but see Morris 2000: 448).

The emphasis on framing emerged as part of a larger effort among scholars to bring issues of culture and identity back into the analysis of social movements (e.g., Johnston and Klandermans 1995). For instance, Verta Taylor and Nancy Whittier (1992) showed how the lesbian feminist movement struggled mightily to define and frame its identity, and how it ended up with several identities depending on how different groups defined their boundaries and consciousness. The consideration of framing also emerged as a corrective to earlier work that failed to recognize that the interests of movement supporters were not objectively given by their social circumstances, including political opportunity structures, but had to be defined, interpreted, and socially constructed (McAdam et al. 1996). In this way, scholars saw that framing had significant consequences for movement outcomes. So, for example, prior to passage of the Nineteenth Amendment, women's groups in the United States were more likely to win suffrage rights at the level of state government when they argued that women would use their voting rights to protect children, homes, and families. In other words, they were more successful when they framed their demands in ways that convinced people that granting women the right to vote would reinforce rather than undermine women's traditional identity and gender roles (McCammon et al. 2001).

Students of organizations, most notably neoinstitutionalists, have taken a similar cultural turn insofar as they recognize that changes in organizational structure and strategy are driven by a logic of appropriateness where proposed changes are likely to catch hold – or even be recognized as viable possibilities in the first place – only if they are consistent with local customs, habits, schema, and routines (DiMaggio and Powell 1983; March and Olsen 1989). For example, Mauro Guillén (1994) explained how the adoption of different models of corporate management varied cross-nationally in part due to how well they resonated with national tradition and culture. This was one reason, he argued, why during the early twentieth century the Germans embraced scientific management, which fitted their Prussian bureaucratic experience, but rejected the human relations model, which was steeped in a Catholic ideology much less familiar to them. Conversely, managers in Spain welcomed the human relations approach because it was consistent with their Catholic and liberal-humanist traditions, which emphasized the importance of social participation, education, and training, but they were reticent to use scientific management, for which there was little resonance due to a relative lack of national bureaucratic traditions at that time.

Despite Guillén's attention to issues of cultural fit, he did not examine whether advocates of the adoption of these managerial models actually engaged in strategic framing to press their interests. In fact, most organizational theorists who stress the importance of cultural and cognitive fit also ignore the issue of framing (e.g., Nelson and Winter 1982: 99–107; Scott and Meyer 1994), perhaps because their work tends to be so structuralist that it does not theorize the importance of actors and agency (e.g., Hirsch 1997; Hirsch and Lounsbury 1997). Nevertheless, given the competition among models that Guillén reported in his cases, one would assume that strategic framing likely occurred and that an analysis of it could have been fitted comfortably into his argument. Yet despite the apparently natural opening for an analysis of framing, particularly in research based on detailed case studies (e.g., Fligstein 1990; Soysal 1994), only a few organizations' researchers have taken the issue of framing seriously. For instance, Dobbin (1994) argued that if proposals for the construction of national railway systems did not resonate with national culture, they typically failed to garner much support. So when British policymakers failed to frame rail policy proposals in terms of their national cultural tradition of individual sovereignty, when French policymakers failed to frame rail policy in terms of their tradition of state sovereignty, and when U.S. policymakers failed to frame rail policy in terms of their traditions of local self-rule and community sovereignty, they lost the policymaking struggle.

Dobbin did not unpack the details of the framing process itself and often reiterated the frequent neoinstitutionalist claim that organizational innovations tend to fail if they do not fit well with their normative environments. Perhaps sensing the need for elaboration, at least a few organization theorists have tried more deliberately to examine the framing process. Maureen Scully and Douglas Creed's work in this volume and elsewhere shows how the movement within corporations for gay-friendly policies depended heavily on framing the issue in terms that resonated with deep-seated public sentiments about equality and fairness as well as with corporate sentiments about how treating workers fairly could improve productivity and profitability (Creed et al. 2002; Scully and Creed in this volume). Neil Fligstein's work (1997b; Fligstein and Mara-Drita 1996) on the creation of the European Single Market project is another good example. He showed that members of the European Commission, in particular its president, Jacques Delors, who sought to develop a single European market, were careful to frame this institutional project in terms deemed appropriate by European governments and business elites. They emphasized how this new institution would involve only new rules of exchange rather than new property rights or governance structures, which would threaten national sovereignty and the interests of industrial actors. Until Delors managed to frame the issue in this manner, the Single Market project had difficulty gathering momentum.

Organization theorists have also intimated how framing has been crucial to the development of new industry niches, such as microbrewing in the United States, where the success of microbrewers depended heavily on their ability to convince consumers that their products had a uniquely desirable identity steeped in the traditions of small-scale craft production rather than the mass production techniques that characterized most beers on the market (Carroll and Swaminathan 2000). Indeed, framing is often about establishing discursive oppositions such as this, as also occurred in France when the characteristics of classical and nouvelle cuisine were juxtaposed by renegade chefs seeking to establish an identity and niche for the latter within their profession (Rao et al. 2001). In some cases framing can be extraordinarily strategic, involving much trial-and-error testing of frames and much counter-framing vis-à-vis the opposition's frames (Campbell 1998; Noakes 2000). For instance, the National Association of Broadcasters experimented in a trial-and-error fashion with several frames before they finally found one that convinced the federal government to preserve the television industry's portion of the broadcast spectrum when others, for example land-based broadcasters such as citizen's band radio operators, sought to reduce it (Dowell et al. 2002). Sometimes framing also can be a hotly contested process within a movement or organization, such as when feminists fighting for the Equal Rights Amendment struggled over whether to connect the ERA with abortion rights issues (Mansbridge 1986).

The point is that framing is a very complex set of processes (e.g., Benford and Snow 2000). Insofar as only a few organization theorists have begun to take the issue of framing seriously, they could still benefit from greater familiarity with this vast and important part of the social movements literature. The results of such cross-fertilization can be impressive. For example, Margaret Keck and Kathryn Sikkink (1998: chap. 1) explicitly blended the insights of neoinstitutionalism with the social movements framing literature to show how institutional practices, such as policies and practices regarding human rights and environmentalism, diffuse internationally, due in part to the efforts of transnational organizations who frame their issues in ways they hope will be irresistible to the governments whose practices they want to change. By stressing the importance of symbolic politics and strategic framing, Keck and Sikkink sought to inject a much stronger dose of agency into the analysis than do most neoinstitutional diffusion theorists (e.g., Boli and Thomas 1999). As a result, their approach is an explicit attempt to better specify the causal mechanisms of diffusion (Risse and Sikkink 1999: 4) – a subject elaborated below in greater detail.

Another area where cross-fertilization might be fruitful involves the more careful specification of the different parts of frames that organizational and social movement entrepreneurs deploy. Some movement scholars have argued that frames consist of at least two important parts. The diagnostic part concerns how problems are defined and where blame for them is located, and the prognostic part concerns how solutions and appropriate strategies for attaining them are defined (Benford and Snow 2000; McCarthy et al. 1996). To my knowledge, relatively few organizational theorists have thought much about the different parts that constitute a frame and how these parts relate to the possibilities for change. One exception is the work done by organizational sociologists on the development of Health Maintenance Organizations (HMOs) in the United States. They show that this new organizational form began spreading during the 1980s only after the problems of cost escalation in the health care delivery system were framed as stemming from the organizational inefficiencies of the old system, and after the HMO solution was framed as being based on a system of private, for-profit, competitive health plans whose operation was consistent with free market principles. In other words, the HMO innovation was institutionalized only after both the health care delivery problem and the solution were framed to fit the dominant neoliberal rhetoric of the day (Scott et al. 2000: 41, 218; Strang and Bradburn 2001).

The fact that frames rarely are constructed out of whole cloth, but rather are fabricated out of bits and pieces of already available repertoires and cultural artifacts, is widely acknowledged in the social movements literature (e.g., Swidler 1986; Tarrow 1994: 130–1). The general idea that people rarely create something truly new but more often cut and paste in innovative ways is an insight shared by organizational theorists that can shed light on another mechanism of social change – diffusion.

Cognitive Mechanisms: Diffusion, Translation, Bricolage

As noted above, social movement scholars have documented how movement structures and strategies often migrate from one setting to another, diffusing across movement organizations (Minkoff 1997b). *Diffusion* refers to the spread of practices through a population of actors. For example, the innovative strategies and tactics of the civil rights movement in Birmingham, Alabama, were so successful in 1963 that they served as a new model for civil rights leaders in dozens of cities throughout the South (Morris 1993: 633). Similarly, Anthony Oberschall (1996) showed how there was a diffusion of opposition frames and popular protest strategies across borders in Eastern Europe as the communist regimes began to collapse in 1989. Doug McAdam (1996) argued that spin-off movements often emerge through a diffusion process whereby the ideational, tactical, and organizational lessons of initial movement organizations spread among subsequent challengers. Organization scholars report much the same thing and have developed complex quantitative models to identify the conditions under which organizational practices diffuse within fields of organizations ranging from groups of business firms to nation states (e.g., Dobbin 1992; Edelman 1990; Strang 1990; for reviews of both literatures see Strang and Soule 1998).

The emphasis in these literatures is on specifying the conditions under which diffusion occurs, the rate at which it happens, the degree to which a new practice permeates a field of organizations or movements, and so on. However, it also involves specifying the mechanisms by which diffusion occurs, such as through coercive, normative, or mimetic processes (DiMaggio and Powell 1983). Diffusion is a cognitive mechanism insofar as it facilitates the dissemination of ideas and models that cause actors to perceive new possibilities or imperatives for action (e.g., Strang and Meyer 1993).

Recent work on organizational bandwagons illustrates the point. Research shows that bandwagons for new management fads, such as quality control circles and total quality management, escalate as old fads are discredited, creating an empty niche for new ones; as a performance gap appears whereby firms fail to meet performance expectations; and as knowledge entrepreneurs, such as journalists, consultants, and academics, offer new organizational solutions to close this gap. As some firms begin to adopt the new solution, others follow suit, not wanting to appear out of step with new trends and not wanting to fall behind competitively by failing to adopt (Abrahamson and Fairchild 1999; Abrahamson and Rosenkopf 1993; Strang and Macy 2001). This research is reminiscent of an older tradition in the social movements literature, which argues that collective behavior such as fads, demonstrations, and riots stems from structural strain, that is, a disjuncture between values or expectations, on the one hand, and structural conditions, on the other hand (e.g., Gurr 1971; Smelser 1962). However, the research on organizational bandwagons recognizes that a gap between expectations and performance is not sufficient to explain the rise of bandwagons. The performance gap as well as new solutions must be articulated and made visible to managers by knowledge entrepreneurs. Moreover, forces for change must be mobilized through framing. In short, there are important cognitive steps involved in the diffusion process.

What is notably absent here is much discussion of what happens when a practice arrives at an organization or movement's doorstep ready and waiting for adoption. Here the story often ends and it is assumed that the practice is simply adopted uncritically and in toto. David Strang and Dong-Il Jong's work in this volume begins to tackle this issue by examining what happens when a new practice first crosses the organizational doorstep. They specify the conditions that accounted for bank employees being willing or not to support new quality initiative practices that arrived at the organization through diffusion. Similarly, Mayer Zald and his colleagues (in this volume) theorize the conditions that affect whether organizational innovations that diffuse through a field are likely to be embraced and implemented seriously, symbolically, or not at all by organizational leaders. Nevertheless, the implication, often explicit for organization theorists (e.g., DiMaggio and Powell 1983; Mizruchi and Fein 1999), is that diffusion results in homogeneous or isomorphic outcomes where organizations or movements within a field gradually converge with respect to their form and function. For instance, John Meyer and his colleagues (1997) argued that the development of a global scientific discourse, embracing the concept of a world ecosystem, caused many national governments to establish environmental ministries during the late twentieth century. However, their analysis omitted any discussion of the national-level political processes that were responsible for this institution building. The problem is that we are left with a black box in which the processes that are actually adopted and institutionalized on a case-by-case basis are left unspecified. In this sense, diffusion appears to be a mindless mechanical transfer of information from one place to another (Rao et al. 2001; see also Haveman 2000: 477). It seems that such neglect is common in the literatures on both social movements and organizations. In a comprehensive review of how the concept of diffusion has been used in these two literatures there is virtually no work mentioned that examines what this process might look like (Strang and Soule 1998).

To be fair, quantitative studies of organizational innovation and diffusion often employ a population ecology perspective and event-history models, which are not designed to capture the processes that I have in mind. Yet if we accept that variation in things such as political opportunity structures and framing cause variation in the structure, strategy, and success of movements and organizations, then it stands to reason that these sorts of things will also cause variation in how the structure, strategy, and success of movements and organizations diffuse across sites (e.g., Andrews 2001).

What is required, then, even in studies such as those of Strang and Jung, and Zald and colleagues, is a specification of the mechanisms whereby models of organization and action that diffuse through a field are translated into practice on a case-by-case basis. By *translation* I mean the process by which practices that travel from one site to another are modified and implemented by adopters in different ways so that they will blend into and fit the local social and institutional context (Czarniawska and Sevon 1996). For example, as neoliberal ideas diffused among countries during the 1980s and 1990s, individual governments tended to adopt different elements of the neoliberal model and blend them into their already existing institutional traditions in ways that resulted in less convergence and isomorphism than most diffusion theorists might expect. So in Denmark, where policymaking was traditionally negotiated at the national level between the state and an array of social organizations, policymakers reformed nationally coordinated labor market institutions by decentralizing but not abandoning them. Labor market policy became coordinated through negotiations between employers and state authorities at the regional level (Swank and Martin 2001). Similarly, Danish industrial policymaking was decentralized rather than abandoned so that close negotiations were still conducted between government authorities, business, and labor unions but at a regional rather than national level (Kjaer and Pedersen 2001). Other countries took very different approaches depending on their own traditions so reform in the areas of economic regulation, labor market institutions, welfare policy, and fiscal policy took a number of different neoliberal forms (Campbell 2001; Kitschelt et al. 1999; Vogel 1996). A few social movement researchers have also suggested that when ideas, practices, or frames diffuse from one place to another they are strategically adapted and fitted to the new context (Benford and Snow 2000: 627). There are enough empirical examples of variation in how these things are translated into practice that we should pay closer attention to specifying at a conceptual level the causal mechanisms involved (e.g., Djelic 1998; Guillén 1994; Lounsbury 2001; Marjoribanks 2000; Soysal 1994).

The foundation for such an analysis of translation already exists in the social movements and organizations literature insofar as both recognize that change in practices generally results from a blending of bits and pieces from a repertoire of elements. This may entail the rearrangement of elements that are already at hand, but it may also entail the blending in of new elements that have diffused from elsewhere. In either case the result is a *bricolage*, that is, an innovative recombination of elements that constitutes a new way of configuring organizations, social movements, institutions, and other forms of social activity (e.g., Balkin 1998: chap. 2; Douglas 1986: 66–7; Levi-Strauss 1966: 16–33).

The notion of bricolage is probably more familiar to social movements theorists than to organization theorists, particularly those who study the discursive processes associated with framing. Notably, Elisabeth Clemens (1996, 1993) showed that during the early twentieth century labor organizers blended elements of several organizational models that were available to them, including fraternal organizations and the military militia, to construct the craft-based union. She also showed that women blended organizational elements of traditional men's clubs, political precinct models, and professional bureaucracies to create new women's political organizations. Symbolic as well as technical elements may be involved in a bricolage. For instance, Martin Luther King Jr. composed a frame for the civil rights movement by blending the Christian doctrine of love with the moral principles of freedom and justice – a frame that resonated with the culture of the African-American church, whose members he was trying to mobilize (Morris 2000: 448). A few organization theorists have also acknowledged how new organizational practices are formed through the process of bricolage (Campbell 1997; Stark 1996). Others have described this process without actually labeling it bricolage as such (Nelson and Winter 1982: 128–34). For example, Haveman and Rao (1997) showed how the California thrift industry evolved through five different organizational forms as a result of the incremental blending and reblending of elements of several important social institutions: principles of mutuality and enforced saving, bureaucracy, and voluntarism. Symbolic as well as technical considerations drove the process, as is often the case (e.g., Campbell 1997). The point is that these studies show how the diffusion of various models and concepts through fields of movements and organizations involved the critical step of being dovetailed into already existing practices by innovative bricoleurs.

The fact that symbolic and technical elements may be blended into a bricolage leads to a more general point. Thinking about diffusion as a process of translation *qua* bricolage should be particularly amenable to students of both social movements and organizations. After all, it is a process that can involve all the different rationalities of action that have drawn attention in these literatures. Social movements and organizations theorists seem to agree that action can be shaped by self-interests, norms, and cognitive understandings (McAdam et al. 1999; Scott 2001: chap. 3). Analyses of translation can accommodate all three. First, translation may involve powerful actors struggling in pursuit of their political and economic interests. Notably, German industrialists and politicians after the Second World War were forced by the United States to adopt antitrust policy based on the U.S. model, but maneuvered to adopt it in a form that did not fundamentally undermine the cartels and business groups that had long been part of the German institutional landscape and in which they had a vested interest (Djelic 1998). Second, translation may involve actors trying to adapt new practices to already existing normative assumptions about how organizations or movements ought to be organized. This was an important reason why during the late twentieth century different European governments devised dramatically different ways to translate a new internationally accepted model of citizenship into institutional practice – a model based on the idea that people living in a community have a right to participate in the politics and public life of the polity regardless of their historical or cultural ties to that community (Soysal 1994). Third, translation may involve actors trying to maintain their cognitive identities. This is a factor that helps explain why unions in different countries decided to oppose different aspects of neoliberalism. Italian unions resisted the elimination of cost-of-living adjustments; Swedish unions resisted the abolition of centralized wage bargaining; German unions resisted an attack on codetermination practices.

In each case, they resisted those aspects of the neoliberal attack that most threatened their organizational identities (Locke and Thelen 1995). The fact that a variety of rationalities may be involved is an especially important lesson for organizational diffusion theorists' who tend to assume that diffusion results from a cognitive process of imitation when, in fact, it can involve a variety of rationalities that need to be disentangled theoretically as well as empirically (Mizruchi and Fein 1999; Suchman 1997). But the more important point is that the concept of bricolage ought to be amenable to scholars regardless of their preference for theories rooted in an analysis of interests, norms, or cognition.

A Related Note on Evolutionary Change and Path Dependence

Recognizing the mechanisms of translation and bricolage offers another benefit. It can help us better understand the dynamics of evolutionary change. Social movement and organization theorists alike have recognized that change is often gradual and evolutionary. Even change that may result from volatile, highly contested processes and that might appear at first to be quite radical and revolutionary often turns out, upon further examination, to be more gradual and evolutionary in the long run (McAdam 1996: 30; Scott et al. 2000: 24–7; see also Campbell and Pedersen 1996). Some argue that such evolutionary change occurs through a process known as *path dependence* in which apparently small or insignificant events or decisions result in an organizational or institutional change that persists over long periods of time and that limits the range of options available to actors in the future (e.g., Clemens 1997: 58–9, 237; Davis and McAdam 2000: 216; Guthrie 1999: 85; North 1990: 93–5; Powell 1991: 192; Roe 1996; see also Stinchcombe 1968: 101–18).

For instance, the initial decision by Thomas Edison and his colleagues to obtain European rather than American financing for the development of early electricity generating technology had profound and largely irreversible consequences for the organizational evolution of the U.S. electric utility industry. The Europeans favored a centralized electricity generation model. As a result, rather than developing small household generators, Edison created big central station technology that gave rise to today's huge electric utility companies and a few large suppliers, such as General Electric and Westinghouse, that provided most of the important products for the industry, ranging from massive generators to common light bulbs. In turn, this precluded subsequent efforts to introduce decentralized technologies, including those that might have been more efficient. Once Edison had made his financial choice the industry evolved along a path that was not easily altered (McGuire et al. 1993).

Economic historians and rational choice theorists have argued more abstractly that path dependence stems from a series of mechanisms that "lock in" actors to a particular developmental path (e.g., Arthur 1994; David 1985; North 1990). Applying this approach to politics, Paul Pierson (2000a, 2000b) has argued that path dependence occurs as a result of several feedback mechanisms through which actors gain increasing returns for behaving in ways that are consistent with how they have acted in the past and, therefore, encourage them to behave similarly in the future. First, political institutions have large start-up costs so that once they are established actors are not likely to seek to change them, especially if they perceive that the chances of other actors joining them to innovate are increasingly slim, given the costs involved. Second, sometimes politicians deliberately build institutions in ways that make them difficult to dismantle. They may, for instance, impose procedural obstacles to prevent others from later changing the institutions that they create. Hence, framers of the U.S. Constitution stipulated that subsequent changes to the Constitution would require not only congressional approval, as does normal legislation, but also ratification by three quarters of the states. This was an important obstacle to ratification of the Equal Rights Amendment in the late 1970s (Mansbridge 1986). Third, once a particular policy style or decision-making approach has been institutionalized, actors accumulate knowledge about how it works. The more familiar and comfortable they become with it, the more hesitant they are to deviate from it. Fourth, beneficiaries of legislative or institutional largesse reinforce institutional behavior that will continue to provide them with benefits. Notably, senior citizens organize to reelect politicians who support old-age pensions and oppose those who favor cutting their benefits and programs.

Scholars who use the path dependence concept often maintain that the operation of these sorts of lock-in mechanisms accounts for evolutionary change (Pierson 2000a: 84; Roe 1996). Most notably, Douglass North (1990: chaps. 1, 8) maintained that institutions that are locked in feed back and constrain actors' choices in ways that generally permit only incremental changes at the margins. These changes accumulate over time altering institutions in an evolutionary fashion. The problem is that this blurs an important distinction between the two concepts. Evolution is a concept that depicts *change*; path dependence is a concept that depicts *stability*. Once we specify the lock-in mechanisms involved in path dependent processes it becomes clear that this concept is far better suited to explaining the persistence of organizational and movement forms and behaviors rather than their transformation (e.g., Pierson 2000b: 265; Thelen 1999, 2000a, 2000b). In other words, path dependence arguments are too deterministic; they specify only the mechanisms that keep history on a particular path, not those that cause it to switch paths (Haydu 1998; see also Roe 1996: 665). How can the situation be improved?

To better link the analysis of change with the notion of path dependence, some theorists have introduced the concept of *critical junctures* – that is, major shocks and crises that disrupt the status quo and trigger fundamental changes (Haydu 1998; Thelen 1999). By itself, this concept is inadequate for explaining change in organizations and social movements. Shocks of the sort that constitute critical junctures explain why major changes occur, but not why more incremental or evolutionary change happens (Thelen 2000a, 2000b). Moreover, the critical juncture approach tends to focus our attention on the key events that may cause actors to want change of some sort, but it sheds little light on the subsequent search process whereby actors weigh their options and decide what sort of specific change they want to pursue now that they confront a critical juncture (Campbell and Lindberg 1991).

The dilemma of explaining how evolutionary change occurs in path dependent ways is resolved when we realize that change often occurs through the process of bricolage. When we acknowledge that new organizational or social movement structures, strategies, and frames are created by recombining elements that are already available in an innovator's repertoire, then we can see how change is simultaneously evolutionary and path dependent. The process is path dependent insofar as the range of choices for recombinant innovation is fixed by the set of elements already at the innovator's disposal. The process is evolutionary insofar as what is created is a new combination of elements, but one that still resembles the past by virtue of the fact that it is made from elements that were already available in the existing repertoire. Indeed, this is precisely how Joseph Schumpeter (1983: chap. 2) conceived of the industrial innovation process and, as noted earlier, this is how students of organizations and social movements have begun to think about change (e.g., Haveman and Rao 1997; Stark 1996). In addition, the more new elements diffuse from elsewhere, become part of the available repertoire, and are translated into the bricolage, the more revolutionary and less evolutionary change becomes. The implication here is that change is a more complex process than is sometimes appreciated; that it is not well represented by a simple evolutionary versus revolutionary dichotomy; and that, instead, it should be thought of more as a complex matter of degree best represented along a continuum (Campbell 2004).

Relational Mechanisms: Network Cultivation and Strategic Leadership

Students of social movements have recognized that in order for collective action to occur activists must utilize mobilizing structures to recruit members, obtain other resources, and disseminate information. By mobilizing structures they generally mean "collective vehicles, informal as well as formal, through which people mobilize and engage in collective action" (McAdam et al. 1996: 3). One of the most important aspects of mobilizing structures is the formal and informal networks that connect individuals and organizations (Tilly 1978: 3). Networks are social structures, that is, sets of social relationships, that shape and constrain people's behavior and opportunities for action. Networks constitute the conduits through which new models, concepts, and practices diffuse and become part of an organization or movement's repertoire and, therefore, become available for use in framing and translation by bricoleurs (e.g., Keck and Sikkink 1998). Networks also help determine the sources of mass support that activists can mobilize. For instance, Roger Gould (1993) found that urban insurgency was mobilized in the Paris Commune in 1871 through social networks that existed in Parisian neighborhoods. Neighborhood ties facilitated mobilization by providing a basis upon which to forge a collective identity against the French government's efforts to control the city through military repression. Similarly, academics and other intellectuals affiliated with movements for new social policies have mobilized through their social networks with policymakers to press for political institutional change (Schweber 1996).

Of course, organization theorists also understand that networks provide the foundation for all sorts of organizational innovation and activity (e.g., Aldrich 1999: chap. 4; Burt 1993). Following Mark Granovetter's (2000, 1985, 1974) classic discussions of network embeddedness and strong and weak ties, Brian Uzzi (1996) showed how firms in the New York City garment district utilized informal networks to mobilize resources, including steady supplies of materials, customers, business information, and more. Uzzi reported that firms that performed the best were those whose networks included both long-term personal relationships and more impersonal, short-term, arm's-length relationships. Similarly, Michael Useem

(1984) documented how networks of interlocking corporate directors provided an important means by which business leaders mobilized in response to political threats to their interests in the 1970s. Annalee Saxenian (1994) showed that the phenomenal success of the computer and microelectronics industries in Silicon Valley was due to the dense web of cooperative interfirm relations that facilitated all sorts of collaboration, information sharing, and cutting-edge technological innovation. Like Gould's analysis of the Paris Commune, Saxenian's story is very much about how success depended on the ability of entrepreneurs to forge a collective identity through tight-knit community networks. Some researchers have recognized that the notion of networks as mobilizing structures offers an important point of cross-fertilization between the organizations and movements literatures (Davis and McAdam 2000).

It is important to see that networks are not always taken as given by activists or entrepreneurs. They may also be cultivated deliberately in order to obtain critical resources, new organizational models, and the like. The process of *network cultivation* is an example of a relational mechanism because it is a process through which networks and thus mobilizing structures are altered (e.g., McAdam et al. 2001: 26). In the social movements literature Keck and Sikkink (1998) showed that international nongovernmental movement organizations often seek to expand their networks to include actors whose resources could be put to work on behalf of the movement to change the policies of recalcitrant governments. Mark Warren (2001) argued that in order for community organizers in the southwestern United States to develop the sorts of social capital required to obtain political resources they had to create networks that bridged diverse racial, religious, and class constituencies and organizations, such as faith-based congregations. In the organizations literature scholars have shown that networks of interfirm alliances are created intentionally so that firms can get the money, market access, technical expertise, and other resources they want (Gulati and Gargiulo 1999).

Organization theorists also have found that networks are formed sometimes in the hope that they will generate resources and innovations in the medium to long term. I have in mind here something akin to what academics do when they "network" at conferences. That is, they try to make new contacts with people who they suspect might be useful to them later, even though they are not sure how or when these contacts will yield benefits. In this case the creation of networks is an investment in the future, rather than a means for obtaining specific payoffs in the present. For instance, local networks of firms have been created sometimes in the hope that the network will eventually generate collective resources even though it is not clear at the time what those resources will be. By the late 1970s Pennsylvania was reeling from industrial decline. Policymakers offered a set of grants and other incentives to bring representatives from business, labor unions, communities, and local colleges and universities together to evaluate the situation and generate new and more effective approaches to the problem. The idea was to create a network of trusting social relations by which new programs could be designed and administered in a more associative and cooperative fashion than had previously been the case, but leaving it up to the network participants to define their goals and solutions for themselves (Sabel 1993). To my knowledge, the intentional creation of networks as investments in the future has not been explored much in the social movements literature, although some scholars have suggested why movements might want to consider doing so in order to forge new identities that might more effectively realize important political gains (Piore 1995). Warren's (2001) work is a notable exception insofar as he shows that community organizers create networks in part to facilitate a needs assessment process in which local community groups are mobilized to determine what the important issues are for them and then to figure out how to act on these issues. In other words, networks are not created with specific predefined goals already in mind, but rather to help people define what their goals are in the first place.

All of this raises the issue of strategic leadership. By strategic leadership I mean more than just people who preside over and maintain already well-established organizations, such as the chief executive officer of General Motors or the president of the National Organization of Women. The sort of leadership I am referring to entails much more innovation and organization and movement building in the first place. In this sense, strategic leadership is equivalent to entrepreneurialism.

Researchers have argued that the social movements literature has failed to theorize the role of strategic leadership – even though leadership is perhaps the most important mechanism linking political opportunities, mobilizing structures, framing processes, and outcomes (Ganz 2000; Morris 2000). Specifically, Marshall Ganz (2000) suggests that the movements literature has not understood how the strategic capacities of leaders, which are crucial in determining movement success, depend on their biographies, networks, and repertoires as well as the organizational contexts within which they operate. As a result, social movement scholars have trouble explaining why some movements with poor resource endowments succeed where those with greater endowments fail, and how some movements succeed and others fail where both confront similar political opportunity structures. Just as Uzzi discovered that a mixture of strong and weak ties was crucial for organizational success in the New York garment industry, Ganz showed that the resource-poor United Farm Workers (UFW), whose leaders were able to cultivate both strong ties to constituencies and weak ties across constituencies, was more successful in organizing Californian agricultural workers than organizations such as the resource-rich AFL-CIO (American Federation of Labor and Congress of Industrial Organizations), which did not have such ties. Strong ties to constituencies provided UFW leaders with information about where to find important resources and support. Weak ties across constituencies provided them with information about people, ideas, and routines that could help them form broad-based political alliances. Similarly, the civil rights movement was most successful in places such as Montgomery, Alabama, where movement leaders were located at central nodes of several indigenous community networks, which provided them with vast communication channels, cultural frames, material resources, and organized followings (Morris 2000: 450). Conversely, opposition against the Equal Rights Amendment ran into trouble in states like Maine where anti-ERA leadership, notably Phyllis Schlafly, was not well connected to the citizenry, was out of tune with the citizenry's attitudes, failed to appreciate how socially liberal the state was, and thus erred in presenting the ERA as something that would encourage homosexuality, gay marriage, and the like (Mansbridge 1986).

Although the business management literature and some of the literature on organizations have not neglected the issue (e.g., Aldrich 1999: chap. 4; Swedberg 2000; Thornton 1999), within the neoinstitutionalist camp organizational theorists also have a blind spot regarding leadership. Despite calls for a theory of the role of institutional or organizational entrepreneurs in organizational analysis (DiMaggio 1988), only a few scholars have begun to pay serious attention. Notably, Fligstein (1997b, 2001b) articulated a variety of general strategies that entrepreneurs will likely deploy depending on whether their organizational fields are well organized and stable or not. Some strategies, he argued, are better suited to and effective in certain organizational environments than others. Furthermore, entrepreneurs with the most "social skill," that is, that ability to devise strategies that can best induce cooperation in others, are the ones most likely to transform organizational fields. However, unlike Ganz, he did not specify the conditions that influence how entrepreneurs devise these strategies and, thus, develop social skill in the first place. Hence, it is not clear in his scheme why one entrepreneur's social skills might be different and more effective than another's. For Ganz, this is the key to developing a theory of leadership.

This is important for issues raised earlier. On the one hand, as both Ganz and Fligstein acknowledge, better understanding the relationship between network structure and leadership can go a long way in bringing agency back into what have typically been rather structuralist accounts of social movement and organizational change, success, and failure (see also Morris 2000). On the other hand, specifying more closely how different network structures influence the strategic capacities of leaders may shed additional light on the process of bricolage and the degree to which it results in evolutionary or revolutionary change. After all, if leaders have only limited ties to their constituency and others outside their immediate movement or organization, then they are less likely to come into contact with new ideas that might expand their repertoires and provide the tools and insights for more creative thinking, innovation, and bricolage (Ganz 2000). This is why being located at the borders and interstices of several networks or organizational fields can enhance the probabilities for relatively dramatic change (Morrill 2003; Piore 1995; Rao et al. 2000). In short, network structure may influence why leaders create one bricolage instead of another.

Finally, a brief remark is in order regarding the usage of the concept "embeddedness" in the movements and organizations literatures. As initially formulated by Granovetter (1974, 1985), actors and organizations were said to be embedded in social relations that afforded them certain opportunities and precluded others. What mattered here were actors' structural relations with each other. That is, embeddedness referred to the position of actors within a network of strong and weak ties. As we have seen, this idea has begun to catch hold in the social movements literature too. However, the concept of embeddedness has been elaborated in several directions (e.g., Streeck 1997). Scholars working in both fields have recognized how being embedded in different institutional milieus can have profound effects on organizational and movement development. These insights can be organized along the lines suggested by Richard Scott's (2001: chap. 3) distinction among the regulatory, normative, and cognitive dimensions of institutions. Cognitive structures limit the range of practices that leaders of organizations (e.g., Fligstein 1990) and social movements (e.g., Ganz 2000) can imagine. Once imagined, normative structures limit what is considered acceptable or appropriate practice for organizations (e.g., Dobbin 1994; Guthrie 1999) and movements (e.g., Skrentny 1998). Lastly, regulatory structures, particularly political ones, as noted above, limit the range of practices that actors can get away with and institutionalize in organizations (e.g., Campbell and Lindberg 1990) and movements (e.g., Della Porta 1996). The point is that there are at least four types of embeddedness that receive attention in both literatures (network, regulatory, normative, cognitive) so there may be insights gleaned in one field about how these operate that may be useful in the other.

Conclusion

The purpose of this chapter has been to identify some of the mechanisms that appear to be operating in common in the worlds of organizations and social movements. This chapter is not exhaustive. First, I have not explored the relationships between mechanisms, although this is worth thinking about some more. For instance, political opportunity structures constrain action in part by providing fairly stable institutional arenas that tend to limit how other mechanisms operate, such as what sorts of strategic framing, network-building, leadership, bricolage, and translation are most likely to occur. Similarly, although I have viewed framing as a very strategic process here, once frames are established and taken for granted, they constitute cognitive structures in people's heads that may further limit the degree to which various network-building, leadership, bricolage, and translation processes are deemed acceptable to the people involved. Overall, then, some mechanisms may operate within constraints established by other mechanisms in a nested fashion.

Second, there are undoubtedly other mechanisms common to both organizations and social movements that are worth examining but that I have neglected. One mentioned briefly above involves the mechanisms associated with population ecology models. Of course, there is a long tradition in organizations theory based on this approach, which specifies how the availability of resources in a field of organizations affects the birth, death, and survival rates of those organizations, and how organizations that are able to establish a resource-rich niche for themselves tend to thrive more than those that do not establish such niches (Hannan and Freeman 1989). Only recently have social movement theorists started to apply these models to their work (e.g., Minkoff 1993, 1997b), even though the attention to resource constraints on movements resonates with their earlier resource mobilization tradition.

Another place to look for parallel mechanisms is in work on the development of organizational forms. Much organizational theory is devoted to identifying the mechanisms through which different organizational forms emerge, such as hierarchies, decentralized networks, and markets. Several theories have been developed accordingly (e.g., Chandler 1977; Perrow 1986: chap. 7; Williamson 1985). Scholars have also been interested in identifying how social movements assumed various organizational forms, again including hierarchy, decentralized networks, and a spontaneous, leaderless form without much organization at all – a form that may bear some resemblance to a market (Gerlach and Hine 1970; Kriesi 1996; Piven and Cloward 1979). Given these strong similarities it may be worth investigating whether the mechanisms identified in one of these literatures can be applied to the other. We might wonder, for instance, whether the mechanisms identified by transaction-cost or principle-agent theorists (or their critics) might shed light on the organization of social movements.

Surely there are other areas of parallel development in these two literatures that might be explored fruitfully. In any case, the important point is that there is already much in common between these two literatures, particularly insofar as they identify similar causal mechanisms, and therefore significant opportunities for cross-fertilization. However, given these parallels, I do not mean to imply that organization and social movement scholars have little else to learn from each other or that there is little value-added to be gained from paying closer attention to each other's work. Indeed, the chapters in this volume suggest quite the opposite. For instance, McAdam and Scott's chapter shows how these two literatures have complementary strengths and weaknesses that, when fully appreciated, can be used to improve research and theory for the study of both social movements and organizations. Moreover, as indicated in this chapter, recognizing the commonalities shared by both literatures can help scholars think more clearly about causality and how it operates.

Calls for cross-fertilization *within* the social movements and neoinstitutionalist literatures have been issued recently. In both cases, strong arguments have been made that by identifying important causal mechanisms it may be possible to find some common ground that will help to better integrate, synthesize, or at least establish the possibility for rapprochement among contending theoretical perspectives, notably rational choice, historical process, and cultural approaches (Campbell and Pedersen 2001; McAdam et al. 1999, 2001). This chapter suggests that a search for causal mechanisms also can facilitate cross-fertilization *between* these two literatures. Insofar as this leads to the identification of relatively generic mechanisms that apply across a broader realm of social phenomena than just organizations and social movements, then their identification also will contribute to the improvement of social theory in general.

Political and Mobilization Context

T he essays in this section have a common theme: the developmental
      dependence of both movements and organizations on the mobiliza-
tion and political contexts in which they develop. By political context we
mean variability in both the formal legal/institutional structuring of politics and the shifting informal elite alignments that define a given historical
period. Mobilization context refers more to the social demographic bases
of local populations. The chapters in this section exhibit similarities and
differences. Three use statistical analyses to show how differences in political and mobilization contexts across all fifty states lead to differences in
outcomes. All of the chapters can be seen as doing a kind of political sociology of the phenomena they are studying. But the chapters are also different
in the concepts they use, in the extent to which events and processes at the
national level are seen as interacting with state-level phenomena, and in the
historical depth explored by the analysis.

   In Chapter 3, "Institutional Variation in the Evolution of Social Movements: Competing Logics and the Spread of Recycling Advocacy Groups,"
Michael Lounsbury studies one aspect of the modern environmental movement as it penetrates organizations and local communities. His chapter
draws upon the concept of institutional logics and on concepts related to
mobilization context. Specifically, he shows that the formation of early state
recycling advocacy groups was enabled by state-level conditions that were
favorable to ecological activism. These early organizations were loosely
connected and promoted a holistic logic of recycling that emphasized a
vision of recycling as a mechanism to restructure capitalistic production
and consumption processes and enable community building and development. As the recycling movement unfolded, it took on a more hierarchical, national character, structured by a new national social movement

organization, the National Recycling Coalition. This national organization promoted a more technocratic logic of recycling that valorized the creation of a mass market in recycling commodities as a way to promote the development of a profitable recycling industry. As a result, the widespread diffusion of recycling advocacy groups was enabled, but mainly in states with high levels of state incinerator capacity. Recycling advocacy groups that emerged under the technocratic logic focused more on implementing recycling programs and engaging in jurisdictional battles with waste-to-energy incineration proponents over the solid waste stream than those organizations founded upon a holistic logic. Lounsbury discusses the implications of his case for organization theory, the study of social movements, and the study of institutional change.

Where Lounsbury is examining the spread, growth, and change of social movement–related organizations, the next two chapters show how laws and policies related to industry and corporations are shaped by political context and social movement processes. Timothy J. Vogus and Gerald F. Davis study how legislation developed to resist the "hostile" takeover, that is, bids for the acquisition of corporations by buyers unacceptable to top management of firms. "Elite Mobilization for Antitakeover Legislation, 1982–1990" examines the spread of state laws regulating hostile takeovers in the late 1980s as instances of political mobilization and social movement activity by state-level corporate elites. The authors argue that a social movement perspective offers a parsimonious, yet comprehensive, set of mechanisms – political opportunity, mobilizing structures, and frame alignment processes – that clarify the conditions under which mobilization will occur and succeed. Vogus and Davis also interpret the adoption of antitakeover legislation as part of an ongoing movement/countermovement between shareholder activists (who opposed state antitakeover laws) and corporate managers (who generally favored them). Event history analyses of the adoption of state laws show that political opportunities (local economic crisis), mobilizing structures (an existing infrastructure), and available frames (prior adoption of an antitakeover statute) predict a state's rate of adopting a statute, the type of statute adopted, and the strength of the legislation adopted.

What does the price of fire insurance sold by insurance companies have to do with social movements? If we believe economic theory, the price of insurance ought to be solely a function of liability risks for different kinds of insurance; but Marc Schneiberg and Sarah A. Soule demonstrate in Chapter 5 that insurance rates are set through state regulation practices that are shaped by movements and politics. Their chapter focuses upon the period in which fire insurance regulations were adopted in most of the states of the union, 1909–30. In contrast to the prior two chapters, Schneiberg and Soule use diffusion models to help trace the development of rate regulation. They also focus more on institutionalization, seen as a process of adoption of routine structures and policies. Organizational analysts have come to view institutionalization in three ways – as an expression of modern rationalized culture, as a process of mimesis, diffusion and emergent order, and/or as a process of negotiation and social reconstruction occasioned by disruptive state interventions. Schneiberg and Soule combine historical analysis and heterogeneous diffusion models of the regulation of insurance rates by the American states to reconceptualize institutionalization as a contested, multilevel process. Four central findings emerge that challenge standard approaches. First, institutionalization here represented a settlement of political conflicts over competing models of organization and the character of economic order rather than the enactment of taken-for-granted principles, as is sometimes implied by neoinstitutionalist theorists. Second, the settlement of political conflicts was not a function of local problem-solving activity, but of efforts by social movements to contest existing arrangements and promote alternative models of market organization. Third, the process of sorting through competing models occurred through interaction at the intra-, inter-, and supra-state levels. Finally, these settlements resulted not in a unitary or isomorphic insurance system, but rather in a fractured field characterized by variations on core themes – a dual community of regulated states – and the persistence of competing logics.

Finally, Elizabeth A. Armstrong examines how institutional fields emerge over time. In Chapter 6, "From Struggle to Settlement: The Crystallization of a Field of Lesbian/Gay Organizations in San Francisco, 1969–1973," she explains how the lesbian/gay movement in this locale arrived at a new institutional settlement in the early 1970s. The crystallization of the lesbian/gay movement in the 1970s around a gay pride/gay rights agenda was enabled by conditions specific to the history of the homosexual movement and the way it intersected with the New Left. The collision of existing homosexual organizing with the dynamism of the New Left produced new identities, new ways of conceiving of homosexual interest, and new organizational models, all of which were crucial to the consolidation of the field. The sudden decline of the New Left in the early 1970s made the political environment easier to read, which allowed gay activists to more easily reach consensus about how to proceed. Early efforts to organize around issues gave way to more successful movements focused on identities. In the typical case, lesbian/gay identity, acknowledging distinctiveness, was coupled with an interest such as biking or music, claiming connection to the broader community. Thus the intersection of existing homosexual organization with the New Left, followed by its rapid decline, produced the right set of conditions for the forging of the new field – the right actors, in the right place and time, with the right models.

3

Institutional Variation in the Evolution of Social Movements

COMPETING LOGICS AND THE
SPREAD OF RECYCLING
ADVOCACY GROUPS

Michael Lounsbury

Students of organizations and social movements recently have highlighted the potential fruitfulness of examining the ways in which ideas and research developments in the organizational theory and social movement literatures can be usefully brought together to advance knowledge (Fligstein 1996; Clemens 1997; Davis and McAdam 2000; Rao, Morrill and Zald 2000). In this chapter, I aim to push such cross-pollination further by reorienting research attention away from the study of institutionalization that has been prominent in both literatures. The institutionalization of social movements involves the transformation of contentious politics that involve tactics such as protest into more conventional forms of political action such as lobbying (Meyer and Tarrow 1998). In organization theory, institutionalization typically refers to the processes by which particular kinds of practices or forms become legitimate and diffuse throughout organizational populations (Strang and Soule 1998). Both literatures have tended to invoke an imagery of incremental change that focuses on how existing social structures maintain stability and elite positions become reproduced.

Recently, some organizational institutionalists have begun to eschew the study of institutionalization and focus more on how qualitative shifts in the core practices of organizations change in tandem with broader institutional beliefs (Scott 2001). The concept of institutional logic has been used to study such shifts and highlight the interconnections between higher order belief systems and lower level material practices and routines (e.g., Friedland 2002). Friedland and Alford (1991: 243) made this dual relationship explicit, discussing societal level logics as "supraorganizational patterns of human activity by which individuals and organizations produce and reproduce their material subsistence and organize time and space. They are also symbolic systems, ways of ordering reality, and thereby render experience of time and space meaningful."

At the level of societies, the capitalist market, the bureaucratic state, and the nuclear family can be conceptualized as logics that constitute the interests of actors and thereby shape cognition and action. At the level of industries, logics consist of common producer "identities and valuation orders that structure the decision-making and the practices of the players in a product market" (Thornton and Ocasio 1999: 805). In organizational analysis, logics have been shown to shape decision making by determining what issues are attended to by decision makers (March and Olsen 1976; Ocasio 1997) and providing the rules of appropriateness that make certain actions or solutions legitimate (March and Olsen 1989).

A number of studies have demonstrated the usefulness of the logic concept as a focal point for analysis. For example, Haveman and Rao (1997) argued that shifts in broader belief systems linked to the emergence of progressive ideology around the turn of the twentieth century led to the creation of new organizational forms in the early thrift industry. Focusing on hospital organizations, Ruef and Scott (1998) highlighted how organizational legitimacy depended upon ownership characteristics that have shifted in tandem with a transformation in health care logics since World War II. Similarly, Thornton and Ocasio (1999) showed how a shift from an editorial to a market logic in the higher education publishing industry led to changes in executive succession practices.

By focusing attention on how organizations are shaped by logics that shift over time, this recent work provides a new direction for the study of institutional processes that emphasizes historical variation and contingency over the inevitability of institutionalization (Clemens 1999; Lounsbury and Ventresca 2002). Further, logic transformation opens up the possibility for status mobility and a reconfiguration of elites and other elements of stratification (Lounsbury 2002), providing a corrective to previous institutional research that has emphasized the robustness of existing institutional structures and incumbents. Drawing attention to the role of broader logics and contexts of action is also consistent with recent directions in social movements research that have extended the resource focus of the political process perspective by creating a more cosmopolitan framework that takes cultural processes seriously – especially through the study of framing (e.g., Armstrong 2002a; Benford and Snow 2000; McAdam, McCarthy, and Zald 1996; Moore and Hala 2002; Zald 2000).

Goffman (1974: 21) defined frames as "schemata of interpretation" that help actors reduce sociocultural complexity in order to perceive, interpret, and act in ways that are socially efficacious. Benford and Snow (2000: 614) argued that "frames help to render events or occurrences meaningful and thereby function to organize experience and guide action." McAdam and Scott (this volume) argue that institutional logics tend to emphasize the power of dominant ideologies and shared cognitive frameworks whereas social movement frames stress challenging ideologies and conflicting beliefs and values (see also Stryker 1994). Even though social movement frames are typically conceptualized as malleable, highly strategic devices that facilitate collective mobilization, that concept suggests an important corrective to the study of logics by emphasizing how broader belief systems may be promoted by challengers and how dominant belief systems are often contested.

In this chapter, I draw inspiration from the focus on challengers that is present in social movement studies of framing and go beyond the analysis of how one logic is replaced by another by highlighting how a new competing logic emerged alongside an existing logic, facilitating a shift in the dynamics of recycling advocacy group creation in the United States. While some advocacy organizations are akin to interest groups that have easy access to the centers of political decision making (Jenkins 1987), the recycling advocacy groups I study are more like social movement organizations (SMOs). A social movement organization is "a complex, or formal, organization which identifies its goals with the preferences of a social movement or a countermovement and attempts to implement those goals" (McCarthy and Zald 1977: 1218). U.S. recycling advocacy groups are an important organizational manifestation of the recycling movement and provide crucial links between grassroots recyclers and governmental bureaucracies which create rules and incentives that authoritatively shape local solid waste practices.

Recently, some social movement scholars have begun to investigate SMO evolution (e.g., Minkoff 1993; Kriesi et al. 1995). For instance, in their study of the activities and structures of SMOs, Kriesi et al. (1995) extended Tarrow's (1998) notion of protest cycle by showing how SMOs change from being more unstructured and protest oriented to more formally structured and professionally oriented over the course of a protest cycle. However, we still know little about the role of SMOs in driving such qualitative shifts or the more proximate mechanisms by which SMOs, especially non-protest-oriented SMOs, change their orientations or practices over time. For social movements researchers, therefore, an analytical focus on institutional variation redirects attention away from the ideologically loaded and teleo-logical conceptualization of social movement institutionalization as coop-tation and towards the specification of how and what kinds of changes occur in social movements over time.

In the 1960s and 1970s, recycling was a marginal practice promoted by activists, but by the 1990s it had become a major for-profit industry. In 2000, there were approximately 10,000 curbside recycling programs, and aggregate revenues from recycling were estimated to be $16 billion (U.S. Department of Commerce 2001). I will focus attention on how the evolutionary dynamics of state recycling advocacy groups shifted as re-cycling was transformed from a marginal activity to a mainstream solid waste practice. More specifically, I will examine how the spread of state recycling advocacy groups was enabled and shaped by the emergence of a technocratic recycling logic that competed with an extant holistic recycling logic.

I argue that the technocratic logic, a dominant ideology, facilitated the spread of recycling practices, providing conditions that were favorable to the creation of recycling advocacy groups that would focus on its implemen-tation. However, the rise of the technocratic logic also shifted the nature of recycling activism and the drivers of advocacy group creation. Recy-cling advocacy groups promoting a holistic recycling logic, a challenger ideology, were initially created in states that were prone to environmental activism, while the subsequent creation of advocacy groups was facilitated by the rise of the technocratic logic, as well as the locations where imple-mentation challenges were greatest as a result of the existence of Waste-to-Energy (W-T-E) incinerators that provided a competing solid waste solution. Even though this shift in causal effects was bound up in the pro-cess by which recycling became transformed into a mainstream industry, it was more proximately driven by the creation of a peak national social movement organization, the National Recycling Coalition, that helped to give rise to the competing technocratic recycling logic and fostered state recycling advocacy group proliferation.

The Emergence of Competing Logics and the Rise of U.S. Recycling

While recycling was considered a marginal solid waste solution in the 1960s and 1970s, today it is a core component of the U.S. solid waste management field. Initially promoted solely by social movement activists, recycling be-came a major for-profit industry by the late 1990s. As part of the process of

Table 3.1. *Two Ideal Types of Recycling*

	Holistic Logic	Technocratic Logic
Ideology	Recycling as a way to restructure society and economy	Recyclables as a commodity
Relationship to other solid waste solutions	Reduce, reuse, recycle	Recycling as a complement to landfilling and incineration
Dominant organizational manifestation	Nonprofit drop-off center	Curbside pick-up (for-profit activity)
Labor	Volunteers	Paid professional staff
Approach to participants	Active/reflective partners	Service recipients
Definition of success	Community-building	Profits/efficiency

the making of a recycling industry, however, there was a shift from a holistic logic of recycling to a situation where competing technocratic and holistic logics existed. Table 3.1 summarizes the characteristics of these two ideal types of recycling logics.

In the late 1960s and 1970s, recycling was bound up in a holistic logic that matched a set of ideas and beliefs with practices. Noticeable signs of environmental degradation and associated health hazards such as those related to pesticides (Carson 1962) and pollution (Crenson 1971) motivated the emergence of a broad-based environmental movement by the late 1960s (Schnaiberg 1973). As part of these developments, attention also was drawn to problems related to population growth and the rapid growth of mass consumerism and discards (Packard 1960). Activists involved in the recycling movement were motivated by these broader societal problems and promoted the development of recycling as a way to restructure the extant social organization of society and economy. Recycling was envisioned as an important mechanism to rebuild communities and achieve social justice, while at the same time restructure capitalist forms of production.

Recycling was practical and educational. It was a vehicle for restructuring our thinking about the determinants of waste in our society. It was a path away from the concentration of political and economic power which treated virgin resources as a grand barbecue of the American continent, and similarly exploited the resources beyond our borders. We began to think about decentralized methods of production with closed-loop production/re-use/recycle systems. (Seldman 1986: 6)

Recycling was viewed as a replacement for other kinds of solid waste solutions such as landfilling and incineration. The mantra of "reduce, reuse, and

77

recycle" which became popular in the late 1980s was in its formative stages in the 1960s. Eco-activists promoting recycling were keen to transform societal consumption patterns and to drastically reduce discards; recycling would be a practical solution for materials that could not be reused. The recycling movement took shape in the creation of nonprofit drop-off recycling centers that were run by volunteers; approximately 3,000 such centers were created in the six months after the first Earth Day on April 22 1970 (Hanson 1972).

The notion of the drop-off center implied that people who recycled had to be active, engaged, and committed to recycling. It was not a trivial exercise to clean and set aside recyclable materials, load up your vehicle, drive to the drop-off center, and unload recyclables into their appropriate piles. Recycling activists believed that if they could convince citizens to actively participate in this way, people would become more reflective consumers as well as more civic minded. The ultimate aim for these movement activists was to use recycling as a way to build their communities. Replacing the prominence of exchange value (the driver of mass consumerism) with a focus on use value, recycling activists not only aimed to better the ecosystem, but to create self-sustaining production systems that were geographically bounded. Further, while nonprofit centers mainly relied on volunteer labor, many recycling activists sought to create a revenue-generating system that would enable recycling centers and processors to hire underprivileged citizens (Gould, Schnaiberg, and Weinberg 1996). Hence, holistic recycling would enable commodity production and consumption flows to be contained more exclusively within a particular community, and thereby reduce a community's connection to broader-scale commodity production systems that featured manufacturing conglomerates and multinationals (Seldman 1995).

By the end of the 1970s, however, nonprofit, volunteer recycling was considered a failure by solid waste management field insiders and the general public (Kimball 1992). Materials to be recycled began to accumulate at recycling centers because there were no outlets for recyclables – supply had outstripped demand. The problem for recycling proponents was to figure out how to build an infrastructure that would facilitate growth in the demand for recyclables. It was not at all certain, however, whether recycling would become instantiated as a mainstream solid waste management solution. If it did become an acceptable solution, it was unclear what form it would take.

While the recycling movement had emerged as a loosely structured set of efforts, mainly on the West Coast in the 1960s and 1970s, in 1978 a national recycling association was created – the National Recycling Coalition (NRC) – that would help to give rise to a new technocratic logic of recycling by working intensively with solid waste management field insiders to make recycling an acceptable mainstream solution (Lounsbury, Ventresca, and Hirsch 2003). Motivated by a couple of inconspicuous sections (sections 5003 and 6002) of the Resource Conservation and Recovery Act (passed by Congress in 1976) that called for the development of new uses for recovered materials and the establishment of federal procurement guidelines favoring recovered materials, Cliff Case, a New York City lawyer, created the NRC with the intent of enabling recycling proponent voices to be heard in broader political debates in the solid waste field. Case aimed to establish a broad coalition along the lines of the Sierra Club that would include for-profit solid waste actors, union representatives, community recycling advocates, and all individuals and organizations with an interest in recycling. While this was a noble aim, Case was an outsider to the core of the ecological activist community – especially that of the West Coast that had already mobilized more formal advocacy groups.

Under Case's direction, the NRC allied with major solid waste haulers such as Browning-Ferris and Waste Management to develop an approach to recycling that would be profitable. To increase demand, the NRC lobbied government agencies to set procurement guidelines that encouraged the use of recycled products such as paper. It also worked with commodity manufacturers through associations such as the American Paper Institute to develop a supporting infrastructure that would make recycling processes cost effective.

Those who promoted this more technocratic orientation to recycling essentially sought to abandon the nonprofit roots of recycling and its holistic logic. Instead of conceptualizing recycling as a way to restructure society and economy, they focused on creating recyclable commodity markets or what has come to be known as secondary materials markets. The NRC sold its ideas about recycling as a complement to landfilling and incineration, creating much consternation in the grassroots recycling community and an enduring tension between technocratic and holistic recyclers. To supporters of the technocratic logic, recycling was not about restructuring the consumption patterns of citizens, but providing an efficient solid waste management mechanism.

As the technocratic logic gained prominence, nonprofit drop-off centers were increasingly replaced with curbside recycling programs and associated for-profit organizations that employed paid professional staff. With curbside recycling, participants no longer needed to be reflective about their activities in the world. Instead, citizens were reconceptualized as service recipients. Even though many curbside recycling programs still require people to clean and sort discards, these programs often are coupled with incentives such as pay-as-you-throw garbage collections that enable people to view recycling as a direct cost savings (this, of course, assumes no-cost citizen labor). Instead of the labor-intensive nature of nonprofit voluntary recycling efforts, therefore, curbside collection relies on free household labor to clean and sort waste, lowering the overall cost to solid waste conglomerates, facilitating the creation of a profitable business. Hence, a focus on profits and efficiency replaced ideas of community building and development that inspired early recycling activists.

While the technocratic logic did enable the rise of a for-profit industry, the holistic logic did not completely disappear. This has been evidenced by the fact that many grassroots recyclers, such as those from California, Oregon, and Washington, celebrate the proliferation of recycling practices, while simultaneously lamenting its contemporary social organization as a "market." In interviews, many grassroots recyclers tied to state recycling advocacy groups noted that a tension continues to exist between the corporatist approach of the NRC and the more activist ideals of some local recyclers who still promote a nonprofit, community-building approach to recycling (Gould, Schnaiberg, and Weinberg 1996). In fact, in 1995, supporters of the holistic logic created an umbrella organization of their own, the GrassRoots Recycling Network, that nominally works with the NRC while at the same time advocating its own local policies and practices. Given that the relationship between grassroots recyclers and the NRC still exists, however, it is best viewed as a form of factionalism as opposed to schism (Balser 1997). Nonetheless, the continued existence of the holistic logic keeps alive hope for the continued development of community-building recycling.

This shift from the holistic to competing technocratic/holistic logics had repercussions for how the recycling movement unfolded. The emergence of the technocratic logic facilitated the mainstream spread of recycling practices in the form of for-profit curbside recycling, but also altered the nature of activism informed by the holistic logic. We now turn to an exploration of temporal variation in the creation of state-level recycling advocacy groups.

Hypotheses: The Shifting Role and Diffusion of State Recycling Advocacy Groups

I have developed hypotheses about how the shift from the holistic to competing technocratic and holistic logics of recycling facilitated a concomitant shift in the causal drivers of recycling advocacy group creation. In the organizations literature, shifts in causal effects have been prominently highlighted in the study of diffusion (Strang and Soule 1998). For instance, there have been a number of studies that focus on how early adopters of a practice have qualitatively different motivations from later adopters. Tolbert and Zucker's (1983) classic study showed that early adopters of civil service reforms were motivated by technical considerations, whereas later adopters were motivated more by a legitimacy imperative that was decoupled from efficiency concerns. Focusing on core-periphery imagery, Menzel (1960) argued that centrally placed actors were early adopters when an innovation was culturally legitimate, but that illegitimate practices were adopted first by "marginal men" who were unconstrained by community norms. Supporting Menzel's arguments, contemporary institutional research has shown that new or illegitimate practices are more likely to be pioneered or adopted by peripheral rather than core organizations (Kraatz and Zajac 1996; Leblebici et al. 1991).

Drawing on historical research and interviews, I have developed grounded hypotheses about how early recycling advocacy group creation under the holistic logic was facilitated by distinctively different factors than later recycling advocacy group creation under the regime of competing logics. Since the state recycling advocacy groups I track gained authorized status among state governmental solid waste officials through their affiliation with the NRC, and the NRC authorizes only one such group per state, the existence of a state recycling advocacy group may be treated as a dichotomous variable. I therefore conceptualize the creation of recycling advocacy groups as a state-level diffusion process.

In the 1970s, the recycling movement initially coalesced on the West Coast in the formation of recycling advocacy groups that promoted the development of holistic recycling through state government lobbying and protest activity. The first advocacy group created was the California Resource Recovery Association (CRRA), founded in 1975. The CRRA was started by a handful of recycling activists in northern California who were pioneers in the creation of nonprofit volunteer recycling programs. Given that recycling was viewed as a fringe practice by mainstream actors in the solid waste management field, CRRA members focused a lot of their energy on enabling their voices to be heard. Their mission was to make recycling a legitimate solid waste solution through the passage of state and local laws and ordinances that would support its development at the local level. One of their most visible successes came with the passage of the 1978 California Litter Tax Law, which created a fund for investment in recycling equipment and training. The vision was to promote holistic recycling through a state nonprofit nexus.

Based on the visible success of the CRRA, recycling activists in the states of Washington and Oregon created similar organizations in the late 1970s. Recycling activists across these three states formed a loosely knitted coalition that provided an active support and advice network. Interviews with recycling activists from this era indicated that efforts to create holistic forms of recycling tended to be located in places where environmental activism was more generally prevalent – such as in California, Oregon, and Washington.

One proximate indicator of the degree of environmental activism in the 1970s was the passage of bottle bills. As Schnaiberg and Gould (1994) have argued, states that passed bottle bills, legislation that was favored and promoted by recycling activists, had more active environmental movements and governments that were more open to the claims of environmentalists. Bottle bill debates heated up in the early 1970s when early recycling pioneers attempted to encourage reuse of materials by getting states to require consumers to pay a deposit on aluminum and glass container purchases, which was refunded upon return of the containers. Container vendors (e.g., soda pop conglomerates such as Coca-Cola) were encouraged to reuse or remanufacture returned containers. The passage of bottle bill legislation provides an indicator of the robustness of environmental activism in a state, especially since container vendors vociferously opposed such legislation.

Hypothesis 1: States that have passed bottle bill legislation will be more likely to experience the creation of a state recycling advocacy group during the holistic logic period.

The emergence of the competing technocratic logic enabled recycling to become a mainstream solid waste solution and shifted the focal point for recycling activism. When the National Recycling Coalition allied with solid waste haulers to construct the technocratic logic of recycling in the 1980s, waste-to-energy (W-T-E) incineration had already taken shape as an authoritatively endorsed solid waste solution. In 1979, the Environmental

Protection Agency (EPA), in an agreement with the Department of Energy (DOE), endorsed W-T-E as a solid waste solution. "These agencies teamed with industry to promote waste incineration through a comprehensive set of commercialization programs and regulatory adjustments, including grants, below market rate loans, loan guarantees, arbitrage and municipal bonding rules, price supports, energy entitlements, guaranteed resale of electricity (Public Utility Regulatory Policy Act [PURPA] rates), and the reclassification of ash as a nonhazardous material" (Seldman 1995: 2354). Further, the Department of Energy created the Office of Commercialization of Municipal Waste to Energy to oversee and promote the creation of 200 to 250 W-T-E plants between 1980 and 1992. The EPA was to provide technical assistance to municipalities interested in building such facilities.

Given the prominence of W-T-E, the NRC decided to promote recycling as a complement to incineration in order to placate solid waste field insiders. The NRC focused its attention on the implementation of curbside recycling programs that would be profitable. They worked hard to publicize successful models and collaborated with solid waste conglomerates such as Browning-Ferris and Waste Management to encourage the creation of curbside recycling programs. Informed by a technocratic logic, curbside recycling gained momentum in the mid 1980s and began to proliferate widely by the late 1980s.

As part of this process, the NRC tried to construct an infrastructure of state-level advocacy group affiliates that would focus on technocratic problems of recycling implementation. While NRC leaders avoided the direct sponsorship of activism associated with the holistic logic, they aimed to incorporate key holistic recycling activists in an effort to build solidarity among all recycling proponents. Cliff Case successfully got extant advocacy groups from California, Oregon, and Washington to join as affiliates. While these affiliates were skeptical of NRC leadership, their affiliation with the NRC gave them more credibility in negotiating and working with their local and state governmental authorities as well as other solid waste insiders who often refused dialogue with supporters of holistic recycling. It was this increased credibility that encouraged recycling advocates in a wide variety of states to create more formal organizational structures and affiliate linkages to the NRC. Even though many holistic recyclers were resistant to the technocratic logic, by affiliating with the NRC as a formal state recycling advocacy group, they had more direct access to policymakers and an opportunity to try to influence solid waste management policy. While some affiliates were more activist than others, the emergence of the technocratic logic provided conditions that facilitated the rapid growth of state recycling advocacy groups.

Hypothesis 2: The rate of state recycling advocacy group creation will be higher under the regime of competing technocratic/holistic logics than during the holistic logic period.

While state recycling advocacy group affiliates often toed the NRC line and promoted the technocratic vision of recycling, many state groups continued to be linchpins in ecology activist networks and were motivated by the concerns of those who promoted the holistic logic. As has been found in the U.S. civil rights movement (Haines 1988) as well as a variety of environmental campaigns throughout the world (Della Porta and Rucht 2002), one key to the eventual success of the recycling movement's efforts had to do with its ability to be effective at both mainstream policy negotiation and grassroots activism (Lounsbury, Ventresca, and Hirsch 2003). While the rise of the technocratic logic and concomitant acceptance of curbside recycling as a legitimate solid waste solution provided an important institutional shift and an impetus for the further creation of recycling advocacy groups, the continued existence of the holistic logic also provided a crucial resource for recycling activists. Many grassroots recycling advocates rejected the official NRC position of recycling as a complement to incineration because it neglected the community-building, nonprofit roots of recycling and embraced W-T-E incineration. Grassroots recycling advocates believed that W-T-E was bad for the environment due to its air emissions and production of toxic ash and would eliminate the impetus for recycling because waste-to-energy incineration is generally a directly competing solution to recycling.

For instance, for W-T-E incineration to be profitable and efficient, a steady flow of garbage is required, especially garbage that burns well, such as paper. This led to the establishment of *flow-control* laws in many municipalities where waste-to-energy facilities were built. These laws guarantee that a certain number of tons of garbage per year will be hauled to the incinerator. In some cases, this completely precludes the possibility of recycling. In Hempstead, New York, in the late 1980s, for example, the local incinerator required 750,000 tons of garbage per year to be efficient and profitable, while the town itself was predicted to generate only 640,000 tons of burnable garbage per year (Besset and Bunch 1989: 232).

While not-in-my-backyard movements inhibited the full-blown proliferation of W-T-E, to which the EPA and the DOE had agreed in 1979, a number of W-T-E incinerators were constructed throughout the country (Blumberg and Gottlieb 1989). Hence, as recycling gained mainstream support from solid waste field insiders who embraced the technocratic logic, many holistic recycling activists were motivated to create recycling advocacy groups to engage in jurisdictional battles with W-T-E proponents over the solid waste stream. Interviews suggested that many recycling advocacy groups spent a good deal of time lobbying local and state governmental officials to promote the advantages of recycling while noting the hazards of incineration.

Hypothesis 3:   States with higher aggregate W-T-E incineration capacity will be more likely to experience the creation of a state recycling advocacy group during the competing technocratic/holistic logics period.

Quantitative Data and Methods

The data set for this study was constructed from archival sources and a survey of state recycling advocacy groups and solid waste officials. The survey queried solid waste and recycling insiders in all fifty U.S. states from 1975 to 1995. There are no cases where states have more than one such organization, since these organizations became "authorized" in the sense of providing a key linking mechanism between the NRC and state solid waste officials. Since I was interested in understanding the diffusion of "authorized" state recycling advocacy groups, the survey tracked if and when such a group was created. I was able to obtain complete data for all U.S. states.

The survey data was corroborated by data on state recycling advocacy groups provided to me by the National Recycling Coalition. While state recycling advocacy groups were created before the NRC was founded, all became affiliated with the NRC over time since it became the peak national association for recycling advocacy. State recycling advocacy groups, however, are completely autonomous entities, in contrast to most national nonprofit organizations, which have a federated structure where somewhat autonomous state and local affiliates are considered important components of an overall bureaucracy that is guided by a national headquarters staff (Zald 1967). That is, state recycling advocacy group affiliations with the NRC are voluntary and can be dissolved at any time.

Dependent Variable   The dependent variable is the rate of state recycling advocacy group creation. Only three states had recycling advocacy groups before 1980. By the end of 1995, thirty-nine states had an advocacy group, the majority of which has been created since 1988 when recycling had begun to diffuse more widely.

Independent Variables   The *bottle bill* variable indicates whether and when a state passed bottle bill legislation. This variable importantly taps into the robustness of a state's environmental activist community or state governmental openness to environmental activism since the passage of bottle bills was heavily promoted by the action of environmental groups. That is, it provides an indicator of a state's political opportunity structure.

State incinerator capacity is a time-varying measure of the aggregate amount of tons per day of waste that could be burned in a state's waste-to-energy incinerators. While movement theorists have tended to emphasize the role of opportunities in facilitating activism, more recent work has begun to give equal attention to the role of threats (e.g., McAdam 1999). In the case of recycling, the existence of waste-to-energy incinerators provide a direct threat to the development and proliferation of recycling practices since incineration and recycling infrastructures compete for access to and control over the solid waste stream. State incinerator capacity, therefore, provides an indicator of the extent to which incineration has been adopted as a solid waste solution in a state, encouraging the mobilization of environmental activists who want to both close down existing and proposed incinerators and promote recycling as an alternative. Incinerator capacity data come from the Environmental Protection Agency. Independent variables are lagged one year and updated annually.

Control Variables   *Waste-to-energy incineration presence* tracks whether and when a state first had a W-T-E incinerator built. *Urban density* measures the degree to which a state is densely populated. This variable, obtained from the Statistical Abstract of the United States, provides a measure of which states are more likely to experience landfill scarcity since the amount of landfill space is directly related to the degree to which a state has densely populated urban areas.

Industry attention to recycling tracks the percentage of articles dedicated to recycling in *Waste Age*. *Waste Age*, a solid waste trade magazine that started in 1970, is the preeminent solid waste management trade magazine. Solid waste managers look to *Waste Age* to provide information on how other municipalities are solving solid waste management problems and to keep abreast of the latest technological developments. As recycling became a legitimate technological solution in the solid waste management field, the coverage of recycling in *Waste Age* increased, creating normative pressures and providing important instrumental information that could encourage the creation of recycling advocacy groups. *Percentage of states with recycling advocacy group* tracks the extent to which state-level recycling coalitions have diffused. This is a standard measure used in the institutional literature to capture isomorphic pressures that shape diffusion (Davis 1991).

I originally included a number of other control variable operationalizations, but omitted them from analyses due to correlational problems with included variables. For instance, I gathered data on the aggregate growth of municipal solid waste, the amount of solid waste recycled, and the overall creation of curbside recycling programs in the United States, but these variables were highly correlated with other time trend variables such as industry attention to recycling.[1] While correlational problems prohibit the inclusion of these variables in the models, those high correlations provide some validation that the variables used are effectively capturing the main contours of the diffusion process. Even if I include these other variables, the basic pattern of results I report remains robust. All control variables are lagged one year and updated annually.

Analysis I used event history analysis to examine the rate of state recycling advocacy group creation (Tuma and Hannan 1984). Since I wanted to explore how causal effects differed across periods, I employed piecewise exponential models that allow the intercepts and the effects of covariates to vary in an unconstrained way across time (see Thornton and Ocasio 1999).[2] The basic functional form of my piecewise exponential event history model is summarized in the following equation:

$$r_j(t) = \exp(\alpha_{jp} + \beta_j X_j),$$

where j is the origin state of no state recycling advocacy group, k is the destination state of recycling advocacy group creation, α_{jp} is a constant coefficient associated with the pth time period, β_j is an associated vector of coefficients, and X_j is a vector of explanatory and control variables used in the analysis.

To account for the shift from the holistic logic period to the competing technocratic/holistic logics period, I established a period break at 1985. I

---

[1] I also tried a standard time trend variable but that is also highly correlated with percent of states with an advocacy group that aims to tap institutional pressures. It is not correlated with the bottle bill variable.

[2] This modeling choice is a conventional solution for analyses that examine shifting causal effects across periods.

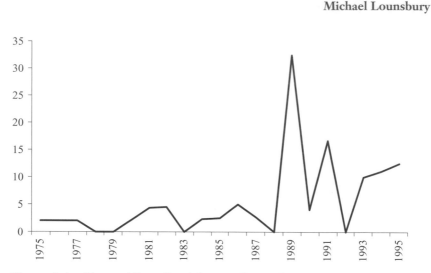

Figure 3.1 Observed Recycling Advocacy Group Creation Rates in U.S. States, 1975–1995

chose this year as a break point because it was the first year that a state recycling advocacy group was created under the auspices of the National Recycling Coalition. This is a key event because the NRC was a key promoter of the technocratic logic and began to encourage the creation of state affiliate groups that would engage in recycling activism that was in accordance with NRC positions. In addition, Lounsbury, Ventresca, and Hirsch (2003) showed that it was around 1985 when recycling began to be perceived and treated as a distinct and viable solution in the solid waste management field. For instance, they showed that recycling became a distinct discourse category by 1985 in *Waste Age*, the main solid waste management trade magazine. Nonetheless, I ran sensitivity analyses for this periodization for three years before and after 1985 and results did not systematically differ.

To verify the appropriateness of my models, I conducted exploratory analyses and performed goodness-of-fit tests (Blossfeld and Rohwer 1995). A variety of other standard nonparametric and parametric models also were run to confirm that the choice of piecewise exponential models was the most appropriate estimation procedure (Wu 1990). In addition, I ran standard logistic regression models of the two time periods separately as a robustness check and the results did not substantively differ from the results I report. Models were estimated by the method of maximum likelihood using the software package TDA (Blossfeld and Rohwer 1995).

Table 3.2. *Descriptive Statistics and Correlations for State Recycling Advocacy Group Creation Analysis*

Variable	Mean	S.D.	1	2	3	4	5	6
1. Waste-to-energy incineration presence	.11	.44	—					
2. Urban density	6.38	7.00	.11**	—				
3. Industry attention to recycling	.35	.90	.09**	.01	—			
4. Log (% of states with advocacy group)	−2.5	1.20	.12**	−.13**	.25**	—		
5. Bottle bill	.18	.38	.09**	.27**	.01	−.04	—	
6. Log (state incinerator capacity)	.74	1.68	.51**	.31**	.13**	.22**	.20**	—

** $p < .05$.

Results

Figure 3.1 plots the observed rates of state recycling advocacy creation from 1975 to 1995. This figure shows that there are clear differences in the rates of advocacy group creation across the periods of interest. In the holistic logic period from 1975 to 1984, the rates remain fairly low. In that period, only nine state recycling advocacy groups were created. In the competing logics period, however, there are dramatic increases in the rate of advocacy group creation, with a large spike in 1989, a slightly smaller one in 1991, and relatively high rates from 1993 to 1995. Twenty-seven state recycling advocacy groups were created in this period.

Table 3.2 reports basic descriptive statistics and correlations. There are no major correlational problems with the variables reported. Table 3.3 reports results of my piecewise exponential event history analysis of state recycling advocacy group creation. Control variables are not significant with the exception of urban density, which significantly affects recycling advocacy group creation in the competing logics period. I expected industry attention to recycling and the percentage of states that already had a recycling advocacy group also to be significant in the competing logics period, but they are not due to the heterogeneity of group creation rates across that period.

Shifting attention to the hypotheses, Table 3.3 shows that the bottle bill variable is significant during the holistic logic period, supporting Hypothesis 1. This indicates that early state recycling group creation did tend to occur in states where environmental activism was more robust and political

Table 3.3. *Piecewise Exponential Event History Analysis of State Recycling Advocacy Group Creation, 1975–1995 (n = 810)*

Covariates	Holistic Logic	Technocractic/Holistic Logics
Constant	−3.530***	−2.997***
	(.764)	(.571)
Waste-to-energy incineration presence	−.407	−.601
	(.869)	(.473)
Urban density	−.087	.068**
	(.086)	(.031)
Industry attention to recycling	−.057	.005
	(.220)	(.010)
Log (% of states with advocacy group)	−3.701	.942
	(10.402)	(1.410)
Bottle bill	1.335**	−.371
	(.762)	(.581)
Log (state incinerator capacity)	−.183	.091**
	(.866)	(.046)
Log Likelihood	−129.27	

Note: Standard errors in parentheses. One-tailed tests are used for hypothesized variables. ** $p < .05$, *** $p < .01$.

opportunity structures were favorable. The increase in the constant term between the two periods in Table 3.3 shows that there is a significant increase in the rate of state recycling advocacy group creation from the holistic logic period to the competing logics period, supporting Hypothesis 2. Finally, the variable tracking state incinerator capacity was negative and not significant during the holistic logic period, but was positive and significant during the technocratic logic period, providing support for Hypothesis 3. This finding indicates that in states where there was more incinerator capacity there was a higher propensity for mobilization around recycling via the creation of a social movement organization.

While these results support the arguments I have made, organizational and social movement scholars also may be interested in the substantive outcomes associated with recycling advocacy groups. In additional unreported analyses of state recycling rates between 1990 and 2000, I found that the existence of a state recycling advocacy group was a positive and significant predictor of growth in a state's recycling rate.[3] This suggests that

---

[3] My analyses of state recycling rates showed that the growth of a state recycling rate was also facilitated by the national growth of curbside recycling programs and the scarcity of

recycling advocacy group creation was not merely a symbolic effort (Meyer and Rowan 1977) to resist the proliferation of waste-to-energy incineration, but that such groups engaged in substantive efforts to increase the prevalence of recycling and were largely successful in those efforts. Overall, these results support my main claims about how the emergence of a new competing logic facilitated changes in the causal drivers of state recycling advocacy group creation as well as the more widespread proliferation of advocacy groups and recycling practices.

Discussion and Conclusion

This study of competing logics and the spread of state recycling advocacy groups showed that the creation of those social movement organizations was shaped by different state-level conditions across periods. During the holistic logic period, state recycling advocacy group creation mainly occurred in states where environmental activism tended to be more robust and where state polities were more receptive to environmentalist claims as proxied by the passage of bottle bill legislation. When the technocratic logic emerged as a competing logic, state recycling advocacy group creation increased, but it also occurred more in states that had built up high incineration capacity, which provided a directly competing infrastructure to recycling. Under such conditions, state recycling advocacy groups emerged to engage in jurisdictional battles over solid waste flows. Echoing Vogus and Davis (this volume), who found that antitakeover statutes were passed as a result of elite mobilization under conditions of takeover threat as well as conducive political opportunity structures, my findings highlight the importance of analyzing threats as well as opportunities in the context of collective action (see also McAdam 1999). The case of recycling, however, further highlights a temporal dimension in that initial recycling advocacy group creation was spurred mostly by political opportunities related to state receptivity to ecological concerns, while later recycling advocacy group creation was motivated by a combination of political opportunities related to the growth of curbside recycling as well as threats having to do with W-T-E incineration.

In contrast to most existing studies of logics that tend to track dominant ideologies (McAdam and Scott, this volume), I draw inspiration from

landfill capacity. Whether a state had a bottle bill was not a significant predictor nor was urban density. The number of incinerators in a state was negative but not significant.

the literature on social movement framing to highlight the role of belief systems tied to challengers. A challenger logic, the holistic logic, provided an important cultural support for the early development of both recycling practices and recycling advocacy groups. In addition, I highlight the actions of challengers tied to the holistic logic that both supported and contested the dominant technocratic logic and enabled the wider proliferation of recycling practices. While I believe that this chapter demonstrates the importance of logics to the study of social movements, it also suggests the importance of attending to the role of challengers and contending belief systems in the study of mainstream institutions.

The emergence of the competing technocratic logic was not exogenous to the practices of recycling advocacy groups, but was promulgated by the National Recycling Coalition, which helped to reshape beliefs about recycling as well as the social organization of the recycling movement from a loosely connected structure of locally autonomous advocacy groups to a more hierarchical national structure with state recycling group affiliates. While a major, for-profit recycling industry emerged, a more simple focus on how recycling shifted from the margins to the mainstream would most likely miss important qualitative changes in movement organization and beliefs that are foregrounded here. Such a shift in research attention away from the study of institutionalization and towards the study of institutional change as involving fundamental shifts in context has a number of implications for organization theory and social movement scholarship.

For instance, a focus on institutional variation and change makes the concept of legitimacy less central for organization theorists. While the concept of legitimacy does provide some utility in tracking how certain practices and behaviors become routine and taken for granted (Suchman 1995; Tolbert and Zucker 1996), contemporary research has tended to conflate it with economic and social forces having to do with resource munificence and dependence. This has detracted attention from the ways in which organizations engage in meaning-making activities and are embedded in broader cultural contexts that enable and constrain the possibilities for action (Clemens 1997). A focus on institutional logics restores attention to broader social structures of resources and meanings and how those social structures themselves change and mediate flows of practices.

To wit, logic-centered analyses usefully expand research on institutional change by moving beyond the false binary opposition between technical considerations and legitimacy-driven isomorphism that has been pervasive in studies of institutional diffusion (e.g., Tolbert and Zucker 1983; Westphal, Gulati, and Shortell 1997; Zhou 1993) by conceptualizing rationality and technical demands as culturally constructed (Clemens 2002; Douglas 1986; Edelman and Stryker forthcoming; Friedland and Alford 1991). As Fligstein (1990) showed, the goals and performance drivers of corporations changed over the course of the twentieth century as dominant leadership backgrounds and related conceptions of control shifted from operations to sales and from marketing to finance. "Institutional theory is not about the leftovers of rational action, the ways in which cultural conventions rush in where means-ends relations are opaque. Rather, institutional logics constitute the cosmology within which means are meaningful, where means-ends couplets are thought appropriate and become the naturalized, unthought conditions of social action, performing the substances at stake within them" (Friedland 2002: 383).

A shift in attention away from the concept of legitimacy also has important implications for research on organizational demography. Organizational demographers have shown that there is an inverted U-shaped relationship between population density (the number of organizations) and the entry rate of organizations (see Hannan and Carroll 1992 for a review). They theorize that the founding of organizations is limited in the early stages of industry formation because new organizational forms lack legitimacy. But as organizations develop a track record and become established, more firms are created. It is posited that increases in organizational density indicate that the new activities and organizational forms have acquired the societal legitimacy necessary for further growth to occur. Once legitimate, founding rates in a new population rapidly increase until crowding effects begin to deter entry. When the number of firms increases to a point that encroaches on the carrying capacity limits of the population's resource space, competition takes over and new entries level off.

Legitimacy in the density dependence thesis, similar to much of the extant research in institutional research, is tightly tied to a focus on resources. While some scholars have noted that the density dependence thesis has not held up across all empirical contexts, has masked unobserved heterogeneity, and has neglected the fine-grained richness of historical process (Baum and Powell 1995; Delacroix and Rao 1994), this study further demonstrates that there might be fundamental qualitative transformations in organizational forms over time that cast a shadow on population ecology findings that assume that organizational forms are static over long historical periods. This study does not analyze the spread of recycling advocacy groups as a founding process tied to changes in resource munificence, but as a diffusion process that highlighted important qualitative shifts over time in causal dynamics. This underscores the need for more historically sensitive institutional analyses of organizational evolution.

A focus on multiple (and competing) logics also highlights the limitations of the concept of institutionalization that places emphasis on the reproduction and stability of social order. Instead of simply being co opted, social movements often become embedded in multiple, overlapping institutions that enable continued struggle for change, albeit in ways that may be hidden and less dramatic than street protests (Lounsbury 2001). Many changes that are driven by social movements and social movement-like processes occur in organizations and require more detailed analyses of how social movement activism takes shape in the everyday realities of organizations (Creed and Scully 2000; Scully and Segal 2002; Zald and Berger 1978). It is important to keep in mind that the "iron law of oligarchy" is not ironclad. Rothschild-Whitt (1979) has noted that advocacy organizations that remain small, rotate leadership and job assignments, and are strongly committed to democratic and participatory values are able to maintain social movement energy over time. Zald and Ash (1966) argued that if oligarchy does develop, the use of adversarial tactics may even increase. For instance, as the Sierra Club became more professionalized in the 1960s, disenchanted eco-activists mobilized to form Friends of the Earth (Fox 1981).

Recent social movements research has aimed to go beyond the ideologically loaded imagery of social movement institutionalization by redirecting attention towards the ways in which social movement outcomes are not only shaped by protest-oriented social movement organizations, but also shaped by a wide variety of mainstream institutional actors (Giugni, McAdam, and Tilly 1999). Meyer and Tarrow (1998: 20) argued that "much of the contention in contemporary societies does not come from movement organizations as such but from campaigns organized by parties, interest groups, professional associations, citizens' groups, and public servants." Della Porta and Rucht (2002) have begun to analyze the complex mix of actors that get involved in environmental campaigns, highlighting the importance of both protest-oriented and professional social movement organizations in promulgating challenges to extant institutions and fomenting or resisting change. McAdam, Tarrow, and Tilly (2001) extended this new sensibility in social movement theorizing by arguing for a process-based focus on the mechanisms by which contention unfolds in a wide variety of contexts (for a critique, see, e.g., Diani 2003 and Taylor 2003).

I am sympathetic to these new directions in social movement research, but also want to emphasize the importance of organizational processes and a focus on broader institutional logics. In an effort to move away from narratives of institutionalization, I stress that the continued existence of the holistic logic suggests that there was not a full and complete transformation of recycling beliefs and practices. While a detailed specification of the ways in which the technocratic and holistic logics continue to be manifest is beyond the scope of this chapter, our knowledge of institutional process and change would be greatly enhanced by research that attends to the multiplicity of social structures of resources and meanings that shape configurations and reconfigurations of social organization (Lounsbury and Ventresca 2002; Mische and Pattison 2000; Schneiberg and Bartley 2001; Stryker 1994). As social analysts, we need to resist the teleological temptation of concepts such as institutionalization and probe more deeply for the fracture lines of institutions and an understanding of the possibilities for ongoing change, whether incremental or epochal.

4

Elite Mobilizations for Antitakeover Legislation, 1982–1990

Timothy J. Vogus and Gerald F. Davis

Elite mobilizations play a key role in shaping the contours of social institutions. Prior research has demonstrated that mobilizations and the resulting struggles between competing elites shape the social structure of markets (Fligstein 1996), corporate governance regimes (Davis and Thompson 1994), and organizations (Fligstein 1990; Zald and Berger 1978). More recent examples in the popular press also demonstrate the use of the tactics of popular social movements by business elites. Corporate elites in the Philippines, dissatisfied with the loss of foreign direct investment and governmental corruption, supported throngs of protesters and helped them stage multiple demonstrations that led to the ouster of President Estrada (Frank 2000).[1] Demonstrations of similar magnitude (also led by the business elite) have recently taken place in Italy (Meyer and Tarrow 1998) and South Korea. A form of elite mobilization was previewed in the United States during the late 1980s, as institutional investors sought corporate governance reform and state legislatures across the country were pressed by coalitions among business and labor to pass legislation to limit hostile takeovers of local companies (Davis and Thompson 1994). In this chapter, we use a social movement framework to study this process as a movement/countermovement dynamic, focusing on the spread of state antitakeover laws among the fifty American states.

State laws regulating takeovers are highly contentious because hostile takeovers are almost always profitable for shareholders of the acquired

---

[1] It is important to differentiate the protests in the Philippines from our case of antitakeover legislation. In the Philippines, the business elite played a more indirect role of logistic and ideological support of a popular movement. In contrast, the business elite in the U.S. states played a much more direct role in effectuating change.

company, and because a regime of contestable corporate control is seen as essential for the vibrancy of the American corporate sector by many scholars of law and economics. In framing takeovers in terms of a "market for corporate control," Manne (1965) argued that takeovers typically happen to badly run businesses where outsiders see a chance to buy the business from its current shareholders at a premium and then rehabilitate it. The managers of the takeover target (who are presumably responsible for its poor performance) may resist the challenge to their control, but dispersed shareholders have few other remedies for bad management. Thus, the takeover market is seen as an essential selection mechanism in a system of shareholder capitalism. Without the possibility of takeovers, the self-aggrandizing empire builders contemplated by Berle and Means (1932) might overrun corporate America: "Protected by impenetrable takeover defenses, managers and boards are likely to behave in ways detrimental to shareholders.... The end result, if the process continues unchecked, is likely to be the destruction of the corporation as we know it" (Jensen 1988: 347). And yet forty state legislatures adopted laws restricting takeovers during the late 1980s, almost always at the behest of local businesses, often in coalition with local labor organizations.

The notion that corporate elites are politically influential is hardly new, as the venerable debate among pluralists, elite theorists, and Marxian structuralists shows (see Mizruchi 1992 for a review). Less recognized is the fact that the influence of the "American corporate elite" varies according to the relevant jurisdiction (cf. Scott and Meyer 1983 on nested levels within societal sectors). Corporate law is made at the state level, rather than the federal level. State corporate law includes the regulation of takeovers of domestic corporations (i.e., those incorporated within the state). Moreover, regardless of the locations of their operations, firms can incorporate in any state, implying that they are able to choose their corporate law regime. In this sense, law is a product, of which state legislatures are producers and corporate managers (and corporate shareholders) are consumers (Romano 1993). Thus, changes in corporate law may be driven by consumer preferences; the relevant question is whose preferences win out, and how. We utilize the three mechanisms of the social movement perspective described by McAdam et al. (1996b) – political opportunity, mobilizing structures, and frame alignment – to ascertain the conditions under which elites mobilize, the form of the mobilization, and the likelihood for success. We also embed the mobilization for antitakeover legislation as a countermovement in the historically rooted and ongoing movement/countermovement between shareholders and managers (cf. Fligstein 1990; Useem 1996).

Our empirical context (the adoption of antitakeover legislation between 1982 and 1990 by U.S. states) is a particularly apt one for utilizing social movement theory, for four reasons. First, it provides an opportunity to extend the study of social movements to the conditions under which elites mobilize and to the factors influencing their success. Studying elite mobilization extends social movement theory beyond its focus on disenfranchised groups and grassroots mobilization and its assumption that elites primarily act as allies, sponsors, and providers of resources. Second, our sample is sufficiently large to quantitatively examine and test the role of political opportunity and threat, mobilizing structures, and framing alignment processes on movement outcomes. Third, it allows us to unpack a dynamic that remains underexplored in the social movements literature – movement/countermovement dynamics (Meyer and Staggenborg 1996). Lastly, it helps to bolster a growing segment of the social movements literature on social movements in and around (business) organizations (Creed and Scully 2000; Zald and Berger 1978).

We also examine state adoption of antitakeover statutes from 1982 to 1990 because it represents a clear example of the political processes surrounding the ongoing struggles and settlements over who controls the corporation. In this instance, the entrenched managerial elites were challenged at the heart of their power – the conception of control of the corporation (Fligstein 1990). That is, the finance conception of control, which emphasized diversification and conglomeration and largely entrenched management, was called into question and ultimately replaced by the "shareholder value" conception of control (Fligstein 1996) propagated by social movement–minded institutional investors (Davis and Thompson 1994). However, prior to the shift in the conception of control, managers partnering with unions, community leaders, and state legislatures were able to both forestall and change the form of its demise through the adoption of antitakeover statutes.

The Contractarian Perspective on Antitakeover Legislation

The contractarian or agency approach emphasizes that corporate structures are embedded in an institutional matrix which insures that the structures that survive are those that maximize shareholder wealth (see Davis and Useem 2002 for a review). Relevant institutions include managerial and director labor markets, compensation systems tied to corporate perfor-mance, markets for corporate equity and debt, a community of securities analysts and institutional investors acting as corporate watchdogs, the mar-ket for corporate law, and the market for corporate control. It is argued that these interlocking institutions orient corporate managers toward the North Star of shareholder value. An essential insight of this approach is that corporate managers enter into this system because they are rewarded for doing so. Without the appropriate rewards this perspective assumes that managers use decision rules that are self-interested (Subramanian 2001). For example, they opt for structures that vouchsafe shareholder interests (e.g., taking on uncomfortable amounts of debt, or putting stern watchdogs on the board of directors, or leaving the firm open to hostile takeover) be-cause shareholders will pay more to own shares in firms that are accountable than in firms where it is hard to get rid of bad managers (Easterbrook and Fischel 1991). Managers, in short, agree to be governed by a system that rewards them for maximizing shareholder value and punishes them for fail-ing to do so. The system works because stock markets are good at placing prices on corporate shares (that is, markets are informationally "efficient"). These markets adjust to reflect the best information available about a given company at any moment, thus rendering true corporate performance in-telligible. If internal control mechanisms fail (e.g., the board fails to adopt appropriate compensation policies to align the interests of management and shareholders), the share price will drop and leave the firm vulnerable to hostile takeover – assuming that such takeovers are possible. While cor-porate managements were largely protected from hostile takeover in the 1960s and 1970s through state-level practices making takeovers onerous, the 1982 *Edgar v. MITE Corporation* decision by the U.S. Supreme Court to outlaw these "first generation" antitakeover statutes ushered in a relatively unregulated market for takeovers. The result was an unprecedented wave of large hostile takeovers in which nearly one-third of the Fortune 500 faced a takeover bid (Davis and Stout 1992), ending only after a large number of states had adopted restrictive "second generation" takeover laws.

In order for agency theory to operate optimally in the realm of corporate law, two features are necessary, efficient capital markets and federalism. As previously noted, efficient capital markets weed out bad governance struc-tures without the assistance of governmental regulation, by guiding vol-untary adaptations by corporate managers. Federalism further reinforces efficiency by creating a market for corporate charters, which places states in competition with one another for corporate franchise revenues generated by domestic corporations. The competition prevents states from overregulating organizational form because states with onerous corporate law will lose firms to more shareholder-friendly states (Easterbrook and Fischel 1991; Romano 1993). (Delaware has been particularly successful in this competition because of its enabling statute, its large body of precedents and sophisticated corporate bar, and its credible commitment to be receptive to corporate needs.) Reincorporation is also a plausible alternative because it is relatively inexpensive (approximately $70,000 in 2001) and typically qualifies as a tax-free reorganization (Subramanian 2001). Firms that incorporate in shareholder-hostile states (such as those with strong antitakeover regulation) are punished with share price declines. According to the contractarian perspective, then, why would a state enact an antitakeover statute? Contractarians offer two possible explanations. First, based on a simple public choice account, states adopting antitakeover statutes might do so based on the relative presence or absence of bidders and targets in their given state. States with more targets will enact antitakeover legislation, while states with more bidders will not. Although potentially plausible, this argument can be empirically rejected because using this logic we would expect Delaware and California (two of the largest incorporators) to have very strong antitakeover legislation. Contrary to this prediction, California has no statute and Delaware has a weak statute that was adopted relatively late and allows new firms to exempt themselves by specifying so in their corporate charters (Easterbrook and Fischel 1991). Second, and more plausibly, the amount of proportional revenue derived from franchise fees should be related to enacting an antitakeover statute. That is, if a state depends heavily upon incorporation franchise fees as a source of revenue it will be less likely to jeopardize these revenues by adopting statutes detrimental to shareholders. This leads to the following hypothesis representing the contractarian perspective:

H1: The greater the percentage of tax revenues derived from franchise fees, the later a state will adopt an antitakeover statute.

We argue that this account is incomplete because it ignores the role of collective action, especially elite mobilizations, in shaping how the institutional "rules of the game" are set. Consequently, by understating the role of collective action the contractarian perspective also slights the historically specific nuances that trigger mobilization, the networks undergirding it, and the frames and ideational elements which speed and broaden its impact.

Shareholders and Managers as Movement and Countermovement

At the heart of the conflict between managers and shareholders is the question, who controls the corporation? The answer has ebbed and flowed throughout the twentieth century as the first third of the twentieth century saw the rise of the Wall Street and powerful bankers which led to populist political action that fragmented finance and ushered in the ascendance of managerial capitalism (Roe 1994). The last quarter of the twentieth century saw the rise of the hostile takeover and shareholder activism.

The Shareholder Rights Movement Emerges

The rise of activist shareholders and institutional investors as a viable social movement has been well documented (Davis and Thompson 1994; Useem 1996). We briefly recapitulate how the shareholder activists resemble a social movement. Tarrow (1998: 2) defined a social movement as "sustained collective challenges against powerful opponents by people united by common purpose through underlying social networks and resonant collective action frames." The shareholder rights movement coincides with each component of Tarrow's definition as shareholders squared off against powerful opponents (managers), united by common purpose (pursuit of shareholder value), with underlying social networks and resonant collective action frames. The shareholder rights movement was born in the mid-1980s amid a free market–oriented Reagan administration, a sympathetic Securities and Exchange Commission, and a thriving market for corporate control enabled by the 1982 *Edgar v. MITE* decision – all of which created a welcoming *political opportunity structure* (McAdam et al. 1996). As public and private pension funds increasingly concentrated shareholdings, they became *mobilizing structures* that facilitated the aggregation of interests and collective action. Lastly, shareholder activists used resonant *cultural frames*, including emphases on corporate democracy, free markets, and economic efficiency as well as a populist characterization of corporate managers as overpaid and unaccountable plutocrats (Davis and Thompson 1994). The confluence of these factors resulted in a viable movement with a coherent agenda.

The Emergence of the Constituency Countermovement and State-by-State Battles

Countermovements exist only to the extent that they are dynamically engaged with an oppositional movement (Zald and Useem 1987). Thus, the shareholder rights movement, which claimed that shareholders are the one true constituency for which corporations are operated, engendered a constituency countermovement asserting that corporations should consider shareholders in tandem with employees, customers, and communities (in the case of hostile takeovers). Three conditions support the rise of countermovements: the movement shows signs of success (e.g., through critical events such as a Supreme Court decision), the interests of some population are threatened by movement goals, and political allies are available to aid oppositional mobilization (Meyer and Staggenborg 1996). As argued above the shareholder rights movement showed many signs of success and had the continuing endorsement of the Reagan administration. However, its pursuit of an active market for corporate control replete with hostile takeovers explicitly threatened the interests of numerous constituencies in local communities including incumbent management, worker, and legislators. As such, there were numerous political allies from the outset.

Zald and Useem (1987: 247) characterized the dynamics of movement/ countermovement interaction as following a "sometimes loosely coupled tango of mobilization and demobilization." As can be seen from the historical contestation over the separation of ownership and control in general and the regulation of mergers and acquisitions in specific, managers and shareholders have periodically faced off to renegotiate the balance of power in the public corporation. The emergence of the constituency countermovement provides an excellent example of Zald and Useem's "loosely coupled tango" because the managers and their allies mobilize only to the extent that there are acute concerns, an organized polity, and effective rhetoric.

Threat and Political Opportunity

Political opportunities are the conditions that encourage, discourage, and shape the likelihood and success of mobilization. They both facilitate movement activity and constrain the range and form of possible action. Political opportunities are historically specific and change over time. They can engender action by creating grievances and incentives for action. Social movements often seek to change the political opportunity structure as occurred in the civil rights movement with the passage of the Voting Rights Act of 1965, which opened insider options as well as outsider tactics (McAdam 1982). Similarly, the constituency countermovement of corporations and unions sought to enact antitakeover legislation to provide management greater latitude of action to answer hostile takeovers and other shareholder insurgencies. The shareholder rights movement also sought and succeeded in expanding political opportunity by altering the law on proxy voting during the 1980s so as to transform corporate governance in a way that counteracted the power of corporate managers (Davis and Thompson 1994).

While mobilization is often triggered by political opportunity, countermovements are primarily triggered by threats. In the context of movements, threats entail the costs a social group is likely to suffer if it does not take action (Goldstone and Tilly 2001). Threats also have an indirect effect by creating political opportunity for protective countermobilization. By viewing threats as the trigger for countermobilization, we are able to analyze why the attempts to enact national legislation precluding takeovers failed and local efforts largely succeeded. Antitakeover legislation on the federal level failed because the threat of hostile takeover was not perceived as a national threat. In fact, the prevailing opinion in the Reagan administration was that takeovers actually enhanced national economic performance and it threatened to refuse to enforce any law regulating takeovers. But as Meyer and Staggenborg (1996: 1645) asserted, "in a federal state where there are numerous institutional sites for making policy, movements often respond to a defeat in one venue by protesting in an alternative arena." The constituency countermovement responded exactly in this way as it moved the conflict to the states.

Managerial elites were much more successful at the state level because they could articulate hostile takeover as an acute threat that posed considerable risks to local jobs and community. Their claims were enhanced because managers could claim residence and played a more central role in the local economy whereas shareholder groups were widely dispersed. These threats also operated indirectly by creating political opportunity by opening the political system to mobilization and broadening the number of elite allies such as local legislators (McAdam 1996).

Protecting local industry was also a full-time job of the state legislatures as the economic crises (e.g., international competition, hostile takeovers, and recession) of the 1980s wreaked havoc on local economies. The effects of raiders and hostile takeovers, both real and imagined, were also being felt on a local level. For example, in Pennsylvania, an early adopter of aggressive antitakeover statutes, Gulf Oil had been taken over in the early 1980s by Chevron resulting in the closing of Gulf's Pittsburgh headquarters and the elimination of thousands of jobs. Tender offers and hostile takeovers are acute threats that make potential job loss salient (especially when a local company is at risk) and can catalyze dormant or otherwise occupied organizations and networks. In general, a hostile takeover attempt of a local company – locally headquartered and therefore having a large effect on the local economy and locally incorporated in order to be governed by a state's corporate law – led to the proposal and adoption of antitakeover legislation because it locally punctuated the ongoing crises of American industry.

Similarly, high levels of unemployment and high bankruptcy rates signal ongoing threats to the workforce and business community and, as such, render states more susceptible to influence. To remedy these conditions, state governments actively seek legislative mechanisms supportive of job security without alienating business leaders. The higher these rates the more exaggerated the climate of insecurity and crisis. Therefore, we hypothesize that acute and ongoing threats contributing to economic crisis will create state political openness to measures perceived to reduce job loss.

H2a: The greater the number of tender offers for firms incorporated and headquartered within a state, the sooner a state will adopt an antitakeover statute.

H2b: The higher the bankruptcy rate within a state, the sooner a state will adopt an antitakeover statute.

H2c: The higher the unemployment rate within a state, the sooner a state will adopt an antitakeover statute.

It is important to note that while our measures approximate levels of objective grievances, political opportunity is theorized as seeing potential for action and is interpretive. While this is an important limitation of our data, in our sample the movement entrepreneurs (i.e., elites) and labor leaders comprising the constituency countermovement interpreted the threats proxied by our variables as threats immediately necessitating redress. For example, "when Dayton Hudson, a Minnesota company, became a target two months later, its managers got Minnesota to hold a special legislative session. Within hours, the state had a new antitakeover bill" (Roe 1991: 339).

While we did not specifically hypothesize an effect of governmental legitimation of a tactic as a source of political opportunity, the legitimation of second generation antitakeover statutes in the *CTS Corporation v. Dynamics Corporation* case shaped and directed other mobilizations because it rendered similar types of legislation constitutional and plausible. Similarly, the enactment of the Equal Employment Opportunity Act made legal mobilization a possible and fruitful tactic for advancing equality in the workplace (Burstein 1991), and numerous court decisions (e.g., *Brown v. Board of*

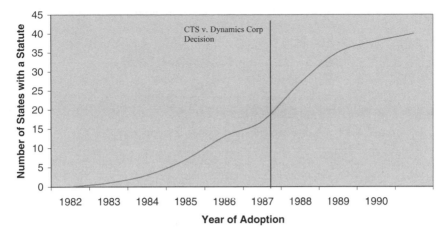

Figure 4.1 Cumulative Antitakeover Statues Adopted in U.S. States, 1982–1990

Education) and new pieces of legislation during the U.S. civil rights movement made tactics plausible that had not been previously viable. Figure 4.1 illustrates the general pattern of adoption of antitakeover statutes, but also illustrates the significant impact of the legitimation of second generation statutes. Prior to the *CTS v. Dynamics* decision, only seventeen states had adopted a statute. Within a year of the mid-1987 decision, thirty-five states had adopted statutes.

Mobilizing Structures

Mobilizing structures are "collective vehicles, informal as well as formal, through which people mobilize and engage in collective action" (McAdam et al. 1996). The mobilizing structures of managerial elites have been the subject of extensive attention, especially by class (e.g., Zeitlin 1974) and social network analysts (Swedberg 1994). Mobilizing structures have long been a cornerstone of social movement analysis because grievances, threats, and opportunities are necessary but insufficient conditions for effective collective action (McCarthy and Zald 1977). In the constituency countermovement both formal organizations such as local Chambers of Commerce and the Business Roundtable and social networks enabled local elites to mobilize quickly and effectively around issues that affect their interests. Many theorists have argued that upper-class clubs serve a similar function in creating cohesion and facilitating action (Domhoff 1998). A representative quote from Romano (1992: 52) illustrates how coupling political opportunity with preexisting organizational capacity led to swift and successful action: "State takeover laws are typically sponsored by a local chamber of commerce at the behest of a local corporation that has become the target of a hostile bid. They are often enacted rapidly, sometimes over a few days in a special emergency session." The swift enactment of state antitakeover legislation in the vast majority of states reflects the depth and effectiveness of these networks and formal organizations. To represent the role of formal organizations in the adoption of takeover statutes we hypothesize:

H3a: *The greater the number of upper-class clubs in a state, the sooner a state will adopt an antitakeover statute.*

The interlock network has a long history in the study of the diffusion of innovations (e.g., Davis 1991) and as a mechanism for creating cohesion and aggregating interests into collective action (see Mizruchi 1996 for a review). Interlocks increase cohesion by bringing individuals into closer contact with one another. When the networks are locally concentrated (connected firms headquartered and incorporated in the same state) they become a potentially powerful force in effectuating institutional change. The denser the interlock network among firms, the greater the capacity of firms to act in similar political ways (Mizruchi 1989). Prior research by Useem (1984) illustrated how the interlock network provided an important mechanism by which managers mobilized in response to political threats to their interests in the 1970s. Based on its ability to create shared interests, similar political action, and its importance in responding effectively to acute threats, we hypothesize

H3b: *The greater the number of interlocks between firms incorporated and head-quartered in a state, the sooner a state will adopt an antitakeover statute.*

Relatedly, the interlock network also plays a powerful role as a source of information transmission and social influence. Interlocks with firms that have adopted an innovation generally lead to subsequent adoption by the interlocking firm because it gains fine-grained information about the innovation that helps it become more familiar with the benefits of adoption and the process for adopting. Ties to prior adopters have been associated with adopting poison pill defenses or securities issued by the board of directors in order to make hostile takeover more difficult by dramatically increasing the potential cost a hostile acquirer would have to pay (Davis 1991), investor relations departments (Rao and Sivakumar 1999), and acquisition strategies (Haunschild 1993). Ties to prior adopters exert social influence by designating an innovation as normatively appropriate and desirable, thus exerting pressure to keep up with current innovations. Thus, when local elites are connected to firms incorporated and headquartered in a state that has previously adopted an antitakeover statute, they gain important information on the benefits of the statute and through processes of social influence come to see these statutes as correct and valid, both of which will lead the local elites to mobilize for antitakeover legislation. Thus, we hypothesize

H3c: The greater the number of interlocks between firms incorporated and head-quartered in a state and firms incorporated and headquartered in the state of a recent adopter, the sooner a state will adopt an antitakeover statute.

Another vital component of quickly enacting antitakeover legislation was strong support by the other key constituency in the countermovement – labor unions. The participation of labor unions plays a crucial role in two ways: first, the rhetoric of saving jobs and preserving the local community institutions becomes more plausible to the extent that labor also partici-pates in the countermovement: second, the greater the percentage of the workforce that is unionized the more readily workers can aggregate their interests in protecting jobs, wield local political clout, and mobilize to enact legislation. Wayne (1990: D1), reporting on Pennsylvania's statute at the time of adoption, stated "Pennsylvania business groups supporting the bill *are aligned with unions seeking to protect . . . their members* and local politicians worried about the impact of corporate takeovers on communities." This partnering of labor, management, and community generates credibility and urgency for adopting statutes. Thus, we hypothesize

H3d: The greater the union density within a state, the sooner a state will adopt an antitakeover statute.

Frame Alignment Processes

Both resource mobilization and political process approaches to the study of social movements and collective action have been critiqued for their inattention to linking the ideational and the structural (Snow et al. 1986). Frame alignment refers to shared schemata of interpretation regarding values, beliefs, and goals that facilitate collective action and help bridge the micro to macro linkage (Snow et al. 1986). Framing consists of three components – diagnostic (constructing a problem in need of redress), prognostic (proposing a solution), and motivational (Snow and Benford 1988). Frames elicit action to the extent that they resonate – align with existing value and belief systems and have relevance to one's "phenomenological life world" (Snow and Benford 1988). The struggle between the shareholder rights movement and the constituency countermovement pitted two frames in direct opposition. The shareholder rights movement utilized frames that articulated free markets, economic efficiency, and corporate democracy and demonized corporate managements as "autocrats" and "feudal lords" to attract supporters. It diagnosed the problem as entrenched empire-building managements that ignored the concerns of shareholders. The solution to the problem was maintaining an active market for corporate control. The rationale for action was the moral inducement to maintain the free market and the promise of increased wealth. The movement also utilized expert testimonials to assist in inducing support (e.g., renowned scholars from the contractarian perspective, pension fund managers, and institutional investors). However, these frames failed to resonate with the public as high language regarding economic efficiency lacked relevance to the "life world" or experiential commensurability for participants and bystanders (i.e., the general public) (Snow and Benford 1988). The movement also lacked empirical credibility, as it is tough to test the claim that the economy is becoming more efficient (Snow and Benford 1988). Pension fund investor Greta Marshall amplified the point: "It's very easy to take a picture of someone out of work because of a takeover, it's very hard, though, to take a picture showing the U.S. economy as a whole becoming more competitive due to takeovers" (McGurn et al. 1989: 3).

The constituency countermovement did not have any of the same troubles, as it articulated specific threats to the local economy – hostile takeovers – as the problem. The proposed solution to the problem was enacting legislation to protect domestic firms from unwanted takeovers. The rationale for action articulated by the framing efforts across the states was the protection of local jobs and local companies from foreign raiders desiring to break up a company and slash jobs for short-term gains. Romano suggested that the frames utilized by the constituency countermovement possessed greater salience for the average constituent because "a news story on a takeover resulting in unemployed workers will...be vividly remembered and considered evidence of the negative effects of acquisitions" (1993: 82). In other words, by design, the frames employed by the constituency countermovement resonated because they were empirically credible (i.e., job loss is easier to observe) and experientially commensurable (i.e., the loss of jobs and/or the destruction of community institutions has great impact on one's "life world"). In addition, the constituency countermovement portrayed shareholder activists and corporate raiders as "rapacious" (Hirsch 1986) and interested only in short-term personal gain.

Given the strong resonance of the constituency countermovement's frames, its proposed solution should be enacted to the extent it is deemed plausible. Plausibility should be most readily conferred in states where there are culturally and politically available repertoires. Repertoires are most available in states where a first generation statute, struck down by the *Edgar v. MITE* decision, was adopted. Thus, we hypothesize

H4: *States that had previously adopted a first generation antitakeover statute will adopt a second generation antitakeover statute sooner.*

Methods

Sample

We collected data on the adoption of antitakeover statutes between 1982 and 1990 for all fifty states. We chose this time frame because it is analytically meaningful for the phenomenon under study. The starting date of June 23, 1982, is immediately following the *Edgar v. MITE* decision that both initiated the large wave of acquisitions and hostile takeovers and outlawed first generation takeover statutes. The end date is also theoretically significant because by 1991 (i.e., the end of 1990) forty of the states had adopted some form of antitakeover legislation and acquisitions had reduced to a trickle: seventeen between 1991 and 1996 with only five classified as hostile (Davis and Robbins 2005). Data on the timing and form of antitakeover statute adoption comes from the Investor Responsibility Research Center (IRRC).

Dependent Variables

Given that we had exact dates for the adoption of each statute we utilized time to adoption as our dependent variable. Specifically, we measured the time from June 23, 1982, until either the adoption of an antitakeover statute or, if a state did not adopt a statute, the end of the study time frame (December 31, 1990). The statutes in our analysis are the following: "control share statutes," which require a vote of "disinterested" shares before an offer can be consummated; "fair price statutes," which prevent an acquiring firm from effectuating a two-tiered acquisition, whereby an acquirer pays a high price to gain control of the corporation and then pays a lower price for the remaining shares; "other constituency" or "directors' duties" provisions, which require consideration of other (nonshareholding) constituencies in the tender offer process; "poison pill endorsements," which allow companies to adopt the poison pill antitakeover defense (Davis 1991); and "freeze out" provisions which institute a waiting period for subsequent business combinations of, most commonly, two, three, or five years. All data on dates of adoption and number of statutes adopted were collected from the IRRC's *State Takeover Laws*.

Independent Variables

Political Opportunity/Threat   We operationalized three measures that we believe capture a state's potential susceptibility to elite mobilization – the *number of first tender offers for fully domestic firms* (i.e., firms incorporated and headquartered within the same state), the *bankruptcy rate*, and the *unemployment rate*. All three of these variables were updated for each year under study (1982–90). The tender offers data was collected from *Compact Disclosure* and includes every first tender offer from 1985 to 1990. For the 1982–84 period we have data on first tender offers for the Fortune 500 (Davis and Stout 1992). While this component of the tender offer data is not as exhaustive, this is not problematic because the takeovers that triggered the adoption of antitakeover statutes were those of the large firms included in these data. Because of the skewed distribution of tender offers, we measured tender offers as the natural log of the number of first tender offers plus unity. Adding unity created valid values for states with zero tender offers. The bankruptcy rate was calculated as the number of bankruptcies in a state (data from Dun and Bradstreet's *Business Failures and New Business Incorporations*) divided by the number of nonfarm firms in a state (data from the Bureau of the Census). We took the natural log of this variable to account for skewness in its distribution. The unemployment rate was collected from the Bureau of Labor Statistics.

Mobilizing Structures   We argued that four variables – *fully domestic ties, ties to fully domestic prior adopters, the number of upper-class clubs and social registries*, and *union density* – help aggregate interests and mobilize collective action through formal networks and formal organizations, respectively.

110

Fully domestic ties were measured as the total number of interlocks between firms incorporated and headquartered within the same state. Ties need to be fully domestic for four reasons. First, corporate law governs firms based on their state of incorporation; therefore, antitakeover statutes are applicable only to firms incorporated in a state. Second, sharing a headquarters state reflects the fact that interlocks are likely to generate local political action only to the extent that both the business and the local citizenry stand to suffer from a hostile takeover. Third, firms headquartered and incorporated in a state are also likely to have stronger ties with a community and, consequently, these firms are likely to wield more influence. Lastly, these conditions minimize the impact of statistical outlier Delaware. Because of the extremely skewed distribution of the number of interlocks within a state, we measured interlocks as the natural log of the number of ties plus unity. Adding unity created valid values for the numerous states with no fully domestic interlocks. We measured board of director interlocks using the same set of firms described in Davis (1991) and at one point in time – 1986. Prior analyses of the interlock network have demonstrated that the total number of interlocks is highly stable over time (Mariolis and Jones 1982). Thus, a point-in-time measure should be representative of the whole period under study. Ties *to prior adopters* were measured as the number of a fully domestic focal firm's interlock partners that were headquartered and incorporated in a state that had adopted an antitakeover statute in the previous year, updated annually. Again, because this measure is extremely skewed, we used the natural log of the number of ties to prior adopters plus unity. The number of upper-class clubs and social registries was coded as the sum of all clubs and registries in a state and collected from Domhoff (1998). We measured union density as the proportion of a state's workforce that belonged to a labor union. Union density was measured for 1983 1986, and 1987. Data were drawn from the Bureau of National Affairs' *Union Membership and Earnings Data Book.*

Frame Alignment   It would be more plausible for a state to enact a second generation antitakeover statute to solve the "problem" of hostile takeovers if legislation had been previously enacted to curb hostile takeovers. Therefore, we measured the plausibility of enacting a new law based on whether or not a state was one of the forty that had adopted a first generation antitakeover statute, which were struck down by the *Edgar v. MITE* decision in 1982. We created a dummy variable for whether a state adopted a first generation statute or not (1 if the state adopted a prior statute, 0 otherwise).

The Contractarian Perspective   The contractarian perspective argues that the adoption of antitakeover statutes results from competition for franchise fees. Those states most dependent on franchise fees should adopt the weakest bundle of statutes, later or not at all. We measured dependence on franchise fees as the franchise fees received by a state divided by total tax revenue. This approach has also been used in prior work that is representative of the contractarian perspective (Romano 1993). This variable was updated annually and we used the natural log to correct for skewness in its distribution resulting from a large outlier – again, Delaware. The data were collected from the Bureau of the Census, *State Government Tax Collections*.

Control Variables

Several factors not included in our hypotheses are likely to correspond with the timing of adopting a statute. Thus, we account for multiple alternative explanations for our hypothesized effects through three control variables that fit broadly under the rubric of state capacity and through the political composition of the state legislatures. State capacity implies that states that are more innovative, larger, and better organized are more likely to adopt any type of legislation irrespective of the other factors in play. We control for state innovativeness using the *Walker innovation index*, which accounts for a state's proclivity to adopt novel legislation (Walker 1969). The Walker innovation index is measured as reported in his seminal article.[2] State size is accounted for by a variable measuring the *number of nonfarm firms* in a state. We use this variable as a control to ensure that our measures of mobilizing structures are not merely a proxy for the size of the business community. The data was collected from the Bureau of the Census and is updated annually. In all the analyses we take the natural log of the variable to correct for skewness. The number of *registered lobbying organizations* is another potential explanation for why a state might adopt an antitakeover statute more quickly. That is, states with better-developed lobbying infrastructures provide formalized channels of influence (i.e., lobbying is likely to be recognized as a legitimate means of shaping public policy) and specific organizations act as mechanisms that facilitate the aggregation of interests and collective action. This variable utilizes data from Gray and Lowery

---

[2] In the original article Hawaii and Alaska were unranked. We imputed the mean to ensure all fifty states had data.

(1996) on the number of registered lobbying organizations in 1990. We use the 1990 cohort of data because prior to that time the data are incomplete. Using the 1990 data is not problematic because although the absolute number of registered lobbying organizations grows dramatically over time, the relative rankings of states remain largely the same between 1980 and 1990. Lastly, the Republican Reagan administration's strong free market stance thwarted multiple attempts by the Business Roundtable to enact federal legislation regulating takeovers. To the extent that Republican-controlled state legislatures share a similar stance with respect to economic issues in general and takeovers in specific, they should be less likely to adopt antitakeover statutes. If an antitakeover statute is adopted, it should be adopted later and the number of laws adopted smaller. We control for *party composition of the state houses* using two dummy variables, one for the state house and one for the state senate (1=Republican-controlled, 0 otherwise). Nebraska, however, has a unicameral nonpartisan legislature. Therefore, we substituted data on the party controlling the state delegation in the national House and Senate, respectively. In the event of an evenly divided state house or state senate, we utilized the party controlling the state delegation in the national House or Senate to break the tie. The data were collected from the *U.S. Statistical Abstract* and updated every election cycle.

Statistical Method

We model the rate of adopting an antitakeover statute using event history analysis. The particular method we employ is the Cox proportional hazards model with time varying covariates. We utilize the Cox model because it does not specify the exact form or distribution of event times and "in the judgment of many, it is unequivocally the best all-around method for estimating regression models with continuous-time data" (Allison 1984: 35). This model assumes that the first event is a fatal event, irrespective of which type of statute is adopted. Thus, for example, poison pill endorsements are treated as equivalent to control share acquisition statutes. While some subtlety is lost, as there are differences in the level of protection from takeovers among the different types of statutes, our second set of analyses using the strength of protection as a dependent variable helps to overcome this limitation. Because we had complete data on adoption dates from the first adoption in this population, there is no problem of left censoring.

Furthermore, our sample contained only a moderate amount of right censoring; 20 percent of the states in our analyses had not adopted a statute by the end of the sample period. This level of right censoring is adequately accounted for by the partial likelihood estimation technique used in Cox models.

Our general modeling strategy was to model adoption of the current year (e.g., 1986) as a function of the previous year's data (e.g., 1985) for our time, varying covariates (bankruptcy rate, unemployment rate, union density, number of businesses, interlocks with prior adopters, and franchise fees/total tax revenue). The other covariates (interlocks, first generation statute dummy, registered lobbying organizations, Walker innovation index, and upper-class clubs) were fixed values that were the same for each state in every model. Lastly, since many statutes were adopted during a hostile takeover attempt, this variable is measured during the same year as the dependent variable. Similarly, the composition of the state legislature of the current year should be most relevant to the adoption of a statute. Thus, this variable also is measured during the same year as the dependent variable.

Moreover, given that there is only a small sample of states ($n = 50$), we are required to use a methodological technique that compensates for the information deficit problem. Following Mintz and Palmer (2000), we utilize a four-step procedure to maximize comprehensive testing of all relevant variables while minimizing the demands on our small sample size in our final models. The procedure is as follows: 1) enter theoretically related variables (e.g., political opportunity), 2) enter all the significant variables from step one into a provisional multifactor model, 3) enter all the significant variables from step two and reenter (individually) each variable dropped after step one into a second-stage multifactor model, and 4) enter the significant variables from step two and step three into a final model. The results for all these analyses are reported in Table 4.2 (see p. 117).

Results

Table 4.1 contains the descriptive statistics and correlation matrix for all the variables used in our statistical analyses. Many of the variables are significantly correlated with each other (as would be expected with time series data) and some are highly correlated with each other. However, regression diagnostics (i.e., the variance inflation factor) yielded no values greater than 3, which makes multicollinearity less of a concern.

Table 4.1. Descriptive Statistics and Correlations for Variables Used in Analyses

Variable	Mean	S.D.	1	2	3	4	5	6	7	8	9	10	11	12	13	14	15
Date of adoption	0.13	0.34															
Tender offers (log)	0.18	0.44	0.19*														
Bankruptcy rate (log)	−2.76	0.60	0.10†	0.06													
Unemployment rate	7.59	2.41	−0.08	−0.16*	0.38*												
Upper-class clubs	0.90	1.79	0.05	0.40*	0.08	0.06											
Number of interlocks (log)	0.56	1.05	0.15*	0.23*	−0.09	0.00	0.48*										
Ties to prior adopters (log)	0.23	0.54	0.12*	0.22*	−0.13*	−0.02	0.28*	0.57*									
Union density	16.43	6.17	0.05	0.02	0.04	0.36*	0.34*	0.34*	0.26*								
First generation statute	0.69	0.47	0.12*	0.07	0.07	−0.08	−0.03	0.25*	0.18*	−0.14*							
Franchise revenues (log)	−1.34	1.84	0.01	0.04	−0.04	0.05	−0.09	−0.10†	0.04	−0.22*	0.15*						
Walker innovation index	0.44	0.08	0.07	0.26*	−0.10†	−0.04	0.57*	0.61*	0.37*	0.56*	0.01	−0.30*					
Lobbying organizations (log)	6.10	0.60	0.09	0.40*	0.17*	0.05	0.52*	0.43*	0.21*	0.18*	0.15*	−0.05	−0.05				
Number of businesses (log)	10.97	0.98	0.12*	0.49*	0.25*	0.13*	0.69*	0.52*	0.34*	0.09	0.23*	0.14*	0.08	0.37*			
Republican-controlled house	0.35	0.48	−0.04	−0.08	−0.15*	−0.39*	−0.31*	−0.21*	−0.10†	−0.23*	0.01	−0.26*	−0.03	0.46*	0.75*		
Republican-controlled senate	0.33	0.47	−0.01	−0.11†	−0.05	−0.18*	−0.14*	−0.08	−0.06	−0.08	0.00	−0.34*	−0.19*	−0.01	−0.15*	0.62*	

N = 308
† p < .10, * p < .05

115

The results of the event history analyses of the rate of adopting an antitakeover statute are displayed in Table 4.2. Models 1 through 5 represent step one in the Mintz and Palmer (2000) procedure where clusters of theoretically related variables (contractarian, political opportunity, mobilizing structures, frame alignment, and controls) are entered individually. These models reveal that only two variables are statistically significant (local interlocks and first generation statute) while two others are marginally significant (bankruptcy rate and union density). Also, only Model 3 and Model 4 are significant as a whole. Model 6 is the provisional multifactor model described as step two by Mintz and Palmer (2000). In step three we ran models with the four significant variables from step two (bankruptcy rate, local interlocks, union density, and first generation statute) and individually reentered each variable dropped after step one. Due to space constraints, we do not report these ten models individually. However, none of the variables individually reentered reached even marginal levels of statistical significance (p < .10). As such, the final model (Model 7), comprised of significant variables from steps two and three is identical to Model 6. We evaluate our hypotheses using Model 7 with all the excluded variables considered statistically insignificant.

Hypothesis 1 posited that states dependent upon incorporation franchise fees would adopt statutes later or not at all. Our results find no support for this hypothesis nor any statistically significant relationship between dependence upon incorporation franchise fees and rate of adopting an antitakeover statute. We also hypothesized that acute economic crises – tender offers for local companies, high bankruptcy rates, and high unemployment – that threaten local businesses and jobs should result in a greater likelihood of adopting antitakeover legislation (Hypotheses 2a, 2b, and 2c, respectively). We found no support for Hypothesis 2a as we found no relationship between the number of first tender offers for local firms and the rate of adopting an antitakeover statute. We discuss this unexpected finding in the next section. Furthermore, we found no support for Hypothesis 2c, which argued that higher unemployment rates would speed adoption of an antitakeover statute. While this finding was unexpected, it likely results from the fact that aggregate unemployment rate imperfectly gauges perceived need to mobilize. Attributions of an acute threat that can readily be redressed as a result of collective action are more likely to result from more sudden (and unexpected) and concentrated threats of unemployment such as downsizings and plant closings. Hypothesis 2b, higher bankruptcy

Elite Mobilizations for Antitakeover Legislation

Table 4.2. *Regression Results Cox Proportional Hazards Regression of the Rate of Adopting an Antitakeover Statute*

	Model 1	Model 2	Model 3	Model 4	Model 5	Model 6	Model 7
Contractarian Perspective							
Franchise	1.01						
revenues (log)	(0.09)						
Political Opportunity							
Tender offers		1.06					
		(0.12)					
Bankruptcy		1.52†				1.61*	1.61*
rate (log)		(0.46)				(0.39)	(0.39)
Unemployment		0.95					
Rate		(0.10)					
Mobilizing Structures							
Upper-class-			0.90				
clubs			(0.09)				
Local interlocks			1.66*			1.42**	1.42**
(log)			(0.37)			(0.21)	(0.21)
Ties to prior			0.95				
Adopters (log)			(0.40)				
Union density			1.05†			1.06*	1.06*
			(0.03)			(0.04)	(0.04)
Frame Alignment							
First generation				2.79**		2.92*	2.92*
statute				(1.18)		(1.50)	(1.50)
Controls							
Number of					1.03		
businesses (log)					(0.33)		
Number of							
lobbying					1.44		
organizations					(0.59)		
(log)							
Walker innovation					5.64		
index					(12.79)		
State House –					0.62		
Republican					(0.27)		
State Senate –					1.41		
Republican					(0.56)		
Likelihood							
ratio	−133.40	−132.09	−125.97	−129.82	−130.10	−121.77	−121.77
Wald χ	0.01	2.29	23.22***	5.89*	5.20	27.18***	27.18***
N	308	308	308	308	308	308	308

Notes: Significance tests are two-tail for controls and one-tail for hypothesized effects.

Robust standard errors are in parentheses.

All models utilize robust standard errors with clustering to account for non-independence of observations.

†p < .10, *p < .05, **p < .01, ***p < .001

rates lead to faster adoption of an antitakeover statute, was supported ($B = 1.61$, p < .05). According to our model, for each percent increase in a state's bankruptcy rate, the rate of adopting an antitakeover statute increases by 0.06 percent. States with a 9.9 percent bankruptcy rate (the seventy-fifth percentile) adopted at a rate 2.4 percent greater than those with a 1 percent bankruptcy rate.[3] The low effect sizes suggest that while bankruptcy rate has a statistically significant effect on the rate of adoption, its effect is largely indirect. The indirect effect of threats and political opportunities, however, is largely consistent with a social movement perspective which argues that perceptions of threats or opportunities encourage, discourage, and channel mobilization (Campbell, this volume).

Our variables representing mobilizing structures generally received support and had a strong practical impact on the rate of adopting an antitakeover statute. First, the number of local board of directors interlocks significantly increased the rate of adoption (Hypothesis 3b, $B = 1.42$, p < .01). For states with two fully local interlocks (the seventy-fifth percentile), the rate of adoption is 268 percent higher than a state with no local interlocks. However, upper-class clubs (Hypothesis 3a) and ties to prior adopters (Hypothesis 3c) did not influence the rate of adoption. Greater union density (Hypothesis 3d, $B = 1.06$, p < .05) also significantly speeds the adoption of antitakeover statutes. This finding indicates labor's participation in the constituency countermovement significantly aided in the adoption of antitakeover legislation. That is, the rhetoric of saving jobs and preserving the local community may have been critical in swaying legislators (i.e., an effective frame), but the actual participation of labor leaders in articulating the frame and mobilizing their membership was also critical. Our variable for frame alignment also received support. Adopting a first generation statute created an available repertoire that later legislatures could effectively capitalize upon (Hypothesis 4, $B = 2.92$, p < .05). The general pattern of support for the social movement hypotheses, when coupled with the lack of empirical support for the contractarian perspective, highlights the importance of collective action in the adoption of corporate

---

[3] The estimated effects on the expected rate of adoption is calculated by $y = \exp\{b_1 z\}$ where y is the multiplier of the rate, z is the natural log of the variable of interest, and b_1 is the parameter associated with the logged variable. For variables that are not logged, the percentages are calculated by exponentiating (i.e., e^B) the coefficients of the regression equation.

law and the inability of the contractarian perspective to account for collective action either theoretically or empirically.

Discussion

Our results indicate that elite mobilization can be usefully studied using a social movement framework. Differences in the threats to established local interests (more bankruptcies) made state legislatures more prone to adopt antitakeover legislation early on, and states' dependence on franchise revenues influenced their corporate law agendas. While the number of tender offers for local companies did not contribute to the rate of adoption of antitakeover statutes, qualitative analysis of individual state histories indicates that tender offers for local companies, especially large corporations often classified as "good corporate citizens," often triggered the process for adopting a statute. For example, several specific takeover battles spurred the adoption of antitakeover provisions: Burlington Industries in North Carolina, Greyhound in Arizona, Dayton-Hudson in Minnesota, Aetna in Connecticut, and Gillette in Massachusetts. Thus, we still argue that political opportunities created by discrete events that disrupt the extant power structure strongly shaped the pattern of adoption. This much might have been expected from a standard public choice account. But what distinguishes a social movement account is its attention to frames and social structures. Movement activity over time bears relatively modest relation to "objective" variation in grievances (Tilly 1978). The world is full of potential grievances, and events taken to be normal in one period are intolerable in other periods. It is when changes in incentives (e.g., from the political opportunity structure) are collectively interpreted as a cause of action by a well-organized set of actors that significant movements arise. Thus, the better organized the local corporate elite (as indicated by the number of corporate board interlocks), the faster the state legislature was to adopt management-friendly legislation regulating hostile takeovers. Labor played a key role in framing the struggle as raiders versus communities and denoting takeovers as prologues to widespread layoffs. Labor also directly participated in creating the legislation as unions mobilized to encourage states to adopt statutes more quickly. Having the available repertoire of a prior statute also facilitated adopting a second generation antitakeover statute.

Given the relatively rapid and widespread diffusion of antitakeover legislation, why didn't the partnership between labor, management, and local communities continue? Romano (1992: 52) noted that "a close examination of the political process of takeover legislation raises serious questions whether employee welfare is a concern in the first place. Business lobbying groups that are the moving force behind takeover statutes uniformly and vigorously oppose plant-closing legislation." That is, the coalition coalesced around a very narrow and specific issue – the hostile takeover – and not a new approach to the corporation. With the combination of the drastic decline of takeover activity in the 1990s (Davis and Robbins 2005) and a healthier economy, a stronger shareholder rights movement weakened the urgency and viability of the countermovement and its coalitions rapidly dissolved. In addition, with antitakeover legislation as the solution the constituency countermovement was not able to extend the frame to other settings (Snow and Benford 1992). More generally, it is likely that countermobilizations (or mobilizations) that coalesce to redress specific threats may be especially fragile. This is akin to what social movement scholars have termed "consensus movements" (McCarthy and Wolfson 1992). These movements enjoy widespread support, and are typically local and geographically bounded, but are typically short lived. In our case, labor and management rapidly banded together and state legislatures nearly unanimously passed antitakeover legislation, but once the perceived threat of hostile takeovers was largely eliminated, the issues that motivated the coalition's formation were ostensibly redressed and demobilization ensued.

While the coalitions of labor and management may have dissolved, the statutes themselves have been remarkably resilient given the contention surrounding their adoption. Thus, the constituency countermovement may provide some insight into what enables institutional settlements (Burton and Higley 1987; Rao 1998) to endure – a diverse movement constituency wielding resonant frames. The adoption of antitakeover legislation has also had lingering effects on the tactics employed during interactions between shareholder activists and managers. After being defeated in state legislatures across the United States, shareholder rights activists changed their discourse and tactics to become mutualistic instead of antagonistic. The relations that have emerged between investors and managers in the United States are now reliant on an ongoing negotiated relation that "serves to achieve what takeover threats, proxy battles, and other blunt forms of 'communication' between owners and companies failed to do in the past ... neither shareholders nor companies could assert unlimited sovereignty over the other" (Useem 1996: 207).

Conclusion

We note two things in closing. First, although we have advocated and found support for a social movement perspective on elite mobilization, our argument has clear affinities with neoinstitutionalist perspectives. Networks are a critical mechanism for the spread of norms and practices among organizations in institutional theory (DiMaggio and Powell 1983), and it is a small step from networks to political mobilization (e.g., Mizruchi 1992). Moreover, while our approach highlights the fragmentation of corporate law in a federated system, Scott and Meyer (1983) noted long ago the importance of specifying the appropriate jurisdiction for the process of institutionalization. As other chapters in this volume indicate, neoinstitutionalism and the study of social movements stand to benefit from closer integration (e.g., Lounsbury, and Scott and McAdam, this volume). Second, as our opening paragraph indicates, the use of the rhetoric and tactics of grassroots social movements, like the more general rhetoric of populism, rebellion, and revolution, has proven to be readily adopted by business for its own purposes (cf. Frank 2001). We await with interest the business response to the anti-globalization movement.

5

Institutionalization as a Contested, Multilevel Process

THE CASE OF RATE REGULATION IN AMERICAN FIRE INSURANCE

Marc Schneiberg and Sarah A. Soule

Institutionalization – the activities and mechanisms by which structures, models, rules, and problem-solving routines become established as a taken-for-granted part of everyday social reality – represents a core sociological process and a central preoccupation for social scientists. Since Selznick's (1957) and Berger and Luckmann's (1967) classic works, understanding institutionalization has itself been understood as a critical agenda for sociologists and social constructionists. Over the last two decades or so, this agenda has been fruitfully pursued by organizational scholars and neoinstitutionalists, who have produced a variety of concepts and images of institutionalization. (For early statements and overviews, see Clemens and Cook 1999; DiMaggio 1988; Jepperson and Meyer 1991; Meyer and Rowan 1977; Schneiberg and Clemens 2003; Scott et al. 2000; Scott 1987, 1994; Zucker 1977; Tolbert and Zucker 1983.)

We work in this chapter to extend and revise these received images. Specifically, we use the case of rate regulation in fire insurance to revise conventional accounts and reconceptualize institutionalization as the product of constitutional struggles – conflicts evoked by social movements over the fundamental character of social, political, and industrial order. In so doing, we join recent efforts to link politics, challengers, and movements with organizational theory and neoinstitutional analysis (Clemens 1997; Davis and Thompson 1994; DiMaggio 1991; Fligstein 1996; Lounsbury, Ventresca, and Hirsch 2003; McAdam and Scott, this volume; Rao 1998; Rao et al. 2000; Schneiberg 1999, 2002; Soule 2003; Zald et al. 2002).

We thank Lis Clemens, Brayden King, Huggy Rao, John Campbell, Dick Scott, Marc Ventresca, Carol Heimer, and Paul Silverstein for their thoughtful comments on earlier versions and presentations of this work. The usual caveats apply.

122

We begin with a description of a key outcome – the enactment of rate regulation laws for a vital infrastructure sector – and briefly treat that outcome from the standpoint of three accounts of institutionalization that frame the organizational imagination about this topic. We begin, in other words, with what looks like a standard diffusion and institutionalization story about public policy. Yet, the standard imagery fails to capture critical features of the production of rate regulation. Accordingly, we then combine historical analysis, logistic regression, and heterogeneous diffusion models of the passage of rate regulation to retell this story and develop an account of institutionalization as a contested, multilevel process. Based on these analyses, we suggest ways to integrate social movements into neoinstitutional research.

Rate Regulation and the Conventional Imagery of Institutionalization – Three Explanations

From 1909 to 1937, thirty-four American states enacted rate regulation laws in fire insurance, a critical infrastructure industry during the nineteenth and twentieth centuries (Schneiberg 1999; Schneiberg and Bartley 2001).[1] These laws enacted *regulated cooperation among private corporations* as the central system of "market order" in the industry.[2] First, they authorized a host of private associational arrangements, data pooling, and cooperative rate-making schemes that for-profit insurers had organized in the late nineteenth century to limit price competition and stabilize insurance markets. Second, they subjected rates and rate-making associations to public oversight and a set of norms regarding reasonable and fair prices. Public oversight typically meant that associations had to file rates and supporting documents with state insurance departments and submit to examination, rate approval, and

---

[1] Fire insurance played a key role in credit and economic development. Steady supplies of fire insurance were vital for commerce and trade in a credit dependent economy, as banks and other lenders required such insurance as collateral and as a condition for mortgages, loans, and short term credit (Brearley 1916; Mowbray 1946). Fire insurance was also a critical support for urbanization: American cities frequently experienced conflagrations in the nineteenth and early twentieth centuries, such as the burning of New York in 1835 and 1845, the great Chicago fire of 1871, and the Baltimore conflagration of 1904. Fire insurance was a central mechanism for financing reconstruction.

[2] By "market orders," we refer to combinations of 1) public policy and governance regimes at the *industry* level (e.g., atomized markets and price competition enforced by antitrust laws), and 2) organizational forms at the *enterprise* level (e.g., private, for-profit corporations, public corporations, cooperatives).

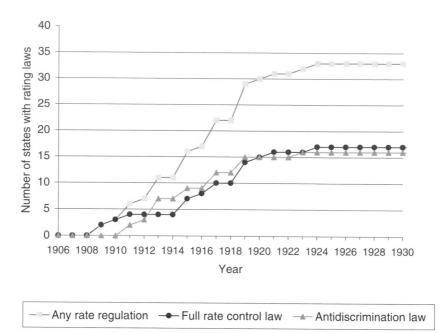

Figure 5.1 Passage of Rate Regulation, 1906–1930

review. It also typically provided for administrative machinery – hearings, grievance procedures, appeals processes – by which consumers or regulators could seek or order changes in rates that were deemed excessive, exorbitant, or unfairly discriminatory. Third, these laws ratified private over public insurance. Architects of regulation endorsed private, for-profit stock corporations as the dominant organizational form for providing fire insurance, while acknowledging a secondary role for consumer owned, not-for-profit mutual insurance companies.

Furthermore, as Figure 5.1 details, enactment of these laws followed the canonical S-shaped diffusion pattern, with a takeoff and rapid diffusion in the early to mid-1910s and a leveling off at the end of the decade, with thirty-three states having enacted these laws by 1924. By the mid-1920s, coupling *private* rate-making associations of for-profit firms with *public* regulation had been established as the taken-for-granted method of governing fire and other property insurance in the United States. In fact, we can plausibly explain how regulated cooperation became the accepted method for ordering insurance using three explanations that have become the starting points for organizational analysis.[3]

Institutionalization as Cultural Expression

Following John Meyer and his colleagues, and the Frank Dobbin of *Forging Industrial Policy*, we could explain rate regulation as the expression of a larger symbolic totality and processes of rationalization – as the enactment of taken-for-granted models of modern social order, replete with their notions of science, efficiency, progress, justice, and the rule of law (Boli and Thomas 1997; Dobbin 1994; McNeely 1995; Meyer and Jepperson 2000; Meyer and Rowan 1977; Meyer et al. 1997; Ramirez and Boli 1987; Skrentny 1996; Soysal 1994). In this view, the adoption of structures or policies reflects *system-wide* cognitive and normative structures – rationalized meaning systems, ontological projects, or visions of order that emerged in the West as a concomitant of modernization. These cultural totalities or meaning systems can be global-level phenomena that represent the rise of a world culture and impinge on nation-states. Or they can be inscribed in national polities as a result of that nation's state-building history. But in either case, institutionalization rests less on actors, their characteristics, or interests, than on how action, interest, and agents themselves flow from accepted mythologies of order and organization.

These modern ontologies authorize particular actors (nation-states, corporations, individuals), projects of progress and rationalized order (efficiency, science, rule of law), and principles of justice (equality, merit, due process). They are instantiated and carried by states, professions, and international nongovernmental organizations (INGOs). They drive organizations toward modal structures and policies, independently of those organizations' characteristics, either *cognitively*, by constituting categories of thought, problem solving, and identity, and rendering only certain problems or solutions thinkable, or *normatively*, by delineating structures and practices to which organizations must conform to be validated as legitimate. In short, the adoption of structures and policies is a systemically rooted, "top-down" process that expresses or enacts increasingly prevalent and taken-for-granted practices, forms, and rationalized meaning systems.

---

[3] These approaches are not mutually exclusive. Scholars, including a number cited in the text, can and do combine elements of each approach in their empirical analyses.

Institutionalization as Diffusion, Mimesis, and Emergent Community Order

Alternatively, following Tolbert and Zucker, Strang, and others, we could explain rate regulation as a policy that a few leading states developed independently, but which then crystallized as a community norm and served as a template for other states to adopt as they managed uncertainty or sought legitimacy (Baron et al. 1986; Davis and Greve 1997; Galaskiewicz and Wasserman 1989; Greenwood et al. 2002; Haunschild 1994; Haunschild and Miner 1997; Haveman 1993; Lant and Baum 1995; Palmer et al. 1993; Soule 1997, 2003; Soule and Earl 2001; Soule and Zylan 1997; Strang 1990; Strang and Chang 1993; Strang and Meyer 1994; Tolbert and Zucker 1983, 1996; Zhou 1993). In this view, institutionalization is a two-stage, "bottom-up" phenomenon consisting of: 1) local problem-solving efforts in which organizations develop or import a new form or policy in response to their own characteristics, politics, and problems, followed by 2) processes of mimesis, theorization, and diffusion by which local solutions spread throughout a field. As the number of adopters increases, as states or professions endorse local solutions, and as actors theorize those solutions, the form or policy gains weight, communicability, and legitimacy. In turn, it becomes a model for other organizations and is eventually established as an accepted norm. Through this process, new baselines emerge to which members must conform as a condition for legitimacy, creating pressures for organizations to adopt the form or policy independently of their characteristics or requirements.

Institutionalization as Shock, Succession, and Politically Reconstructed Order

Finally, following Fligstein, Edelman, and others, we could explain regulation as a response to crises generated by state interventions – interventions which disrupt existing practices, create uncertainty, and evoke claims making and political struggles over jurisdiction and control, as different groups or professions seek to establish their preferred practices or conceptions as the new dominant logics (Campbell and Lindberg 1991; Edelman 1990, 1992, 2003; Edelman et al. 1999; Fligstein 1990, 1996; Hoffman 1999; Kelly and Dobbin 1999; Mezias 1990; Sutton and Dobbin 1996; Scott et al. 2000; Sine and David 2003; Sutton et al. 1994). Generally exogenous, these interventions include the passage of laws, court rulings, and the creation of new agencies. Such acts, in turn, either ban specific practices or impose broad but ambiguous mandates that create uncertainty for organizations. And in so doing, they produce shocks to the system that spark politico-cultural processes – sense- and claims-making activities, searches for new solutions, and a succession of players, forms, and logics as groups mobilize to gain power in organizations and fields by framing situations in ways that require their expertise.

Here, too, isomorphic mechanisms figure centrally. Faced with uncertainty, organizations engage in mutual monitoring, fueling diffusion among peers, feedback, and endogenous, self-reinforcing processes of reborrowing in which private responses to state interventions become models for subsequent intervention. Likewise central are connections among organizations, flows of personnel, and fieldwide associations of aspiring professionals and managers, who assert analyses, endorse certain options, codify their own models, and work to shape debate in their bids for control. Both dynamics foster convergence and consolidation around a particular logic or conception. Yet as the advocates of this view stress, new interventions and reversals are possible, leaving us with an image of institutionalization as a punctuated process of intervention, disruption/succession, and political reconstruction.

These three explanations all provide plausible accounts of the development and key features of rate regulation in insurance. Consistent with a view of institutionalization as rationalization or expression of modern ontologies, actors in insurance used the language of efficiency and political order to justify private, for-profit corporations, and the language of merit, equality, impartiality, and science to critique and defend rates and rate-making associations. In fact, rate regulation was posed and accepted as a means to promote scientific rate making – as the culmination of a project that aimed to eliminate guesswork, gambling, and politics by basing rates on actuarial laws, inspection, and the statistical analysis of pooled loss data. Moreover, consistent with arguments about diffusion and emergent order, states extensively monitored developments in other states, holding investigative hearings to scan their environment, and explicitly modeling their legislation on other states. Finally, consistent with an image of shock, struggle, and political reconstruction, rate regulation emerged in response to antitrust or anticompact laws that disrupted existing governance systems, sparked struggles for control of the industry's rate-making machinery, and induced mobilization and the advocacy of new models by the professions.

Yet, closer inspection of the case leads to a different view, one that looks back to DiMaggio's (1991) classic study and builds on work by Berk (1994), Carruthers and Babb (1996), Clemens (1997), the Dobbin of Dobbin and Dowd (2000), and Rao (1998), which documents the centrality of multiple models of order in the institutionalization process. Our view also draws on work that conceptualizes institutional orders as constituted by plural and competing principles and logics (Friedland and Alford 1991; Heimer 1999; Klienman and Vallas 2000; Orren and Skowronek 1999; Schneiberg 2002; Scott et al. 2000; Stryker 2000), and on recent efforts by Scott, McAdam, Zald, and others to link organizations and institutions with politics and social movements.

The rest of this chapter revises conventional accounts of institutionalization. We will highlight four findings: First, the institutionalization of rate regulation represented a settlement of political struggles over competing models of organization and the character of economic order rather than an expression or enactment of taken-for-granted principles. Second, this settlement and its underlying conflicts were products not of local problem-solving activity, but of work by social movements to contest existing arrangements and promote alternative orders and forms. Third, the processes of sorting through competing models and crafting a settlement were driven, shaped, and made possible by conflicts and institutional dynamics occurring at multiple levels in the American polity, that is, by developments at the intra-, inter-, and supra-state levels. Finally, these settlements constitututed not a unitary or isomorphic insurance system, but rather a fractured field characterized by variations on core themes – a dual community of regulated states – and the combination, recombination, and persistence of multiple logics and forms.

Rate Regulation as a Contested, Multilevel Process

In the United States, *states* were the pivotal arenas for insurance politics and the production of rate regulation. The centrality of states stemmed partly from the federal character of the American polity: as points of authoritative decision making, states constitute a locus of private organizing, coalition building, public debate, and collective representation. Moreover, following the 1869 Supreme Court decision in *Paul v. Virginia*, insurance was regulated by the states, not the federal government, and was exempt from federal antitrust law until 1944 (Lilly 1976; Patterson 1927; also Harrington 1984; Meier 1988).

Rate Regulation as a Settlement of State-Level Political Conflicts

Rate regulation emerged as a product and a settlement of political conflicts and debates that were evoked within the states by insurance company efforts to govern markets privately, via price fixing and data-pooling associations. Fire insurers associated with unusual vengeance during the nineteenth and early twentieth centuries. They did so both to achieve monopoly control and to manage market failures produced by unregulated price competition. In price competitive markets, insurers not only under-produced critical collective goods, such as pooled loss data, they also drove rates below loss costs, depleting reserves, and leaving the industry vulnerable to waves of bankruptcies when conflagrations occurred (Schneiberg 1999). To solve these problems, companies and agents formed over one thousand data-pooling bodies and rate-making associations. By the 1880s and 1890s, they consolidated a workable, nationwide system of collective self-regulation and private price control (Parker 1965; Wandel 1935).

Not surprisingly, associations and price controls evoked protests, public debate, and counterorganization by consumers, agrarians, business groups, and public officials in the states (Brearley 1916; Grant 1979; Handy 1916; Meier 1988; Schneiberg 1999, 2002). Consumers resented paying high rates, especially because insurers could neither explain nor justify their rates. This fueled legitimacy crises, and widespread complaints that rates were extortionate and discriminatory. It also fueled counterorganization both in the market – in the form of roughly 3,500 consumer-owned insurance mutuals – and in the political area. From 1885 to 1910, twenty-three states passed "anti-compact" laws – antitrust measures that specifically targeted the insurance industry and banned association or cooperative price fixing in fire insurance. A few states adopted statist rate-making regimes that displaced private decision making about prices. And from 1909 to 1915, nine states held public investigations of insurers' pricing practices, subjecting the industry to renewed scrutiny and critique. (See Figure 5.2.)

These dynamics reflected constitutional struggles over insurance markets within the states and crystallized around three competing models of order. Emphasizing insurance market failures, companies and public officials located mainly in urban northeastern states advocated an *associational model of order* (Streeck and Schmitter 1985), a system of insurance based on for-profit stock corporations and private, unregulated cooperation among those firms. Some small firms contemplated regulation as a mechanism for tempering competition and protecting themselves from

129

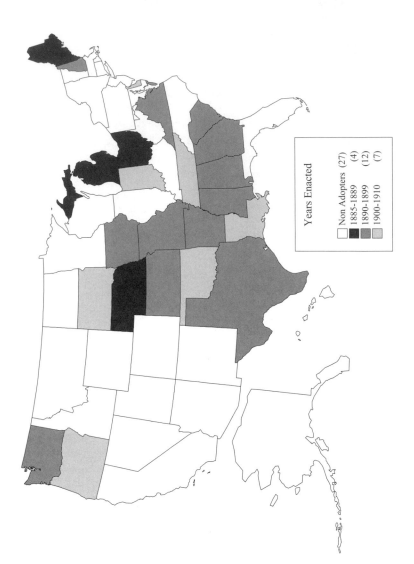

Years Enacted

	Non Adopters (27)
	1885-1889 (4)
	1890-1899 (12)
	1900-1910 (7)

130

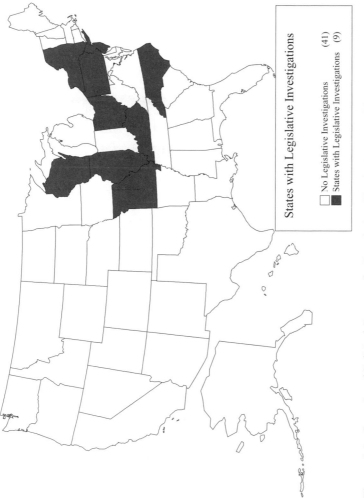

Figure 5.2 State-Level Political Contexts for Regulation. *Top*, Anticompact Measures, 1885–1910; *Bottom*, Legislative Investigations, 1909–1915

larger rivals. But larger stock insurers dominated industry discussions, and fears that state intervention would exposes rates to "politics" prompted the industry to close ranks to reject regulation for purely private self-regulation.

In contrast, consumer groups, agrarian interests, and state officials in midwestern, southern and plains states rejected association for an *antitrust or anticompact model of decentralized market order* that called for market deconcentration, state-enforced price competition, and the promotion of local mutual alternatives to for-profit corporations. These actors saw the "insurance combine" as the problem rather than the solution to the rate problem, and were hostile toward for-profit corporations organized by eastern and foreign interests. Industry opponents in Kansas, Texas, Kentucky, Oklahoma, and Louisiana also resoundingly rejected association. They combined anticompact measures with a *statist model of order* in which public authority displaced private decision making, either by taking over rate making as a state activity, or by denying associations a role and regulating *individual* firms' rates directly (Hobbs 1925, 1941–2; Merritt Committee 1911; Riegel 1916; Schneiberg and Bartley 2001). Both policies were part of broader programs for reconstructing industrial order along more decentralized, regionally based, and locally self-governed lines.

Initially, consumers, agrarian interests, and key institutional actors rejected stock companies' market control efforts with little qualification. Yet, in the late 1890s and early 1900s, public debates and political struggles over the "insurance trust" generated new theories, a movement for scientific rate making, and a host of structural reforms, including schedule rating, collective bargaining, and fire prevention (Heimer 1985; Schneiberg 1999). These reforms fundamentally altered the structure and practice of stock company associations. They formalized rate making, creating possibilities for impartial and equal, rule-based treatment of risks and property owners. They tied rates to inspection and documented hazards, fostering objective assessments and merit-based pricing that penalized property owners for fire-breeding facilities, carelessness, or other morally *hazardous* behavior while rewarding policyholders for improvement and prevention. They also provided consumers with means for securing rate reductions from stock companies *within* the associational system.[4] And as these reforms altered

---

[4] Companies bargained collectively with consumers and public officials, offering rate reductions in exchange for consumers' eliminating hazards. Firms also formed prevention associations to provide consumers and lawmakers with information and technical support for reducing losses.

associational practices, they transformed the political dynamics of insurance governance: consumer groups and public officials began to cooperate with insurance associations in rate-making matters and came to accept associations and price control as the price of good insurance. By the early 1910s, a compromise and a new model of "regulated cooperation" emerged in which consumers, business groups, and public officials were willing to authorize association in insurance markets *provided* that private associations were publicly regulated and monopoly power contained.

Rate regulation was a product and a settlement of the public debates and trust-busting politics evoked by insurance associations at the state level. It appeared in nearly 80 percent of states with anticompact laws and in every state that held a public investigation. Further, it was theorized – and enacted – as a quid pro quo in which consumers and officials abandoned statism and trust-busting policies, and granted insurers the legal right to associate, in exchange for the industry's submitting rates and rate-making associations to public disclosure, supervision, and appeal (Meier 1988; Merritt Committee 1911; NCIC 1915 (adjourned meetings 1914): 19–24; 1915; Riegel 1916, 1917; Rose 1967).

The rate regulation settlement combined multiple regulatory principles and organizational forms, articulating the projects and logics advocated by conflicting groups into a single, complex package. For consumer groups and public officials, the public oversight element was both a mechanism for assuring rational and equitable rates, and the condition for conceding to companies' insistence on association. "It is perfectly certain," wrote New York's Merritt Committee in its effort to theorize a settlement, "that the public has a right to demand and is going to demand that in turn for the right to combine that companies shall furnish equitable rates . . . *if companies are allowed to combine then it must be only on the assurance that rates will be equitable*" (Merritt Committee 1911: 72, 65–6, emphasis in original).

In fact, regulation for outsiders was an alternative to statism or market deconcentration, a synthesis of principles that let consumers, business groups, and states capture the benefits of association. "It would be unfortunate for the public," the committee elaborated,

if a condition of open competition in rates were forced by the State. The safe policy to follow . . . is to recognize the good which flows from *combination well regulated*. . . . It is therefore recommended that no anti-compact bill be passed, but that in place thereof a statute be enacted that will permit *combination under State regulation*, such regulation to stop short of actually fixing the price at which the companies shall sell their insurance, but which be of such a positive nature that all forms of discrimination shall cease. (Merritt Committee 1911: 124–5, emphasis added)

Further, the architects of "regulated combination" looked to supplement these safeguards by cultivating a small competitive segment in the industry, and combining organizational forms, that is, by promoting mutual insurers who worked closely with consumers to prevent fire and reduce loss costs (Heimer 1985). As the committee explained,

to keep rates from becoming excessive . . . it is important that this beneficial and regulative form of competition should be retained and increased if possible. This can be done . . . by opening the way to a free competition by the factory mutuals and miscellaneous mutuals. . . . Such companies can unquestionably, if they receive proper supervision, exert a very wholesome influence in the direction of economy and the prevention of fire. (Merritt Committee 1911: 108–9)

Conversely, for stock companies, regulation was the price for association. Stock insurers fought for purely private cooperation. But threats of statism made it clear that the industry could lose control of rate making entirely, prompting insurers to accept the rate regulation compromise. "There is a *middle course*," a company official noted in 1913,

between the two extremes of State rate making, [and] complete company control of rate-making without the steadying influence for its control of laws and State supervision to hold the rate-making body up to a full sense of responsibility for its action to the representatives of the people. The necessary joint control and balancing of influence can, I think, be secured by leaving the companies selection of the person who shall make rates, but giving to the Superintendent of Insurance the power of examining . . . the power to compel removal of discrimination in rates [and] jurisdiction to review complaints. (Riegel 1916: 69, emphasis added)

As contestants converged on this middle way, states repealed or abandoned statist and anticompact measures. Struggles over competing orders gave way to struggles over regulatory reform, and trust-busting politics largely disappeared from the industry.[5] Again, rate regulation was a product and a settlement of constitutional struggles in the states over the character of insurance market order.

---

[5] The last major episode of trust-busting conflict in the states was in Arkansas in 1905, beginning a nearly three-decade-long period in which antitrust was virtually absent from the industry. Statist politics ran their course from 1909 to 1916, when that option disappeared from the agenda.

Politics and Settlements as Products of Social Movements

As we will show shortly, anticorporate politics within states combined with inter- and supra-state dynamics to produce the convergence just described. Yet treating politics as exogenous, and moving from the internal politics of states to diffusion and consolidation, neglect a key feature of this institutionalization process: internal politics, the geography of conflict, and the presence of multiple logics were the direct result of social movement activity. *Regulation as a settlement, and the underlying political conflicts that produced it, were themselves the product of work by movements to contest corporate combination and the "insurance trust," and to promote instead more decentralized, regionally balanced, and self-sufficient forms of economic development.*

Institutional sociologists including Fligstein, Dobbin, and Dowd have showed how antitrust politics shaped the development of firms, markets, and regulation in the United States. But in focusing on effects, they have treated antitrust laws and politics as exogenous, largely untheorized shocks. Such a practice shifts attention away from critical processes by which policies and forms emerge and are institutionalized – via movements and collective action. And in the case of antitrust laws and regulation, both in the economy in general, and insurance in particular, it was the anticorporate, agrarian protest movements of the late nineteenth century – the Patrons of Husbandry or the Grange and the Farmers' Alliance – that launched the institutionalization process and the political conflicts underlying state intervention and regulation.

At stake here was the dramatic concentration of economic power in the United States after the Civil War. As financial and state institutions channeled funds and development opportunities toward northeastern metropoles, firms relentlessly pursued combination and consolidation, first in infrastructure sectors, then in heavy industry (Berk 1994; Chandler 1977; Fligstein 1990; Lamoreaux 1985; Roy 1997; Sklar 1988). Consolidation and uneven development, in turn, squeezed farmers, manufacturers, and merchants in the Midwest and South, depriving those regions of credit and access to markets, and devastating their economies. In so doing, consolidation fueled protest, populist revolts, and anticorporate movements. Peaking, respectively, in the 1870s and 1890s, the Grange and the Alliance represented the two main waves of agrarian revolt in the United States, and served as the key platforms for mobilizing political challenges against the emerging corporate order in the last quarter of the nineteenth century (Buck 1913; James 1999; Ostler 1993; Sanders 1986, 1999; Schwartz 1976).

135

Both movements were formidable forces in the states and at the national level. At its 1875 peak, the Grange had over 450,000 *families* as members, with the heaviest concentrations in the upper Midwest. The Alliance peaked at more than twice that amount, with 1,053,000 families as members in 1890, and strong support in Midwest and plains states (*Appleton's Annual Cyclopedia* 1891: 301; Tontz 1964:147). Moreover, both movements rejected corporate liberalism or the dominance of giant national corporations in favor of "regional republican" (Berk 1994) programs of decentralized regional development based on thriving market towns and a "cooperative commonwealth" (Goodwyn 1978) of farmers, local manufacturers and independent producers. Drawing analogies across sectors, the Grange and the Alliance cast the problems facing the Midwest and South as the result of corporate combination and the economic strangleholds placed on independent producers by railroads, "middlemen," and "trusts." To solve these problems, Grangers and the Alliance pursued a combination of antimonopoly politics and cooperative or mutual self-organization in the marketplace, introducing new logics, models of market order, and organizational forms into the economy.

Agrarians were ambivalent about politics, and third-party politics in particular, sometimes opting instead for nonpartisanship and local private organization, including cooperatives, state exchanges, and insurance mutuals (Clemens 1997; Ostler 1993; Schneiberg 2002; Sanders 1999; Schwartz 1976). But politics was essential for securing the institutional and regulatory conditions for decentralized regional development. Thus, agrarian statism appeared in the Grange laws and in struggles over federal railroad regulation. In addition, antitrust laws to safeguard local economies from predatory corporations were an enduring centerpiece of the agrarian program (James 1999; Sanders 1999). Embracing market deconcentration, the Grange and the Alliance pursued antitrust models at the state and federal levels, ranging across sectors, including the railroad, oil, and schoolbook trusts, and fire insurance. Whether it was the Grangers in Wisconsin or the Alliance and the Populists in Kansas and Texas, it was these movements' efforts to contest insurance associations in the states and assert alternative conceptions of control that fire insurers feared when they spoke of the dangers of "politics" associated with regulation (Grant 1979; Kimball 1960; Schneiberg 1999).

The analysis in Table 5.1 confirms the central role agrarian movements played in provoking politics at the state level and expanding the models and forms on the insurance associations' agenda. The dependent variable

Table 5.1. *Effects of Agrarian Protest Movements on Anticompact Measures in Insurance, 1885–1910*

	Model 1	Model 2	Model 3	Model 4	Model 5
Constant	−0.6995	−1.057	−0.3376	−0.8651	−1.642
	(0.5753)	(0.7298)	(0.6089)	(.6664)	(1.266)
Controls					
Population	−2.69e-4	−9.93e-4	−4.34e-4	−8.25e-4	−1.22e-3
	(6.26e-4)	(6.97e-4)	(6.08e-4)	(7.14e-4)	(1.37e-3)
Size of farm economy	0.00105	−0.000425	0.000926	0.000659	0.00451
	(.00197)	(0.00164)	(0.00181)	(0.00167)	(.00398)
Populist vote	0.0329*	0.0237	0.0234	0.0167	−0.0017
	(0.0187)	(0.0198)	(0.0178)	(0.0159)	(0.00217)
Patrons of husbandry					
National Grange members		0.2846**			
		(0.1268)			
State Grange members			0.0167		
			(0.0192)		
Number of local Granges				3.1055**	
				(1.580)	
Farmers Alliance					
State Alliance members					0.00449**
					(0.00211)
Number of observations	40	38	38	38	23
Log likelihood	−24.644	−18.681	−23.256	−20.326	−10.603
Pseudo R^2	.1111	.2893	.1153	.2268	.3340

* $p < .10$, ** $p < .05$.

is whether or not a state passed an anticompact law targeting rate-making associations in fire insurance from 1885 to 1910. We use logistic regression as this is the appropriate method for a dichotomous dependent variable, as we have here. See the Appendix at the end of the chapter for a discussion of variables and their measurement.

Consistent with past research, states were more likely to pursue anticompact measures where the Grange and the Alliance were strongest: controlling for population, the size of the farm economy, and the populist vote in a state, increasing the number of Grange and Alliance members per state increased the odds of a state enacting an anticompact measure, as did increasing the number of local Granges.[6] Similar results flow from an

---

[6] In Model 1, populist vote has a positive effect on anticompact measures, which is consistent with prior research on antitrust policies (James 1999; Sanders 1999). Adding Grange and

analysis of mutual insurers (Schneiberg 2002): mutuals were most numerous in states where the Grange and the Alliance had the greatest number of members or chapters, and where anticorporate forces were strong enough to secure political victories against trusts and corporations like anticompact laws in insurance and Granger regulation for the railroads. In short, institutionalization and the politics that fueled rate regulation as a settlement were driven in the first instance, not so much by independent local efforts to solve governance problems, but by conflicts resulting from social movement activity that challenged existing arrangements and placed alternative logics and forms on the states' agendas.

Institutionalization as a Multilevel Process

Furthermore, the production of rate regulation as a settlement of these conflicts was a *multilevel process* driven, shaped, and made possible by developments not just within states, but also at the inter- and supra-state levels. There emerged a call and response among states in which politics and outcomes in one affected politics and the options considered in others. Moreover, intrastate politics escalated into national-level conflicts, producing outcomes there that closed off certain options and made the rate regulation settlement possible.

Interstate Dynamics   The interstate story hinged on events in four states: Kansas, Texas, New York, and Kentucky. All four states became centers of attention and served as reference points for other states, albeit in very different ways.

In 1909 and 1910, populists in Kansas and Texas extended anticompact measures by enacting populist-statist forms of rate regulation (Grant 1979; Hobbs 1925; Riegel 1916). Kansas bypassed insurance associations to regulate companies directly, and put the power to order *general*, across-the-board rate reductions in the hands of the insurance commissioner, a power he promptly used to mandate statewide rate cuts of 12 to 14 percent. Texas took rate making out of private hands altogether, delegating that function to a state board. Neither law authorized industry associations or enacted the combinations of principles or quid pro quo settlement that regulation

---

Alliance measures in models 2 through 5 wipes out the effect of populist vote, which is consistent with the association between populist politics and these movements. The results for Grange and Alliance membership are not sensitive to controls.

would become. Instead, both were populist, anticorporate measures that substituted state control for private cooperation.

These events sent shock waves through the system, evoking fierce company opposition, mobilization by industry opponents, and threats of populist regulation in other states. In 1910, Missouri considered a Kansas measure, and Louisiana adopted a measure modeled on the Texas law. Moreover, two states that never passed anticompact laws, Illinois and New York – "the home of the insurance combine" – launched the first legislative investigations into fire insurance, holding extended public hearings.

New York's "Merritt Investigation" and its 1911 rating law reflected and amplified interstate processes, and were critical for the emergence of rate regulation as an institutional settlement. A direct response to populist measures in other states, the investigation was a vehicle through which New Yorkers observed and focused attention on developments elsewhere. The Kansas and Texas laws occupied center stage in the investigation, as did anticompact measures in the Midwest (Merritt Committee 1911: 43–5, 51–4, 76–7). The investigation was also an occasion for New York to reflect on principles advocated by reformers, activists, and actuaries, and to *distinguish* itself from other states. Indeed, New York's investigation and 1911 law served to *preempt* pressures for populist rate laws and *theorize* a different model of insurance order.

That New York would continue to reject an anticompact path was a forgone conclusion (Merritt Committee 1911: 43–50). Moreover, the committee and legislature also rejected measures that took insurance provision or rate-making powers out of private hands or authorized the state to alter rate levels. Led by Robert Wagner, one group of lawmakers pushed a Kansas-like provision to create a state bureau with powers to change rates that were "unreasonable, excessive, arbitrary or unwarranted" (Merritt Committee 1911: 130–1). But insurers feared that granting that power to the state would foster "politics" and prevailed on the committee to limit the state's authority. "This is a very dangerous power," it wrote, "it might be used for political purposes. . . . [He] who exercised the power would have effective pressure brought to bear upon him from only one direction, that is, to reduce the rates, while at least in certain emergencies the situation would demand an increase" (Merritt Committee 1911: 52, also 77).

The committee also stressed the lack of administrative capacities, noting how "the State does not possess and could not obtain, except with great pains and expense, the expert knowledge upon which to make rates properly" (Merritt Committee 1911: 77, 51–2). Thus, private, for-profit stock companies were quite appropriately the dominant organizational vehicle for providing insurance and making rates.

Yet, regulation was too firmly entrenched on the public agenda and external pressures too strong for legislators simply to reject regulation for association. Accordingly, New York's lawmakers developed the model of "regulated cooperation," enacting a 1911 law that authorized private associations, while subjecting those associations to regulation. In addition, the architects of regulated cooperation hoped to further discipline associations via a competitive fringe of mutual companies. In effect, New York crafted the combination of principles and quid pro quo settlement that became the cornerstone for rate regulation. Moreover, it did so in a way that stock companies could accept. It endorsed private provision and rate-making association. And unlike Kansas, it denied its superintendent powers to order *general* rate reductions, limiting his authority to changes in *particular* rates that were found, after a hearing, to discriminate unfairly between risks of "like hazard and character" (Spectator Company 1911–12; New York State Insurance Department 1911–15).

Politically, New York's law and investigation were preemptive, *moderate* responses to Kansas and Texas by a procompany state. Institutionally, they provided other states with a circumscribed, "antidiscrimination" regulation option for settling their insurance conflicts, a specific template, and an extensively theorized conception of control to guide those efforts (Schneiberg 1999). Articulated by industry reformers, regulators, and the emerging actuarial profession, and fully aired in the Merritt investigation and report, this conception distinguished insurance from other sectors and theorized the sector as a scientifically administered, quasi-public market. It viewed insurance as a tax system that pooled community funds and covered the losses of the few via small "tariffs" on the many. It defined principles of merit and equality for allocating the tax and setting rates that reflected the loss costs a risk or risk class imposed on the community. It denounced price competition as subversive of the insurance function. And it envisioned a scientific system of rate making, overseen by the state, in which prices were set by associations and expert actuaries, based on the inspection of hazards and the statistical analysis of classified loss data.

While New York's law only partly implemented this vision – insurers blocked efforts to require them to disclose classified data – the Merritt report and law marked a turning point in insurance regulation and became the center of attention nationwide. New York joined Kansas and Texas as a referent for other states. Theories of regulated cooperation and scientific rate making expressed by the report were incorporated by investigations in other states, and framed discussions within the National Convention of Insurance Commissioners (NCIC) (Wisconsin State Federation of Labor 1913; NCIC 1915: 119–40; Riegel 1916: 68–70, 1917: 190–3; Spectator Company 1915–25). In 1913, three states passed laws like New York's. In 1915, three more followed suit, and by 1923, sixteen had passed antidiscrimination measures. In effect, New York's answer to the rate question proved satisfactory for a range of actors outside the state, and served as the model for the formation of an "antidiscrimination" community of states (see Figure 5.3).

However, the New York law did not satisfy demands for more comprehensive public control in midwestern states. In fact, theories of scientific rate making publicized by the Merritt report helped amplify criticism of companies' failure to base rates on the systematic analysis of loss costs (Merritt Committee 1911; NCIC 1915, App. 119–56). In 1912, Kentucky enacted a statist measure, sparking intense conflict, an insurance boycott that nearly shut down the whiskey trade, and a new regulatory settlement (Kentucky 1912, 1913, 1914, 1916, 1917; Louisville Board of Trade 1912; Spectator Company 1912–16; Riegel 1916: 64–5:1917: 188–9).

In this settlement, companies returned to the state and accepted regulation in exchange for lawmakers' abandoning statism and recognizing company associations as the primary rate-making authority. Enacted into law in 1916, the Kentucky settlement ratified regulated cooperation. But the law also added new principles to the mix, creating a substantial variation on that regulatory theme. It empowered the state board *both* to order the removal of rates that discriminated unfairly *and* to order *general* rate reductions if the business in Kentucky showed more than a reasonable profit. In addition, the law required the board to base its rate orders on five years' of premium and loss data, insulating regulation and rate orders from political considerations.

The Kentucky regulatory settlement signaled the end of statism in fire insurance. Moreover, in implementing a rationalized, data-based rate regime, the 1916 Kentucky law extended scientific rate making. The law thus met *consumers'* demands for broader protection, *reformers and regulators'* calls for rational or objective rates, and *companies'* interests in insulating rates from politics. As such, the Kentucky law provided other states with a comprehensive settlement of insurance matters – a "full rate control" alternative to New York's limited measure. By 1924, seventeen states had adopted versions of this alternative, leaving rate regulation states split between

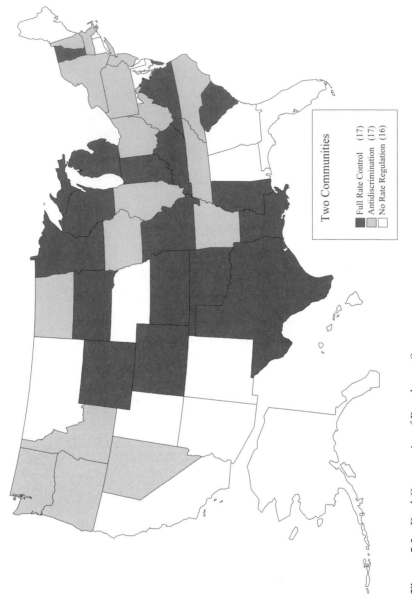

Figure 5.3 Dual Community of Regulatory States

Two Communities

Full Rate Control (17)
Antidiscrimination (17)
No Rate Regulation (16)

antidiscrimination and full rate control measures (see Figure 5.3). Like Kansas, Texas, and New York, Kentucky became a center of attention and produced a model for other states.

National-Level Dynamics   The evolution of regulation from Kansas and Texas through New York to Kentucky was by no means assured. Instead, the development of the full rate control settlement, and the survival and diffusion of rate regulation in any form hinged decisively on two developments at the national level.

First, key national actors endorsed rate regulation. In 1914, the U.S. Supreme Court ruled in *German Alliance Company vs. Lewis* that insurance "was affected with a public interest" and that the states had the right to regulate insurance rates (Riegel 1917: 188; Hobbs 1941–2; Crane 1962: 55–7). In December, the National Convention of Insurance Commissioners seconded the Court's endorsement with its own and threw its weight behind regulated cooperation, further theorizing the model of regulated cooperation, and promulgated model rating laws (Meier 1988: 60; NCIC 1915, New York Adjourned Meeting: 17–25; Chicago Adjourned Meeting: 11–22; Wandel 1935: 135–6).

The *German Alliance* case stemmed from insurers' decision to challenge the Kansas rate reduction orders and the states' jurisdiction over rates in federal court. As intended, this strategy translated state-level conflicts over insurance into the national arena. But the Supreme Court endorsed states' rights, the principle of regulated cooperation, and the theory of insurance as a quasi-public market. This endorsement strengthened the hand of advocates of regulation in the states, ensuring that rate regulation would remain a viable option in the states. The NCIC follow-up amplified these national-level pressures and focused lawmaking in the states onto crafting local settlements, both by codifying regulated cooperation and by generating model laws that were quickly adopted by Pennsylvania and six midwestern states (NCIC, Chicago Adjourned Meetings 1915: 11–12).

Second, the NCIC and the National Board of Fire Underwriters (NBFU) reached an accord that consolidated scientific rate making, created supra-state structures, and increased states' capacities to implement a rate regulatory settlement. This accord was part of the Kentucky settlement, and was reached in 1915, when the NBFU agreed to form an Actuarial Bureau that compiled and distributed firms' premium and loss data for various classes of risks, on an annual basis, for each state (Brearley 1916; NCIC 1915: 78–9; Riegel 1916: 21–2 1917: 219). This structural innovation transformed the terms of political trade at the state level. Classified data gave consumers and regulators a way to evaluate rates and resolve rate conflicts on an objective basis, increasing their willingness to authorize associations. It also let associations defend rates against populist pressures, addressing companies' fears that regulators would play politics with prices. In effect, this accord created system-wide administrative capacities, making it possible for each state to institute a rationalized, data-based regime of rate review. In fact, states incorporated the accord into their rating laws. Over seventy-five percent of the full rate control laws passed or amended after 1916 required companies to file classified experience with the state, either directly or through the Actuarial Bureau, and/or required the commissioner to base rate orders on classified data (Hobbs 1925, 1941–2; Spectator Company 1916–44).

Outcomes of Institutionalization

Instituting rate regulation was a contested, multilevel process. Rate regulation was a response to – and a settlement of – political conflicts in the states over competing models of insurance. These conflicts were evoked by insurers' decisions to pursue private association, and efforts by agrarian forces to use the statehouses to subject an infrastructure industry to alternative models of economic order. Moreover, sorting through these models and converging on a settlement was a multilevel matter. State-level politics and investigations were the foundation for adopting regulation. Yet states influenced other states. And the diffusion of the settlement rested on bargaining, organizing, and on articulating and endorsing models at the national level.

After 1916, rate regulation and its rationales rather than statism, anticompact principles, or the agrarian program framed the discourse and politics of fire insurance governance, becoming a taken-for-granted baseline for the industry. But the community that emerged was a *fractured or multiply ordered* one (see Figure 5.3). A few states – notably Texas, California, and Nebraska – remained outside the rate regulation orbit, serving as repositories where alternatives quietly persisted through the mid-1940s. Even more importantly, *the rate regulation settlement itself assembled, incorporated, combined and recombined multiple and even competing governance logics (private association, public regulation) and organizational forms (for-profit corporations, mutual companies)*. Regulatory states themselves fell into two camps, reflecting important variations of dominant themes. And the fires, while banked, were not put out completely, as occasional flare-ups in New York, Virginia, and Missouri nudged some antidiscrimination states into the full rate control camp and tested some limits on the rate regulatory settlement. Systemic conflicts over order were absent from the industry through World War II. But settlements, we suggest, are provisional affairs that incorporate multiple principles rather than establish, once and for all, a single, comprehensive, and encompassing industrial culture.

Modeling Institutionalization in a Multilevel, Event History Framework

As the preceding discussion makes clear, states' decisions to adopt rate regulation laws were governed by political conflicts within the states over insurance market governance, and by intra-, inter- and supra-state effects. Here, we use the *heterogeneous diffusion model*, discussed elsewhere (Greve, Strang, and Tuma 1995; Strang and Soule 1998; Strang and Tuma 1993), to incorporate all three types of effects in a single event history model. This model predicts the *rate* of state-level adoption of rate regulation laws. In the absence of time dependence, the model is represented as:

$$r_n(t) = \exp\left(\alpha'\mathbf{x}_n + \sum_{s \in \tau(t)} \beta'\mathbf{v}_n + \sum_{s \in \tau(t)} \gamma'\mathbf{w}_s + \sum_{s \in \tau(t)} \delta'\mathbf{z}_{ns}\right)$$

In this model, n refers to those states that have not yet adopted a rate regulation law and s refers to those states that have already adopted a law. We capture institutional effects at the state, inter-, and supra-state levels using the four vectors in the diffusion model above. We also develop measures of political-institutional factors at the intra-, inter- and supra-state levels based on our historical analysis of the fire insurance industry. The sources of our data are described in detail in the Appendix to this chapter. Data availability led us to analyze the adoption of rate regulation from 1906 to 1930.

State-Level Effects

To capture *state-level* effects, we use the propensity vector (x_n) and a set of variables measuring the characteristics of states and the institutional dynamics *within* states that might influence their decisions to adopt rate regulation. We include measures of state-level characteristics in the propensity vector as we would in a traditional event history model. First, we include a dummy variable for whether or not a state enacted an anticompact law or legal injunction that specifically targeted fire insurers and their rate-making practices. Second, we include a dummy variable for whether or not a state conducted a public probe into insurance rate-making practices during the 1909–15 "era of legislative investigations." Both variables tap the development *within* a state of public criticism, effective anticompany politics, and a crisis of legitimacy regarding the industry and its associations. Since our historical analysis suggests that regulation emerges as a settlement of legitimacy crises and political conflicts over the insurance trust, we expect the presence of anticompact politics and legislative investigations to increase the likelihood of rate regulation (Schneiberg 1999).

We also considered including the social movement determinants of the anticompact laws analyzed in previous section. But careful consideration of the specific mechanisms by which agrarian protest movements affected rate regulation led us to omit those variables from the rate regulation models. Committed to anticompact measures and statism, the Grange and the Alliance were neither the architects of the rate regulation settlement nor played a direct role in its production. That job fell to industry reformers, actuaries, and regulators who theorized and advocated the rate regulatory settlement in response to threats of anticompact measures and the controversies that surrounded insurance governance. As stressed, the Grangers and the Alliance critically affected the production of this settlement. But they did so *indirectly*, fueling politics, legislative investigations, and anticompact laws that, in turn, impacted the rate regulatory settlement. Accordingly, we model the adoption of rate regulation as the direct effect of anticompact measures and investigations, including these movement outcomes or proximate causes rather than the movement variables themselves in our diffusion models.

We did, however, include two state-level control variables. First, we control for the assets of insurance companies doing business within a state. This measure captures a variety of factors that might affect rate regulation including the market structure (size, number of firms, and heterogeneity), the stakes involved in regulating, and the political strength of insurance forces (see Schneiberg and Bartley 2001 for details). Second, following Amenta et al. (1992), we also include here a measure of the administrative capacity of the state in insurance matters – a dummy variable for whether a state has a specialized, stand-alone insurance department as opposed to folding insurance regulation into a more general department such as the state treasury. In general, administrative capacities and a stand-alone state department create both a state constituency for expanded regulation and the ability to regulate in a reasonably reliable fashion (Schneiberg and Bartley 2001; Skocpol and Finegold 1982; Skowronek 1982). Having an insurance department should thus increase the likelihood of regulation.

Interstate Effects

To capture *interstate* effects, we use the susceptibility, infectiousness, and proximity vectors. These three vectors tap different dimensions of interstate influence.

Susceptibility   The susceptibility vector (v_n) lets us examine how characteristics of states that have not yet adopted a rate regulation law might render those states more open or vulnerable to influence by other states. This vector measures potential adopters' susceptibility to these laws by creating, in effect, an interaction term between the cumulative number of adopting states and state-level characteristics. One implication of our analysis is that states that conduct legislative investigations or have experienced anticompact struggles over insurance associations are more likely to be influenced by rate regulatory actions in other states. Investigations are a mechanism by which states scan their environments, and both investigations and anticompact struggles indicate the mobilization of constituencies who are searching for alternative solutions to the insurance rate problem. We also expect that states with administrative capacities would be more likely than states without such capacities to adopt rate regulation in response to other states' initiatives. We thus include in the susceptibility vector dummy variables for anticompact laws, legislative investigation, and the presence of a stand-alone insurance department. Note that the appropriate model specification requires that measures in the susceptibility vector are also included in the propensity vector.

Infectiousness   The infectiousness vector (w_s) lets us determine whether certain states are more likely to be imitated or copied by others. The historical record suggests that some states were more central or influential to other states puzzling or struggling over whether and how to regulated rates. In particular, our historical analysis suggests that rate regulation by four states – Kansas, Texas, New York, and Kentucky – sent shock waves across the entire nation and became referents for other states. Those states' regulatory actions were closely watched by players in other states, figured especially centrally in public debates, and precipitated regulatory activity by states throughout the system, albeit for different reasons. Thus, we include here a measure for the infectiousness of these four states.

Diffusion The proximity (z_{ns}) vector captures a different aspect of interstate influence by examining how the actions of states in some grouping affect the actions of other states in that group. We use the proximity vector to examine whether rate regulation was more likely to diffuse *within* "populist" and more "procompany" subcommunities of states than between those categories. As our historical analysis suggests, adopters fell into a group of procompany states who enacted moderate "antidiscrimination" forms of rate regulation or a group of populist states who passed more powerful "full rate control" laws (see Figure 5.3). Following Sanders (1986, 1999), we developed a measure of state membership in populist versus procompany political communities. In particular, we used Sanders' classification to code states into three political-economic groups – the industrial "core" which housed the nation's major industrial and financial corporations, the agrarian-based "periphery," and "diverse." The rationale for these measures derives from our analysis and from Sanders, Grant (1979), and Schneiberg (1999): from the 1890s through the 1910s, regulatory politics in general and in insurance were profoundly shaped by a broad and self-conscious social movement in which "peripheral" agrarian and largely populist southern and midwestern states sought to use politics and regulation to contest the concentration of corporate power in the heavily industrialized "core" states of the Northeast and the Great Lakes region. In effect, struggles over concentration divided the nation into highly salient "regions" – groups of states that shared common economic interests, political stances and parties, reformers and reform policies, and that formed subcommunities of emulation and coordinated problem solving. As Lant and Baum (1995), Soule (2003), and Strang and Meyer (1994) point out, theorization or classifications that identify organizations as similar or in the same category can constitute those organizations as cognitive or institutional communities of peers, creating pathways for emulation, and enhancing diffusion within those groups. Accordingly, we expect the adoption of rate regulation by populist (peripheral-agrarian or anti-compact) states would increase the likelihood that other populist states would adopt rate regulation, but have no effect on the rate of adoption by pro-company (core-industrial or non-anticompact) states, and vice versa.

Supra-state Effects

Finally, to capture *supra-state* or *national-level* institutional effects, we include in the propensity vector a set of period effect dummy variables that indexes the occurrence of system-wide events such as the emergence of national-level bargains, the building of supra-state administrative capacities, and the endorsement or promulgation of model laws by national associations. First, we include a dummy variable for the year 1915 to tap the endorsement of rate regulation by two key actors. At the end of 1914, the Supreme Court decided to ratify the states' right to regulate fire insurance rates, which was immediately seconded by the National Convention of Insurance Commissioners, which promulgated a "Model Rating Law." Second, we include a period effect dummy variable for 1916–30 to capture the agreement between the National Board of Fire Underwriters and the National Convention of Insurance Commissioners to establish a national actuarial bureau. As seen, this agreement settled a key issue in the struggle over regulation – the issue of how to evaluate rates – producing a system-wide increase in the states' capacities to regulate rate making and generally increasing actors' willingness to accept rate regulation. We expect both dummy variables to increase the rate of adoption of rate regulation throughout the system.

Results

Table 5.2 includes six different models designed to examine intra-, inter-, and supra-state pressures on states to adopt rate regulation laws. The effects of the intra-state factors are consistent across the six models. In all of the models except Model 4, the presence of an anticompact law increases the rate of adoption. States which banned cooperative rate making in fire insurance between 1885 and 1910 were quicker to adopt rate regulation than those that did not. Similarly, states that conducted public investigations of insurance rate-making practices had higher rates of rate regulation than those that did not. In all but Model 5, the coefficient for the legislative investigation dummy variable is positive and significant. This finding dovetails nicely with findings from the historical analysis that states that subjected the industry to public scrutiny and debate were quicker to regulate rates. In fact, these findings support our earlier findings that rate regulation in insurance was a product – and a settlement – of public debates and political struggles over insurance market order within the states.

Table 5.2. *Intra-, Inter-, and Supra-State Effects on the Adoption of Rate Regulation, 1906–1930*

	Model 1	Model 2	Model 3	Model 4	Model 5	Model 6
Intercept	−3.44***	−3.46***	−4.85***	−4.95***	−4.80***	−4.47***
	(.49)	(.50)	(.87)	(.94)	(.86)	(.80)
Intrastate effects						
Anticompact law	.90**	.93**	.87**	1.01	.84**	.89**
	(.38)	(.39)	(.39)	(.65)	(.39)	(.39)
Legislative investigation	1.61**	1.56**	1.20**	1.21**	.54	1.53***
	(.48)	(.49)	(.50)	(.51)	(1.10)	(.55)
Insurance commissioner	−.46	−.47	−.53	−.53	−.51	−.61
	(.43)	(.43)	(.43)	(.43)	(.43)	(.44)
Total assets (log)	−.01	−.01	−.01	−.01	−.01	−.01
	(.01)	(.01)	(.01)	(.01)	(.01)	(.01)
Interstate effects						
Intercept		−.02	−.04	−.04	−.05	−.12**
		(.03)	(.04)	(.04)	(.04)	(.05)
Diffusion within political		−.02	−.01	−.01	−.01	−.01
subcommunity		(.05)	(.05)	(.05)	(06)	(06)
Influence of KY,			.82**	.83**	.83**	.81*
TX, NY, KS			(.35)	(.34)	(.34)	(.32)
Susceptibility –				−.01		
Anticompact				(.79)		
Susceptibility –					.06	
Investigation					(.08)	
Supra-state effects						
Institutional						.81
endorsement, 1915						(.75)
Institution of National						2.04**
Actuarial Bureau,						(.96)
1916–29						
Likelihood ratio vs.	17.94	18.16	25.64	25.71	26.13	30.04
constant rate						

* p <.10, ** p =.05, *** p =.01.

The findings likewise support the argument that interstate institutional dynamics also shape regulation. While Models 2 through 6 in Table 5.2 show that there is no evidence in the proximity vectors for the diffusion of rate regulation within the political subcommunities of core, periphery, and diverse, there *is* consistent evidence that certain states were more influential than others. Kansas, Texas, New York, and Kentucky were very much leaders in rate regulation. As the positive and significant coefficients in the infectiousness vector of Models 3 through 5 show, the adoption of laws by these four states was quickly followed by other states. By passing statist measures, Kansas and Texas exerted influence through the system, emboldening populists and reformers elsewhere and creating a credible political threat to insurance interests in other states. New York, the home of fire insurance interests, responded with an antidiscrimination measure, a political settlement that served as moderate model for other states puzzling over whether or not to adopt rate regulation. In contrast, actors in Kentucky found this relatively weak system of controls unsatisfactory, and settled instead on a "full rate control" law, providing other states with a model that more fully reflected the principles of scientific rate making and public control.

Models 4 and 5 include measures designed to capture the third dimension of interstate dynamics: were states with anticompact laws or legislative investigations more susceptible to regulation than those that had none? As noted, factors in the susceptibility vector are analogous to an interaction between the cumulative number of adopters of regulation and the state's internal characteristics. Models 4 and 5 show that states with anticompact laws or investigations are not more susceptible to rate regulation.

Model 6 examines the extent to which national or supra-state factors affects states' decisions to adopt rate regulation. First, we examine whether or not the endorsement of rate regulation in late 1914 by the Supreme Court and the National Convention of Insurance Commissioners, coupled with the latter's promulgating a model rating law, affected states' decisions to regulate. Model 6 indicates that this factor, as measured, is not significant, although the coefficient for these national-level events is in the expected positive direction.

Second, we examine whether or not the 1915 accord between the National Convention of Insurance Commissioners and the National Board of Fire Underwriters affected states' decisions about rate regulation. As discussed, this accord established a national Actuarial Board, creating system-wide administrative capacities for data-based regulation and significantly extending the logic of scientific rate making. Model 6 indicates that, in fact, this national-level development has a positive, significant, and particularly powerful influence on states' decisions to adopt rate regulation. Taken together, these models confirm our historical analysis of rate regulation.

Discussion and Conclusion

Combining historical analysis with heterogeneous diffusion modeling, the foregoing study of insurance rate regulation provides a view of institutionalization that differs substantially from conventional accounts of this process. First, the institutionalization of rate regulation represented a *settlement* (McAdam and Scott, this volume; Sanders 1986; Schneiberg 1999; Zysman 1994) of political conflicts over competing models of organization and the basic character of political, social, and economic order. Second, this settlement and its underlying conflicts were *products of social movement mobilization* to contest existing arrangements and advance alternative logics, models, and organizational forms. Third, sorting through those competing models and producing an institutional settlement was a *multilevel process* resting on conflicts, theorization, and partial settlements at the intra-, inter-, and supra-state levels. Finally, what emerged from these processes was a *multiplex, fractured institutional field* characterized by recombinations of multiple logics and forms, antithetical principles, and variations on core themes.

Figure 5.4 diagrams our conception of institutionalization, highlighting a number of contributions our work makes to existing research. First, by conceptualizing structuration and the production of market orders as result of an interaction between movement mobilization and institutional

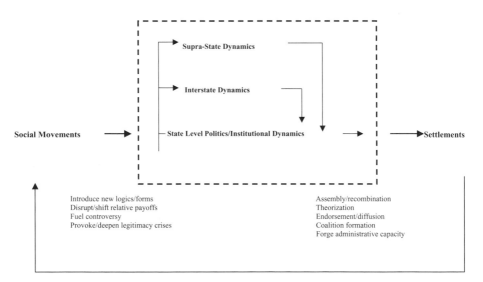

Figure 5.4 Social Movements and Institutionalization

processes in organizational fields, we build on the insights of McAdam and Scott, Campbell, Zald, Lounsbury, and others in this volume and develop one set of possibilities for integrating organizations and movements research. As our analysis shows, challengers and movement mobilization are vital "inputs" or instigators of institutional processes, for example, by promulgating critiques and introducing alternative logics into a setting, movements can fuel controversies, political conflicts, and crises of both cognitive and sociopolitical legitimacy, shattering the taken-for-granted character of existing arrangements, and using state power to contest or ban organizational practices (see also Baum and Powell 1995; Davis and Thompson 1994; Stryker 2000; Suchman 1995). Moreover, as carriers of new analyses and organizational forms, movements can foster theorization, transform the terms of policy discourse, and spark mimicry and diffusion, while providing actors in fields with templates and cultural resources for recombination, industry construction, and the (dis)assembly of political and economic regimes (e.g., Armstrong 2002; Campbell 1997; Clemens 1997; Lounsbury, Ventresca, and Hirsch 2003; Rao et al. 2000; Schneiberg 2002; Soule 2003). Furthermore, as potentially deeply disruptive forces, movements can fundamentally transform the payoffs or "relative prices" of alternatives for actors within fields, fostering new coalitions, and prompting new settlements or equilibria. Indeed, whether by fostering generative political conflicts, introducing new logics, or shaping the broader political-cultural terrain, social movements constitute critical inputs and determinants for core institutional process. And in fueling the dynamics just described, movements propel fields toward new combinations and settlements – combinations and settlements that incorporate or reject challenger agendas and principles, thereby creating conditions for reduced or renewed mobilization in subsequent periods.

To be clear, in developing this conception, we seek neither to consign movements to extra-institutional status, nor to draw any hard and fast line between movements and institutional processes. As our case suggests, movements do number as important "antecedents to (de)institutionalization" (Oliver 1992) and give shape to the black box of "pre-institutional" processes (Tolbert and Zucker 1996). Yet movements also can enter into or develop within fields, deliberately exploit institutional processes, and shape institutionalization or deinstitutionalization at any stages. For example, movements can act as institutional entrepreneurs, theorizing problems and solutions, and serving both as architects of settlements and as vehicles for diffusing or legitimating already theorized forms (Clemens 1997;

Schneiberg 2002; Soule 2003). Furthermore, movements also can use their capacities for mobilization and disruption to help sort through various options, however they get onto the agenda. Further still, movements can be institutionalized as a part of a system's ongoing routines and their organization or associations incorporated within fields as recognized and legally sanctioned insiders (Streeck and Schmitter 1985). Conversely, as others in this volume suggest, elites within fields might deliberately support or organize intra-, inter-, or extra-organizational movements to realize their ends. And there is reason to believe that conventional organizations within fields are increasingly structured like social movements, further blurring the boundaries between institutional and extra-institutional domain. But for our purposes here, these lines were sufficiently clear to show, at a minimum, how challenger movements can underlie, instigate, and even constitute core institutional dynamics.

Second, our analysis of institutionalization as multilevel process has implications for subsequent research on core institutional phenomena, including the development and diffusion of policies and organizational forms. The specific effects and mechanisms cited here may apply mainly to the case of insurance regulation. Yet our framework and modeling strategy for analyzing multilevel dynamics can be applied more broadly. Most simply, our approach suggests that future state-level research on market organization and other forms of public policy can and should consider state, interstate, and supra-state level political and institutional effects (Amenta et al. 1992; Schneiberg and Bartley 2001; Soule and Zylan 1997). Indeed, state-level research that fails to consider all three levels of effects cannot clearly document whether state-level factors have independent effects on outcomes, and risks mistakenly attributing inter- or supra-state forces to state-level political or institutional dynamics.

In addition, our approach can be fruitfully applied to other outcomes and other kinds of multilevel systems. Research on the institutionalization in work organizations of grievance procedures and other rights-based governance mechanisms makes a compelling case for effects at the firm, interfirm, and national levels, making significant progress toward documenting the multilevel character of this process (Davis and Greve 1997; Dobbin et al. 1993; Edelman 1990, 1992; Edelman et al. 1999; Fligstein 1990; Sutton et al. 1994; Sutton and Dobbin 1996). We also would expect at least three levels of institutional effects in transnational settings, particularly to the extent that the global institutions develop and deepen (Strang 1990; Soysal 1994; Meyer et al. 1997; Boli and Thomas 1997; Jang 2000). Recently, scholars have made important theoretical advances in addressing the shift from relatively autonomous nation-states to nested transnational systems (Boyer and Hollingsworth 1997), and the development of international dynamics of diffusion, emulation, and transformation, centered around the export and partial incorporation of American models of capitalism (Djelic 1998; Djelic and Quack 2003). Again, the specific factors and mechanism involved vary, but there is clearly a warrant for employing a multilevel perspective on institutionalization to analyze the national, subnational, international, and global-level determinants of this process.

Furthermore, our approach can be elaborated both to analyze "bottom-up" and "top-down" dynamics in nested systems. The insurance case illustrates a bottom-up dynamic: movements, external shocks, or local innovation activate political and institutional responses *within* a state, generating state-level outcomes that influence other states, crystallize *inter*-state structures, and fuel organization, debate, and the creation and endorsement of models at the *national* level. Conversely, a more "top-down" process can obtain. It can begin at the national level and work down toward organizations within a country, as was the case with personnel procedures during World War I (Baron et al. 1986) and the adoption of equal employment opportunity/affirmative action policies (e.g., Edelman 1990, 1992). Or it can begin at the inter- or trans-national level and work down toward nation-states, as with the exporting of American mode in the post–World War II era (Djelic 1998; Djelic and Quack 2003). In the first case, national- or field-level events such as a new federal law evoke system-level activism by national associations, experimentation with policies or structural forms within individual organizations, and the emergence of peer pressures and interunit dynamics as organizations monitor one another's behavior and converge on common solutions. In the second, the emergence of the United States as an exemplar for Western European modernizing elites accompanied the consolidation of an international diffusion network, fostering transnational normative standards and processes of recombination and transformation within nation-states. Similarly, top-down dynamics can occur as movements organize at the highest levels and target super-ordinate systems, as is the case in recent years with transnational movements and advocacy networks (Keck and Sikkink 1998; Smith, Chatfield, and Pagnucco 1997; Tarrow 2001a).

Equally important, our approach can be elaborated to analyze how the dynamics and trajectories of institutionalization differ across structural contexts. For example, institutionalization is more likely to unfold

155

as a multilevel and multicentric process in *federated* systems, such as the American polity, where authority is multicentric, than in unitary polities, where top-down effects might dominate, or in decentralized or fragmented systems, where a lack of connectivity or intermediate authority might induce diverse but largely uncorrelated and relatively weak pockets of institutionalization. Indeed, a potential strength associated with a federated system is that institutionalization processes can be launched or sustained at one or more levels, with or without the support of a central state (Dobbin and Sutton 1998; Jepperson and Meyer 1991). At the same time, however, the presence of multiple platforms and ports of entry create possibilities for broadly organized but competing projects, the development of institutional contradiction within or across levels, and the institutionalization of multiple, even contradictory, industrial orders (see also Berk 1994; Herrigel 1994; Schneiberg 2002).

Third, our approach has two important implications for research on diffusion and the mechanisms of interorganizational influence. First, diffusion can be a profoundly political process. Actions or events in one organization or state can highlight new possibilities for challengers in other organizations or states, fostering organizing and theorization by champions of alternatives within those units, as well as public discourse, institutional entrepreneurship, and internal political struggles. Such influence can occur without direct ties between units, or it can emerge from an institutionalization project in which activists and institutional entrepreneurs use adoption in their home organizations or states to promote models, support challengers, expose injustice, and exert normative pressures in or on other organizations and states. Moreover, actions that dramatize new possibilities or problems might evoke countermoves by elites in other organizations or states, even in the absence of an independent internal challenge. Should established powers in one unit see developments in others as threatening, misguided, or irrational, adoption by "peers" will promote rejection, processes of distinct, or preemptive alternatives – "negative diffusion" or "heteromorphism"– rather than mimesis (Soule and Earl 2001). Further still, debates and legitimacy crises in one location can produce reforms, structural innovations, or new principles that actors in other organizations or states can use to reach their own compromises and settle their own internal political and institutional conflicts. In each of these cases, organizations monitor other organizations, but diffusion is driven by the political dynamics of opposition, argumentation, contestation, and compromise.

Second, actions by organizations or states can activate and crystallize structures of interorganizational or interstate influence. Existing work on state policy finds that some states are recognized leaders and others followers, suggesting heterogeneous diffusion and an interstate role structure in which some states are more influential or susceptible to influence than others (Eyestone 1977; also Davis and Greve 1997; Strang and Soule 1998). Structure also can result from processes of distinction or differentiation, which push organizations or states away from an interorganizational system based around a dominant model or simple leader-follower structure toward other configurations, including core-periphery and multiple subcommunities, in which organizations or states form distinct reference groups, follow different paths, and implement competing or complementary models (D'Aunno et al. 1991). Cleavages could emerge on a variety of bases. But once cleavages develop, organizations or states will not form a single, homogenous community of influence or diffusion. Instead, organizations will observe, influence or be influenced by those in the same category, subcommunity, or region (Lant and Baum 1995; Soule and Zylan 1997; also Greve 1995), and deem actors in other categories as irrelevant or inapplicable, dampening normative pressure and the diffusion of models across types. Here, too, diffusion – and institutionalization more generally – occurs often, if not inevitably, as deeply political and even highly fractured, rather than purely cognitive, connective, or isomorphic processes.

Finally, thinking of these processes and their outcomes as partial or successive settlements of constitutional politics reintroduces "hot" models of action and agency into institutional analysis, while highlighting the provisional and fractured character of taken-for-granted social reality. Viewing extant arrangements and their emergence as settlements foregrounds how institutionalization can rest on articulation, layering, bricolage, and recombination rather than homogenization or convergence (Campbell 1997; Clemens 1997; Djelic and Quack 2003; Klienman and Vallas 2001; Morrill 2003; Orren and Skowronek 1999; Sabel and Zeitlin 1997). Institutionalization as process or outcome may represent less a development of consensus than a linking, combination, or recombination of different models, principles, groups and projects, an articulation or convergence that preserves ambiguity and multiplicity and contains a range of possibilities for subsequent assembly, reassembly, and recombination. Indeed, thinking in these terms takes us full circle, extending the theoretical bases for integrating politics and movements with organizations and institutional analysis. Viewing extant institutions as complex, potentially contradictory articulations not only lends itself directly to understanding the multiple, competing, and conflicting interests and logics that underlie their production. It also leads directly to an understanding of how institutions reshape movements, either by incorporating key demands and principles, and channeling contestation into narrower channels, or by providing movements with multiple logics and levers for creating legitimacy crises, mobilizing more extensively, and mounting broader institutional challenges.

Appendix

Data Sources: Logistic Regressions for Anticompact Laws

Data on whether or not states passed anticompact laws that specifically targeted fire insurance associations and rate-making practices from 1885 to 1910 came from Handy (1916), Wandel (1935), and Spectator Company's *Fire Insurance: Laws, Taxes and Fees* for 1900 to 1915, an annual report summarizing insurance laws by state. (See Figure 5.2, states with anticompact measures). We measured size of state using population per state in 1880, size of farmer economy using the value of farm property per state, and populist vote using the number of votes per state for People's Party presidential candidate James P. Weaver in 1892. These variables let us examine the effects of social movements variables on the log odds of a state enacting anticompact measures after controlling for the size of a state, economic factors and politics, notably the electoral strength of populist forces in a state.

Data for the population per state in 1880 and the value of farm property came from the U.S. Bureau of the Census *Tenth Census of the United States* (1880) and the *Statistical Abstract of the United States* (1912). Data on populist vote came from the *Statistical Abstract of the United States* (1909: 36). Data on peak Grange membership, number of family members, and number of Granges in 1875 came from Buck (1913) and Tonz (1964). Data for Farmers' Alliance membership came from *Appleton's Annual Cyclopedia and Register of Important Events of the Year 1890* (1891: 301). All independent variables were measured in the 1000s.

Data Sources: Heterogeneous Diffusion Models of Rate Regulation

Data on whether and when states passed rate regulation laws and the type of laws passed came from Spectator Company's *Fire Insurance: Laws, Taxes*

Table 5.A1. *Summary of Rate Regulation Laws*

State	Year	Type	State	Year	Type
Kansas	1909	Full	New Hampshire	1917	Antidiscrim.
Texas	1909	Full	Ohio	1917	Antidiscrim.
Louisiana	1910	Full	Oregon	1917	Antidiscrim.
Missouri	1911	Full	South Carolina	1917	Full
New York	1911	Antidiscrim.	Wisconsin	1917	Full
Washington	1911	Antidiscrim.	Colorado	1919	Full
Massachusetts	1912	Antidiscrim.	Indiana	1919	Full
Arkansas	1913	Antidiscrim.	Nevada	1919	Antidiscrim.
New Jersey	1913	Antidiscrim.	North Dakota	1919	Antidiscrim.
North Carolina	1913	Antidiscrim.	South Dakota	1919	Full
West Virginia	1913	Antidiscrim.	Tennessee	1919	Antidiscrim.
Iowa	1915	Antidiscrim.	Vermont	1919	Full
Michigan	1915	Full	Virginia	1920	Full
Minnesota	1915	Full	Wyoming	1921	Full
Oklahoma	1915	Full	Idaho	1923	Antidiscrim.
Pennsylvania	1915	Antidiscrim.	Mississippi	1924	Full
Kentucky	1916	Full	Illinois*	1937	Antidiscrim.

* Not included in the event history analysis.

and Fees for 1900 to 1950. We corroborated our coding using surveys of insurance rate legislation conducted by industry analysts and investigating committees in 1911, 1916, 1925, and 1941 (Hobbs 1925, 1941–2; Merritt Committee 1911; Riegel 1917, 1927). (See Table 5.A1).

Data on the assets of companies doing business within a state came from Spectator Company's *Insurance Year Book, Fire and Marine* (1900–40), annual reports on nearly every fire insurance company operating in the United States, including their states of operation. Based on these reports, we assigned companies to states, creating for each state a list of companies licensed to do business there and the assets of each company. Multistate firms were coded as present in each of the states in which they were licensed to do business. We collected and compiled this data from 1906 1910, and then every five years until 1929, using linear interpolation to obtain values for years in between these dates. The *Year Books* listed data as of December 31 of a year, so we lagged all the market variables by one year. We used *Best's Insurance Reports: Fire and Marine* for the same years to fill in missing data on states of operation. When data was missing from both sources, we used evidence from earlier and later years, information on company size, and county-specific company names to infer its state(s) of operation.

Data on whether or not states conducted a legislative investigation came from historical materials provided by Brearley (1916: 115–32) and information contained in the *Proceedings of the National Convention of Insurance Commissioners* (NCIC 1915: 119–44). Data on anticompact laws used the sources and methods described above. Data on whether or not a state had a stand-alone insurance department came from tables in Spectator Company's *Insurance Year Books* listing state officials with authority in insurance matters. We coded the state as having a stand-alone insurance department if a position specific to insurance (not concerned with other state functions) was listed.

Data for coding states into political-economic groups (core vs. periphery, anticompact vs. non-anticompact) for the diffusion analysis came, respectively, from Sanders (1999) and the Spectator Company's *Fire Insurance: Laws, Taxes, Fees* for 1900–15. Information on the dummy variables for the endorsement of rate regulation by the Supreme Court and the NCIC and the institution of the Actuarial Bureau came from the historical materials presented in Riegel (1917), the NCIC *Proceedings* (1915 (adjourned meeting 1914): 17–25; April 1915: 22), and Crane (1962: 56–7).

We fit models for the passage of rate regulation for 48 states from 1906 to 1930. We begin with 1906 as it precedes the enactment of the first rate regulation law and is the first year for which good data on all variables exists. Serious proposals for regulating rates began circulating around 1900 or so. We end with 1930 because format changes in significant sources deprived us of good measures on key variables and because thirty-three of the thirty-four states that passed rate regulation had already done so by 1924. For further details about variables and their construction, see Schneiberg and Bartley (2001).

6

From Struggle to Settlement

THE CRYSTALLIZATION OF
A FIELD OF LESBIAN/GAY
ORGANIZATIONS IN SAN
FRANCISCO, 1969–1973

Elizabeth A. Armstrong

In 1969 gay liberation was new and exciting. The collision between existing homosexual organizing and the New Left had transformed activists' understandings of what could and should be accomplished by organizing on behalf of homosexuals. In this moment of intense energy the ideologies of the movement were contradictory. Gay liberationists wanted both to solidify gay identity and to demolish sexual identity categories altogether. They wanted both revolution and civil rights. By 1972 the revolutionary and anti-identity currents of the movement were on the wane. Many scholars have remarked upon the transformation of gay liberation from a radical movement into one focused on identity building and gay rights (Altman 1982; Bernstein 1997; Epstein 1987; Escoffier 1985; Gamson 1998; Seidman 1993; Vaid 1995). Affirming gay identity and celebrating diversity replaced societal transformation as goals. This turn toward identity building was accompanied by rapid political consolidation and the explosive growth of a commercial subculture oriented around sex. For the first time, gay organizations agreed upon a national gay rights agenda and moved aggressively to pursue common goals in the political arena.

This sudden transformation of the movement is puzzling. How did the movement come to settle in this way at this moment? How, in general, does settlement occur? This question, in both its general and specific forms, can best be addressed by drawing on both social movement and organizational theory, as "weaknesses in one field . . . might be redressed by insights from the other" (McAdam and Scott this volume: 5). Institutionalists have studied institutional reproduction, social movement scholars have studied

Thanks to Doug McAdam, Mayer Zald, Huggy Rao, Ann Mische, and Melissa Wilde for comments on earlier versions of this paper.

challenges, but few have examined the role of conflict in producing new orders.[1] Scholars of revolutions and social movements have focused on the sources of revolutions and social movements, while treating the return of order after a cycle of social protest as a natural consequence of the decline of factors facilitating movements.[2] Along with other scholars, many of whom are represented in this volume, I attempt to integrate organizational and social movement scholarship in order to advance our understanding of institutional change.

McAdam and Scott, and Campbell, argue in this volume that integrating organizational and social movement theory is eased by overlap and commonality between the fields. Campbell (this volume: 42) points out that organizational and social movement literatures theorize the "mechanisms by which organizations and social movements develop and change" in similar terms. Thus, both literatures would expect political opportunities, framing, and strategic leadership to be factors in field crystallization (Campbell this volume, see also McAdam and Scott this volume). And they are, as I will show. However, both social movement and organizational sociologists often implicitly assume a stable political opportunity structure. I argue that framing and strategic leadership operate differently in unstable institutional environments, and that understanding how they do so is central to understanding processes of field crystallization. Stable political environments encourage, discourage, and channel action more predictably than unstable environments. Framing is a more difficult task when it is unclear with what actors should resonate. Unstable situations often bring multiple cultural strands into contact and generate feelings of possibility that allow for more creative cultural recombination, or bricolage. And, as Fligstein argues, strategic leadership is both more important and more difficult under conditions of uncertainty (Fligstein 1997a, 1997b, 2001b; Swidler 1986, 2001).

In addition, neither social movement nor organizational sociology pays sufficient attention to temporal processes. While Campbell (this volume) does not claim that the mechanisms he discusses are exhaustive, his neglect of temporality might lead others to neglect it as well. The unfolding of process over time plays an important role in both of the cases that McAdam

---

[1] Institutionalists have noted the weakness of their theories in accounting for change. See Brint and Karabel (1991), DiMaggio (1988, 1991), Fligstein (1997a: 29), McAdam and Scott (this volume), and Powell (1991: 197). In recent years, scholars have begun explaining institutional change. For examples, see Clemens (1999), Clemens and Cook (1997), Fligstein (1990, 2001a), Schmidt (forthcoming), and Rao (1998).

[2] Stinchcombe (1999) criticizes this tendency in research on revolutions.

and Scott (this volume) discuss, but the theoretical importance of time is not highlighted in their analyses. Elsewhere McAdam reveals that he is highly cognizant of the importance of temporality in social movement processes. In a coauthored piece, McAdam and Sewell argue that "the precise sequencing of actions over the course of a few hours or days and the particular contingencies faced by actors at particular times may have structuring effects over a very long run" (2001: 102). Historians and historical institutionalists have also emphasized the importance of temporality (Buthe 2002; Pierson 2000a; Sewell 1996; Thelen 2000). Events unfold and occur in time, in particular sequences and over long or short durations.

In the pages that follow I demonstrate the power of environmental, framing, strategic leadership and temporal mechanisms by employing them to explain how and why the field of lesbian/gay organizations crystallized as an identity and rights movement instead of a revolutionary one.

Explaining Field Settlement

Studying institutional crisis is central to the study of social change. Durable social arrangements often consolidate as periods of upheaval come to a close. In 1991 Walter W. Powell hypothesized that, "when change does occur . . . it is likely to be episodic, highlighted by a brief period of crisis or critical intervention, and followed by longer periods of stability or path-dependent development" (1991: 197; Stinchcombe 1965). Similarly, William H. Sewell, Jr. (1996) has observed that major changes tend to occur around dramatic crises and monumental historical events. This section discusses existing theories of field crystallization, contrasting structural approaches with more process-oriented approaches. Before describing these competing theories of field crystallization, I first discuss the concept of the "field" and the identification of stable and unstable fields.

Identifying Crisis and Stability

Stable fields are "organized around local rules of action and conceptions of membership" (Fligstein and McAdam 1995: 2–3).[3] These local rules are

---

[3] For definitions and discussions of fields see Bourdieu (1977), DiMaggio (1983), DiMaggio and Powell (1983), Fligstein (1990, 1996, 2001b), Fligstein and McAdam (1995), McAdam and Scott (this volume), Meyer and Rowan (1977), Mohr (1992), Schmidt (forthcoming), and Scott (1994, 1995).

institutionalized; they are "stable and self-reproducing," and provide shared understandings about the goals of an enterprise, who can participate in it, and how the enterprise is to be pursued (Jepperson 1991: 145; Swidler 2001: 202). Actors' identities and interests are produced by and stabilized by fields. These "rules of the game" benefit some actors more than others, providing some with more resources and power than others. Differences in power are created by and depend upon fields. Fligstein argues that "preexisting rules of interaction and resource distributions operate as sources of power" (2001b: 5).

A field is in crisis, is "unsettled" (Swidler 1986, 2001), or experiencing a "structural dislocation," "rupture," (Sewell 1996: 845) or "critical juncture" (Campbell, this volume) if "major groups are having difficulty reproducing their privilege, as the rules that have governed interaction are no longer working" (Fligstein 2001b: 26). Sewell sees such moments as characterized by uncertainty about how to proceed, because "no one [can] be entirely sure what actions [are] safe or dangerous, moral or wicked, advantageous or foolish, rational or irrational" (1996: 848). Actors often experience these crises as emotionally unsettling (Sewell 1996: 865).

The process of moving an arena from a state of disorganization to a state of organization has been referred to variously as field structuration, consolidation, institutionalization, or crystallization (DiMaggio and Powell 1983). Zysman (1994) refers to the process of arriving at new institutional settlements. Campbell (this volume) refers to "lock in." Unsettled moments are usually, but not always, brief and quickly resolved. Established rules enable actors to pursue orderly lines of action with a reasonable degree of certainty about the consequences of action (Swidler 1986, 2001).

Because fields do not exist independently of actors' collective conceptions of them, the stability of a field is always at risk. Small ruptures are usually "repressed, pointedly ignored, or explained away" (Sewell 1996: 843), but there always exists the possibility that ruptures might escalate and become threatening. DiMaggio explains that "large-scale cultural changes may be caused by large-scale, more-or-less simultaneous frame switches by many interdependent actors" (1997: 15). The wholesale abandonment of the rules of the game is relatively rare because those who benefit usually continue to engage "in actions that have always worked to their advantage" until (and often beyond) the point when it is clear that their old strategies no longer work (Fligstein 2001b: 37). This devotion to the rules of the game sometimes operates as a self-fulfilling prophecy. By acting as if the rules of the game still apply, dominant actors are sometimes able to restabilize the field.

"The distinction between continuity and change [in fields] is one of degree, not of kind" (McAdam and Sewell 2001: 121), which makes the task of distinguishing between stable and unstable fields difficult. Fields also evolve through "the accumulation of small revisions" in the course of institutional reproduction (Sewell 1996: 843; see also Clemens and Cook 1999). Stable fields are dynamic; they must be able to "neutralize" and "reabsorb" challenges presented by changing environments (Schmidt forthcoming; Sewell 1996: 843).

Processes Producing Field Settlement

Most research on how political opportunities, framing, and strategic leadership shape movements and organizations assumes relatively stable arenas. However, understanding field crystallization requires theorizing action under conditions of uncertainty. How does order reemerge when it is no longer possible for actors to determine what the consequences of action are likely to be? This section discusses how framing and strategic leadership operate differently in unstable institutional environments, and how both are dependent upon temporal processes.

Arguments about political opportunity structures' effects on organizations and movements rest on the premise that environmental rigidities enable some possibilities and block others. While the influence of political opportunity structures on action is viewed as indirect (as actors must first define opportunities in order to act), scholars generally assume that the strategy and structure of movements will reflect environmental constraints and opportunities.

Political process models are intended to analyze how actors respond to political environments in flux. Authors such as Doug McAdam (1982) have demonstrated that it is often when environments shift, opening up new opportunities, that movements emerge. But even models attentive to the dynamism of political opportunities often assume that the evolving environment continues to be predictable and transparent. In short, political opportunity structure models assume institutionalized environments.

Existing explanations of field crystallization tend to refer to a background institutionalized order to account for the shape of the new field (Brint and Karabel 1991: 346; Carruthers and Babb 1996: 1578–9; Rao 1998: 918; Starr 1982: 8). As Rao explains, "when multiple frames and forms vie with each other, why one form is chosen and why other roads are not pursued hinge on larger constellations of power and social structure" (1998; 912). Brint and Karabel found that the field of American community colleges developed in relationship to four-year colleges and business organizations (1991).

But in times of severe upheaval it is often not clear what is possible and what it is not. These are situations in which the rules of the game are called into question. The more thoroughly the rules have broken down, the more challenging it is for actors to reach agreement, because the more uncertainty there is about how to disagree, and the less binding the results of contestation (Morrill 1991; Stinchcombe 1999).

Just as actors organize their action in response to environmental rigidity, they also respond to environmental uncertainty. Action is less predictable when it is not clear which strategies are likely to be effective and which are not. Actors tend to experience these moments of environmental uncertainty as "crisis." Crises tend to generate extreme emotion, both positive and negative (Sewell 1996). Sometimes cognitive restraints on imagining alternative ways of doing things lift, opening up a moment of collective creativity (Armstrong 2002a; Sewell 1996). The high emotion and collective creativity of the moment can generate action that appears irrational once order is reestablished. These moments are sometimes characterized by the intersection of cultural currents usually kept distinct (Armstrong 2002a). The combination of a sense of possibility and the presence of multiple cultural options generates particularly creative forms of bricolage. Bricolage refers to the "innovative recombination of elements that constitute a new way of configuring organizations, movements, institutions, and other forms of social activity" (Campbell this volume; see also Clemens and Cook 1999). However, the lack of clear environmental signals about the consequences of action may generate conflict about how to proceed. Thus, crisis may be highly creative but also paralyzing. In general, the desire for action to have predictable results leads most actors to have an investment in the reestablishment of order.

Research on framing typically has assumed the existence of stable cultural repertoires which strategic actors attempt to resonate with in order to accomplish their goals (Benford and Snow 2000; Snow and Benford 1988, 1992; Snow et al. 1986). Framing is based on the notion that "activists must frame issues in ways that resonate with . . . supporters. . . . Frames mediate between opportunity structures and action because they provide the means with which people can interpret the political opportunities before them and, thus, decide how best to pursue their objectives" (Campbell this volume: 48–49). This suggests that a stable political opportunity structure exists to be interpreted. Framing is more difficult when the environment is uncertain. Actors may find it useful to build a variety of ambiguous frames, investing little in any of them, in situations where it is not yet clear which coalition or set of rules will organize the arena. In these circumstances, successful framing activity may not be so much about resonating with a stable aspect of culture, but about being able to "realign" and shift allegiances rapidly. The activity of framing under conditions of uncertainty may involve guesswork, intuition, and rapid adjustment.

Consequently, strategic leadership is more difficult under conditions of uncertainty (Fligstein 1997a, 1997b, 2001b; Swidler 1986, 2001). Social skill is "the ability to induce cooperation among others. Skilled social actors empathetically relate to the situations of other people and in doing so, are able to provide those people with reasons to cooperate" (Fligstein 2001b: 112). "Some social actors are more capable at inducing cooperation than others" (Fligstein 2001b: 112). Fligstein points out that "in fields where there is little internal turbulence or external threat, it is possible that social skill matters less for the reproduction of groups" (2001b: 117). When fields are in crisis, actors struggle to clarify differences, forge agreements, and mobilize consensus. They circulate a variety of different possible solutions. Coalitions try to convince others to get behind the frame they have proposed. The ability of new groups to consolidate fields depends "on their being able to convince a large number of actors that changing the rules is in their interest" (Fligstein 1997b: 403).

Temporality matters by shaping the ways in which actors and frames intersect with shifting political opportunities. Whether or not a field "locks in" may depend on whether actors and frames manage to come together before a particular window of opportunity closes. If actors with the right cultural tools happen to be in place when an opportunity emerges, a field may form. Political opportunities are not static but active, flowing, changing processes. Opportunities have to be grabbed when and where they present themselves. Thus, it matters precisely where and when opportunities occur in time and space. They are moments of possibility that may or may not present themselves to actors again in precisely the same form.

Sewell's work on revolutionary France vividly demonstrates how temporality matters. He found that without a unique confluence of circumstances, the taking of the Bastille would not have been a "world-shaping" event. This outcome depended on what Sewell refers to as "conditions peculiar to the circumstance." Sewell builds his understanding of the importance of particular conditions on the work of Marshall Sahlins, who used "the term 'structure of the conjuncture' to refer to the particular meanings, accidents, and causal forces that shape events – the small but locally determining conditions whose interaction in a particular place and time may seal the fates of whole societies" (Sewell 1996: 862; see also Sahlins 1981 and Jacobs 1996). While Sewell does not refer to "fields" or "field settlement" in his work, his theory can be seen as illustrating the role of contingent sequences of historical events in field crystallization.

The Study

One question motivating the collection of the data analyzed here was why lesbian/gay organizations in San Francisco seemed to be diversifying over time instead of homogenizing, as predicted by DiMaggio and Powell (1983). I created a database of all lesbian/gay organizations existing in San Francisco from the years 1950 to 1994 by coding listings of organizations in periodicals, resource guides, and directories.[4] This data set provided an exhaustive record of the forms of organization extant at each point in time.

After constructing the data set, I attempted to measure the diversification of the field. It gradually became clear that the organizations were not similar enough to each other even to identify dimensions along which it was meaningful to measure diversity and homogeneity. Comparing homosexual organizations founded in the 1960s with those founded in the 1970s was like comparing apples and oranges. However, if I looked only at organizations formed after 1972 it was possible to measure their homogenization and diversification. This indicated a relatively sudden increase in the coherence of this collective project in the early 1970s.

Once I realized this, I turned to describing and explaining the crystallization of this field. Stinchcombe noted in 1965 that "organizational types generally originate rapidly in a relatively short historical period, to grow and change slowly after that period" (1965: 168). The forging of new fields tends to be associated with the development of new organizational forms and the rapid proliferation of these organizations. The sudden proliferation of organizations in this case provided a vivid picture of field founding: the

---

[4] See Armstrong (1998, 2002b) for more details on the construction of the data set.

emergence of guides to lesbian/gay nonprofit organizations provided another indicator of field crystallization.[5]

To those familiar with the history of the lesbian/gay movement in the United States, the notion that there was a rupture in the late 1960s and early 1970s is hardly surprising. All accounts of the development of the gay movement confirm the existence and importance of this rupture. I analyzed both archival and secondary sources to provide a detailed description of the shift. Once I described the crystallization of the field, I turned to primary and secondary sources to analyze why it crystallized when and how it did.

Successful institutionalization tends to produce the view that the resulting settlement was natural or inevitable – that the outcome could not have been otherwise (Clemens 1997; Schmidt forthcoming). Sometimes the fact that a particular arena was ever organized differently is forgotten. I attempt to dislodge the assumption of inevitability in this case by developing counterfactuals – by pointing out the various paths the gay movement might have taken if events had unfolded differently. To reconstruct the feel of open-endedness that characterizes social life on the ground and in the moment – when actors do not know how things are going to turn out, and when, in fact, outcomes are not yet determined – it is important to rely on evidentiary materials created in the heat of the moment, and to be skeptical of accounts constructed after the fact.

The Crystallization of the Lesbian/Gay Movement

Homophile organizations that were formed in the 1950s mark the beginning of a continuous thread of organizing on behalf of homosexuals in the United States (D'Emilio 1983; Licata 1981; Marotta 1981; Martin and Lyon 1991).[6] They hoped to improve life for homosexuals by educating the mainstream public (Bernstein 1997, 2002; D'Emilio 1983; Epstein 1999). After brief experimentation with secretive structures borrowed from

---

[5] Organizational researchers see resource guides as an indicator of the existence of a field (DiMaggio and Powell 1991; Mohr 1992: 42). Guides provide evidence that participants are aware of being involved in a common enterprise, and evidence of the ways that participants conceive of their enterprise. Guides to nonprofit lesbian/gay organizations did not exist before the early 1970s.

[6] Homosexual organizations formed in the 1950s were not the very first such organizations in the United States. Adam discusses a homosexual rights organization which existed briefly in the 1920s (1987: 42). See also FitzGerald (1986 [1981]), Blasius and Phelan (1997), and Stein (2000).

Communist Party organizations, homophile organizations modeled themselves on public nonprofit organizations (D'Emilio 1983). They adopted names that conveyed little explicit information about sexual identity, such as the Society for Individual Rights, the Daughters of Bilitis, and the Mattachine Society. By adopting conventional organizational forms, particularly winning legal incorporation, they endeavored to enhance the legitimacy of their cause (D'Emilio 1983). Homophile activist Marvin Cutler boasted in 1956 that Mattachine was "incorporated under the strict requirements of California law, to insure impeccable propriety and civic non-partisanship at all times" (1956: 10).

Although usually dated from the Stonewall riots that took place in New York in late June 1969, the gay liberation movement had been under way in San Francisco since at least April of that year (Armstrong 2002b; Murray 1996; Stryker and Van Buskirk 1996). Often treated as merely another outgrowth of the New Left, gay liberation was deeply influenced by and embattled with the preexisting homophile movement (D'Emilio 1983; Duberman 1993; Marotta 1981; Stein 2000). Contemporary accounts focus on gay liberation as the source of a politics of gay pride centered on "coming out," but at the peak of the movement gay liberation also saw itself as part of a broader New Left coalition bringing about a revolutionary transformation of society (D'Emilio 1983; Jay and Young 1992 [1972]; Kissack 1995).

At its peak, gay liberation was composed of three analytically distinct currents.[7] Gay power sought the overthrow of capitalism and the creation of a liberated society in which sexual identity categories would no longer be necessary. Gay power activists, who saw themselves as gay revolutionaries, fought for sexual liberation for all, not just for rights for gay-identified people. This strain of gay liberation, organized around a redistributive political logic, was deeply indebted to the socialist ideas of the New Left. Gay power activists saw themselves as a vanguard, as part of a movement that would improve society for everyone, not just for a particular group. While gay power activists endorsed coming out, they did not see the affirmation of gay identity as the end goal of sexual politics. They saw the creation of gay identity as merely a step toward the goal of getting rid of sexual identity categories altogether (Altman 1993: 239). Gay power activists believed that

---

[7] Marotta (1981) developed a more complex categorization of the strains of gay liberation ideology. I borrow the distinction between gay power and gay pride from Teal (1995: 68).

"everyone is gay, everyone is straight," and that gay liberation should lead to "a far greater acceptance of human sexuality and with that . . . a decrease in the stigma attached to unorthodox sex and a corresponding increase in overt bisexuality" (Altman 1993: 246). Consequently, in their view, "Gay, in its most far-reaching sense, means not homosexual, but sexually free" (Young 1992 [1972]: 28).

In contrast, a second strain of gay liberation, which I refer to as gay pride, saw the solidification of gay identity as the primary goal of gay politics. Gay pride endeavored to build gay culture and community through forming support groups and other kinds of gay organizations. Dennis Altman (1993: 242) described the difference between gay pride and gay power as follows: "The liberal sees homosexuals as a minority to be assisted into a full place in society. The radical sees homosexuality as a component of all people including her- or himself." Gay power activists thought all revolutionaries should come out as gay, thus contributing to the blurring of sexual identity categories. Gay pride activists felt that only those individuals sincerely interested in same-gender sexual relations should come out.

The third current, inherited from the homophile movement, believed that the situation of gays could be improved through single-issue interest group politics seeking rights. Gay rights activists identified themselves primarily as gay and worked to improve life for gay people. Gay rights activists were never convinced that revolution was the answer. Indeed, they were often skeptical about how homosexuals would fare under socialism.[8] They believed in the reform of the current system, and advocated working within mainstream institutions. Gay rights activists criticized gay power's attention to issues other than those of concern for homosexuals. They questioned whether other radicals would reciprocate and take up homosexual issues. Gay rights activists rejected violent means in favor of working within the political system and engaging in clever cultural "zaps." Gay rights activists tended to see the building of identity as a necessary precursor to institutional politics, while gay pride activists saw engaging in gay rights politics as a way to build gay identity.

Radical gay liberation fell into disarray in 1970 (D'Emilio 1992a; Humphreys 1972). As it disintegrated, a more moderate gay movement

---

[8] This concern manifested itself in a debate within gay liberation about the quality of gay life in Cuba. See Jay and Young (1992 [1972], section 6) and Teal (1995: 77).

crystallized. In the early 1970s, observers noted that it seemed like something new was forming. Sociologist Laud Humphreys noted that in 1970, "the old-line, civil-libertarian thesis and the gay liberationist antithesis began to produce a synthesis" (Humphreys 1972: 123). *The Advocate*, a prominent Los Angeles gay newspaper, proclaimed in September 1971 that

Between the hard conservatives and the intolerant radicals, young Gays are finding the middle ground productive. From coast to coast, they are building new organizations modeled after New York's highly successful and active Gay Activists Alliance. The formula: just enough structure and planning to have a sound foundation but not so much that action is impossible. Also, most new groups are limiting their activity to gay-oriented issues, rather than tackling all the world's ills at once. It seems to be a formula that can win the widespread support that the GLF's (Gay Liberation Front) were never able to get.

This new coherence in the gay political project manifested itself in a variety of ways. It sparked the rapid proliferation of a diversity of new gay organizations. These new organizations had more specialized names reflecting a continuously unfolding variety of new identities and subidentities, such as Affirmation Gay/Lesbian Mormons, Gay Asian Pacific Alliance, Straights for Gay Rights, Gay American Indians, Digital Queers, and the Bay Area Bisexual Network (1995). Organization names included elaborate identity information and represented specialized subidentities. These organizations included gay religious organizations (e.g., the Metropolitan Community Church, founded 1970), gay self-help organizations (e.g., Gay Alcoholics Anonymous, founded 1971), gay hobby organizations (e.g., San Francisco Front Runners, founded 1974), and gay parenting groups (e.g., Lesbian Mothers' Union, founded in 1971). The use of bold sexual identity terminology in organizations' names illustrated their new devotion to pride and identity building. The sudden explosion of support groups, which were unheard of before 1970, created contexts in which individuals could discover and express themselves.

The changing density of various kinds of homosexual organizations provided another confirmation of the timing of the consolidation of the gay identity movement. Figure 6.1 shows the decline of both homophile and gay liberation organizations and the proliferation of gay rights and gay pride organizations. The existence of multiple kinds of organizations in the years from 1969 to 1972 indicates the unsettled nature of the field, which coalesced in the early 1970s.

The creation of resource guides in the early seventies also indicated field crystallization. While the community published bar guides throughout the

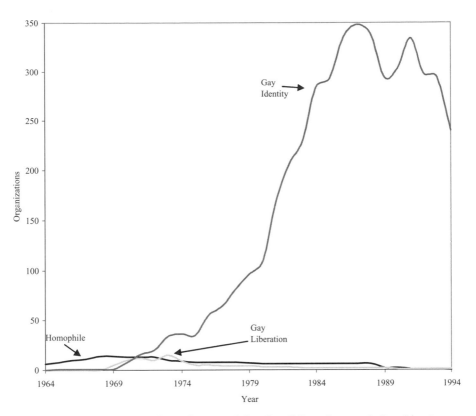

Figure 6.1 Total Number of Homophile, Gay Liberation, and Gay Identity Organizations in San Francisco, 1964–1994

1960s, the first guides to list both nonprofit and commercial organizations were published in 1972. *Gayellow Pages*, the first national guide to both nonprofit and commercial organizations to be published annually, was first published in 1973. These guides listed bars and bathhouses as well as political and cultural organizations, revealing that gay activists saw their project in terms of the expansion of all kinds of gay social space.

Today, lesbian/gay freedom day parades occur in all major U.S. cities and some small towns each June. The intent of the founders of the parades was to commemorate the June 1969 Stonewall uprisings in New York. Organizers of the first parade in New York in 1970 defined the event as an opportunity for the gay community to show its pride, its unity, and its diversity. San Francisco organized its first freedom day parade in 1972, and has had a parade every year since. Each year the original language of "pride," "celebration," "unity," and "diversity" appears in parade themes and mission statements.

The year 1972 also marked the first time, after years of effort, that a national conference of homosexual organizations reached a consensus on a political platform (Humphreys 1972: 165). In February 1972, at a National Coalition of Gay Organizations, jointly sponsored by New York's Gay Activists Alliance and Chicago's Gay Alliance, eighty-five organizations from eighteen states agreed on a Gay Rights Platform in preparation for the 1972 elections (Humphreys 1972: 162). Never before had a national conference of gay organizations been able to agree on a gay stance. Throughout the late 1960s multiple attempts had failed to produce such a consensus (Humphreys 1972: 165). Together, these indicators provide strong evidence of field consolidation in the early 1970s. The next section explains how this outcome came to pass.

Explaining Field Crystallization

The movement that developed in the 1970s and 1980s was not the only kind of movement that could have been organized on behalf of homosexuals. Even in 1969, when much of the groundwork for the contemporary lesbian/gay movement was in place, the shape (and even the existence) of the future movement was not fully determined. Activists might have endorsed a more revolutionary option, as did some aspects of the New Left. Or the movement could have split off into different wings, as did the women's movement. It is also possible to imagine internal conflict destroying the movement altogether. The crystallization of a field of lesbian/gay organizations was not inevitable, but a result of political decisions made within a historically specific context. Below I demonstrate that framing and strategic leadership were much more difficult at the peak of the New Left. Thus, the decline of the New Left, which made the political environment more transparent, rapidly changed the environment in which activists struggled to arrive at the best way to proceed. The timing of the intersection of homosexual organizing with the New Left, and of the decline of the New Left, played a crucial role in determining what actors, political approaches, and possibilities intersected. Even slight differences in the way events unfolded might have led to different convergences among actors, political models, and political possibilities that could have channeled the movement in a different direction.

How Possibility Paralyzes

Few would dispute that the 1960s was a time of great cultural and political upheaval in the United States. The generalized nature of the cultural crisis called into question the rules of multiple arenas. Debra Minkoff described "an open environment for social action that was (and is) unmatched in U.S. history" (1999: 1669). Todd Gitlin, who was deeply involved in the New Left, described "the hallucinatory giddiness of the late Sixties...whose sheer wildness, even now, seems the stuff of another century...people were living with a supercharged density: lives were bound up with one another, making claims on one another, drawing one another into the common project." The expansive feeling of possibility expanded the boundaries of the thinkable, producing "unraveling, rethinking, refusing to take for granted, thinking without limits..." (Gitlin 1987: 7). Wini Breines, also an activist, echoed Gitlin's description of the moment: "We believed that we were going to make a revolution. We were convinced that we could transform America through our political activity and insights. ...A deep enthusiasm characterized our faith in our own political and social power....The new left opened everything to scrutiny" (1989: xxi-xxii).

The relaxation of beliefs about the impossibility of major structural change in the United States, combined with the intense interaction characteristic of crisis and the intersection of distinct cultural traditions, created an unusual context of collective creativity (Armstrong 2002a). The encounter with the New Left introduced homosexual activists to new ways of thinking about organizing around sexuality. Introduction to an identity logic generated new strategies such as coming out, pride parades, rap groups, and cultural zaps. Coming out, the practice of revealing one's sexual identity for psychological, cultural, and political gain, seems obvious now. However, until homosexual activists were able to conceive of the public revelation of sexuality as politically productive, the practice did not and would not have developed. These new strategies developed through bricolage, in this case the combining of elements of the New Left with homosexual movement approaches.

The encounter between the New Left and the homophile movement was historically contingent. Had homophile politics not collided with the New Left, say, because of an earlier decline of the New Left, it is not certain that strategies such as coming out would have been created. Cornerstone assumptions of contemporary gay politics owe much to the fact that an existing homosexual movement collided with the New Left early enough in the New Left's lifespan for the gay movement to experience the full creative benefit of involvement with this encounter. The cultural tools needed to forge the lesbian/gay movement field were created in the encounter between existing homophile organizations and the New Left.

However, this moment of creativity also generated political conflict. The intersection of the New Left and a preexisting homophile movement generated the view that gay liberation could not be achieved without simultaneously addressing class, race, and gender inequality. In 1969, it was very difficult for activists to assess what was politically possible. The fate of the New Left was not yet clear. Some still felt that revolutionary change was possible, while others had lost faith, and still others had never been convinced. Activists fought about what was politically possible as well as about what was politically desirable. It was difficult to ascertain whether it made more sense to support the gay power frame which aligned the gay movement with the New Left and its revolutionary project, or to support gay rights and gay pride frames which resonated more readily with fundamental features of the American political environment. In 1969, though, in the midst of the excitement of the moment, the limits of the politically possible were opaque.

Throughout the fall of 1969 and the spring of 1970, conflict between the various strands of gay liberation escalated. In November 1969, a faction of New York's Gay Liberation Front (GLF) split off to found the Gay Activists Alliance (Dong 1995; Marotta 1981: 142). The issue which brought the crisis to a head was whether the Gay Liberation Front should support the Black Panthers (Dong 1995; Marotta 1981: 135, 142; Teal 1995: 78). Gay liberation activists on the West Coast also faced the Black Panther issue. According to Rt. Rev. Michael Irkin, the November 15, 1969, March for Peace revealed

a clear division in the ranks of the Homosexual Liberation Movement as represented by the Committee for Homosexual Freedom, the Gay Liberation Theatre, the Gay Liberation Front, and some other groups. [This] became clear to all during the rally at the Polo Grounds when, during the speech of David Hilliard of the Black Panther Party, dissension broke out when some of our members, among them the author of this article and some others under our banner, joined with other pacifists in shouting down David Hilliard's speech with cries of "Peace, Now!" while others showed their support of his statements with clenched-fist salutes and cries of enthusiasm (Irkin 1969: 8).

Irkin was critical of the Black Panther Party, while the gay power activists were enthusiastic supporters. Irkin felt that "under the pretense of speaking for peace, [Hilliard had] called for violence. . . . We cannot see that violence, in any man's hand, is any less violence" (Irkin 1969: 9). In response, Irkin clarified the ideological differences internal to gay liberation: "[The Committee for Homosexual Freedom] at present has among its members many who have not come to any particular socio-economic or political philosophy. While the majority of our members . . . call themselves socialists, I know personally of at least a few members who believe that capitalism should continue in some modified form" (Irkin 1969: 8). Similar conflicts about related issues occurred in late 1969 and 1970.

Thus, the encounter between the New Left and the homophile movement created potentially paralyzing internal conflict. The intensity of the conflict could have become debilitating, as it did for other parts of the New Left. By introducing new cultural possibilities and making the context difficult to read, this unsettled moment escalated the social skill required to arrive at a stable way of organizing around sexuality. This provides an example of how unstable political environments influence action differently than stable environments. In stable environments actors may be able to assess opportunities and constraints with reasonable accuracy. In unstable environments this is less possible. Uncertainty may generate intense conflict about how to proceed, as it did among gay activists in 1969. However, this particular case does not allow us the opportunity to see if and how activists are able to stabilize political projects in uncertain environments, as the environment grew more predictable with the rapid demise of the New Left in 1970 and 1971.

The Timing and Rapidity of the Decline of the New Left

In the 1960s many movement activists believed the United States was on the verge of radical social change (Gitlin 1987). This optimism faded quickly as the sixties came to a close. Scholars point to the election of Richard Nixon as a political turning point: "The 1968 election of Richard Nixon signaled a turn away from the supportive political agendas associated with the Kennedy-Johnson decades, and as antiwar and student movements escalated, a period of intensive political retrenchment began" (Minkoff 1995: 65). By the early seventies, it was clear that revolutionary change was not likely.

Students for a Democratic Society (SDS) "burned up and out in a spectacular fashion" in 1969 and 1970 (Echols 1992: 22; Polletta 2002). Echols noted that "the conventional sixties' story line," developed by white male leaders who have written on the New Left, tends to equate the disintegration of the SDS with the end of "radicalism," finalized by the "February 1970 Greenwich Village townhouse explosion" (1992: 23). Humphreys and Echols also pointed to the Kent State killings later that year as a common marker for the end of radicalism (Echols 1992: 23; Gitlin 1987; Humphreys 1972).

Feminists Wini Breines and Alice Echols de-emphasized SDS in their accounts of the radicalism of the times and claimed that male leaders exaggerated "the significance of the collapse of SDS at the end of the decade" (Breines 1989: xv; Echols 1992).

What is overlooked in accounts that focus on the fate of SDS as an organization is the mass movement after 1968, regional and local activity not dependent upon a national organization, students organizing and grass-roots activists (including women and people of color), the counterculture, and the significance of the birth of other movements such as the women's liberation and gay movements. (Breines 1989: xv)

Alice Echols argued, "if one's narrative is conceptualized around the idea that radicalism was simply played out by the decade's end, then there really is only token narrative space available for women's liberation (or for the Chicano, Native American, or gay and lesbian movements)" (1992: 13). Breines and Echols have a point. Radicalism did survive beyond 1970, but the demise of the SDS in 1970 marked a fundamental shift in the nature of activism and the optimism associated with it. Activism shifted away from an effort to bring about a socialist transformation of society, and away from Marxist-influenced, class-oriented, redistributive politics.

While opportunities for some forms of political action contracted in the late sixties and early seventies, other opportunities began to expand. Debra Minkoff has shown in her work on women's and racial-ethnic organizations that while it became more difficult to form and maintain protest organizations, the environment improved for more moderate service and policy advocacy organizations. She argues that: "The increasing efforts at law and order during the Nixon administration and into the 1980s did not so much repress collective action as channel it into more institutionally acceptable organizational activity" (Minkoff 1995: 74).[9] Minkoff, drawing on the work of Jenkins and Walker, pointed to the improved "funding opportunities" for

---

[9] Minkoff (1995) cites Haines (1984), Jenkins and Ekert (1986), and McAdam (1982). See also McCarthy, Britt, and Wolfson (1991) and Meyer and Imig (1993).

"interest groups and a broader range of policy advocacy organizations" in the seventies (1995: 55).[10] Foundations increased their level of support for nonprofit organizing. "Congressional reforms that began in the early 1960s gradually decentralized authority, creating broader opportunities for non-profit advocacy" (Jenkins 1987: 301). In 1969 and 1976 the tax deductibility of contributions to nonprofit organizations involved in political advocacy were liberalized (Jenkins 1987: 301). McCarthy, Britt, and Wolfson (1991) describe the emergence of a "tangle of incentives" pushing movements toward nonprofit organizational forms.

While more radical socialist ideologies lost their luster, the pursuit of ethnic group equality and civil rights remained viable. Together, the Civil Rights Act of 1964, the Voting Rights Act of 1965, and the Equal Employment Opportunity Act of 1972 enhanced the political utility of an ethnic self-characterization. An ethnic framing of gay identity and an orientation toward gay civil rights fit nicely with the structure of American politics (D'Emilio 1992 [1972]: xxvii; Epstein 1987: 2; Gamson 1998: 20). Epstein noted that "This 'ethnic' self-characterization by gays and lesbians has a clear political utility, for it has permitted a form of group organizing that is particularly suited to the American experience, with its history of civil-rights struggles and ethnic-based, interest-group competition" (1987: 2).

In addition, the cultural permissiveness introduced by the 1960s survived well into the 1970s. A revolution in the sexual mores of heterosexual Americans, particularly the young, was ongoing. The broader cultural focus on authenticity, therapy, self-actualization, and "doing your own thing" supported an acceptance of gay identity and lifestyle as one possible result of a search for a "true self."

How the Rapid Decline of the New Left Mattered

The most commonsensical story about how the decline of the New Left mattered for the gay movement is that it simply accommodated to a political environment growing more conservative. In an essay drafted in 1991, historian John D'Emilio argued that

one reason [for the demise of gay power] is that the soil that fertilized GLF, the radicalism of the 1960s, was drying up rapidly. The belief that a revolution was imminent and that gays and lesbians should get on board was fast losing whatever momentary

---

[10] See Jenkins (1985a, 1987) and Walker (1983).

plausibility it had. By the early 1970s, the nation was entering a long period of political conservatism and economic retrenchment. With every new proclamation of revolutionary intentions, radicals compromised their credibility. (D'Emilio 1992b: 245)

The plausibility of this account is difficult to dispute. And, indeed, it is part of the story. The decline of the New Left revealed a political environment more transparent and more conservative than what had gone before. In this new context, gay activists found gay power's revolutionary vision less plausible than gay rights or gay pride approaches.

However, simply pointing to the implausibility of revolutionary change is an incomplete explanation. Not all parts of the New Left responded to the change in the political environment by modulating their notions of what was possible and desirable. Some parts of the New Left remained committed to revolutionary visions. Some even turned to violence. Why gay activists found it relatively easy, compared to other New Left activists, to turn away from a multi-issue social justice vision still must be explained. The answer lies partially with the timing and rapidity of the decline of the New Left. Gay activism intersected with the New Left long enough to benefit from the tremendous creativity of the moment but not so long as to enable many gay activists to become deeply invested in the more radical political project.

As mentioned above, the encounter between the homophile movement and the New Left provided the crucible in which the gay pride model, emphasizing coming out and identity expression, was forged. The existence of this model provided an alternative to the radical gay power approach – an alternative that became increasingly appealing as its mobilizing power started to become obvious. In New York, the Gay Activists Alliance (GAA) staged highly successful cultural zaps. The GAA, tailored to the "'hip' homosexual mainstream" was "activist but nonviolent, imaginative, cool, and very successful" (Humphreys 1972: 160; Marotta 1981: 146). In San Francisco, the Society for Individual Rights (SIR) was aware of the successes of the GAA in New York. In June 1971, the SIR's publication, *Vector*, expressed admiration for New York's GAA, while criticizing New York's GLF. The *Vector* editor indicated that the SIR needed to adapt to stay vital: "Gay liberation is on the move and if SIR does not stay aboard it will go the way of the Mattachine Society" (*Vector* 1971: 4). SIR organizers situated themselves in a parallel position to New York's GAA. Activists observed what seemed to work and imitated it.

The SIR experienced immediate success with the gay pride formulation. In June 1971 the SIR organized a "work-in" at the San Francisco Federal Building. This ingenious demonstration involved homosexuals (with signs on their lapels identifying themselves as such) volunteering their services to the government "until they were 'fired' by the Security Guards. For a time, Uncle Sam had homosexuals working for free in the IRS, Federal Employment Information Center, the US Printing Office Book Store, and homosexuals working as Indian Guides, and elevator operators. The Federals went into a 'panic' when a homosexual tried to be a janitor, by pushing a broom across the lobby" (Broshears 1971: 1). This demonstration was organized to protest "what SIR's president, Bill Plath, called 'an unjust government policy in refusing to employ homosexuals'" (Broshears 1971: 1).

Thus, part of the reason that gay activists turned away from gay power was that an exciting alternative existed. That this alternative existed, and was beginning to reveal its potential, is a consequence of the timing of the intersection between homophile and New Left movements. People are less likely to abandon a line of action, even one that is doomed, if they do not have an alternative available. However, people do not always support even the most exciting alternatives if they are already deeply committed to another approach (Wilde 2004). And, here, timing played a role in gay activists' relative lack of commitment to radical politics.

The intersection between homosexual organizing and the New Left was brief, limiting homosexual commitment to a revolutionary agenda. By the time gay liberation emerged in 1969, signs of the decline of the New Left were evident. Gay activists witnessed the pitfalls of revolutionary politics without experiencing the series of events that led other movements down that path. Some gay leaders, such as New York's Jim Owles, were self-conscious in their efforts to try to prevent the gay movement from repeating what they saw as the mistakes of other branches of the New Left. In a 1971 statement, Owles made the case that trying to create an ideologically homogenous movement would be a mistake. He asserted that "few of us are anxious to see a uniform and monolithic movement develop out of the foundations we have laid. We have seen other mass movements develop in this direction in the past, only to be torn apart by internal struggles over ideology and leadership, eventually to fail in achieving their goals" (Humphreys 1972: 126–7). Owles saw efforts to develop ideological consensus to be dangerous, potentially leading to movement factionalization. Thus, the relatively late emergence of gay liberation in the cycle of protest, combined with the very rapid decline of the New Left, helped protect the gay movement from the fate of kindred movements.

The enthusiasm of gay activists for the gay power perspective also was reduced by the reaction of other movements to this attempted alliance. Gay activists reported painful experiences of homophobia within the New Left. Jim Owles, one of the founders of New York's GAA, experienced the New Left as "viciously antihomosexual":

> When [gay liberationists] did go out to other actions – let's say a support rally for the Panthers or the Young Lords or the more radical groups – . . . they were still getting spit at. The word faggot was still being used at them. They were relegated to 'back' roles, and were told, 'Don't come out in front! We don't want our groups to become known as homosexual things.' That happened in other groups: in women's lib the lesbians are told, 'Get in the back. We don't want women's lib to be identified as a lesbian movement.' It was just one put-down, spit-in-the-face thing all the way. And I just couldn't do that. . . . (Teal 1995: 297–8)

Owles was explicit that this treatment contributed to his desire to work in a single-issue organization because in this brief moment of experimentation activists learned that linking homosexual interests with those of other minorities could lead to rejection. The New Left never fully incorporated gay liberation because of the challenge it posed to its gender and sexual politics.

Even with the mixed reception gay liberation received from the women's movement, women's liberation was, of all the various strands of the New Left, most akin to gay liberation. Women's liberationists were already discussing the need to break away from a male-dominated New Left movement by the time gay liberation emerged (Echols 1989: chap. 3). The separation of women's liberation from the New Left decreased the likelihood that gay activists would make a deep commitment to revolutionary politics. If the New Left would not take women's issues seriously, what hope could gay activists have that homosexuality would be taken seriously? In addition, by splitting off from the New Left, the women's movement modeled a possible path for the gay movement and shaped the relationship between women's and gay movements. Just as the women's movement separated from the Left, lesbians turned away from participation in gay politics toward a separatist lesbian feminism (Martin 1970). The departure of women from the gay movement increased the likelihood that the gay movement would turn to a single-issue rights politics. Lesbian involvement in gay liberation militated toward a multi-issue politics because women were more likely to argue that issues of gender and sexuality both needed to be addressed.

Thus, the abandonment of the gay power agenda by gay activists was partly a pragmatic response to a changing environment. Activists wanted the gay movement to survive this tumultuous moment. In this moment when multi-issue movements were floundering, gay activists saw the turn away from multi-issue politics as key to survival. However, pragmatism cannot fully explain the abandonment of gay power. A lack of commitment to radical politics, partially a result of the timing of the decline of the New Left, also played a role. The late development of gay liberation in the cycle of protest meant that the intersection between the homophile movement and the New Left was brief. This, in turn, meant that the vision of gay interest as inextricably connected to the interests of those oppressed in terms of gender, race, and class was tentative. This vision did not stand much of a chance as gay activists witnessed the failures of more radical approaches, and the successes of the gay pride and gay rights approaches. All of these features of the situation guided activists away from gay power approaches. The lack of appeal of gay power was not inevitable, but a result of the specific historical circumstances.

The fact that white middle-class men created and experimented with gay power politics suggests that a different formulation of gay interest was possible. Interests are constructed and reconstructed, and do not emerge directly from identity, which is itself an historical and political accomplishment. Some gay men were, and still are, advocates of a multiracial, multi-issue social justice politics. A view that assumes that the way actors interpret their interests can be derived from an objective analysis of social structure cannot explain the existence of the many middle-class white men who were and are devoted political radicals.

The abandonment of gay power by many (although not all) gay activists had both immediate and long-term consequences for the movement. In the short run, it reduced conflict internal to the gay movement, and thus, the social skill needed to forge agreements. Given the intensity of the conflict internal to gay liberation in 1969 and 1970, the continuation of those conflicts could have destroyed the movement. Attempting to reach agreement on goals and strategy in an uncertain political context might have led to a slow, contentious movement death. The timing and rapidity of the decline of the New Left meant that activists encountered this new (albeit more conservative) environment in a highly mobilized state. For most, turning to the more moderate gay pride and gay rights approaches did not feel like "selling out," but felt ripe with fresh possibilities. Thus, the rapid decline of the New Left in the early 1970s meant that the political environment became more transparent before activists were worn down by years of disagreement. Thus, the sharp decline of the New Left and the associated rejection of gay power played a pivotal role in the dramatic crystallization of a gay rights/pride agenda and the explosive growth of the gay movement in the 1970s.

Because of the sharpness of the rejection of the gay power agenda, the gay movement became more aggressively single issue than it might otherwise have become. This has had long-term consequences for the inclusivity of the movement. The turn away from gay power meant the abandonment of a politics that saw race, class, and gender politics as inextricably linked with sexual liberation. The race, class, and gender implications of this turn were not lost on activists at the time. The split of the GLF in New York occurred around the issue of the Black Panthers, giving the conflict between gay pride and gay power a distinctively racial cast. When interviewed in the 1990s for the documentary *Out Rage '69*, African American activist Bob Kohler talked about his feelings about the founding of the GAA as if the events had happened yesterday. He explained that, in his view:

[The Gay Activists Alliance] was formed as a class thing. It was formed because of class and because of race.... The dirty little secret of the gay movement is how and why the GAA was formed.... They wanted white power. And so they let the freaks, the artists, the poets, the drag queens, the street people, the street queens, the blacks, and the colored people keep the GLF. We're going to go form this thing that is going to change laws. That is a good idea. Change laws. But it was mainly reformist. The vision was broken. The vision went. (Dong 1995)

Kohler's palpable sense of loss was fueled by the knowledge that for a brief moment the possibility of a fundamentally different kind of gay identity and movement existed. Middle-class white men experimented with a way of thinking about sexual identity and interest that would have aligned their interests with those disadvantaged in terms of gender, race, and class. But this experimentation had little time to develop. The decline of the New Left shut this conversation down by resolidifying earlier formulations of class, race, and gender interest and identity.

The rapid response of gay activists to the restabilizing of the political environment suggests how much easier it is for people to act collectively (or to agree that it is too dangerous to act collectively) when they receive clear signals from stable environments about the likely consequences of action. Framing and strategic leadership are difficult in unstable environments. This case also provides an example of the role of temporality in field settlement. While the gay movement abandoned gay power partially because of the pragmatic assessment of political possibility, activists also were guided away from gay power because of *the particular timing and sequence of events*. Had the decline of the New Left unfolded in a different way, activists might have built a more radical (and unsuccessful) movement, or perhaps no movement at all. What we take for granted as the obvious and inevitable way of organizing around sexuality is only one possible outcome.

Discussion and Conclusion

A historically specific sequence of events enabled the crystallization of the lesbian/gay field in San Francisco in the early 1970s. A rapidly changing political environment in the late 1960s engendered a sense of nearly infinite possibility, which, in turn, generated both creative bricolage and internal conflict within the gay movement. Many ways of framing the movement seemed possible and it was difficult to assess which would resonate with surrounding movements and the larger political environment. Thus, strategic leadership at this moment was extremely difficult.

This moment of possibility ended abruptly, when actors suddenly found themselves in a much more predictable environment in the very early 1970s. The task of framing then became easier as it was more obvious which frames were likely to resonate with the larger political environment. While the stabilization of the environment curtailed creativity, the earlier period had generated many creative ideas about how to organize around sexuality. Strategic leadership in this case involved accurately reading the environment and acting to streamline the movement to take advantage of political possibility. Thus, the highly uncertain environment generated creative ideas but also conflict and paralysis, while the more transparent environment curtailed creative activity, but encouraged strategic thinking by allowing activists to select which frames would resonate in the new context. The rapid change in the political environment meant that possibilities that existed in one moment did not in the next. In order to take advantage of these fleeting possibilities it was necessary for actors to be there with cultural tools ready. Actors and frames intersect in contexts created by the unfolding of events over time.

The use of social movement and institutional theory in the explanation of field crystallization has implications for future theoretical development and empirical scholarship. Theoretically, the analysis here suggests that common mechanisms identified by organizational and social movement scholars are a powerful starting point in the analysis of organizational and social movement development and change. However, the analysis here also suggests that both intellectual arenas are much better at understanding social action under conditions of social order than in conditions of serious social upheaval. Both social movement and organizational scholars should attend more closely to the problem of action in conditions of uncertainty, and to sources of innovation and creativity. The analysis also suggests the importance of temporality to processes of field transformation. A variety of social movement theorists currently are focusing on such issues as the roles of place, identity, and emotion in movements (Goodwin, Jasper, and Polletta 2001; Polletta and Jasper 2001; Sewell 2001). It would be a mistake if the intersection between social movement and organizational theory neglected the insights of these scholars and developed an approach based on the shared resource/rationalist basis of much social movement and organizational theory. The third party to this new intersection between social movement and organizational sociology is culture. Attending to culture means attending not only to framing processes, but also to the sources of cultural repertoires, and the ways in which culture is constitutive of structures, institutions, identities, interests, grievances, goals, and strategies.

A focus on processes also has methodological implications. New settlements form through contentious social and political processes. The more that established arrangements are disrupted, the more contentious the process is likely to be. This approach suggests the examination of questions such as: what the rules of the game were before the field was thrown into crisis, how the field became unsettled, who the various actors with stakes in new framings of the field were, how the interests and identities of these actors were reconstructed through the political process, how actors constructed events to be consequential, what the alternatives were that actors were promoting, how one solution or another succeeded at organizing the field, and how the processes unfolded through time.

Studying field transformation and using theory from both institutional and social movements is consistent with the suggestion that social movement scholarship move away from narrow studies of the internal processes of movements (McAdam, Tarrow, and Tilly 2001). Social movement and institutional processes and theories are inextricably connected: we need to understand change to understand social order, and vice versa. Drawing simultaneously on the theories developed in both of these sociological traditions provides a powerful set of analytical tools. These approaches enable the explanation of field transformation in a variety of arenas in society, including economic, political, cultural, medical, educational, and sexual arenas.

Social Movement Organizations: Form and Structure

M uch of the literature on social movements focuses upon the determinants of participation. Why do some people with certain characteristics participate, while others who seem similar do not? How are some successful social movements able to generate involvement from bystanders and transform this potential into activism and, even harder, long time commitment, while other movements burn out? Clearly, social movements that endure for any length of time take on an organizational framework, morphing into social movement organizations (SMOs). SMOs appropriate many of the features and so share many of the advantages of formal organizations, including a known location and group of participants, recognition as a more or less legitimate player, and some continuity of mission and routines. By the same token, SMOs share many of the problems of other formal organizations. How is organizational authority sustained, especially as leaders turn over? What resources – financial, human, technical – are critical, and how are they combined across different SMOs? What is the division of labor between professionals and nonprofessionals, between staff and volunteers? How are SMOs organized across large geographical and geopolitical boundaries? How do they change over time? How do different SMOs sharing related goals that are part of the same movement (e.g., the environmental movement or the women's movement) cooperate, compete, and conflict with each other?

As we noted in the Preface, a concern with the organizational side of social movements goes back at least to the beginning of the last century. Scholars such as Michels (1962 [1911]) were concerned with the extent to which movements developed self-reproducing authority structures. Moreover, movement leaders took a strategic and organizational view of how movements were to proceed over the long haul. Lenin's (1969 [1902])

189

famous pamphlet, "What Is to Be Done?" presented an argument about the intersection of strategy and organizational form. Weber (1968 [1924]) was intrigued by the role of charisma in the creation of new organizations, and gave careful attention to the ways in which charisma must be routinized – either traditionalized or rationalized – if the movement is to be sustained. In spite of this history, it remains the fact that the literature on organizational theory has only occasionally been used to frame the issues of research on SMOs. All too often, when movements are sufficiently successful to become stable organizations, movement theorists lose interest. As elaborated by McAdam and Scott in Chapter 1, scholarship on movements and organizations all too often remains segregated – published in different journals and volumes and taught in different courses by faculty members who rarely attend to one another's ideas or concerns.

An early and important exception to this differentiation, if not outright segregation, characterizing relations between scholars and fields is the resource mobilization perspective developed during the 1960s by McCarthy, Zald, and colleagues. (Much of this work is collected in Zald and McCarthy 1987; see McCarthy and Zald 2001 for a recent review.) Their approach drew particularly on Selznick's (1948, 1949) institutional approach to organizations as well as organization theory more generally. Other scholars interested in activism at the local level, especially of the kind promoted by Saul Alinsky's Industrial Areas Foundation (Warren 2001), have paid close attention to the organizational aspect of activism.

Zald also pioneered in applying social movement concepts and arguments to the analysis of processes internal to organizations (Zald and Berger 1978). Related work in organizations employed a social conflict model to examine political processes within organizations (e.g., Dalton 1959; Gouldner 1954). In general, however, organizational students, such as March (1962) and Pfeffer (1981), who have examined power processes, drew on scholarly sources other than social movement theory for inspiration. It is only as organizational scholars have come to see social movements as sources of new ways of organizing and as generators of organizational change that the relevance of research on social movements has come to be appreciated.

The two essays in this section illustrate some of the continuing but newer ways in which social movement scholars draw on organizational concepts to examine the structuring of social movements. (The two concluding sections, in particular Section IV, will show the ways in which students of organizations are learning from movement scholars.) Although similar in this broad sense, the following essays are quite different in their focus. The first, in Chapter 7 by John D. McCarthy, shows how the concept of a franchise, originally developed as a form of business organization, can be used to understand the relationship of social movement organizations at the local level to national level SMOs. The second, by Jackie Smith, examines the organizational manifestation of transnational social movements.

National social movement organizations with widely dispersed local affiliates have been common since the turn of the twentieth century, and they have continued to proliferate in recent years. Early in the twenty-first century, approximately one quarter of local SMOs in the United States are affiliates of national organizations. Yet little scholarly attention has been directed at describing their common structural forms, the demography of the population, or the contrasting organizational logics that lead their founders and leaders to prefer one structural template to another. The recent emphasis upon professionalized national SMOs has diverted attention from an exploration of the role that local affiliates of national franchise SMOs play in facilitating individual activism. In Chapter 7, "Persistence and Change Among Federated Social Movement Organizations," John McCarthy makes national SMO franchises and their affiliates his substantive focus. He describes and explains the evolution of the population of national SMO franchises. After placing national franchises in context with respect to the potential variety of SMO forms, McCarthy proceeds to establish the prevalence of this affiliate form among local SMOs with members. A number of key dimensions of SMO franchise structure are explored, including a commonly recognized name and symbol, articulation between organizational levels, locus of member loyalty, territorial hegemony, locus and scope of control over financial affairs, the selection of goals, tactics, and operating procedures, and core technologies. The aim is to develop hypotheses about how national groups determine the optimum number of local affiliates. Possible explanations include the changing meaning of membership, the extent of vulnerability of national offices to liability for the actions of local affiliates, and the shifting nature of the primary task specializations of national franchise SMOs. Together, McCarthy's several hypotheses offer a multifaceted explanation for the decline in recent years in the average number of local affiliates of national SMO franchises.

In Chapter 8, "Globalization and Transnational Social Movement Organizations," Jackie Smith takes a quite different look at the spread and transformation of an SMO form, examining social movement organizations in a global context. The end of the Cold War brought important changes to the global political arena. Military security issues declined on the international agenda as environmental, economic, and social issues came to the fore. At the same time, the decline of superpower conflict created space for new attempts at multilateral problem solving. Her essay explores how these changes at the global level have affected the ways people organize transnationally to promote political and social change. Using data from the *Yearbook of International Associations*, Smith examines changes in the size, issue focus, geographic makeup, and organizational structure of the population of transnational social movement organizations (TSMOs) in recent decades. Although human rights and environmental concerns predominate on TSMO issue agendas, during the 1990s more groups adopted multi-issue organizing frames rather than a single-issue focus. A shift toward a greater emphasis on economic issues also occurred. The major divide in the global system between core and periphery is reflected in the population of TSMOs, but the data show that survival rates are more strongly linked to access to inter-governmental organizations and the legitimacy of groups than to the North-South divide. If the most recent patterns continue, however, the global South may be relatively less well incorporated into transnational organizing efforts. Past trends towards increasing percentages of TSMO members and headquarters in southern countries slowed or were reversed in the latest period. And more groups are organizing within, as opposed to across, regions than was true in the past. Finally, the data show a consistent trend towards greater decentralization in the organizational structures adopted by TSMOs.

These two essays make a convincing case for the relevance of organizational theory for the study of social movements.

7

Persistence and Change Among Nationally Federated Social Movements

John D. McCarthy

> While the implications of mass production and large scale administration fill the literature on organizations, the mass production of organizations itself – the cloning of a common set of practices in geographically dispersed units, which is what a chain does – has gone largely unnoticed. (Bradach 1998)
>
> A major problem facing companies with valuable brand names is controlling the actions of agents throughout the organization to assure the continued value of the trademark. (Brickley and Dark 1987: 403)

National social movement organizations (SMOs) with widely dispersed local affiliates have been common since the turn of the twentieth century when prototypical groups such as the National Association for the Advancement of Colored People (NAACP) were founded. Social movement groups like them have continued to proliferate up to the present. At the turn of the twenty-first century, I will show, approximately one quarter of local SMOs in the United States are affiliates of national ones. The majority of those local affiliates work to mobilize members and adherents for collective action projects. This portrait of the U.S. social movement sector, however, is at odds with increasingly widespread understandings of the predominant modern social movement form – "advocates without members" (Putnam 2000 and Skocpol 1999a) – and images of typical recent citizen behavior – "civic disengagement." The several intersecting puzzles that emerge from these contrasting images motivate the analyses that follow. In spite of the growth of professional social movement forms, why has the federated form that mobilizes local adherents and members remained a popular one among social change entrepreneurs as they have formed new

Jerry Davis, Erik Johnson, Andrew Martin, Assata Richards, Jackie Smith, Mark Wolfson, and Mayer Zald each provided helpful comments on earlier drafts, for which I am grateful.

SMOs? Has the form undergone noticeable changes in recent decades? What key theoretical mechanisms are most important in accounting for the persistence and change of the SMO federated form? I draw upon the insights of organizational sociology as I seek to understand how regulatory and other environmental influences shape the evolving nature of the population of federated SMOs in the United States. Ultimately, of course, the level of citizen activism is importantly dependent upon this population of organizations.

Images of the Post–World War II Evolution of the SMO Form

Impressions about the evolution of the population of SMOs over recent decades have been shaped by the great attention paid to examples of highly professionalized forms. For instance, Ralph Nader's Center for Auto Safety served as a prototype for Mayer Zald and me (1973) as we sketched the parameters of the professional social movement organizational form. Such groups have no members, depend upon grants for financial support and are run by experts who advocate the interests of a class of consumers, in this case, automobile owners.[1] Subsequently, Theda Skocpol (1999) has made the Children's Defense Fund (CDF) the poster child of the professional SMO form. Headed by Marian Wright Edelman, the CDF depends upon grants to fund its extensive advocacy on behalf of poor children, and has no members, either individual or organizational.

Many other well-known SMOs founded during the recent period do have members, but, as many have argued, membership for many of them consists mainly of financial support from afar (Putnam 2000, Skocpol 1999). Public Citizen, Inc., a key SMO of Ralph Nader's present extended network of organizations, is a classic example of this form. It raises most of its resources through direct mail solicitations, and those who donate to the group become members as a result. Other SMOs combine these checkbook members with a more traditional membership base. So, while Mothers Against Drunk Driving (MADD) claimed 3,200,000 members in 2002, the vast majority of them were neither local members nor local volunteers, but, instead, were individuals who had responded to telemarketing appeals for support of the organization and were counted as members only because they had donated money to MADD.

---

[1] Nader has during the last three decades spawned a wide variety of advocacy organizations similar in form (see Powers 1984).

Such forms of membership are not devoid of meaning for many members who join these organizations (see Minkoff 1997a and Smith 1998), and, as I have argued earlier (McCarthy 1987), the weak social ties that are established by such connection are regularly utilized to mobilize grassroots lobbying campaigns.[2] Nevertheless, membership of this kind rarely provides the opportunity for widespread activist involvement for members, nor is it likely to provide any face-to-face contact among checkbook members or between them and SMO leaders.

Widespread images of SMOs *without members* and with *checkbook members* have drawn attention away from both an empirical and a theoretical focus on more traditional SMO forms, and, as a result, have provided a distorted picture of the recent evolution of the population of national SMOs. SMO entrepreneurs have continued to create groups that do have membership of the more traditional kind which seek to recruit citizens into activist involvement in their local communities. Describing the persistence and change within the population of federated organizations is an important task because citizen engagement heavily depends upon the opportunities to participate that are presented to citizens by SMOs (Klandermans 1997; Verba et al. 1995). It is nationally federated SMOs with local chapter memberships that will be the major focus of attention here, since their constituent units make up a major segment of the population of local SMOs. I begin, however, by placing them within the full hypothetical range of SMO forms before I try to establish their prevalence.

Toward a Taxonomy of SMO Forms

I will return to a discussion of other characteristic dimensions of SMO structure, but in enumerating the range of SMO varieties, I focus here, consistent with my concern about federated forms, exclusively upon the hierarchical and geographical scope of SMO structures and whether or not they include membership. By hierarchical scope I mean whether a group includes any combination of local, state, regional, and/or national organizational units. By geographical scope I mean whether a group includes any combination of hierarchical levels across diverse locations. The first panel of Figure 7.1 pictures the full range of these possibilities for SMOs with

---

[2] Grassroots lobbying campaigns have become common in the United States. Business groups and interest groups of many varieties use similar techniques for mobilizing wide, if fleeting, activism on issues. Inept campaigns are known among professional grassroots lobbyists as "Astroturf."

Organization type

	I: Classic National Federation / I (a): National Professional Federation	II: State/Regional Federation / II (a): State Professional Federation	III: Centralized National Federation / III (a): Centralized National Professional Federation	IV: National Federation Without Locals / IV (a): National Professional Federation Without Locals	V: National Direct Membership / V (a): National Professional SMO	VI: State/Regional Direct Membership / VI (a): State Professional SMO	VII: Freestanding Locals / VII (a): Local Professional SMO
With Local Members / **Without** Local Members							
National Group	X		X	X	X		
State/Regional Groups	XX	X		XX		X	
Local Groups	XX	XX	XX				X

Figure 7.1 Logical Possibilities of SMO Organizational Form, by Hierarchical and Geographical Scope, Groups *with* and *without* Local Individual Members

members. For the moment let us ignore the mechanisms through which units across hierarchical and geographical levels are tied to one another, and the criteria of individual membership. Organizational units within and across any configuration of hierarchical and geographical levels would be included, as would SMOs with individual members of any kind. Within each type the presence of an X indicates that at least one organizational unit exists and two Xs indicate that multiple units exist at the specified hierarchical level.

Type I is the prototype of the classical SMO federated structure. Mothers Against Drunk Driving (MADD), the National Organization for Women (NOW), and the National Association for the Advancement of Colored People (NAACP) are examples of this form.[3] Each has a national headquarters, many state-level subunits, and a great many local chapters. Each group enrolls individual members. The Industrial Areas Foundation (IAF) and the Pacific Institute for Organizer Training (PICO), two congregational-based community-organizing networks, are other examples of a somewhat different variety. Each has a national headquarters, many local groups, but only a few state-level structures that serve to coordinate its local groups within states. In each case local groups enroll congregations and parishes as members and the individual members of those churches are deemed members. SMOs that enroll blocks of members are quite common.

The state federation (Type II) and the centralized national federation (Type III) are variations on the classical federation form in that they each include local chapters which are connected to either a regional or a national unit, but not both. I suspect that the centralized national federation is rare in the United States because of the typical decentralization of many political and social functions. As well, many classical federations began as state federations before they achieved national scope in chapter representation. For instance, MADD and the Association for Children for Enforcement of Support (ACES) began by proliferating chapters in the state in which they were founded (California for MADD and Ohio for ACES), and only thereafter began to develop chapters in other states, and subsequently state and regional offices in geographical areas of local chapter strength. It is the federated membership forms that are the substantive focus of my subsequent analyses.

---

[3] SMOs referred to in this and succeeding discussions are included in Table 7.1 with information on founding date, subunits, and membership, if any.

The national direct membership form (Type V) is one of those that have received so much recent attention. Public Citizen, Inc. is a good example of the type. In 2002 the group did not list a membership figure. Rather, membership dues of $20 guaranteed a subscription to *Public Citizen News* with a circulation of 150,000. I suspect that pure examples of this type are relatively rare, since many such groups tend to subsequently form state and/or local affiliates. An example is the National Abortion Rights Action League (NARAL). Originally the group resembled Public Citizen with a membership mobilized exclusively by direct mail solicitation and a Washington, D.C., headquarters staffed by paid and volunteer employees. As the abortion conflict shifted to the state level, NARAL proliferated state-level units, with 29 of them in 2002.

Freestanding locals (Type VII) are those locally based SMOs without formal affiliation to other organizations, although local SMOs may be affiliated through more temporary coalitional relations with other local SMOs. Local groups with no extralocal ties are probably the most numerous kind.

A full enumeration of SMO types includes a replication of those displayed in the first row of Figure 7.1, each similar in hierarchical and geographical form but lacking individual members. There are many variations of the professional social movement organization (McCarthy and Zald 1973), seen in the second row of Figure 7.1. Several of them are not federations. The Children's Defense Fund (CDF) epitomizes the national professional type, VI (a). Lacking systematic evidence, it is difficult to determine how common the State Professional type, VI(a), may be, but a recently formed California group, Children Now, appears to be a state level clone of the CDF. Its professional staff lobbies on children's issues at the state level and, like the CDF, it has no individual members.

Estimating the prevalence of the several professional federated SMO forms is difficult, but they are certainly rare compared to the classical national federation. They probably are not as common as nonfederated professional forms, but examples can be found. For example, the Partnership for a Drug Free America at present displays a national professional federated form with a national headquarters, state-level groups in most every state, and many local groups that are affiliates. The partnership does not have individual members, but mobilizes individuals and groups for state and local projects.

Describing the persistence and change of federated forms of SMOs in recent years would be facilitated by the existence of systematic enumerations of the social movement sector (SMS), for all of the SMOs in the United

States in a time series covering the last three or four decades, but nothing approaching such a data set now exists. This explains why we must struggle to describe the recent evolution of the SMS with particular attention to federated forms.

Local Affiliates of Classic National Federations: Glimpses of the Dark Matter

The difficulties in gaining empirical purchase on all of the SMOs that make up the SMS are well known to scholars of social movement organizations. In contrast to profit-making organizations, there is no comprehensive registration requirement for not-for-profit organizations, an important subset of which are SMOs. Formal Internal Revenue Service (IRS) charitable status (mostly 501(c)3 and 501(c)4 for SMOs) creates a class of registrants for which some organizational information is gathered and disseminated. But the filing of this information by registrants is notoriously incomplete, especially among smaller groups. Large numbers of small, usually local, organizations do not register. As a consequence, it is very difficult to develop estimates of the extent of local SMOs of the various types in the United States. It was the frustration at how this state of affairs has limited discourse about nonprofit organizations mostly to the large national ones that led David Horton Smith (1997) to speak of the "dark matter" of the nonprofit world – a very large part of the sector (in numbers of organizations, if not total revenues)[4] is hidden from view by a distorted map of its demography.

To overcome these well-known difficulties I have sought evidence developed through a number of different strategies to illuminate the prevalence of federated local outlets of national SMOs. Each approach generates estimates indicating a very strong presence of federation locals.

Enumerating Geographical Areas[5]　　Kempton and his colleagues (Kempton et al. 2001) carried out a comprehensive attempt to locate all of the local environmental groups in two areas: the Delmarva Peninsula (the peninsula that forms the Chesapeake Bay, which includes portions of Delaware,

[4] The size of SMOs is inversely proportional to their numbers, as is the case for other populations of organizations (Aldrich 1999).

[5] Kirsten Gronbjerg (1992) completed an exhaustive version of this approach by attempting to enumerate the local population of nonprofit social service organizations in Chicago.

Maryland, and Virginia) and the state of North Carolina. They followed up their census by contacting a sample of groups from each area. Twenty-four percent of the respondent groups on the Delmarva Peninsula were chapters of national groups as were 14 percent of those in North Carolina. The researchers were much more confident in the exhaustiveness of their Delmarva estimate, suggesting that their figure of about a quarter of the local SMOs being affiliates of national ones is the more accurate.

Bob Edwards and Kenneth Andrews (2002) also have enumerated environmental groups in North Carolina, and their preliminary estimates suggest that the number obtained by Kempton and his colleagues is probably an underestimate. Their data, based upon a more thorough enumeration of local North Carolina groups, yields an estimate much closer to that of Kempton and his colleagues for the Delmarva area – about 27 percent of the local environmental groups were chapters of national organizations.

Enumerating the SMOs of a Movement   Edwards and Foley (2002) recently analyzed a survey sample of peace movement organizations (PMOs) that were listed in a directory that had been compiled in an attempt to enumerate all such organizations in the United States in the mid-1980s. They found that of the small-budget, non-national groups, most of which were local, 41 percent were affiliated with another organization. If the proportion of local PMOs that are affiliated in any way is similar to that of the environmental locals enumerated by Kempton et al., then we arrive at an estimate of 24 percent of the local PMOs being affiliated with national movement organizations.

Information on Nationals with Local Outlets Based on IRS Filings   A number of researchers have used IRS nonprofit filing records in an effort to describe populations of SMOs (see Brulle 2000). The use of these records presents many difficulties, some of which I have already described. First, a large proportion of groups simply have not applied for and received nonprofit tax status, so they are not included in such records. Edwards and Foley (2002) estimated that more than 40 percent of the PMOs do not have formal nonprofit tax status.

Second, there is another problem inherent in developing estimates of the extent of penetration into local communities by classic national federations – many national groups apply for "group exemptions" and file group IRS tax returns; most such affiliated locals, then, do not file separate returns. The IRS labels the chapters of groups that so file "subordinate organizations." MADD, for instance, files a group exemption, as do many other federated SMOs.

An analysis was carried out by the National Center for Charitable Statistics (NCCS) (1997: 405–8) of the 1996 IRS Business Master File in order to estimate the extent of affiliate organizations. They concluded:

Although the number of parent organizations is small (1,772 in 1996), the number of affiliates is quite large. There were 126,864 affiliates on file with the IRS in 1996, up from 89,584 organizations listed in 1991 – a 42% increase. *Nearly one in five charitable 501(c)3 organizations in 1996 was an affiliate.* (Italics added.)

Most affiliates do not file 990 returns, those that are filed annually describing a group's revenues, expenditures and personnel. According to the IRS Business Master File, 21,169 organizations (17 percent of all affiliates) filed an IRS return within the preceding three years. Of the 105,695 organizations without returns, nearly 73,000 had completed the IRS biannual survey and indicated that their gross receipts were below the filing threshold of $25,000. Another 19,800 did not file because they held religious affiliations. About 13,100 organizations could not be positively tracked. Most likely, these organizations either have ceased to be active or are included on their parent organizations' group returns. (NCCS 1997: 406)

This evidence buttresses that of areal and movement enumerations suggesting that a sizeable proportion of local SMOs, approaching one quarter of them, are subunits of national, or at least, multistate, super-ordinate umbrella SMOs.

Estimating the Prevalence of National SMOs with Local Chapters from the Encyclopedia of Associations The *Encyclopedia of Associations* began publishing in 1958 and has been published annually for many years. It is also now available on the Web as the Associations Unlimited database (http://www.galenet.com/servlet/AU). The *Encyclopedia* seeks to list self-descriptions of all national nonprofit organizations in the United States, and has been used widely by scholars (e.g., Minkoff 1995, 1997).

In Table 7.1 I have assembled, primarily from the *Encyclopedia*, a set of groups listed in 2002 as working for social change. Many of them have local chapters and local members. A quick glance shows that many such groups estimate memberships that are probably primarily local ones. For instance, 9to5, which organizes female clerical workers, and ACES, which organizes women who have difficulties collecting child support from ex-spouses, each show a plausible number of local members, approximately

Table 7.1. *Selected Examples of National SMOs with Local Outlets (Current estimates unless otherwise specified)*

SMO Name	Year Founded	Members	State/ Regional	Local
MADD	1980	3,200,000	37	300
9to5	1973	13,000		25
ACLU	1920	275,000	53	200
Bread for the World	1973	44,000		400
Common Cause	1970	220,000	41	
NAACP	1909	400,000		1802
NORML	1970	80,000	80	
NOW	1966	250,000	50	500
Pax Christi	1972	14,000	29	500
YAF	1960	55,000		200
Gray Panthers	1970	40,000		60
ACES	1984	40,000	8	400
John Birch Society	1962	50,000		4,000*
PFLAG	1981	80,000	14	425
NRLC	1973		50	3000
IAF				75†
PICO				14†
DART	1982			17†
Gamaliel	1968			28†
Million Mom March	2000			40–45
NARAL	1969	400,000	29	
People for the American Way	1980	290,000	3	
Public Citizen	1971	150,000		
Habitat for Humanity	1976		15	1470
Amnesty International, USA	1961	300,000	1,800	400
Students for a Sensible Drug Policy	1998			132

Note: Except as otherwise indicated, all estimates are from Associations Unlimited or from the named organization's Website, March 2002.
* Estimate by Oliver and Furman (1990) for 1983–84.
† Estimates from various organizational Websites and Warren and Wood (2001).

500 per chapter for 9to5 and about 100 per chapter for ACES.[6] On the other hand, a group like MADD lists more that three million members; this contrasts with my estimates, based upon mid-1980s surveys of chapters, of a total of 25,000 to 40,000 somewhat active local members and volunteers

[6] It has been suggested (Oliver and Furman 1990) that local activist groups probably rarely engage even 100 members in any but the most superficial ways.

Table 7.2. *Percentage of Public Affairs Groups Listed in the 1995 Encyclopedia of Associations with Members and without Members, by Founding Period*

Founding Period	With Members %	Without Members %	N*
1969 and before	89	11	499
1970–1979	86	14	690
1980–1995	79	21	894
TOTAL	84	16	2,083

* The 1995 *Encyclopedia of Associations* lists 2,178 public affairs organizations, but only 2,083 of the entries include the founding date of the organization.

(McCarthy, Wolfson, and Harvey 1987). Most of the members of MADD listed in 2002 are members only through their donations to the group. Table 7.1 provides a picture of the range of currently active federated SMO groups. It shows extraordinarily wide variability in the number of local chapters, a subject to which I will return.

Tables 7.2 and 7.3 display membership data on all of the groups listed in the 1995 *Encyclopedia of Associations* in the "Public Affairs" category. Not all of the national groups that we might categorize as SMOs are included in this category, and many groups which are included are not SMOs.[7] Nevertheless, examining this list provides a rough glimpse of the extent of federated structures, and the extent of local chapters. Public Affairs groups made up a little over 9 percent of all groups listed in the 1995 *Encyclopedia*. In all, eighteen categories of groups are listed. Public Affairs shows the highest rate of growth in numbers of any category of groups from 1959 to 1995 – there were more than eighteen times as many groups listed in 1995 as there were in 1959 (Baumgartner and Leech 1998: 103).

I have divided the total population of Public Affairs groups into three founding periods: 1969 and before, 1970 to 1979, a decade of rapid growth in the founding of such groups (Walker 1991); and 1980 to 1995. For each organization, we know the number of regional, state, or local groups as well as whether or not the group had members.[8] We do see a pattern that matches

[7] Some groups which we might consider to be SMOs are listed under categories such as civil rights and liberties, conservative, disarmament, feminism, gay/lesbian, human rights, peace, religious freedom.

[8] Data of this form raise difficulties of interpretation as a result of left censoring – excluding groups that were founded earlier but have since disappeared. As a result the patterns shown here must be interpreted with caution.

Table 7.3. *The Number of Regional, State, and Local Units for Public Affairs Groups with Members Listed in the 1995 Encyclopedia of Associations, by Founding Period*

Founding Period	Regional Groups			State Groups			Local Chapters			Any Unit	
	% with	Mean	Median	% with	Mean	Median	% with	Mean	Median	% with	N*
Before 1969	12	77	6	12	35	38	13	343	62	28	443
1970–1979	12	17	7	11	38	32	13	120	29	25	592
1980–1995	12	33	6	12	28	10	14	111	23	28	706
TOTAL	12	36	6	12	33	20	13	170	30	27	1,741

* The 1995 *Encyclopedia of Associations* lists 2,178 public affairs organizations, but only 2,083 of the entries include the founding date of the organization. Of these, 1,741 have members.

the widespread image of a trend toward the founding of nonmembership SMOs over time. In the latest period, as seen in Table 7.2, there is a smaller proportion of new organizations founded with any kind of membership, 79 percent of the groups formed after 1979, than in the two earlier periods, 89 percent and 86 percent respectively. Nevertheless, it is notable that groups with any sort of individual membership, despite their declining proportion of groups founded, remain by far the most common kind of new group, even in the most recent period.

Yet, as seen in Table 7.3, for those groups founded *with any kind of membership*, no change is evident in the proportion of groups with any kind of affiliates over the three time periods. The proportion of national groups that have any regional, state, or local groups appears to remain remarkably stable (12 percent with regional and state groups and 13 percent with local groups). About a quarter of new groups founded in each period have affiliates at some level. Based on this population of national groups enumerated in 1995, then, we have some evidence to suggest that the rate of founding of federated SMOs with members has not declined during the past several decades, as the focus upon the emergence of professional SMOs has suggested.

Table 7.3 displays the average number of regional, state, and local groups listed for these organizations, by founding period. Since the distributions are highly skewed, the medians are most interpretable. Notably, there is no change in the number of regional affiliates by founding period. Most notable, however, is the pattern of decline in the median number of local chapters for groups founded after 1969. It falls by more than half between the first and second periods, then a bit more in the most recent period. That decline for groups founded during the last period may simply indicate, however, the length of time it takes a nationally federated group to complete the establishment of a desired number of local chapters. It is possible that a desired upper limit has not yet been achieved by many of the newly formed groups. The same logic for caution should guide interpretation of the precipitous decline in the median number of state groups, from thirty-two for groups founded during 1970–9 to ten for the 1980–95 period. In any case, the pattern most germane to the question I have raised is the marked decline in the median number of local chapters for groups founded after 1969.

The several sources of evidence assembled here make a strong case that a significant proportion of local SMOs are actually affiliates of national ones. Additionally, while national SMO federations continue to be founded, the ones founded during more recent years on average have created fewer local chapters. Examples of classic national federations founded during each time period under study are included in Table 7.1. The NAACP and the John Birch Society, founded in the first period, and the National Right to Life Committee and Habitat for Humanity, founded in the second period, each display substantial numbers of chapters (1,802, 4,000, 3,000, and 1,470, respectively). I have not been able to locate a federated SMO founded during the last two decades that has created chapter affiliate numbers of this magnitude.

These empirical patterns suggest the continuing importance of some mechanisms governing federated SMO formation and strategy as well as the increasing importance of new mechanisms at work in the more recent periods. I now turn to accounts of the evolution of the predominant structural dimensions of federated SMO forms, and the logics of local chapter expansion in recent periods.

Instability and Common Structural Sources of Tension and Conflict Within Classic Federated Social Movements

Sector Instability   SMOs in general, and federated SMOs in particular, represent highly unstable organizational forms. As a result, the population of federated SMOs can be expected to be especially sensitive to the environmental, cognitive, and relational organizational mechanisms that shape the structures and processes of any population of organizations (Campbell this volume). This instability is importantly the result of relatively weak state regulation of the sector, the multiple origins of federation constituents, and ongoing conflicts between central structures and constituent federated units.[9]

First, as Gaffney noted in his discussion of the formality of relations between affiliates and national nonprofits, "Non-profit organizations, being considerably less concerned with regulations and taxes, and not at all concerned with profit distributions, and being tied together through beliefs and social objectives, are likely to create informal, indistinct, and uncertain forms and systems of organization" (1984: 26). While nonprofit organizations in general and SMOs in particular are increasingly more likely since

---

[9] Minkoff (1999) demonstrated a remarkable stability in organizational social change strategy among women's and racial ethnic national SMOs, but was not able to trace similar rates of change in organizational structure among the groups.

Gaffney made this observation to display a concern with regulation and ever better elaborated and documented organizational forms (McCarthy et al. 1991), they remain relatively free of state surveillance and control. The consequence is a more heterogeneous range of federation structures and a high rate of experimentation with alternative structures.

Second, mature federated SMOs can be the result of a top-down process of formal chartering of local affiliates, a bottom-up process of coalition formation among previously freestanding local SMOs, or some combination of the two processes. Each of these federation origins brings with it tensions associated with issues of autonomy and control. The parameters of these tensions are typically written into organizational governance documents that vest more or less control over the SMO's name, organizational form, group activities, and, especially, financial matters with affiliates as opposed to federation headquarters. The two major federated SMOs associated with the citizens' movement against drunk driving, MADD and Remove Intoxicated Drivers (RID), illustrate these alternatives. MADD has developed mostly by chartering new local affiliates with clear guidelines about how local groups may operate, and may withdraw the charter of a noncompliant chapter. RID, on the other hand, represents a coalition of previously independent local groups, many of which jealously guard their independence (McCarthy and Wolfson 1996). During the last decade, however, many local groups have switched their allegiance from one federation to the other.

Third, such instability stems, importantly, from conflict over authority and control relations between national headquarters and local affiliates, regardless of the dynamic origins of a federation. Federations typically are beset with chronic conflict over such issues, as is well illustrated in the histories of Committee for a Sane Nuclear Policy (SANE) (Katz 1986), the Anti-Saloon League (Kerr 1985), and the Southern Farmer's Alliance (Schwartz 1976). The many structural tensions inherent in classic national federations lead these organizations toward regular reassessment and tinkering since the reality of creating formally organized structures for creating social change typically evolves through a series of contested choices. Such conflict creates great instability and probably accentuates the impact of institutional mechanisms upon resulting SMO forms.

Sources of Tension and Conflict Within Federations   Each of the key dimensions of the classic federated social movement form can become the subject of contention among the constituent units of a federation. The great advantages of federated structures, widely dispersed mobilization around shared goals with common strategies, are inevitably accompanied by problems of coordination and control. Many of these dimensions mirror features of the for-profit franchise form (Bradach 1998), and similar tensions around them beset franchises, as well.

A Commonly Recognized Group Name (Logo and Acronym)   When collective actors choose a name for their formally organized efforts they create an image about the purposes their group embodies. This is as true for SMOs as it is for firms. SMO group names typically include "citizen" and commonly convey group-ness with terms such as "league," "committee," and "federation." Many such names become household words when they yield pronounceable acronyms, such as ACLU (American Civil Liberties Union), SDS, PFLAG (Parents and Friends of Lesbians and Gays), NOW, PETA (People for the Ethical Treatment of Animals), MADD, SANE, or commonly understood nicknames, such as Amnesty and Habitat. Many times names are chosen in the early stages of organization building and then change as the purposes of the SMOs evolve. For instance, MADD initially stood for Mothers Against Drunk Drivers, and was subsequently changed to Mothers Against Drunk Driving. NARAL initially stood for the National Association for the Repeal of Abortion Laws. It was later changed to the National Abortion Rights Action League, and subsequently the National Abortion and Reproductive Action League, all the while maintaining fidelity to its original acronym. In a short but organizationally eventful period of seven years the emergent National Emergency Committee of Clergy Concerned About Vietnam, begun early in 1966, became Clergy and Laymen Concerned About Vietnam (CALCAV) later that year, Clergy and Laymen Concerned (CALC) in 1970, and, ultimately, Clergy and Laity Concerned (still CALC) in 1972 (Hall 1990).

When an SMO develops dispersed units, commonly recognized names can be very useful for a variety of reasons. The name serves, of course, as a sense of common identity among activists beyond symbolizing who the activists are (Clemens 1997). A group of citizens in a small community speaking in the name of a well-known, widely dispersed national SMO can gain immediate credibility. Its presence in a local community can also signal, yet again, the deep local support that the national conglomerate commands. Widely dispersed groups using the same name are, as a consequence, interdependent with units in other locations. Because using the same names implies that groups are speaking with a single voice, inevitably disputes arise as to the conditions for the use of the SMO name. As well, new groups that form under the name of a nationally known group have distinct advantages (McCarthy and Wolfson 1996).

A brief comparison between MADD and RID is instructive here. MADD very strictly regulates the use of its name by local groups. Unless a group complies with a very elaborate set of guidelines of operation, its right to be a chapter of MADD can be withdrawn, as has happened with a number of local groups. Others have voluntarily chosen to give up the use of the name and the associated rights, reminiscent of the dispute between national SANE and several of its early chapters that chose to disaffiliate (Katz 1986). For the local MADD groups, the name is usually seen as an incredible asset, and the right to use it in pursuing collective action is typically given up only reluctantly. On the other hand, some local RID groups that have voluntarily affiliated with the national organization are rather casual in their use of its name and associated logo. Several of these groups established strong local reputations in the fight against drunken driving before they affiliated with national RID. In these cases the national leaders are the ones encouraging local groups to, as they phrase it, "Fly the RID Flag." Their inability to enforce the use of the name and logo reflects the nature of central RID's relationship with its affiliates, as will be discussed below.

The symbolic importance of a group name and the advantages that accrue to those who can use it are seen also in the series of struggles around the control of CORE in recent years. The Congress of Racial Equality, a centralized national federation, became a widely respected SMO during the heyday of the civil rights movement (Meier and Rudwick 1973). When control of the SMO fell into the hands of Roy Innis, who pursued very different purposes while engaging in deceptive fundraising practices, all the while using the public legitimacy that attached to the organizational name, several other civil rights leaders tried, unsuccessfully, to wrest back control of the organization from Innis (Rule 1981). Had Innis pursued these purposes with a different organizational name, it is unlikely that any effort to oust him would have been made.

The great advantages of nationally known social change name brands, however, do not mean that all franchise-like SMOs make it a requirement of affiliation, or even necessarily promote it. A good example is the Industrial Areas Foundation (IAF) groups (Rogers 1990; Rooney 1995; Warren 2001; Warren and Wood 2001). These are the widely admired local congregation-based community organizations that seek to organize and empower poor communities by knitting together local congregations and parishes, the best known of which are Communities Organized for Community Service

(COPS) in San Antonio, and BUILD in Baltimore. Local groups are relatively tightly coupled to the national IAF organization through both its control of the appointment of local lead organizers and ongoing indoctrination of leaders in its signature tactics of community organizing. Each local group has its own distinct and locally resonant name and only rarely prominently displays its status as an affiliate of IAF. As a consequence, despite the presence of IAF groups in many communities across the United States, the IAF does not have very wide national name recognition. Newly formed groups, therefore, must establish themselves one by one at the local level without the benefit of preexisting local knowledge of the IAF approach. On the other hand, those same newly forming groups do not carry the potential baggage of their successful co-affiliates in other communities, which, in some cases, has been quite controversial.

It is not obvious how common the IAF practice is among SMO federations since we do not usually recognize the local affiliates of groups that do not operate under clearly projected names and symbolic images. It is worth noting, however, that an early study of for-profit franchise contracts found that only a few more than half of them included any restriction on the use of franchiser trade names (Udell 1972).

Articulation Between Hierarchical Levels   Analysts of SMOs have often discussed the distinct levels of organizational structure that many of them display (Lofland and Jamison 1985; Oliver and Furman 1990; Young 1989; Zald 1970a). I have chosen to focus primarily on federations that have at least two levels, including one national and one local. The local groups are usually referred to as chapters or locals. National offices are sometimes called headquarters, national, or central.

As SMO structures are established and evolve, there are commonly recurring debates about whether and how to best structure geographically dispersed groups into smaller regional, state, or county combinations as well as which intermediate levels of structure, if any, will be most useful in pursuing group goals. A variety of factors shape this ongoing decision making. These include the correspondence between an SMO's strategy and purposes and the appropriate political unit or units of focus. Many groups combine their local units by congressional district because they invest great energy in attempting to influence the national legislative process. The National SANE/Freeze clustering was organized on this principle. The Southern Farmer's Alliance, an earlier SMO displaying franchise-like features, was organized by county because it was seen as the most appropriate

210

political unit for clustering local groups (Schwartz 1976). Regional clustering that crosses state boundaries is also common, as it was for many of the
groups enumerated by Kempton and his colleagues (2001) that operated on
the Delmarva Peninsula. For many groups, however, state seems to be the
most appropriate choice, especially because of the great decentralization of
policymaking in the United States.

Another contingency in the choice of subnational combination strategies is the historical evolution of geographical concentration. SANE, for
instance, developed state units where its chapters were most highly concentrated, New York and California. MADD developed state-level structures
as the concentration of local groups progressed. ACES developed regional
clusters based upon their naturally occurring concentration so that coordinators could most efficiently travel between local chapter locations.

It is my observation that very few, if any, SMOs develop more than three
levels of structure, but it is quite common for them to develop at least
one level of intermediate structure between nationals and locals. A primary
issue once such an intermediate level is created is how it maps onto the
authority structure of the SMO. By the late 1980s MADD, for instance, had
developed quite a few state units – they listed 37 such units in 2002. These
units, while staffed by state activists, reported directly to the national office,
as did the local chapters. The state units did not serve as an intermediary
level of authority in the relations between the national organization and the
local chapters. In the case of ACES, regional coordinators were appointed
by the central office and did serve as intermediate levels of authority and
decision making. Authority relations between levels of SMO structure are
not typically transparent, so as a result it is quite difficult to estimate modal
patterns at any point in time and even more difficult to describe changes in
those patterns.

Locus of Local Member Loyalty   Federated SMOs show a variety of patterns of individual membership, with several possibilities stemming from
the multiple levels of organizational units. These include most prominently:
1) membership in a local automatically means that one is also a member
of the larger entity; 2) membership in the local is one form of attachment
to the national, but the same individual, at the same time, may be directly,
without intermediation, a member of the national; 3) a resident of the catchment area of a local chapter may be a member of the national SMO without
any connection to the local group; and 4) one becomes a member of the
SMO by virtue of attachment to a local, but cannot be directly a member

of the national, which is constituted only of organizational members. This synthetic analytic review of the range of membership types, however, may suggest more order to such designations than actually exists. Gaffney (1984: 24), in his review of issues of legal liability among nonprofit entities such as federated SMOs, noted, "Procedures for becoming a member are often left unclear, as are procedures for terminating their status. Many persons become unwitting members of a non-profit organization, under that organization's bylaws, by subscribing to a magazine or making a donation."

The second wave of the Ku Klux Klan (KKK) exhibits a classic example of the first form of membership noted above. Local groups enrolled members in the KKK. They became, as a result, members of the national organization. Their connection with the national SMO was mediated through state groups. One could join only through membership in a local group (Chalmers 1987; Wade 1998). This was also the case for the NAACP (Gaffney 1984). Many modern SMOs, however, exhibit a combination of the second and third types of membership, where individuals may join local groups, and thereby become members of the national organization, or they may join the national organization directly through the mail. Sometimes individuals may do both. This means that in the territory of any local chapter affiliate there might exist SMO members who are connected to it and/or to the national organization. This is the case for MADD, and also for the ACLU, producing a pattern of bifurcated membership.

This combination is, I believe, the far more common pattern among recently formed groups than the more traditional one seen in the KKK, and it probably is also common among groups that were formed earlier but have adapted to the advent of modern technologies. Direct mail and telemarketing technologies have become common among SMO federations, since they can provide relatively stable flows of resources. There are several probable consequences of bifurcated memberships for federated nationals and their chapters. For example, it may put them in competition for members' resources. Until MADD developed a resource distribution formula acceptable to local chapters, it experienced great conflict between locals and the national office over the proceeds of national telemarketing and the rules governing local fundraising. In addition, conflicts may develop over access to national and local membership lists.

The Southern Christian Leadership Conference (SCLC), Habitat for Humanity, and the IAF are examples of the fourth type, multitiered structures that are organizations of organizations. For these groups, while local members can develop an intense identity with a national movement, there is no conception of membership in a national organization. Instead, individuals are members of local units that affiliate as corporate members of broader structures, or as in the case of Habitat, project volunteers (Baggett 2001).

Local Territorial Hegemony   Local SMOs often compete with other local groups pursuing similar social change goals for volunteers, members, financial contributions, gifts in kind, and the attention of mass media, political elites, and the general public (Zald and McCarthy 1980). Affiliation with a widely recognized national or regional SMO may improve a local SMO's competitive position. This is even more likely if the national SMO is favorably viewed among the segment(s) of the local population that the local SMO seeks to mobilize. Therefore, it can be to the advantage of a local SMO to obtain a guarantee that other SMOs occupying the same niche – that is, groups using the same or highly similar tactical, strategic, and operational formulae, and using the same name – will be excluded from the local area in which the SMO operates. So there may be strong incentives for local chapter leaders to oppose the proliferation of additional groups in their communities. Territorial hegemony is widely imagined as one of the key features of for-profit franchise chains, but Udell's (1972) early survey of franchise contracts suggests that it is not a defining characteristic of them, since he found less than 60 percent of the contracts to include any reference to "exclusive territory."

From the point of view of the central SMO headquarters too, it may be desirable to allow only one affiliated SMO to operate in a particular locality. To sanction more than one can lead to difficulties of coordination and control for the central headquarters, to the extent that several local chapters in the same community may compete with one another for members and resources, as well as notoriety.

In practice, federated SMOs do restrict the number of affiliates in a particular geographic area. MADD, for instance, did not allow more than one chapter in a county, although it created a new form that it called "satellites," allowing spin-off groups to pursue specific projects in large and densely populated counties where a chapter already existed. SMOs that use block mobilization through churches and other preexisting social formations to create local groups, on the other hand, may be less likely to depend upon such an exclusive mechanism. Sometimes, it is probably the operation of local norms that limits local expansion. The rapid proliferation of Students for a Democratic Society (SDS) chapters across college and university campuses during the late 1960s (Sale 1973) suggests such a pattern. In the space of a very short time several thousand local chapters of SDS were formed, but there was almost no duplication of chapters on the same campus.

Most federated SMO local leaders probably have a good sense of the scope of their group's territorial coverage, and can easily name the geographical boundaries from which it recruits and which it serves. As well, funding sources such as foundations typically ask groups to specify their target areas. The Catholic Campaign for Human Development, for instance, asks applicants who propose to organize the residents of poor communities to specify the area they intend to serve and from which they intend to recruit members (McCarthy and Castelli 1994). When I surveyed MADD chapters in 1986, there was no more than one chapter in any U.S. county. When asked to describe the boundaries of their territory by listing other counties and/or parts of counties within which they recruited members, all respondents were able to do so without difficulty. Most groups conceived their recruitment catchment area to be broader than their residence county. In 1985 15 percent of all U.S. counties had a local anti-drunk driving group (either MADD or RID) and those counties included 55 percent of the U.S. population. Their recruitment counties, on the other hand, included 24 percent of U.S. counties containing 67 percent of the U.S. population. Calculating the geographical coverage of these groups (a total of about 400) by their penetration of media markets showed that their activities would have been covered in markets that included 95 percent of the U.S. population (McCarthy et al. 1987).

Locus and Scope of Financial Control   A key dimension of central-local relations for federations is the degree and scope of the national headquarters' control over a local chapter's financial affairs. Theoretically that control may range from very little, with almost no monitoring (as with SDS, where the central office had more than enough trouble just keeping an updated list of current affiliates), through simple reporting requirements, all the way up to extensive controls that entail spot auditing. In practice, since most SMO affiliates have relatively little in the way of financial resources, central SMO control over the finances of local affiliates tends more toward the looser control end of the continuum. There are, however, reasons to suggest that national leaders of some federated SMOs have a great stake in the control of local financial affairs.

When I surveyed local MADD chapters in 1986, I discovered that their median annual revenue had been about $1,300 in the previous year

214

(McCarthy et al. 1987). While some of the local member dues were supposed to be remitted to the national office, in the aggregate that sum was an insignificant part of the total budget of the national office, which at the time was about eight million dollars. About 15 percent of the local chapters reported annual revenues of more than $25,000, the trigger to requiring freestanding nonprofits to file IRS reports. This portrait of local chapter finances mirrors the analysis of the IRS survey of nonprofit affiliates discussed earlier (National Center for Charitable Statistics 1997). They found that 17 percent of the local affiliates had annual budgets under $25,000. None of the local chapters we surveyed owned any property. Some rented space, many used loaned space for an office, and many other groups were located in the home of the chapter president.[10]

If MADD is at all typical of national SMO federations, then, whatever extent of control they might exert over local chapters is probably not motivated by an effort to mobilize greater revenues through local dues pass-through mechanisms, but rather by concerns of fiduciary responsibility.[11] On the other hand, earlier federated national offices, such as those of the KKK and the Anti-Saloon League, were motivated by such concerns since they depended to a great extent upon dues pass-through. With the ascendance of other revenue streams for contemporary SMOs, such as direct mail, telemarketing, and grants from many institutional sources, dependence upon dues from local chapters appears to have declined in importance in recent years.

This does not mean, however, that federation national offices have no interest in the financial affairs of local affiliates. Since they are both symbolically and legally connected to their local affiliates, national federation leaders have cause to worry about both the notoriety associated with financial scandal and potential fiduciary responsibility. First, federation name brands can be tarnished by financial scandals that involve local affiliates, providing an incentive to avoid them.

Second, many local chapters enjoy a tax–exempt/tax-deductible (501(c)3) status by virtue of their affiliation with the central federation. This is

---

[10] Udell's (1972) review of for-profit franchise contracts showed, in contrast, how central financial pass-through arrangements are to those franchiser-franchisee relationships.

[11] It is important to note that the central office's financial control over a federation local is often rather weak compared to that seen in business versions of the franchise form. One reflection of this is the fact that central MADD has at times sponsored contests among its chapters in order to encourage greater adherence to the central office's financial reporting requirements.

common as the IRS data on affiliates, discussed above, demonstrated. Such an arrangement provides the federation headquarters with another incentive for exerting some degree of financial control as a result of its fiduciary responsibility for its component parts. For example, local affiliates of national groups that file group exemptions are subject to limitations on the amount of money that can be spent on lobbying for passage of state legislation. Therefore, restrictions are imposed by the central organization, as they are by MADD, to protect the whole organization's 501(c)3 status, as the federal tax code and subsequent rulings impose limits on the expenditures of funds for lobbying by tax–exempt/tax–deductible organizations (see McCarthy et al. 1991). Gaffney (1984) termed this general issue the problem of *ascending liability*. He reviewed the substantial case law and appellate rulings about the conditions under which religious denominational structures can be held liable for the behavior of their congregational affiliates. I have been unable, however, to find much trace of litigation over ascending liability for SMO federations. This does not guarantee, however, that federated SMO leaders are not privy to legal advice by lawyers from the "nonprofit bar" couched in terms of financial liability, since many nationally federated SMOs have very "deep pockets" indeed.

One strategy by which a national federation may escape the legal fiduciary responsibilities of ascending liability is to design local affiliates as stand-alone legal entities. This is the strategy used by Habitat for Humanity (Baggett 2001). Before achieving affiliate status a local Habitat group must apply for its own individual 501(c)3 designation. The national group, then, is shielded from financial responsibility for the behavior of local groups, if not from the damage to the group's reputation that might stem from local financial mismanagement. This structural strategy is not, however, a very common one among federated SMOs.

Selection of Goals, Tactics, and Operating Procedures Federation leaders provide templates to local affiliates that allow them to pursue somewhat uniform approaches to social change in diverse locations. National groups develop signature tactics along with a menu of interrelated goals that are offered to chapters as suggested lines of action, along with structural and operational templates. The issues of control of affiliates, analogous to those confronting for-profit franchises, that were raised above are central to a federation's ability to effectively provide a standard social change product. There are a number of control mechanisms that are commonly employed, including 1) formalized templates, 2) chartering procedures, 3) choosing and training leaders, and 4) monitoring.

Several devices are employed by national leaders aimed at creating some uniformity in goals and tactics among local chapters. These include the preparation of written materials describing them and, probably more importantly, face-to-face interaction between national and local leaders. MADD, for instance, holds regular workshops for local leaders where many of them are assembled for several days where sessions on goals, tactics, and operating procedures are offered. I have attended several of these sessions and they typically are staffed by some combination of experienced local leaders, outside consultants, and national office employees. Many of the sessions are based upon the explicit premise that local conditions vary tremendously, so that leaders must adapt the general templates that are offered to their own specific local circumstances. A wide range of video, audio, and written material is made available at these workshops, much of it produced by the central office or by supporting organizations or agencies, such as insurance companies and the National Highway Transportation Safety Administration.

Standard operating procedures were also specified in a MADD Chapter Handbook, which included rules about accounting and record keeping, as well as the recruiting and training of volunteers. During its rapid growth phase, MADD required a program of self–study – a sort of correspondence course – for the presidents of chapters in the process of forming or chartering a local affiliate (Meyer 1970). Prospective chapter leaders were required to go through a number of stages before a chapter could become a fully chartered MADD group. The same is true for ACES, which provides a seventy-five-page Chapter Handbook to each chapter leader describing the structure of the organization, responsibilities of officers, dues and fundraising policies, and procedures for recruitment of members and volunteers. Habitat for Humanity has developed an even more elaborate chartering process. Baggett says of this process, "From start to finish the affiliation process takes from nine to twelve months. The intentionality, comprehensiveness and sheer length of the process is a function of Habitat International's deep concern that its affiliates be formed as full-fledged incarnations of the Habitat ethos.... [The process is outlined in] a two volume orientation handbook ... [that describes] no fewer than seventy-seven steps" (2001: 75).

In the middle 1980s the primary contact between MADD's central office and local leaders was the chapter affairs coordinator. The occupant of that position was in regular telephone contact with leaders across the country, traveled widely, making visits to local groups, and made an effort to monitor the activities of those groups that displayed signs of weakness or major deviation from the central office's understanding of appropriate behavior by chapters.

As MADD matured into the late 1980s the group experienced conflict between the central office and chapters over a number of issues including fundraising techniques and appropriate behavior. National leaders were particularly concerned with fundraising behavior since the national group had been heavily criticized for its fundraising practices. As well, the national leaders regularly reminded local leaders about the lobbying and partisan political activity restrictions that inhered in their status as affiliates of MADD through its formal IRS registration. Many local leaders were active in lobbying their state legislatures, and few of them came to the drunk driving issue with any previous political experience. It was this particular combination of vigorous agency and political naivete that caused the national leaders, and their lawyers, so much concern.

One national leader used the "herding cats" imagery to capture what she saw as the difficulties of keeping chapters in line and effectively working toward what the national office saw as important goals, most importantly community awareness of the drunk driving issue. Ultimately, the national office had the weapon of taking control of a recalcitrant local chapter, and, in several notorious cases, MADD central took possession of the offices, files, and finances of chapters, installing new replacement leaders.

In contrast to MADD, the Industrial Areas Foundation's control over goals, tactics, and operating procedures is more direct through its choice of a local chapter's "lead organizer." These IAF staff are recruited, trained, and evaluated in a variety of organizing tasks before they are given responsibility for a local affiliate (Warren 2001). Rather than attempting to establish bureaucratic control through extensive written regulations, monitoring, and social control, the IAF instead selects and intensively trains "community organizers." Candidates are screened and then given a probationary period of training. If they are retained they move through a series of apprenticeship positions where they work with more experienced organizers until they are assigned responsibility as a "lead organizer," who is the main representative of the IAF in the local group. As organizers move through this elaborate system they undergo ongoing training in the principles of the IAF, so that local groups tend to employ quite similar technologies of organizing poor communities.

IAF groups take an interest in a wide variety of local issues including education, housing, and crime. An ongoing deliberative process that includes a wide representation from constituent groups determines which issue any particular group chooses to pursue. The process by which issues are chosen and the template for building a local group and involving the group in local politics are highly uniform across the IAF groups, and appear to also characterize the groups that make up other congregation-based networks of community organizations that have modeled their approach after the IAF (such as Gamaliel, DART, and PICO). For all of these groups the template for federation operation is embedded in the experience of the "lead organizer." As a result, the proliferation of local chapters occurs much more slowly for them than for groups such as MADD, where chapter proliferation occurred far more rapidly. Table 7.1 includes crude estimates of the number of congregation-based community organizations for each of the four national networks named above, and, as can be observed, the total number of local chapters still does not reach the number of MADD chapters.

Core Technologies   SMO federations can be usefully characterized by their primary specialization along the lines of Minkoff's analyses of women's and racial/ethnic SMOs (1995). She distinguished among advocacy, service, and protest emphases. Many groups combine one or another of these primary approaches to social change, and an exhaustive typology probably would include a number of other primary approaches. Public education or community awareness, for instance, has been a primary concern for MADD, what Klandermans (1997) termed "consensus mobilization." Local MADD chapters display a variety of mixes of these general emphases, as do local IAF groups. Some of them, for instance, are much more deeply involved in providing low-cost housing than others. Pursuing each emphasis requires different skills and is more or less labor intensive. For example, Habitat for Humanity's work is especially labor intensive, which explains why the group reports mobilizing hundreds of thousands of volunteers each year (Baggett 2001). The key dimensions of core social change technologies are 1) the extent to which they are labor intensive, and 2) the extent to which any volunteer, no matter their human capital, can contribute useful labor (Oliver and Marwell 1992). These features of social change core technologies shape federation decisions about the recruitment and deployment of volunteer and paid labor.

Processes Shaping the Population of Federated SMOs

Patterns of national federation births and deaths along with organizational change on the part of surviving SMOs shape the characteristics of the population through time (Aldrich 1999; Scott 2003). There are certainly many cases of what Rao and his colleagues (Rao and Singh 1999; Rao et al. 2000) call weak speciation, by which they mean partial innovation in organizational form. These variations may occur at founding, and also may occur as national federations adapt and adjust their many features over time. My approach to federation formation and change emphasizes both agency and the central importance of institutional processes (Scott 2001).

Organizational Mechanisms   I highlight three mechanisms that together form the backbone of my hypothetical account of the patterns of change and persistence in the population of SMO federations over recent decades: 1) political opportunity/societal sectorization; 2) state regulation of non-profit organizational forms; and 3) internal organizational and membership imperatives of federations. The operation and impact of these mechanisms was illustrated in the foregoing discussion of structural tensions within federated SMOs.

Political Opportunity/Societal Sectorization   The relatively decentralized structure of the U.S. state and the consequently fragmented and dispersed sites of public policymaking offer multiple hierarchical and geographical targets for SMOs aiming to influence public policies (Campbell this volume). Since the early part of the twentieth century movements such as Prohibition (Kerr 1985) and suffrage (McCammon 2002) have created classic federated structures penetrating U.S. states and localities. Scott and Meyer (1991) showed the similar proliferation of multiple levels and organizational units among public organizations, professional associations, and firms, and went on to spell out how organizations that operate in such fragmented and complex environments can be expected to, in turn, develop more complex internal structures. As well, the growing policy importance of the federal level in the latter half of the century has, in general, led to greater centralization of authority and finances across institutional organizational sectors.

State Regulation   While state regulation of nonprofit organizational forms is not as pervasive as for profit-making ones, the extent and impact of state regulation have been growing in recent decades (McCarthy et al. 1991). Such regulation has effects upon both the strategy and the structure of SMOs (Cress 1997), operating primarily through Internal Revenue Service rules governing registered nonprofit organizations. While many freestanding local and some state level SMOs may not be formally registered with the IRS, very few nationally federated SMOs remain "unofficial." The likelihood of registration for such groups expanded dramatically through the last three decades with the consequence that during that time SMOs were increasingly likely to be concerned with the relevant regulations as they structured and restructures themselves. Central to these concerns have been issues of ascending liability, or the responsibility of national federations for the actions of local affiliates.

Internal Organizational Imperatives of Federation Forms   Social movement analysts have tended to ignore issues arising out of the consideration of federated structures.[12] On the other hand, organizational researchers have devoted extensive attention to a set of parallel issues in for-profit "federations" or "chain" structures. Because federated SMOs are nonprofits, however, the framing of some issues of central concern to those who study for-profit franchising is not directly germane to federated SMOs. For instance, the literature on for-profit franchising has been dominated by an exploration of the logics that govern decisions by national franchisers to expand either by contracting with independently owned local franchisers or by creating wholly owned outlets (or some combination of the two forms). (e.g., Baucus and Baucus 1996; Brown 1998, Kaufmann et al. 2000; Oster 1996; Williams 1999) Nevertheless, the issues raised by such analyses are quite relevant to the dilemmas faced by the leaders of federated SMOs (Brickley and Dark 1987). A key problem for both franchise and federation leaders is ensuring the integrity and uniformity of the organizational product. The franchise solution allows local owners (affiliate leaders) to partake in the profits of the enterprise. This solution is not possible for local SMO affiliates that, first, are nonprofit groups, and, second, are unlikely to generate high levels of resources in any case. Choosing the wholly owned outlet solution for a franchiser carries with it diverse problems of controlling the behavior of local agents. Solving these problems through monitoring, for instance, may be quite costly. Federated SMOs, however, have no alternatives to creating monitoring systems in order to attempt to control the behavior of local affiliates. They do not, typically, have the luxury of surplus resources that for-profit franchisers do for carrying out such tasks. The high priority and extensive resources that federated SMOs devote to the control of affiliate behavior, then, are illuminated by franchise studies. An

---

[12] For notable exceptions, see Zald (1979a) and Zald and Ash (1966).

SMO that seeks to create a federated structure cannot avoid confronting the ongoing difficulties of the control of local agents.

Hypotheses   These hypotheses are motivated by a search for the logics by which leaders *choose their desired number of local chapters*, as well as the tasks that those chapters create for local members. In for-profit franchises the increased profits derived from adding additional organizational units can be expected to lead to expansionary approaches possibly dampened only by competition and by issues of coordination and control. On the other hand, it appears clear that SMO federation leaders have placed governors on chapter expansion in recent years. I will specify some families of logics that appear to affect that choice, and then develop some illustrative hypotheses for each family.

Member Logics   It is clear that the meaning of local individual membership for federated SMOs has changed during recent decades, as has membership in SMOs more generally. This change has strong implications for how federation leaders think about whether to invest resources in expansion of the number of local affiliates. This insight makes sense of evidence I have collected from local MADD affiliates. In my 1986 survey, it became clear that many of the groups invested rather little effort or thought in recruiting local members beyond the twenty they needed to be chartered as a chapter. In my 1990 survey I asked the direct question, "In the last year did your group make any systematic effort to recruit members?" More than 40 percent of the groups' leaders answered no, and the majority of those that answer yes had not put great effort into doing so.

H1: To the extent that a national SMO federation does not need local members as a source of financial support, it will be less inclined to encourage extensive proliferation of local chapters, and, therefore, decisions on chapter proliferation will be governed by other organizational logics.

H2: To the extent that a national SMO federation does not need local members as a source of financial support, its decisions about whether to encourage extensive recruitment of local members will be governed by other organizational logics.

I have worded these hypotheses to apply to individual federated organizations. However, to the extent that federated SMOs in general do not need members for financial support, these processes will have consequences for the entire population of federated SMOs.

Organizational Control Logics   When federation national offices are tightly coupled with their local affiliates through an IRS group exemption or explicit written agreements, those offices become liable for some behavior and activities of their chapters. Those liabilities may be financial, or have financial consequences, or they may be regulative, through the possibilities of sanctions by IRS. In fact, it is not easy to find many cases where federated nationals have suffered such consequences because of their potential liability. Nevertheless, many federation leaders are especially sensitive to such possibilities. Organizational decision making based upon these contingencies is likely to be especially affected by institutional processes through professional contacts between national leaders, through the aid of movement technical assistance providers, and through the solicitation of advice from the "nonprofit bar."

H3: National federations that are tightly coupled (e.g., those that file group exemptions and/or have written agreements that connect them) with their subordinate chapters will tend to limit the number of local chapters they form because chapter proliferation expands their vulnerability to violations of IRS regulations, and, hence, their IRS charitable status.

H4: National federations that are tightly coupled with their subordinate chapters will tend to limit the number of chapters they form because chapter proliferation expands their vulnerability to civil liability claims based upon the behavior of local groups.

Core Technology Logics   The activities that federation affiliates choose to emphasize have consequences for the task structures they create and, therefore, the extent to which they need local members for something other than their ability to contribute financial resources. Volunteer labor is most useful at the local level, but organizing and maintaining it can be quite demanding (Oliver and Marwell 1992). To the extent that local groups specialize in media strategies to create public awareness or lobbying rather than approaches that entail offering labor-intensive services or mobilizing many citizens for political participation, there will not be such a great premium for continuing to expand local chapters or to expand the number of local members in them.

H5: National federations that specialize in providing a labor-intensive, volunteer-based local service will encourage the proliferation of local chapters.

H6: National federations that specialize in mobilizing citizens to participate in elections will encourage the proliferation of local chapters and the size of their membership.

H7: National federations that specialize in advocating for a social movement constituency will tend to limit the number of local chapters they form.

H8: National federations that specialize in lobbying in national legislative, executive, and judicial forums will limit the number of local chapters they form.

H9: National federations that specialize in lobbying in state legislative, executive, and judicial forums will proliferate more local chapters.

Other Organizational Logics The families of logics I have emphasized, of course, are not exhaustive. Logics of appropriateness (Clemens 1993, 1997), comity, territorial hegemony, and professionalization are others that might be explored to find additional factors relevant to the calculus of determining a preferred number and geographic mix of local affiliates. I have ignored, for example, the trend toward professionalism, but the increasing professionalization of leadership in SMOs generally (McCarthy and Zald 1973), and most likely, in local affiliates of national federations, also may affect the preference for a desired number of affiliates and/or their task structures.

Conclusion

I have assembled evidence suggesting both persistence and change in the federated SMO form in the United States in recent decades. In spite of the widely trumpeted growth of social movements without members, the nationally federated SMO with local members is alive and well, such that at least 25 percent of local movement groups are affiliates of such federations. On the other hand, federated SMOs of recent vintage appear to have developed fewer state, regional and local affiliates. This is the case, I argue, because there now exist important constraints upon national federations that diminish their enthusiasm for expanding the number of local affiliates. As a result, we find very few modern social movement federations to have more than three to four hundred local chapters. At the same time, the changing rationales for enrolling local members have also probably dampened efforts to expand the number of members. I have ignored two other common species of nationally federated nonprofit organizations, labor unions and churches. Each of those populations of organizations operates under a quite different regulatory regime than do federated SMOs, while, at the same time, they confront similar tensions inherent in their common federated organizational forms. Comparative analyses of the persistence and change among SMOs, churches, and labor unions might, then, allow an assessment of the importance of those contrasting state regulatory regimes. A primary motivation for exploring persistence and change among social change federations is the important consequences the number and task structures of its local affiliates may have for societal wide levels of citizen activism. Organizational logics, then, through the multiple dimensions I have discussed, have apparently led to a reduction in the total supply of opportunities for citizen activism provided by federated SMOs.

8

Globalization and Transnational Social Movement Organizations

Jackie Smith

The transnational integration of markets and political institutions, especially prevalent in recent decades, presents new challenges for organizations of activists seeking to protect their existing rights or entitlements or to advance new claims against power holders. As national markets dissolve into a growing global marketplace, national governments have turned increasingly to international organizations to negotiate new rules about the boundaries of state authority. These interdependent and parallel processes of "globalization" (global market integration) and "internationalization" (the increasing importance of relations between nations)[1] substantially transform the character of the organizational fields in which social movements seek to pursue their interests. This chapter draws from the insights of social movement and organizational scholarship to analyze the changes in the global political economy that are most relevant for social movement actors. It explores whether and how these changes have influenced the character of the population of transnational social movement organizations.

The expansion of the global economy reduces the capacities of states (some more than others) to define and enact their own internal economic policies. It thereby prevents the state from carrying out its traditional functions of regulating the national economy and ensuring the welfare of its citizens. Moreover, the global legal and political environments increasingly constrain the range of policy choices available to national decision makers.

Support for this research was provided by the American Sociological Association-National Science Foundation Funds for Advancing the Discipline Program, the World Society Foundation, the Joyce Mertz-Gilmore Foundation (human rights organization survey), and by the Aspen Institute Non-profit Sector Research Fund (survey of transnational affiliates).
[1] This distinction between internationalization and globalization is drawn from Daly (2002).

As the effective sources of authority in the global polity shift from the national level, groups seeking to challenge existing policies and distributions of power must adapt their strategies and structures to this transformed organizational field.

Globalization forces states to reduce their role in economic planning and decision making in favor of global "free market" forces as reflected in international trade agreements such as the General Agreement on Tariffs and Trade (GATT) and now the World Trade Organization (WTO). This is especially true for the poor states of the global South. By reducing the state's role in the economy, globalization undermines national democratic decision making, because it removes important decisions about things such as labor or environmental standards and even government purchasing choices from local political control (for review, see Wallach and Sforza 1999).

Internationalization also shifts policy decisions from local and national to transnational settings by producing agreements among national governments to address shared problems such as environmental degradation, crime, weapons trading, and disease. As states enter such agreements, they effectively shift some of their authority to supranational institutions. An important difference between the global political institutions and those defining the global economic order, however, is that the WTO and international financial institutions such as the International Monetary Fund (IMF) and the World Bank have far greater enforcement capacities than do institutions such as the United Nations and the treaty bodies under it.[2] Also, the latter two organizations are governed by a system of voting that is weighted by a country's financial stake. Thus, the richer countries have an obvious advantage here and have sought to move key policy decisions into those bodies.

This increasing formalization of transnational economic and political relations through the expansion of global treaties and international organizations has occurred during a time of rapid growth in the organization of all sorts of social relations both within and across national boundaries (see, e.g., Boli and Thomas 1999; McCarthy and Zald 1977; 2001; Minkoff 1995; Walker 1991). Thus, as governments have developed new ways to

---

[2] The WTO and NAFTA have built-in dispute settlement mechanisms that allow for the automatic enforcement – through economic sanctions and/or fines – of decisions put forth by their panels of judges. In contrast, the United Nations requires proactive responses by member governments to take action to enforce international law.

coordinate their policies and address transnational problems, private sector and civil society groups have evolved in similar ways to maximize their goals and to respond to their changing social environments (cf. Powell and DiMaggio 1991).

The following section examines the ways that expanding political institutions affect the organizational field and therefore the strategic options available to social movement actors and how they alter the organizational demands of political challengers. Next, I describe the population of transnationally organized social movement organizations, or TSMOs, to establish whether we do indeed see adaptations to this changing environment. Finally, using survey data from selected subsets of TSMOs, I explore some of the key organizing challenges for transnational organizations face as they attempt to mobilize across national boundaries and affect change in the global polity.

Organizational Imperatives of Globalization

As governments turn increasingly to global institutions such as the World Trade Organization and the United Nations to resolve shared problems, social movement actors seeking to change local and national practices find that they must look beyond their national boundaries to do so. The global political context both expands and complicates the strategic choices available to those hoping to promote political and social change. In the terms of organizational theorists, we should expect that the nesting of states within a broader and increasingly influential interstate system – which itself introduces new institutional actors and governance structures – would change the broader *institutional logic* that governs the organizational field in which social movements operate (see, e.g., chapter by McAdam and Scott, this volume). This means that we also should see changes in the ways social movement actors carry out their struggles.

In particular, we can expect that social movement organizations – viewed by many as key building blocks of social movements – will become increasingly transnational in structure. This process parallels the transformation of contentious politics during the rise of national states (cf. McAdam, Tarrow, and Tilly 2001; Tilly 1984). For instance, within a global institutional setting, efforts to shape the practices of a particular government require international legal or scientific expertise, understandings of the rivalries and practices of interstate political bargaining, and capacities for mobilizing protests and otherwise bringing simultaneous pressure against multiple national governments.[3] Interstate politics, in other words, has a dynamic and logic of its own, and social movement scholars need to refocus their analytical lens to account for an organizational field that transcends national boundaries.

The logic that drives interstate politics requires that activists develop organizations that can facilitate broad, cross-cultural communication while managing diversity and coordinating joint action around a shared agenda. These demands differ sharply from those required of most national-level movement organizations. We should not be surprised, therefore, to find that social movement organizations devoted especially to transnational-level organizing and political action play key roles in global-level contentious politics. A growing body of empirical evidence on transnational protests allows us to evaluate this assumption. For instance, a growing number of case studies point to the presence of transnationally organized groups or at least transnational coalitions of associations in major global change campaigns (see, e.g., Fox and Brown 1998; Keck and Sikkink 1998; Khagram, Riker, and Sikkink 2002; Smith and Johnston 2002). To explore in detail the relations between transnational and national SMOs, we must examine key "episodes" in transnational or global contentious politics and analyze relationships among the key organizations. Table 8.1 does this by summarizing some of the central organizational actors and their various roles in the 1999 "Battle of Seattle" against the expansion of the WTO. This event has come to represent the first major – though by no means the first – confrontational protest at a global political site.

I have categorized each organization according to the extensiveness of its transnational ties. If there are any transnational ties, are they informal and sporadic or are they somehow formalized and routinized within the organization? Are these transnational ties peripheral or central to the day-to-day operations of the organization? Thus, we can distinguish among the organizational participants in the Seattle mobilization in terms of how exposed they were to regular and direct transnational exchanges. The next question then is whether or not the extensiveness of transnational ties was associated with different forms of participation in this particular episode of collective action. Do transnational organizations perform different tasks than do more locally organized SMOs?

---

[3] For more on the political dynamics of social movements within nested national and interstate politics see Rothman and Oliver (2002), Smith, Chatfield, and Pagnucco (1997), and Tarrow (2001a).

Table 8.1. *Mobilizing Structures and Divisions of Labor in the "Battle of Seattle"*

Type of Transnational Tie	Movement Mobilizing Structures*	Major Roles
No formal transnational ties	Local Chapters of National SMOs (e.g., NOW) Neighborhood Committees United for a Fair Economy	Public education Mobilizing participation in protest Localizing global frames
Diffuse transnational ties	Direct Action Network Reclaim the Streets Ruckus Society Coalition for Campus Organizing	Public education Mobilizing participation in protest Localizing global frames Tactical innovations and diffusion
Routine transnational ties	Public Citizen Global Exchange Rainforest Action Network United Students Against Sweatshops Council of Canadians Sierra Club	Public education Facilitating local mobilization by others Tactical innovations and diffusion Articulating and disseminating global strategic frames Research/publication of organizing materials Facilitating transnational exchanges Monitoring international institutions
Formal transnational organization	Greenpeace Friends of the Earth International Forum on Globalization Third World Network Peoples Global Action 50 Years is Enough Network Women's Environment and Development Organization	Public education Facilitating local mobilization by others Articulating and disseminating global strategic frames Research/publication of organizing materials Facilitating transnational exchanges Monitoring of international institutions Coordinating transnational cooperation Cultivating and maintaining global constituency Global symbolic actions

Note: This list is illustrative, not comprehensive.

* Organizations vary a great deal in their levels of formalization and hierarchy. For instance, Friends of the Earth and Greenpeace have well-defined organizational structures and institutional presences while groups such as Peoples Global Action resist forming an organizational headquarters, and Reclaim the Streets seeks to sustain a loose, network-like structure relying heavily on electronic communications.

Source: Adapted from Smith (2002b).

The general pattern that emerges from this table is that groups with less routinized and formalized transnational ties were indeed more involved in mobilizing local participation in the Seattle protest event. The educational activities in which they engaged drew largely from the strategic framing and information dissemination done by groups with more extensive transnational ties. In contrast, more of the work of groups with routine transnational ties or with transnational organizational structures was devoted to facilitating such mobilizing work by other groups. Groups with transnational ties enabled transnational exchange of various kinds by producing newsletters and Web sites that provided information about the work of activists in various countries, as well as by bringing activists from different countries for speaking tours and other forms of direct transnational contacts. In the Battle of Seattle, for instance, People's Global Action organized a "People's Caravan" that traveled across the United States in the weeks before Seattle to participate in local teach-ins on the WTO and its effects on various peoples around the world. The People's Caravan relied upon and complemented local organizations, which provided the meeting venues, audiences, and resting places along their route. Groups such as the Women's Environment and Development Organization (WEDO) provided funds, training, and otherwise enabled activists from poor countries to attend global meetings and to speak at public rallies and to participate in organizing workshops such as those held during the 1999 WTO meeting.

Broad changes in the organization of the state and society are seen as having substantial impacts on the ways that people might wage political struggles, and they have contributed to the professionalization of social movement organizations and to the now widespread formation of social movement organizations to advance these struggles (see McCarthy and Zald 1977; Tilly 1984).[4] Alongside globalization processes, we find an expansion in the numbers of SMOs (and other types of organizations) that incorporate members from different countries (Boli and Thomas 1997; Smith 1997). SMOs and their transnational counterparts (TSMOs)[5] are carriers of

---

[4] In practice, social movement organizations vary tremendously in the extent to which they adopt formal bureaucratic structures and hierarchical leadership. My use of the term "organization" includes both highly bureaucratic groups such as Amnesty International and self-consciously decentralized and nonformalized groups such as People Global Action.

[5] TSMOs are at least minimally formalized organizations that involve participants from more than one country whose purpose is to "change some elements of the social structure or reward distribution, or both, of a society" (McCarthy and Zald 1977: 1218). Prominent examples of TSMOs are Greenpeace and Amnesty International.

movement ideas, cultures, and skills. They are not the only actors in social movements; they are joined during times of movement expansion by church and school groups, unions, and other social groups (see McCarthy 1996). But by understanding their structures and discourses we can gain insights into broader social movement dynamics and capabilities. The consistent rise in the numbers of TSMOs during the latter half of the twentieth century suggests that political challengers see sufficient benefits in developing and formalizing transnational ties to justify the relatively higher costs of long-distance organizing. As was seen with the rise of national SMOs in the eighteenth century, we would expect that these transnational organizations and their interactions with other global actors will have important influences on the ways that people engage in politics in the global political arena (cf. McAdam, Tarrow, and Tilly 2001).

The Changing Population of Transnational SMOs, 1970s–2000

The argument outlined above would lead us to expect that the quickening pace of global integration and the related changes to the relevant organizational field will generate more extensive efforts by social movement actors to develop formal transnational organizations to defend against unwanted forms of global integration and to shape global processes in ways that complement their goals. Below we examine changes in the population of TSMOs in order to assess the extent to which this expectation is borne out. Table 8.2 presents the counts of TSMOs identified in various editions of the *Yearbook of International Associations* (Union of International Associations), the most comprehensive census of all international organizations, including governmental, business, and civil society groups.[6]

The population of TSMOs has expanded dramatically, especially in the past three decades.[7] While fewer than 200 TSMOs existed in the 1970s, there were nearly one thousand such organizations by 2000. However, the

[6] For more details on this source and its relevance to these claims, see Boli and Thomas (1999) and Smith (1997).

[7] This pattern parallels the growth of other international nongovernmental organizations (INGOs). It also likely is influenced by the expansion of national-level social movement sectors. Although we lack systematic data with which to compare growth in national and transnational SMO populations, existing theories and research (see, e.g., Fisher 1993; Minkoff 1995) support the claim the past three decades have seen an expansion in the numbers of both national and transnational organizations. Moreover, research on transnational organizing suggests that this is dependent upon strong national-level movements (e.g., Lewis 2002; Sikkink 1993).

Table 8.2. *Growth and Issue Focus of Transnational Social Movement Organizations*

	1973 N = 183		1983 N = 348		1993 N = 711		2000 N = 959	
	No.	%	No.	%	No.	%	No.	%
Human rights	41	22	89	26	200	28	247	26
Environment	17	9	43	12	126	18	167	17
Peace	21	12	37	11	82	11	98	10
Women's rights	16	9	25	7	64	9	94	9
Development/ Empowerment	8	4	15	4	52	7	95	10
Global justice/Environment	7	4	13	4	30	4	109	11
Multi-issue organizations*	18	7	43	12	82	12	161	17
% change from prior decade	30		90		104		42 (est. to 2003)	

* This categorization overlaps some of the categories above – especially the global justice category.
Source: Yearbook of International Associations.

data for 2000 suggests that the very rapid growth of TMSOs in the population that was seen during the 1970s and 1980s has slowed. We examine some reasons for this below, but first we should consider the issues around which these TSMOs organize. Human rights TSMOs constitute the largest segment of the TSMO population, and they consistently remain around 25 percent of all TSMOs during the four periods examined here. In contrast, we found fairly rapid growth in the environmental and economic justice movement "industries," particularly in the most recent decades. The most dramatic change, however, is in the number of TSMOs that adopted "multi-issue" goals such as "environment and development" or "human rights to development" rather than the more traditional, single-issue focus. The number of multi-issue groups doubled during the 1990s (growing at twice the rate of the overall TSMO population), and in percentage terms, they rose from less than 10 percent of all groups in the 1970s to 17 percent in 2000.

I want to explore some of the reasons why we are seeing these two broad shifts in the TSMO population, namely, a declining rate of growth and a shift from single-issue to multi-issue organizing frames. When considering why the population's growth rate has slowed, we must account for the important development at the 1992 United Nations Conference on Environment and Development that produced a change in the *environmental mechanisms* (see Campbell, this volume) relevant to social movement actors. This institutional change allowed more direct access by national and subnational groups to United Nations forums. Before that time, only international organizations could obtain "consultative status" with the UN, which allowed them access to international meetings as well as to important documents on international negotiations and UN practices (see Willetts 1999). This effectively reduced the benefits of transnational association for some groups, which may have found it easier to make direct appeals to international organizations rather than to submerge their own organizational interests within a broader transnational framework. Moreover, once the UN began to credential national and subnational groups, this paved the way for their greater access to other international organizations.

The shift to multi-issue organizing frames is another interesting development, and one that might be explained by changes in the *relational mechanisms* that are at work in this organizational field. Specifically, over time we see a growing number of organizations representing a growing number of individual activists engaging in more international meetings and other exchanges, often with the self-conscious aim of generating networks of ties to other activists and organizations. These networks and the exchanges they produce have contributed to a growing awareness of global interdependencies (see, e.g., Young 1991) or a transformed understanding of movement issues that arises from the experience of activism itself. We might categorize this changed awareness as a *cognitive mechanism* that contributes to the changes in the broader environment.

Such cognitive processes have been documented in other, national, movements as well. For instance, Marullo and his colleagues (1996) found that peace movement organizations in the United States tended to adopt more complex, multi-issue frames over time. They interpreted these frame shifts as attempts by SMOs to maintain the interest of activists who had confronted the limitations of previous organizing frames (in this case, the nuclear freeze) and whose activism had led to a greater appreciation for the complex relationships between U.S. military spending and its interventionist foreign policy. Multi-issue organizations may also be a response to attempts to build transnational ties that can include activists with quite different political and cultural backgrounds. As groups form and extend inter-group and inter-personal ties across national boundaries, they find that they must re-frame their ideas about the causes of and solutions to the problems they hope to address. In many cases, we see processes of *diffusion, translation, and bricolage* at work (see, e.g., Bandy and Smith 2005). These processes are also well documented in Rothman and Oliver's (2002) analysis of transnational environmental and indigenous rights coalitions in Brazil,

Table 8.3. *Organizational Structures of TSMOs*

	1973 %	1983 %	1993 %	2000 %
Federation structure	50	38	28	18
Coalition structure	25	31	43	60

Source: Yearbook of International Associations.

in the work of Alison Brysk (1996, 2000), and in Rupp's (1997) analysis of the international women's movement.

Another factor in the slowing TSMO growth may be the organizational structures adopted by TSMOs. Transnational organizing requires substantially greater resources than does more locally oriented action. Not only is this due to larger communication and transportation costs, but it also results from the need to bridge linguistic and cultural distances within the organization. We can expect to find organizational structures aimed at limiting these transaction costs. The *Yearbook* data allows us to determine the ways that TSMOs structure their relationships with members. Table 8.3 displays the changes in these organizational structures. The more centralized, "federated" structure involves the division of the organization into national sections that are certified by the international secretariat. Typically national sections have a national monopoly on the organization's name (e.g., Amnesty International-USA), contribute a predetermined share of their resources to the international secretariat, send national delegates to international meetings, and agree to follow a set of international guidelines regarding political claims, governance, and activities. In contrast, what I refer to here as the "coalition" form reflects a more *decentralized* and informal structure. There are fewer requirements for conformity with a broad set of organizational rules, goals, and procedures as defined in the organization's secretariat or international office. While coalitions vary tremendously in the extensiveness of their shared commitments and in the ties between organizational affiliates and the international headquarters, the main feature of this form is that affiliates are asked to adopt a relatively limited shared ideological framework, and they maintain fairly wide autonomy within the coalition framework.

The most dramatic change in the TSMO population over the past three decades is that these groups are adopting the more decentralized and informal coalition form. It is probably no coincidence that this same phenomenon is happening in the corporate sector, as firms seek to maximize the ability of their diverse regional and national operations to adapt quickly to changing market forces (see, e.g., Sklair 2001). The coalition form accelerates decision making and therefore adaptability of groups by decentralizing authority within the organization. In a rapidly changing and uncertain political context, such flexibility is essential.

How can these changes in the organizational structure of TSMOs help explain the patterns of growth we found in Table 8.2? First, the more common, decentralized coalition structure would allow more national groups to participate in transnational associations without major changes in their preexisting routines and agendas. Joining transnational coalitions brings rather minimal financial costs, and for many groups the commitments of time and other organizational resources can be determined by the affiliate organization itself. The returns on coalition membership include access to strategic information and frames, access to policymakers, and the enhanced solidarity that comes from being part of a transnational collectivity of diverse local struggles (see, e.g., Cullen 2003). For some groups, there may be even greater benefits such as assistance with global-level mobilization and attendance at international conferences, financial and strategic resources for global work, greater local and international legitimacy, and enhanced opportunities to participate in transnational meetings. In sum, given the logics governing the global organizational field, the coalition form can reduce the start-up costs to groups seeking to extend their work into the global arena. With an almost unlimited capacity for expansion, coalitions can absorb new participants more readily than can the more rigid and centralized federation structure (see, e.g., Murphy 2002).[8]

Coalition structures also encourage the framing of goals and issues in ways that extend their possibilities for attracting the broadest possible base of affiliates. Thus, the shift to multi-issue frames may reflect this need to organize from a constituency of activists that crosses major geographic, political, cultural, and ideological divides. By limiting the degree of ideological conformity among affiliates to a limited consensus around a specific set of aims, coalitions create spaces where a more diverse range of organizations can join transnational collective efforts without abandoning their own

---

[8] Interestingly, an unsystematic survey of the foundings of transnational groups suggests that quite a few of them were formed by activists who began their careers in major transnational federations such as Amnesty International or the International Confederation of the Red Cross, but left these groups because of their rigid and hierarchical structures. The former helped spawn many groups, including Equality Now and Peace Brigades International, and the latter inspired Medécins Sans Frontierès (see, e.g., Smith, Pagnucco, and Romeril 1994).

Table 8.4. *Subregional Versus Transregional Organizations*

	North Only	South Only	Both North and South
Number of organizations	211	87	531
% of all organizations (N = 829)	25	10	64
Age (mean years)	18.6	17.5	32.6
(median)	12	13	22
% formed during 1990s	45	36	20

Source: Yearbook of International Associations, 2000.

organizational constituencies and missions. Thus, with fewer organizations, coalitions can accommodate a broader and more diverse constituency.[9]

Another dimension of TSMO organizational structure is the extent to which they are organized on a global versus a regional level.[10] Boli and Thomas's analysis of the more general category of international nongovernmental organizations (INGOs) showed a growing tendency for these groups to organize along regional lines. They argued that regional organizing enjoyed the "practical advantages of shared language, culture, and history as tools for mobilization with respect to the larger world." In their view, the broader world culture and its institutional artifacts define an overarching framework within which "world culture authorizes and compels organization at diverse levels" (1999: 31–2). The question remains, however, as to whether this pattern is reproduced among that segment of the INGO population that is devoted to social change goals. To evaluate this, I examined TSMO memberships in terms of their locations within the global North, the global South, or in both Northern and Southern regions. While various regional categorizations are possible, this North-South division distinguishes between the "core" of the global economic and political order (the North) and the "periphery" states that have more recently been incorporated into this world order. It assumes, generally, that the central interests and histories of each region differ in ways that are likely to affect the shape of political mobilization. Table 8.4 presents the distribution of TSMOs according to their regional scope.

---

[9] Whether or not this enhances political effectiveness is a separate question. Looking at national groups, for instance, Gamson (1990) found that more formalized and centralized organizations (i.e., federations in this study) were more successful at achieving their goals.

[10] This section is based upon a similar discussion in Smith 2004.

We see in this table that most TSMOs are organized interregionally, that is they incorporate members from both the global North and the South. However, the growth rates among *intra*-regional organizations exceed those of the interregional groups. While nearly one half of North-only TSMOs and more than one third of South-only TSMOs were formed during the 1990s, only one fifth of all interregional TSMOs began their work in the 1990s. This pattern could reflect a growing *polarization* among transnational social movement organizations along the major structural divide in the world system, meaning that social movement actors have been unable to mitigate or overcome the major lines of inequality in the global system.

On the other hand, this pattern could also reflect a change in the relevant relational mechanisms, as we may find that more regional organizations play a *bridging* role for transnational organizations. This would be consistent with the expectations of Boli and Thomas and other world culture theorists. Regional structures facilitate the aggregation of diverse interests of local actors in order to more effectively integrate local and regional interests into global-level negotiations. They make it easier, in particular, for groups whose language or historical experiences differ most dramatically from the dominant Western influences on world culture to define their interests within the world cultural framework and to devise strategies for fostering their regional interests. Indeed, intergovernmental conferences may encourage region-specific organizing by the fact that they hold regionally based preparatory meetings before major global conferences and by their emphasis on regional representation in their formal structures and negotiation processes. Further research is needed to assess the underlying dynamics behind this organizing pattern, but certainly this regionalization of TSMO structures will impact the nature of transnational mobilizations yet to come.[11]

Organizational Integration and Its Challenges

The net effect of the changes in the global organizational field and the changing mechanisms at work here is that a much larger societal infrastructure

---

[11] A slightly higher percentage of intraregional groups were organized in the area of human rights, and this is an issue along which Northern and Southern activists tend to be divided between an emphasis on civil and political rights versus economic and social rights. More North-only groups were organized around environmental issues, whereas South-only groups were more likely to focus on development and economic justice issues. This may signal that highly contentious issues create the strongest incentives for actors to organize within similar cultural, ideological, or geographic groupings.

exists for the transnational dissemination of information and exchanges between people from different national backgrounds.[12] If we can view each organizational unit as an indicator of a variety of social interactions across national borders, then these figures reveal substantially more frequent transnational communication and dialogue in the 1990s than in earlier decades. Such transnational dialogue is essential to cultivating ideologies and identities that will appeal to an international movement constituency.

But how *global* are these associations? Do they serve to reinforce the "opportunity hoarding" (Tilly 1998) found across many societies, where already privileged groups reinforce their influence and advantages, while weaker groups see minimal gains as they fall farther behind? Western Europeans and North Americans are clearly overrepresented in TSMOs, and most organizational headquarters are based in those regions (principally in Western Europe). However, there is some evidence of a gradual shift towards greater representation of Southern citizens in TSMOs (Sikkink and Smith 2002; Jackie Smith 1997). Case studies also suggest that, within TSMOs and other transnational coalitions, the influence of Southern activists has been increasing (Fox 2002; Gray 1998; Wirth 1998).

Regardless of their geographic scope, the extent to which TSMOs can produce transnational relationships that are meaningful for political contention depends upon the types of activities taking place within them. Does the transnational character of these associations trickle down to affiliates in different countries? International organizations in particular must overcome distinct challenges to cultivating a unified organizational purpose that can motivate collective action. Organizational *integration*, in other words, cannot be assumed by the mere presence of a transnational organizational structure, but rather varies in the degrees to which an organization produces the cognitive shifts necessary to overcome diversity, distance, economic barriers, and political fragmentation (Young 1991). Young argues that both technological advances and changes in perceptions of global interdependence will make the internal cohesion of transnational associations less problematic.

To assess the internal dynamics of transnational SMOs, this study draws from two different mailed surveys of TSMO leaders and their local and national affiliate organizations.[13] One survey addressed leaders of

---

[12] This secion draws from analyses reported in Smith (2002b).

[13] Further details on these surveys and additional findings from them are available in Smith (2002b).

transnational human rights SMOs and the other focused on the organizational affiliates of EarthAction, a TSMO working on global environment, development, and human rights issues. The human rights survey, conducted during 1996, examines the transnational headquarters of all human rights TSMOs, providing evidence about their human rights frames, contacts with interstate institutions, resources, and geographic makeup. The survey response rate was just over 50 percent (144 responses), and there was no systematic difference in the response rates of groups based in the global South as compared with Northern-based groups (see Smith, Pagnucco, and Lopez 1998). However, most human rights TSMOs were based in the North (103 versus 41 Southern TSMO respondents).

EarthAction's principal focus is on supporting multilateral solutions for global environmental and economic justice problems. It distributes "action kits" to its affiliate or "Partner Organizations," providing them with background information and action suggestions. EarthAction actively solicits input from affiliates as it plans its campaigns, which include global negotiations such as those on climate change and local struggles such as the Ogoni people's resistance to the Nigerian government and multinational oil companies. The survey was conducted during 1998, and achieved a response rate of 52 percent (209 responses). Comparisons of the pool of respondents with nonrespondents found no systematic differences in organizational location, size, structure, or duration of ties with EarthAction. However, as one might expect, respondents tended to be somewhat more active partners than were nonrespondents.[14]

Internal Communications

Transnational SMOs vary tremendously in the intensity of interactions they represent. Some TSMOs may have only quadrennial meetings of national representatives of their members, while others may have bi-weekly conference calls among leaders and/or frequent electronic communications with local individual or organizational members. Some may have the resources to conduct extensive electronic and mailed communications, while others may

---

[14] The measure used here was a dummy variable indicating whether or not the group had made any contact with EarthAction (e.g., by sending newsletters or news clippings about their campaigns or returning postcards indicating that they took action on an EarthAction campaign) or responded to earlier attempts by EarthAction to contact them prior to the survey. Thirty-five percent of respondents and 22 percent of nonrespondents had made prior contact with EarthAction international offices, a significant difference.

Table 8.5. *Frequency of Transnational Communications*

Activity	Number of Times Group Engaged in Activity During 1995*	
	Quarterly or Less (%)	Monthly or More (%)
Issue background papers or action alerts to members	40	23
Contact organizational sections or members	28	40
Contact other nongovernmental organizations	20	54

* No statistically significant differences were found between groups based in the global North and those in the global South.

Source: Human Rights TSMO survey (N = 144).

have more uneven electronic contacts and infrequent postal exchanges. For instance, the frequency of EarthAction contacts depends to a large extent upon its success at fundraising for its various campaigns. So what can we say generally about the significance of the transnational linkages represented by this collection of groups? Table 8.5 displays the responses of human rights TSMOs to questions about the frequency of contacts with organizational affiliates.

This table shows that most groups maintain fairly frequent contact with their affiliates at the local and national levels. Ninety percent of all transnational human rights organizations responding indicated that they have at least quarterly contacts with members through background papers, action alerts, or other contacts. Seventy-nine percent indicated contact with members beyond quarterly communications. In addition, most TSMOs are actively engaging in contacts with other organizations in their environment. The human rights survey showed that more than half of all groups engage in at least monthly contact with other nongovernmental organizations. Such contacts indicate relationships that link actors and identities to global human rights frames and arenas.

Certainly the rise of electronic communications over recent years has facilitated transnational organizing. Indeed, Warkentin (2001) argued that progressive groups advancing global agendas helped pioneer the application of these technologies in the service of a global civil society. Nevertheless, given the wide disparities in access to Internet communications even within the highly industrialized countries, we should expect great inequity in the use of electronic communications by Northern and Southern TSMOs and their affiliates. The data we have in these surveys supports this contention, although the gaps may not be as wide as some might anticipate. Among the human rights TSMOs surveyed in 1996, just 44 percent reported use of electronic communications (e-mail and/or Internet). Comparing geographic differences, we see that 30 percent of Southern-based groups and 49 percent of Northern-based groups reported access to electronic communications.[15] A somewhat higher percentage of EarthAction affiliates reported access to electronic communications.[16] Overall, 59 percent of respondents reported that they used e-mail, and 50 percent reported use of the Internet. Here again, geographic differences were not as great as one might expect. While 80 percent of Northern groups used e-mail, about half (51 percent) of Southern affiliates reported doing so. Disparities on Internet usage were greater: 77 percent of Northern groups, compared with 39 percent of Southern ones, reported using the Internet. Eighty-two percent of European and 79 percent of North American partners reported that they used e-mail; African partners reported the least access to e-mail, 35 percent. Asian groups were next at 41 percent. Nearly three-quarters of Latin American Partners and 62 percent of partners in the Pacific have e-mail.[17]

One thing that is clear is that the "digital divide" between Northern-based and Southern-based TSMOs is far smaller than that for the general society. The 1999 UN *Human Development Report* showed that more than 26 percent of the U.S. population and around 7 percent of the populations of other industrialized Northern countries were Internet users, compared to less than 1 percent of the populations of countries in the South (UNDP 1999: 63). But without further knowledge of the class backgrounds of groups with access to communications technologies, we cannot say whether or not

---

[15] Differences were statistically significant at the .05 level (t = 2.13).

[16] Some of this difference might be due to expanding access to electronic communications as the 1990s progressed. The different sampling frames of these two studies also may account for some differences. The transnational organizations may be more heavily reliant upon electronic communications than some of the many more locally organized groups in the EarthAction survey. Indeed, a comparison of EarthAction affiliates that transcend national boundaries shows that a significantly higher percentage of transnational affiliates than local and national affiliates used email (72 percent vs. 52 percent) and the Internet (69 percent vs. 41 percent). (Mean differences are significant at .01 level for both comparisons.)

[17] Use of the Internet was again less common: only one-quarter of African and Asian partners reported use of the Internet, while around three-quarters of European, Latin American, and North American partners were Internet users.

the comparatively small technology gap between Northern and Southern TSMOs is simply a result of their location within an educated cosmopolitan middle class (see, e.g., Tarrow 2001b).

It is also worth emphasizing that new communications technology alone cannot produce the kinds of commitment and understanding that are essential for sustained collective action. "The revolution will not be e-mailed," according to People's Global Action (2000). Jocelyn Dow, founder of a women's organization in Guyana and a board member of the international Women's Environment and Development Organization, argued that "if we are not careful, we lose the texture of information. One of the most important things for women is to continue to meet globally, because there is nothing that better challenges any misguided notion you might have than to meet a person in her actual skin. We have to live each other's reality. [Global] conferences have a capacity for energizing what I call the agenda of defiance" (quoted in Thom 2000: 32).

My own contacts with affiliates of transnational organizations corroborate this widespread desire for human connections and its importance to solidarity building. EarthAction affiliates, for instance, quite frequently ask the organization to organize conferences for their partners to meet each other. Directories of affiliates have been very popular within the organization as a means of promoting more direct exchange.[18] Despite the vast distances between activists, the need for personal contact remains important for motivating and sustaining collective action. Transnational organizations facilitate this contact.

In sum, despite the higher costs of transnational activity, this evidence suggests at least a capacity for fairly routine transnational communications between the headquarters and the local or national affiliates of TSMOs. Without more qualitative data we cannot say much about the content of these communications, but at the very least they suggest that TSMOs actively incorporate routine information exchanges that are necessary for effective transnational cooperation to develop.

Perceived Obstacles to International Cooperation

The following two tables explore some of the obstacles that participants in transnational organizations perceive in their efforts to build transnational

---

[18] Brown and Fox (1998: 455–6) reported similar conclusions from their study of transnational coalitions working to oppose World Bank projects and policies.

Table 8.6. *Organizational Integration Survey Items: Human Rights TSMOs*

	% "Often or Always True"
Our organization has difficulty maintaining contact with some members because of the costs of transportation and communication	20
It is difficult to involve many of our members in decision making because of language differences	10
Cultural differences among our members make it difficult to agree on joint statements or actions	6

Source: Human Rights TSMO Survey (N = 144).

Table 8.7. *Organizational Integration Survey Items: TSMO Affiliates*

	% "Often or Always True"			
	North N = 56	South N = 156	Reg./Global N = 79	Local/Nat'l N = 130
Financial limitations prevent us from taking action on EarthAction campaigns	51	64	44	62
Language differences make it difficult for us to use EarthAction materials	14	14	12	15
We have difficulties relating global issues to people's everyday concerns	26	42	27	45

Source: EarthAction Survey (N = 209).

cooperation around social and political change goals. Table 8.6 lists items from the survey of transnational headquarters of human rights groups regarding perceptions of financial, linguistic, and cultural obstacles. Responses to similar questions by EarthAction affiliates appear in Table 8.7.

These responses indicate that financial limitations are perceived as a relatively small obstacle to transnational work by human rights groups. In contrast, the EarthAction affiliates were more likely to report strong financial constraints on their abilities to participate in transnational campaigns. The contrast between the two surveys is probably explained by the fact that the human rights groups are transnational associations whose principal purpose is to promote global organizing around human rights goals. Therefore, their organizational budgets are likely to account for the expenses involved in maintaining regular contact with widely dispersed affiliates. In contrast, many affiliates of EarthAction are small, local groups attempting to address the global dimensions of their local concerns or trying to connect their local efforts with those of other activists. Few have very large budgets, and much of the efforts taken on behalf of global campaigns must come out of regular organizational budgets that leave little room for new outreach or campaign efforts.

Not surprisingly, Southern affiliates were considerably more likely to report having financial limitations on their activities than were Northern groups. This is at least partially related to the fact that Southern groups were more likely than Northern ones to be local or national in orientation and that the more locally oriented groups also tended to report greater financial limitations on their transnational participation.[19] Organizations oriented towards local and national activities can be expected to face difficulties in shifting scarce organizational resources to global campaign efforts.

Linguistic differences were reported to be a much smaller problem for all groups involved. This may be because EarthAction produces materials in three languages, and many human rights organizations reported the use of multiple working languages. One additional reason may be that the infrequent and written communications representing many of the interactions taking place within most TSMOs do not require the same facility with language that direct interactions or verbal exchanges do. It might also reflect a rather limited engagement of affiliates or members in decision making or complex negotiations about organization strategy and activities.[20] Further research is needed to assess the relevance of language differences as a barrier to organizational integration.

A greater difficulty for transnational affiliates was in relating their local concerns to global campaigns. Southern affiliates and local groups especially reported much more frequent difficulties in this area. Certainly this disparity hinders equitable North-South integration into transnational organizations. It suggests a need for greater efforts to articulate and develop strategic connections between local interests and relevant global political processes. In other words, if they are to better integrate groups that are most dependent upon their transnational organizing work – local and

---

[19] Seventy-two percent of the survey sample of Southern affiliates, compared with 38 percent of Northern affiliates, were organized at the local or national levels.

[20] The finding could also be a result of the fact that response to the surveys was more likely from groups with leaders who speak or read English, French, or Spanish.

Southern affiliates – TSMOs such as EarthAction must make efforts to enhance strategic frames so that they better demonstrate local-global connections and suggest feasible local actions. Comparing responses to this question by groups that were less active in EarthAction campaigns with those that were more engaged revealed that groups engaging more frequently in global campaigns found fewer difficulties making global-local connections. Thus, efforts to assist groups to make such connections may encourage them to take more concerted action on EarthAction's transnational campaigns.[21]

Conclusion

This study set out to explore the ways that a changing global environment affects the dynamics of social movement organization. The processes of global political and economic integration alter the organizational field in which social movements operate, and even locally oriented social movements require some level of awareness about, if not involvement in, global-level political institutions. This is especially true for activists in the global South, at the periphery of the global economy, where the policy autonomy of national governments is increasingly limited (see, e.g., Robinson 1996; Walton and Seddon 1994). Thus, we expected that transnationally organized SMOs would fill a particular niche in the social movement sector[22] by providing specialized information and articulating global strategic frames.

The expansion of global institutions has encouraged the rapid growth of transnationally organized social movement organizations. These TSMOs reflect the key conflicts at work in the global political economy, as most groups focus on issues of human rights, environmental preservation, and economic empowerment/justice. Over the past several decades, the form

[21] Comparisons of mean responses by groups taking part in at least half of the campaigns listed in the survey with those taking up fewer than half suggest, not surprisingly, that more active groups found greater benefits from EarthAction resources and campaigns. Differences between the more and less active affiliates reached or approached significance on the following claims: that "EarthAction helps us link local issues to global negotiations," (p. < 10); that their work relating to the UN has increased since joining EarthAction (p < .05); and that EarthAction materials aided their work with other NGOs and the media (p < .10).

[22] I use the term "social movement sector," following McCarthy and Zald (1977), to refer to the aggregate of all organizational and individual actors that are advocates for *any* social movement industry.

of transnational SMOs has become more decentralized and adaptive, indicating that these organizations are responding to a changing and uncertain global environment.

Within transnational SMOs, we find that language and cultural differences constitute a relatively minor obstacle for organizers, suggesting that these groups have internalized effective cognitive mechanisms to bridge their internal differences. But while cognitive matters were less problematic, financial limitations were of greatest significance to the affiliates of TSMOs rather than to the transnational organizations themselves. Moreover, affiliates in the global South and locally organized affiliates–those on the periphery of this organizational field–had the most difficulty relating to global organizational initiatives.

We might ask, in closing this chapter, about the extent to which the population of TSMOs can be expected to grow or shrink in relation to major galvanizing events (such as the September 11, 2001, attacks, the anti-WTO protests in Seattle, or the outbreak of a major war). Do old groups respond to new issues and conditions that emerge, or must new groups be formed to accommodate new surges of interest in an issue? Analysts of organizations and of world culture (see the contributions in Boli and Thomas 1999) have argued that global institutions themselves motivate new transnational organizing efforts by restructuring institutional logics and by staging international conferences and other fora where governments reflect on major global problems and their possible solutions. Indeed, we see surges of new organizational formations in the years immediately preceding and following these kinds of events. My focus on more recent years prevents a systematic analysis of this question, but it supports the world cultural theorists' expectations that organizational growth will follow changes in the broad institutional and cultural framework of the world polity. In this sense, organizational growth likely will be more tied to institutional events or transformations than to more contingent events such as the September 11 attacks. Of course, to the extent that the September 11 tragedy has generated collective responses within international organizations, it too could have consequences for the population of transnational organizations advocating for social and political change.

In short, the global political context has important consequences for social movement challengers, not the least of which is the problem of devising organizations that are effective at mobilizing a broad and diverse global constituency and providing them with significant avenues for participation in global political debates and decision making. The protests against the global trade regime in Seattle showed the extent of popular interest in expanding democratic input into policy that is increasingly made in international organizations. But we lack the infrastructure for formal democratic participation in global-level policy debates. TSMOs have attempted to fill this institutional vacuum by providing some of the few opportunities for popular scrutiny of and participation in decisions that increasingly affect our day-to-day lives.

Understanding these organizations and their operations will help uncover the likely dynamics of global change and of the routes to greater democratization of global institutions, perhaps along lines similar to those seen with the rise of the modern democratic states of the West. However, as social movement actors strive to promote greater "internationalization," or the strengthening of democratic institutional structures that make inter-state policies more transparent and accountable to popular constituencies, they must face the competing process of "globalization." The concentration of resources in the hands of a few multinational corporations and the class of elites that controls them alters the nature of the struggle between the holders of capital and those demanding greater popular input into the actions of states. The work reflected in this volume, and in the broader literatures in organizational studies and social movements, has provided some useful tools for helping discover the dynamics that drive change in this global polity and for providing us with some insights into the types of organizational structures and strategies that are likely to be most effective in this political arena.

Movements Penetrating Organizations

Organizational scholars have had to begin to take more account of social movements because, in their myriad forms, they have been an important source for organizational change. Indeed, a case can be made that, along with technological, market, and political policy changes, social movements have been a major engine in the transformation of organizations. Movements have this impact on organizations through several mechanisms and processes. As forces acting in the wider environment, movements contribute to the reconstitution of organizational fields. For instance, the consumer movement of the early twentieth century contributed to the development of norms and standard-setting bodies for industries producing consumer products (Rao 1998). Similarly, among its many manifestations the progressive movement contributed to the enactment of child labor laws, the development of municipal building codes, and the transformation of city and state agencies that regulate industries (Keller 1990; Skowronek 1982). Movement activists or sympathizers external to organizations also attempt to affect organizations directly: they organize boycotts, pursue publicity campaigns, and bring lawsuits to attempt to change policy. Finally, members of organizations who also have professional and personal affinities to movements attempt to work within those organizations to change policies and procedures. In some cases, organizations are obliged not only to listen to and negotiate with movement members, but to hire persons sympathetic to their interests (Hoffman 2001 [1997]).

The chapters in this section employ a variety of different but overlapping lenses to consider the topic of how movements impact organizations. In Chapter 9, Mayer N. Zald, Calvin Morrill, and Hayagreeva Rao attempt a broad synthetic overview of, in their terms, how social movements impact organizations. David Strang and Dong-Il Jung, in Chapter 10, examine how the Total Quality Movement, aimed at upgrading organizational products and core technologies to improve performance, fared in one large corporation. And Maureen A. Scully and W. E. Douglas Creed, in Chapter 11, examine the vicissitudes of activism in several large organizations in the area of greater Minneapolis. They show how identities and symbolic resources were shaped and reconfigured as gays and lesbians pursued changes in domestic benefit policies.

Zald, Morrill, and Rao argue that the large social movements of the last half-century, such as the environmental movement, the women's movement, and the civil rights movement, have contributed to changing the way we think and act. Much of their impact occurs through changing organizational practices and policies. Yet, they argue, we do not have an adequate theory or framework for understanding how social movements directly and indirectly impinge on and operate to change organizations. Moreover, since organizations will differ in their response to social movement demands, an adequate theory must take into account variations in organizational response. Their chapter presents a middle-range, synthetic conceptual framework to help us understand the impact of social movements on organizations. It draws upon a variety of literatures, including implementation theory, legal mobilization theory, compliance readiness theory, neoinstitutional theory, and political opportunity theory. The first section discusses the myriad ways in which movement activities external to the organization come to bear on organizations. In particular, they discuss how movements contribute to the reshaping of institutional fields through cognitive, normative, and regulative reconstitution. They also discuss direct impacts of movement activism – for example, strikes and boycotts – as they differ from indirect impacts, such as those involving changes in the consciousness of relevant professionals and other participants. The second section presents a schematic model of how differences in the environments of organizations combine with leadership commitments and organizational resources to shape organizational responses. This section combines implementation theory with managerial decision theory. Finally, in the third section, Zald and colleagues propose an "open polity" framework to explain organizational responses to movements. This model recognizes the permeability of organizational boundaries that older models tended to ignore.

The broad theoretical synthesis developed by Zald and colleagues is followed by a concrete historical and quantitative study. In "Organizational Change as an Orchestrated Social Movement: Recruitment to a Corporate Quality Initiative," Strang and Jung conduct an in-depth study of one organization to explain the vicissitudes and relative lack of success of an attempt to respond to and incorporate elements of a widespread movement to change organizations. The Total Quality Movement generated much excitement in the United States during the 1980s and 1990s, and elicited the participation of a wide variety of companies seeking competitive advantage (Cole and Scott 2000). Many such attempts at organizational change take the form of "orchestrated social movements," where elites seek to set social movement-like processes in motion rather than establish new organizational rules or roles. Such a process is in distinct contrast with the diffusion of reforms such as ISO 9000, which rely more on top-down certification and pressure from exchange partners (Mendel 2002). In the American quality movement, change initiatives are apt to be rolled out with symbolic support and vague references to long-term career and organizational benefits, but few material resources. A small cadre of professionals plays the role of activists, involving workers and managers in training sessions and problem-solving teams. The hope is that positive feedback between the converted and the unconverted will lead to new ways of working that will become self-sustaining. They examine one such process, that of a "quality initiative" at a global financial services corporation. A survey of bank employees indicates that attitudes to the program reflect individual values, forms of personal involvement, experience with related programs, expectations of program durability, and the attitudes of co-workers. Strang and Jung argue that the fragility of the quality initiative is explained in part by its difficulty in recruiting adherents, coupled with the fact that workers rather than managers are its strongest supporters.

Where Strang and Jung examine a social movement initiated by managerial elites, in "Subverting Our Stories of Subversion" Scully and Creed focus on the efforts of grassroots activists in several organizations located in the same metropolitan area to push for the adoption of gay-friendly policies. Drawing upon previous theory and research, they show the importance and interrelationship of three important concepts – the construction of social identities, the creation and diffusion of repertoires of action, and the role of symbolic resources. The construction of social identities is one of the bases for social movement mobilization by active agents. Scully and Creed found that everyday encounters in which agents begin to share and thereby mold the distinctive and, often, prosaic elements of an identity help to legitimate that identity. As identities are forged, they lead to the creation and diffusion of repertoires of action. Not only did domestic partner benefits partially diffuse among organizations in a field, but activists' tactics, such

251

as "stealth legitimation," diffused as well, enabling some organizations to be deeply involved in the issues even if they were not yet adopters. In many ways, the adoption/non-adoption distinction becomes a less crucial outcome than the mobilization of agents and tactics. Symbolic resources, such as discourse and framing, are tools for action. Frames from the political realm are sometimes adopted wholesale and sometimes translated and manipulated by agents pursuing change in local workplace settings. Together, these three themes begin to construct a richer narrative of how social movements are carried forward by grassroots organizational members.

9

The Impact of Social Movements on Organizations

ENVIRONMENT AND RESPONSES

Mayer N. Zald, Calvin Morrill, and Hayagreeva Rao

In some measure, much of the social change we have witnessed in America and elsewhere during the last several decades can be attributed to social movements, large and small. The civil rights movement (CRM), the environmental movement, the women's movement, and the gay rights movement are among the larger and more visible motors of social change. Other, less visible, movements also have promoted significant changes in social policy, raised our consciousness about issues and problems, and even altered our behavior in everyday life, at home, with friends, and at work. The anti–drunk driving movement, the coalition of groups opposed to smoking, the movement for pay equity reform, and the animal rights movement may not have loomed as large on the political landscape as other movements, but they have significantly contributed to changes in the way we live. Movements that developed as spin-offs or amalgams of larger movements also have led to social change. Consider, as examples, the environmental justice movement, which emerged as an outgrowth of the environmental and civil rights movements, or the movement for pay equity reform, which grew out of the interplay among the CRM, the women's movement, and the more progressive streams of the labor movement. Of course, social movements are themselves created out of broad social processes and social forces, and are accompanied by diffuse political and social processes that contribute to social change. Nevertheless, it is useful to ask *how* and *where* social movements contribute to social change.

We are indebted to Amy Binder for her remarks at the conference and to participants in the Social Justice and Social Movements Seminar at UC Irvine, especially Yang Su and David S. Meyer.

Although largely ignored by the theoretical literature on social movement theory, much of what could be counted as social change occurs in *organizational behavior* via *organization policy*. As Perrow (2002: 1) reminded us, much of our individual and collective experiences are constituted by organizations in which they "provid[e], on their own terms, the cradle-to-grave services that communities and small organizations used to provide." Within this vast organizational population, some organizations quickly adopt policies that are consonant with the visions of "right" behavior articulated by movement leaders and activists. In these instances, change is woven into the formal structures, strategies, and, in some cases, the daily routines of organizations. Examples along these lines include adopting domestic partner benefits in concordance with the demands of the gay and lesbian rights agenda, banning smoking on an organization's premises, and changing laboratory procedures for using animals in medical experimentation. On the other end of the spectrum are organizations that resist movement imperatives. They continue to pollute long after antipollution statutes are adopted. They ignore demands for an end to sex discrimination in hiring, or for equal pay for equal work. Still other organizations articulate policies that seem to support movement goals, and establish programs and offices that suggest concern with changing the organization consonant with movement demands, yet see little change in the behavior of employees or in the implementation of policy directives (Edelman 1992). Conversely, since the members of organizations are also participants in the larger society and culture, practices and discourses in organizations can change without formal enunciations and adoptions of organizational policy.

Against this backdrop, this chapter addresses two large and interrelated questions: First, how do social movements' demands for change affect organizations? Second, what determines how organizations respond to those demands? Our aim is to present a middle-range synthetic theoretical framework that accounts for and charts the conditions under which movement-related policies and practices are adopted and enacted (or resisted) in organizations. The framework melds several literatures, but they can be classified as coming from two directions. The first literature addresses how social movements lead to changes in the *environment* of organizations, such that the abstract or not-so-abstract demands of movements are translated into more or less authoritative norms and directives attached to sanctions and surveillance. A second literature investigates aspects of an organization's internal life, thought of as an *organizational polity*, that facilitate or inhibit the incorporation and enactment of movement demands.

All organizations with any distinguishing boundary can be subjected to political analysis; thus, the impacts of movements on voluntary associations, government agencies, religions, schools and school systems, and for-profit corporations are all subject to our analysis. However, in this chapter, we focus upon corporate and formally hierarchical organizations that contain identifiable managers, display internal differentiation, and manifest autonomy vis-à-vis other organizations and agents.

To answer our first question about movement impact, we specifically draw upon implementation theory, neoinstitutional organizational theory, legal mobilization theory, and social movement theory. To answer our second question about organizational response, we draw upon a political perspective of organizations (Zald 1970a, 1970b; Zald and Berger 1978), but one that is more attentive to both overt and covert coalitional possibilities in organizations, as well as to the links between internal organizational levels and groups and external professional networks, associational affiliations, and institutional processes. Although we distinguish between the organization and its environment, we view the "boundary" between them as more or less permeable; they are linked through the identifications and affiliations of actors, the normative and ideological commitments that actors within the organization share with those outside, and a variety of boundary-spanning organizations, processes, and actors. Social movements thus impact organizations not only by contributing to changing the costs and benefits of pursuing certain policies and practices, but also by changing the orientations and attitudes of organizational members. That means that we must pay attention to how movements contribute to the transformation of discourse, culture, symbolic categorizations, and frames.

A word about how this chapter relates to prior work on the impact of movements on organizations: Most of the studies with which we are familiar analyze single movements and often focus upon a limited number of organizations. In *From Heresy to Dogma*, for instance, Hoffman (2001 [1997]) investigated the growth of modern environmentalism to trace its vicissitudes in one large oil/chemical firm. As illuminating as case studies can be for gaining in-depth understandings of single social phenomena, they may be less useful for establishing empirical generalizations that cut across different empirical domains. Since enacting movement-related goals requires adopting policies that have different costs, are differentially subject to surveillance and monitoring, and have different ideological matrices of resistance, a study of one movement could have little bearing upon the problems of other movements. A second limitation of prior studies, from our perspective, is that they sometimes focus upon one end of the problem rather than seeing the problem whole. Mary Katzenstein (1998), for instance, has done an excellent study of the confrontation of two resistant organizations, the Catholic church in America and the U.S. military, with modern feminism. Katzenstein's vantage point, however, largely resided within the organizations, with little attention to the larger social movement and its legal/institutional environment. We contend that movements and organizations must be seen in interaction. Movements and the political/administrative/legal processes that they unleash or accompany establish constraints and opportunities that shape the environment of organizations, which, in turn, are also shaped by organizational responses to external and internal demands for change.

At a theoretical level, our work most resonates with that of Michael McCann (1994, 1998), Hoffman (1999, 2001, 2001 [1997]), and the collection of essays edited by Hoffman and Ventresca (2002). McCann examined the impact of the pay equity reform movement upon organizational salary practices. He focused on the interplay of legal change and judicial rulings, movement activists and the community support for activism, and organizational change. We use his work as a springboard to broaden the analysis in two ways. First, we theorize a wider range of movement policy objectives. Second, we consider a broader range of internal organizational processes. Yet McCann had an important part of the story right: Although he undertheorized both organizational structures and resistance, he treats both the environment and the organization as variable.

The essays collected in Hoffman and Ventresca used neoinstitutional theory to recast our understanding of the impact of the environmental movement, including policy processes, the construction of institutional fields, and organizational responses. Although our focus is somewhat more on the determinants of organizational response, is more comparative, and draws upon different theoretical literatures (e.g., implementation theory, the literature on legal mobilization), our understanding of the interaction of environments and organizations substantially overlaps with theirs.

The analysis unfolds in three parts. In the first section, we examine three ways in which movements influence organizational environments: (1) through changing categorizations, justice claims, and consciousness–raising, and by changing the assumptions about right actions and routine grounds and practices; (2) through direct surveillance and sanctions by movement-identified groups and activists; and (3) indirectly through movement influence on public policy and agencies that constrain or facilitate organizational responses. In the second section, we present a "stylized" model of organizational compliance. The model presents a schematic analysis of how organizations respond to environmental pressures for movement-related compliance. It treats organizations as more or less unified actors whose responses to differential pressures vary according to organizational commitments (or resistance) to the intents or goals of the movement and organizational capacity (financial, administrative, etc., resources). Finally, our third section explores the processes through which organizational commitments are reached. We frame our analysis in this section around the concept of organizations as "open polities," which provides analytic leverage for understanding the various ways movement issues get on organizational agendas. It treats organizational commitments as an enactment process through which members with different statuses and authority, as well as connections to the larger society, process and create demands for organizational change and compliance.

Organizational Environments: Movements, Culture, Law, and Implementation

Movements manifest themselves and influence organizations via three mechanisms. First, movements bring to public attention grievances and problems in the larger society as they influence the framing and understanding of legitimate claims for organizational change; that is, they contribute to change in the cognitive and affective grounds of action. Second, movement activists and adherents, (i.e., those who identify with movement goals and orientations even though they are not involved in particular social movement organizations (SMOs) or networks of activism), individually or collectively attempt to convince organizational authorities to change policies and practices (e.g., through boycotts, protests, lawsuits, blockades, publicity campaigns, etc.). Third, movements participate in politics and attempt to change laws and establish government agencies to enforce or facilitate organizational change. In these circumstances, agencies and courts become the carriers of movement aims. These different kinds of activity can be seen as part of the reconstitution of organizational fields. Movements contribute to the redefinition and constitution of agencies, institutions, and practices in the environment of organizations, and to the internal practices and structures of organizations. Organizations are part of and contribute to that redefinition and reconstitution.

The Early Phase of Movements: Consciousness and Framing

In the early phases of a movement – more precisely, since few movements begin *de novo*, in the early phases of the current manifestation of a movement – organizational members, as participants in the larger society, begin to hear about a movement's definitions of issues and grievances. They may or may not perceive the relevance of movement claims for their own organizational functioning. Institutional fields (see Scott and McAdam, this volume; Rao, Morrill, and Zald 2000) and their cognitive and normative underpinnings may have been constituted with little regard to movement claims; or, indeed, they may be subject to normative definitions which the movement actively disputes. It is in this sense that the early moments of a movement can be seen as a consciousness-raising period in which the grounds and goals of action are challenged and new definitions of roles, relationships, and practices are proposed. In this early phase, movement-related activists and adherents directly have impact on a few targeted organizations. Many organizations, by contrast, will have little knowledge of movements and their claims unless mass and specialized communications media publicize movement events and claims. (See McCarthy, Smith, and Zald 1996 for a review of the relationship of movement activities and media coverage to the public agenda.) Moreover, a movement's early phases often accompany a welter of ambiguity and counterclaims regarding potential policy implications and legal status. Conflicting claims generated from opposition and partisan groups can further pull targeted organizations hither and yon in the crux of interpretive processes regarding movement aims and implications. In some instances, even before a movement develops a large presence, some organizations may respond to movement demands, either because internal elites quickly accept the justice of the movement claims or because they experience negative consequences from not complying. Negative consequences can be economic, social, or moral.

Direct Action

If a movement is even moderately successful, it establishes a presence in the public consciousness. Its general goals or aims become attached to labels or basic frames, SMOs, and leaders that in some sense represent or come to act as "flag-bearers" for the movement. Moreover, SMOs and networks of activists typically develop a set of tactical repertoires and venues through which they pursue intermediate and long-term goals. SMOs can directly attempt to get organizations and individuals to change, or attempt to affect the climate of opinion, and press for political and administrative changes. At the same time, sympathizers in other arenas provide support to the movement (e.g., churches, foundations, government officials) and can also press for change. Whether in concert or not with SMOs, legislators can conduct hearings and introduce legislation, and office holders and administrators can introduce administrative decrees and regulations that translate the more abstract goals of the movement and specific movement demands into legal and administrative remedies and programs.[1] In these cases, movements can be thought of as having had an indirect impact on organizations, through their contribution to the development of state policies, regulations, and programs.

Obviously, movements vary in their presence in different communities and organizations. In a large, diverse nation such as the United States, the ability of movements to survey and bring pressure on organizations will vary enormously depending upon the socio-demographics of the community and organizations, and on the support or hostility to movement goals present in the community. Indeed, movements exhibit a geographic and regional dimension that structures the local environment of organizations. In general, movements with a larger presence in the local community (as indicated by a larger number of adherents with mobilizable resources and by an organized presence) are likely to make more demands on organizations for change than they are when they have little support in the local community. At the same time, organizations in the local community vary in their vulnerability to movement demands, according to their dependence upon the community for support and relevant resources (Jacobs, Useem, and Zald 1991).

Even if a movement has demobilized, in the sense of containing fewer active organizations and groups pressing for change, it still can have significant impact through the bureaucratic and legal mechanisms that have been established. Moreover, movements may have appeared to demobilize, in the sense of very visible protest, even though they actually have just developed relatively stable organizations and a more conventional repertoire of action. It is also possible, however, that the political, legal, and administrative instrumentalities adopted are inadequate to the task. Proclamations

---

[1] Although they come from different starting points, see the extent to which Einwohner (1999), Skrentny (2002), and Wolfson (2001) overlap in focusing upon specific practices and regulations that are promoted by movement activists and/or by officials and administrators.

and policies can be advanced that at best give symbolic reassurances, with few concrete mechanisms for achieving change. Resources may be committed while the intractability of problems go unrecognized; remedies may be based upon mis-specified and inadequate technologies. Whether or not bureaucratic and legal mechanisms are established that actually seem to meet the objectives of a movement depends upon adequate policy implementation and the dynamics of legal mobilization. It is to these issues that we now turn by drawing from the literatures on implementation theory and legal mobilization – both of which developed somewhat separately from the main lines of organizational and social movement theory.

Implementation Regimes

Social scientists (typically sociologists and political scientists) developed implementation theory in the 1960s and 1970s in response to the shortcomings of federal programs designed to redevelop urban communities and negate the effects of poverty on life chances (Mazmanian and Sabatier 1989; Nakamura and Smallwood 1980; Pressman and Wildavsky 1979). The literature also grew out of the assessment of federal programs aimed at changing classroom performance by teachers of disadvantaged populations via new curricula, especially in mathematics and the sciences (Williams and Elmore 1976). A number of emphases emerged in the literature. The most prominent of these concentrated on the conflicting and often ambiguous objectives written into laws and the administrative regulations created to put laws into place. Questions about the clarity of purpose and the relationship of legislative goals to appropriate technologies or instrumentalities were raised. A second emphasis grew up around the amount and appropriateness of resources committed to the task. What positive and negative sanctions were mandated, and were the administrative agencies given enough resources and powers to induce compliance? Third, implementation theorists took seriously the social characteristics of target populations and some even regarded such characteristics as the *key* factor in "successful" implementation (Nakamura and Smallwood 1980). How much did legislation depend upon achieving agreement with a number of community groups and interests, possibly with conflicting interests? How big and diverse was the target population? How easy was it to know and reach the target population, whether organizations or individuals? Yet another issue concerned the very definition of implementation "success." Empirical studies documented the utter failure of governmental programs in which neither the end result nor process goals were met during implementation (e.g., Pressman and Wildavsky 1979). Conceptually or operationally defining success, and then empirically demonstrating success (either in terms of process or outcome), proved difficult. Finally, especially in the case of implementing change in schools, the literature drew attention to the human dimension, especially informal social relations that sometimes enabled and at other times constrained change efforts: How did programs reach the classroom through teachers and principals? What were the teacher training programs (inside and outside of a particular school or school system) and professional mentoring resources that sometimes led to effective adoption of new programs, but which also sometimes led to a transformation of programs that was unforeseen in their original design? This last emphasis especially opened up the topic of networks of contention and partisanship that crossed organizational, professional, and social boundaries. Although it is difficult to render a brief summary on the current status of the implementation literature, there has been increased emphasis upon the role of professional networks inside and outside of organizations and upon the ways in which internal organizational arrangements can facilitate or impede the adoption of new programs (Hill 2000; Lin 2000).

One useful way to organize the disparate streams of work within the implementation literature can be found in Robert Stoker's (1991) *Reluctant Partners: Implementing Federal Policy*. Using game theory, Stoker demonstrated how government policies can be understood as operating within different "implementation regimes" that contain various degrees of cooperation, information flows, and sanctioning mechanisms. Collecting social security taxes can be accomplished through a relatively straightforward bureaucratic regime because the government has vast and regular information available about wage earnings in established businesses and sufficient sanctions, should they need to be applied. Where, however, cooperation is hard to achieve and information complex and ambiguous, a very different set of relationships develops between the government and targeted groups and organizations. In school desegregation cases, cooperation has been difficult to achieve and a judge's ability to know whether court orders have been carried out has been limited. Indeed, it is in these contexts that special masters have been appointed to monitor and guide compliance with court orders. Stoker also noted that multiple federal agencies, as well as state and local governments, can share responsibility for federal policy. Implementation regimes thus reflect this complexity.

Although we do not fully utilize Stoker's analysis, some of its implications are crucial for our argument. If a simple bureaucratic regime can be set up that gains widespread compliance, political and social movement partisans can retire from the field. For instance, social security resulted from various historical movements and political activity, and there is continual political activity to defend the program and call for its enlargement, contraction, or change (Skocpol 1992). But there is relatively little need for continual social movement pressure to justify the collection of taxes and disbursement of benefits. (Of course, we recognize that there has been a small fringe movement of businesses and other partisans that deny the legitimacy of federal collection of social security and income taxes; we also recognize that the system has been largely unsuccessful in collecting social security taxes from households not registered as businesses.) Wherever policy is well institutionalized, almost complete demobilization can occur and yet the movement, in one sense, continues to achieve its goals. Even if movement leaders and key constituencies are not satisfied with the bargain encapsulated in a bureaucratic program or in a regulatory policy and agency, the movement can demobilize and accept stasis. Indeed, an iron triangle of industry, agency, and legislative oversight can eventually become dominant; the agency is captured by the clientele (Sabatier 1975).

Yet, as Sabatier and Mazmanian (1983) argued, and as Baumgartner and Jones (1993) brilliantly demonstrated empirically, stable policy arenas get disrupted as scandals occur, as the public agenda changes, and as events pose challenges to the iron triangles. Social movements and mobilized interest groups remobilize. In some cases, the enactment of policy fuels the continuation of the movement, although in a different form, since legislation may provide support for the continuing involvement of interested parties. Advisory boards and community participation requirements provide yet another impetus for partial mobilization. Indeed, policy can create a demand for mobilization in communities where little prior mobilization had occurred. Demobilization also can occur for reasons unconnected with the enactment of legislation and the implementation of policy (e.g., adherents and activists lose interest and shift attention to other issues; movement organizations and their leaders lose local credibility or broader legitimacy, given shifting normative and cultural currents).

It is important to note that the establishment of implementation regimes can directly implicate movement and organizational strategies. The legal/administrative apparatus may legitimate or delegitimate movement-related activists and agencies (see Marx 1979; McCarthy, Britt, and Wolfson

1991; Wolfson 2001). Governments can provide advocacy and a formal role in governance for community groups, or they can bar them from participation. Similarly, an implementation regime that focuses upon procedural compliance can permit an organization to comply on paper, with little commitment to actualizing programs (Edelman 1992). Where bureaucratic oversight is not feasible and/or where surveillance is difficult, compliance based only on state action is likely to be nonexistent or weak. But some basis in law can encourage activists to attempt to use the law to press for change. Studies of legal mobilization address this issue.

Legal Mobilization: Using the Law for Pursuing and Resisting Movement Goals

During the same period that implementation theory developed as a response to governmental efforts to facilitate community development and ameliorate poverty, students of the law began to ask how successful social movements were in making "rights claims"; in essence, could the courts be used as instruments of movements? Somewhat separately, those studying the Supreme Court (e.g., Becker and Feeley 1973; Wasby 1970) began to raise the issue of compliance readiness; why do some organizations quickly comply with the rulings of the court (e.g., *Miranda* and desegregation rulings), while others do not? In *Social Movements and the Legal System* (1978), law professor Joel Handler was somewhat skeptical of the ability to use courts to achieve social change because, he argued, they were usually restricted to due process oversight, not substantive intervention. When legislation did not directly mandate a particular organizational provision of benefit or service, courts could not intervene.

The legal mobilization literature, a loose confederation of interpretive perspectives on law and society, enlarged the scope of thinking about the impact of law on organizations by recognizing what McCann (1994: 7) called the "constitutive role of legal rights both as a strategic resource and as a constraint for collective efforts to transform or 'reconstitute' relationships among social groups." Underlying this observation is a sense of the dynamic role of law and policy regimes in shaping consciousness regarding the social world, individual and collective identities, and strategies for social change (Espeland 1998). Thus, law can act as an important resource for social movements operating around and in organizations. However, the legal mobilization framework does not posit a top-down view in which law "authorizes" social change or is an unambiguous resource once the "laws on

263

the books" or the "rulings in the judicial records" are given a favorable read by employees or movement lawyers (Fuller, Edelman, and Matusik 2000). Law is rarely an exclusive or unilateral force in social practice, especially related to social change (McCann 1994: 8). Rather, law is often indeterminate, and "legality" (the way individuals and groups orient themselves to law in social practice) is pluralistic, sometimes reproducing social hierarchies and sometimes challenging them, but always embedded in social practices and contexts (Ewick and Silbey 1998). Thus, lawyers and activists, both inside and outside organizations, can make diverse claims about the appropriate distribution of social benefits and burdens to organizational members, and can broach "legally" grounded strategies for achieving those claims in wildly divergent ways. Organizational authorities also can approach the very same sources of law as activists do (e.g., judicial rulings, legislature, administrative mandates) in divergent ways. Moreover, legal arenas vary as to whether lawyers have incentives to bring cases. When class action suits are allowed, when penalties include extensive monetary damages and provisions for the payment of lawyers, lawyers can intentionally or unintentionally become the carriers of movement goals, even if the direct regulatory power of state agencies is limited.

Taken together, the concepts of legal mobilization and implementation regimes provide a conceptual terrain that helps us understand how movements "get" into organizations and influence compliance with movement goals. Implementation regimes constitute a salient source of environmental pressure for organizations to comply with movement demands. However, since laws are open to multiple interpretations, the commitment to movement goals of organizational authorities and elites becomes a crucial variable that helps explain organizational responses. Organizations differ in their compliance capability, and their financial, material, and cultural resources. We need to ask how organizational capacity and commitment interact with environmental pressure to affect forms of compliance.

A Stylized Model of Organizational Compliance

As a first cut at explaining movement impacts on organizations, we present a stylized model to explain organizational responses to movements by focusing on the compliance readiness of organizations as it interacts with the strength of sanctions and surveillance in the environment. Assuming knowledge of movement goals, compliance readiness can be thought of as consisting of two components, ideological commitment (or agreement) and organizational capacity. Ideological commitment is the extent to which the top executives or the dominant coalition (Cyert and March 1963) of the organization are sympathetic to the goals of the movement and believe they can legitimately make claims for organizational change. Crudely, we propose a dichotomous treatment, low or high commitment. (Obviously, a more complex treatment could be used, including a neutral ground and more or less intensity of negative and positive commitment.)

Organizational capacity refers to the organization's financial and human resources, as well as the administrative knowledge and capabilities to implement procedures and programs relevant to movement-related goals. If, for instance, compliance with environmental regulations requires large capital investments, some organizations may not have the wherewithal, and, therefore, may go out of business, or stall and attempt to evade compliance, even if ideologically they are in agreement with the movement's goals. Or, organizations may not contain staff with requisite skills or administrative know-how to put in place movement-related programs. Here we again treat capacity in dichotomous terms as high or low.

We also treat organizational environments in simplified terms. Where direct and indirect surveillance and sanctions are well organized, severe, and certain, we can think of the environment as presenting compelling (high) pressures for compliance. Where they are disorganized, weak, and uncertain, the environment presents few (low) pressures for compliance.

What of the forms of organizational response? The new institutionalism reminds us that just as orientations to the law can be pluralistic, organizations can respond to external expectations in a number of ways (Edelman et al. 1991; Meyer and Rowan 1977). Organizations can respond by symbolic conformity, with little change in actual organizational procedures. Thus, leaders can give speeches or do public relations work that implies organizational conformity, even while the core procedures relevant to the expectations are not changed. On the other hand, when leaders have resources available and are tied into industry networks, if they are opposed to movement goals, they can proactively oppose the movement. They also can organize collectively to change the policies, to get more sympathetic regulators appointed, to de-fund regulatory agencies; and they can attempt to restrict the usages of class action legal remedies.

Table 9.1 presents a typology of organizational responses as a function of the amount of environmental pressure and organizational capacity and commitment. Where commitment and capacity are low and sanctions and surveillance are weak (Type A: Low Pressure, Low Capacity, Low

Table 9.1. *Varieties of Organizational Compliance*

Type	Properties	Organizational Response
A	Low pressure Low capacity Low commitment	Disregard movement demands or treat movement as irrelevant
B	Low pressure Low capacity High commitment	Early attempts to implement movement objectives
C	Low pressure High capacity Low commitment	Some compliance or thwarting of movement
D	Low pressure High capacity High commitment	Symbolic compliance of low cost items
E	High pressure Low capacity Low commitment	Evasion
F	High pressure Low capacity High commitment	Compliance on low cost items
G	High pressure High capacity Low commitment	Early resistance
H	High pressure High capacity High commitment	Maximum compliance

Commitment), we would expect organizations to disregard movement demands. Here, the movement is treated as largely irrelevant, although executives who believe the movement is likely to lead to increasing pressures could develop resistance strategies. For example, the antichild labor movement in the United States during the early part of the twentieth century was treated as irrelevant by business firms even though two million children worked in factories, mines, and fields. The National Child Labor Committee formed in 1904 to raise awareness, but for the next three decades, the Supreme Court and Congress were at odds over child labor regulation. Only in 1938, with the enactment of the Fair Labor Standards Act, did children become legally excluded from dangerous work (Saller 1998).

Our expectation is that maximum compliance occurs when commitment is high, capacity is high, and external sanctions and surveillance are high (Type H in our table). Of course, if commitment and capacity are high when movement aspirations first hit the public scene, surveillance and sanctioning apparatuses are likely to be easily developed. This is the case in what has come to be called "consensus movements" (McCarthy and Wolfson 1992; Schwartz and Paul 1992). The movement against drunk driving provides a useful example of a consensus movement. Few people, if any, support driving while inebriated. But even in the case of consensus movements, there is apt to be some, perhaps even substantial, resistance to specific practices and programs advocated by movement activists. For example, producers of beer, wine, and spirits have stoutly resisted recommendations offered by Mothers Against Drunk Driving to regulate advertising on radio and at sports events. The more a movement presses for substantial changes in purveyor practices and marketing, the greater the resistance will become.

Our expectations for responses by organizations with characteristics that locate them in the other cells are less clear than at the extremes. Nonetheless, we hypothesize possible patterns for these cells. Organizations located in Type B (Low Pressure, Low Capacity, and High Commitment) are likely to generate early attempts to meet movement objectives, especially if costs are low; they will be early innovators, but large organizational changes will not occur. An example might be the T-Group movement–a human relations movement that used leaderless group discussion to promote democratization and teamwork in organizations. Senior executives in companies who were highly committed to these values were the first to adopt training programs, but were unable to refashion the culture of the organization because of low external pressure, and the lack of incentives and resources within their organizations (Kleiner 1996).

The combination of characteristics of organizations in Type C (Low Pressure, High Capacity, Low Commitment) leads to two possibilities: one might be some compliance; but organizations also might use their capacity to actively thwart whatever external pressures develop. In the early phases of the quality movement, for example, American firms possessed the resources to implement change, but a combination of low commitment and the lack of external pressure from movement activists led to minimal compliance, and thwarted the goals of the movement (Cole 1999). Managers in many U.S. firms overlooked quality as a competitive factor and denied Japanese superiority. Instead, they attributed the performance of Japanese firms to Japanese access to cheap capital, government support, and the manipulation of currency rates. Managers also believed that high quality and low cost were contradictory goals, and that diminishing returns would come from additional increments of quality (Cole 1999). Many American managers perceived the model of continuous quality improvement as impractical.

Organizations located in Type D (Low Pressure, High Capacity, High Commitment) have a high likelihood of compliance on low-cost items, and a great deal of proactive symbolic compliance and culture change in organizations. An example might be the antisweatshop movement of the 1990s that sought to ensure the prohibition of child labor and prison labor in Asia and Africa in the international apparel industry. Although apparel manufacturers such as Nike and Reebok swiftly adopted codes of conduct in order to safeguard their reputations, compliance on costlier items, such as factory inspection by the merchandiser or company-hired external monitoring, appeared at a slower rate (Elliott and Freeman 2000).

The combination of pressure, capacity, and commitment of organizations in Type E (High Pressure, Low Capacity, Low Commitment) leads to maximum evasion and internal delaying tactics, which sometimes coalesce into proactive external resistance. If compliance is costly, the organization may refuse to comply and even close down or redefine itself. In the case of the environmental movement, while there has been high external pressure on target industries such as automobiles, automobile firms have adopted delaying tactics in the development of energy efficient cars, nonpolluting technologies, and substitute technologies due to the dearth of resources and commitment (Moore and Miller 1994).

Organizations in Type F (High Pressure, Low Capacity, High Commitment) are likely to comply on low-cost changes, but defer or move at a slower rate in implementing higher-cost changes. If, for instance, relevant external actors are empowered to make facilitation grants, organizations in Type F are more likely to take them than are organizations in Type E. Thus, the women's movement achieved success in transforming the occupational and educational opportunities for women by attaching the goals of gender equality to the earlier antidiscrimination victories of the civil rights movement and by changing the cultural template about equal opportunity and women's capabilities. Although some occupations or specializations within occupations remain largely closed to women, or not sought by them, (e.g., firefighters, long-distance truck drivers, coal miners, heart surgeons), other lines of work have become open to women. Yet, more subtle organizational processes continue to be beyond rectification and solution (Davis 1999). Thus, the attempt to eliminate hostile work environments, the need to change mentoring relationships, the problems of work/family tradeoffs, and the subtle ways in which the masculine or macho culture and networks of organizational elites create glass ceilings are beyond easy fixes (Davis 1999).

Organizations in Type G (High Pressure, High Capacity, Low Commitment) are likely to resist early, even launching proactive resistance activities. Where, however, the costs of continued resistance are great, these organizations have the capacity to implement changes, especially where the changes are of a more technical and bureaucratic nature. Without a change in commitment, however, more culturally based changes that alter foundational premises for action are likely to be resisted. An example is the animal rights movement, where, in a short time, a very dramatic and indeed violent movement gained compliance from medical schools and research institutions around the country that initially sought to resist the movement (Jasper and Nelkin 1991). Although the more activist members of the movement were anathema to medical school and pharmaceutical laboratory personnel, supported by governmental regulations and professional norms, rapid changes in the handling of laboratory animals occurred, even though the more radical goals of stopping the usage of animals in the laboratory did not occur.

As we noted earlier, this stylized presentation simplifies a much more complex set of possibilities. The range of responses is too limited, there are response sets possible in each condition, and these sets can overlap across conditions (although it is highly unlikely that the response sets overlap across *all* conditions). Second, the table presents a static conceptualization of what is necessarily a dynamic, over time, process. Thus, commitment can lead to an allocation of resources that changes capacity; and the development of capacity can change commitment. Imagine a situation where an organization hires personnel to meet regulatory demands and where the personnel then rise in the organization and become part of the dominant coalition, thus influencing its commitments. Moreover, commitments are entangled with affiliations. Thus, mid-level professionals and functional managers may participate in external trade associations and professional organizations that shape organizational commitments (see Lounsbury 2001; Rosenkopf, Metiu, and George 2001). Similarly, organizational responses feed back on sanctions and surveillance, if the organization and the industry affect the movement and government policy. Third, the table ignores the complexity of organizational fields. A field can be rife with contradictory and ambiguous normative prescriptions, and these can be changing in different directions. Finally, the table assumes a uniform or singular organizational response. Although a model of a unitary organization may be heuristically valuable, it ignores a wide variety of possible commitments, power/authority constellations, and interpretive schemata that may be distributed across organizational units. Personnel in different locations and statuses in the organization can have differing views of what the organization should be doing and what its capacities are, they can make different "reads" of what laws and rules mean relevant to organizational routines (Fuller, Edelman, and Matusik 2000), and they can be differentially positioned to support or block attempts to move the organization for or against movement objectives (Morrill, Zald, and Rao 2003). All of these sources of variation in the organizational responses represented in Table 9.1 suggest that the internal processes of organizations, especially those of a political and contentious nature, need to be conceptualized. It is to this task that we now turn.

Movement Demands and Political Process in Organizational Polities

What are the processes and organizational structures that shape how particular organizations respond to movement demands? How do the changes in discourse and direct and indirect attempts to implement movement goals affect the commitments and procedures of organizations? How do they get *inside*? We can begin to answer these questions by examining the limits of an earlier attempt to think about social movements in organizations. Zald and Berger (1978) theorized organizations as analogous to societal polities with constitutionally defined social structures, interest coalitions, distributions of rights and duties, and, most importantly, governance systems of authority and control. They drew from resource mobilization theory to conceive collective action in organizations as purposive, interest-driven responses to social injustice and attempts at change, rather than only spontaneous outpourings of grievances as in earlier collective behavior traditions. Moreover, they examined the opportunities and constraints that different organizational polities presented, including responses by authorities, control systems, available material and cultural resources, and social networks. However, there is a need to extend Zald and Berger's insights on four counts.

First, as with much of organizational theory, Zald and Berger focused upon organizational identities and positions, ignoring that most members have salient identities in and with other social groups, categories, and statuses. Racial, ethnic, gender, community, professional, occupational, and class identities, and the networks and associational lives connected to these identities and statuses, are powerful determinants of organizational members' responses to movements and the incorporation of movement goals and ideologies in organizational contexts.

Second, although Zald and Berger mentioned, in passing, other dimensions of organizational structure, the core of their analysis focused upon the hierarchical dimension of structure, that is, top management conflicts (coups d'état), middle management and professionals (bureaucratic insurgency), and lower participants (mass rebellion). Thus, they do not systematically bring in the functional, spatial, and institutional linkages and structures that effect the location, diffusion, and resolution of social movement claims.

Third, the imagery used by Zald and Berger stressed highly organized and overt instances of collective action, missing covert forms of individual and collective action that can be tacitly coordinated. Morrill's (1995) study of conflict in the upper executive ranks is instructive in this regard. Almost none of the conflict he identified involves more than a few participants and most of it is barely visible, yet it occurs often and can have significant impact on entire organizations. Moreover, as Meyerson's (2001; Meyerson and Scully 1995) analysis of "tempered radicalism" demonstrated, feminists in organizations often operate through loose networks and subtle co-action to push the organization towards providing a more sympathetic milieu for women. Morrill, Zald, and Rao (2003) took this insight one step farther by attempting to think more systematically about the covert and almost invisible co-action aspects of resistance and conflict in organizations as they relate to overt forms of "voice" (Hirschman 1970).

Finally, Zald and Berger relentlessly focused on collective action generated by internal issues in the organization. While these issues may be linked to the larger economy and to the changing position of the organization and its products and technologies in the larger industry, they paid little attention to the connection between internal mobilizations and actions and the external environment. Yet, for our purposes here, such attention is central.

What is needed is a conceptualization of organizations as open polities. Zald's earlier (1970, 1972) analysis of organizational political economies may be helpful in this regard. It might be useful to conceptualize organizations as overlapping polity arenas, in which internal structures and processes are linked to external fields, agents, and norm-defining institutional processes. An open polity approach thus can be thought of as applying a political process or opportunity approach to organizations, as Kurzman (1998) did. In the next section, we draw on the notion of open polity to deepen our

271

analysis of how organizations respond to the emergence of social movements and the processes that unfold as they impact organizations.

Open Polities

The polity of an organization (or its political system) emerges out of three interconnected dynamics: the constituting norms and commitments of an organization, its formal or legitimated system of authority, and its informal power and influence systems (Zald 1970a, 1970b).[2] Constituting norms (whether written or not) include product and clientele commitments, central organizational routines, and authority or governance norms. Authority or discretion is allocated to both positions and offices held by individuals and groups (e.g., committees, boards, panels). The notion of an *open* polity thus facilitates analysis of the *interplay* between movements and organizations because it treats the boundaries of organizations as porous and permeable. Indeed, to the extent that groups and organizations external to the focal organization have significant control, power, and authority over it, the "external" units may be conceptualized as part of the polity (just as the polity of a colonized nation includes the colonizer *and* subalterns). It is one in which actors and groups in different locations in organizations, operating within a variety of institutional processes and rules, and linked by identity and networks to movement issues and to external actors, come to pursue or resist movement-related goals. Organizational members with their multiple identities and their different locations within the organization perceive and process pressures from social movements (loosely defined), and define the internal problems and issues within organizations. They also reach out to actors and agencies in the environment of organizations to enlist them in specific conflicts and issues within organizations. They call on consultants, lawyers, professional accrediting agencies, regulatory agencies, and the media to bolster their positions within organizations. (Of course, the analysis of organizations as open polities also focuses attention to how organizations process *any* pressures or possibilities for organizational change, not only social movement–related changes.)

---

[2] For several decades, explicitly "political" approaches to organizations have declined in macro-organizational theory. Neither neoinstitutional theory nor population-ecology work made political processes or structures central to their concerns. There is some evidence of a revival of interest in political analysis in recent years (McAdam and Fligstein 2003; Stryker 2000).

Open polities vary along a number of dimensions that are relevant to how organizations process external and internal pressures for change. One relatively gross distinction is between corporate hierarchical organizations and federated and associational (partnership) forms. The latter two facilitate open conflict, schisms, and factions in a way that the former does not (Zald and Berger 1978). Indeed, it could be argued that the constituting norms accompanying each of what, in common parlance, are treated as "natural types" (e.g., hospitals, schools, religious organizations), exhibit distinctive modes of political processing. However, there also is variation in organizational polities of a fine-grained sort. Thus, for instance, corporate hierarchical organizations vary in the number of divisions that they have, in the extent to which divisions have autonomy in policy formulation over different domains, and in the linkage structures (e.g., reporting systems, committee structures, cross-unit team structures) that tie the divisions to one another and to the central office.

These variations ought to lead to differences in the ways in which organizations process movement demands. For instance, even if the dominant coalition within the executive elite is relatively committed to moving in the direction desired by a social movement, if divisions have great autonomy in policy areas relevant to the movement, recalcitrant divisions may be slow to accommodate. In universities, for example, it is very common to find the upper administration promoting diversity and affirmative action, while individual departments and schools may pay little attention to these issues. (Our sense is that physical science and old-line humanities departments – classics and philosophy – have resisted or ignored the blandishments of the upper administration more than social sciences and the more politically engaged humanities disciplines.) Thus, the criteria for undergraduate student admission, which is centrally controlled, can reflect great attention to having a diverse student body while faculty hiring demonstrates great variation across departments with regard to this issue. Similarly, some schools or departments may show great environmental awareness, while others barely show any.

At this point in time, we are not prepared to develop a theory or model about how and when organizational polities respond to movement demands; there are just too many types of issues that generate implementation/organizational adoption contingencies. But we can suggest some guiding questions and issues. Are organizational elites drawn from and/or connected to groups that are committed to or opposed to movement goals? Have the elites, as a group, publicly avowed or disavowed commitment to the goals? Has the organization given great autonomy to units with regard to enacting practices related to movement goals, or are policies and practices created that extend throughout the organization? If separate staff offices have responsibility for practices related to the movement's goals, how much authority does the office have in relationship to units? Are staff offices perceived as influential over relevant organizational practices, or are they limited in their ability to develop programs and require participation? Are there monitoring systems in place that specify the dimensions of expected behavior and "measure" over time the extent of effort to achieve desired outcomes? Is the organization embedded in a local community that has a substantial base of movement supporters? The more these questions are answered positively, the more we would argue that the organizational polity supports or is committed to movement goals.

In the remainder of this section we discuss three issues, alluded to earlier, that help us see the complexity of linking external "demands" and internal processes: co-action and caucuses, legal ambiguity and legal remedies, and executive commitment and professional transformations.

Co-action and Caucuses

Organizational membership implies, to some extent, the suppression of nonorganizational identities. A clichéd slogan might read: "We are all employees, working for the betterment of the organization." But the suppression of nonorganizational identities fails in the face of the importation of gender, ethnic, race, religious, and political markers and expectations into the organizational arena. Since workers need jobs and are rewarded, sometimes, for performance in those jobs, the assertion of nonorganizational identities into those jobs and making claims on the organization can be viewed negatively and punished.

In the first instance, asserting claims related to movement goals can be tempered by the desire to get ahead, or at least to remain in good standing. Even before that, if an identity is stigmatized, any acknowledgment of an identity can inhibit co-action – whether it is the search for mentors, the mutual support of group members, or the development of caucuses that actively seek policy changes that promote movement goals. Since organizational members closer to the top are usually expected to identify more with organizational goals (e.g., vice-presidents are expected to be more loyal and committed than maintenance staff), members of an identity group that climb in an organization will typically be expected to distance themselves from the goals of identity groups (LaNuez and Jermier 1994). At the same time, there are two conditions under which the emergence of identity groups and identity claims are facilitated. First, as noted above, the claims of the movement can be facilitated by strong community support. Second, internally, the executive cadre may be committed to movement goals.

Legal Remedies and Legal Ambiguity

When surveillance is high and sanctions are certain, organizations will have little wiggle room with regard to the law (Calavita, Pontell, and Tillman 1996). Much of the time, however, law is much more of an "open text" (especially with regard to civil rights laws), and activists outside of organizations as well as relevant staff within organizations can argue for the adoption of policies that are not strictly mandated by law. Much has been made of the extent to which personnel officers (in the modern parlance, human resources staff) played a role in the reinterpretation of affirmative action and diversity policy (Kelly and Dobbin 1999). Moreover, as Edelman, Abraham, and Erlanger (1992) noted, legal counsel have facilitated the adoption of pro-movement policies as protection against liability, even if the current status of the law denies such need—a kind of protective insurance against a future reading of the law. Both of these interpretations pay no or little attention to the pro- or anti-movement orientation of the relevant staff. Indeed, staff members typically are portrayed as pursuing a professional project that is long divorced from an activist stance issued by a relevant movement. One can well imagine a school counsel in a Southern city, for instance, arguing for delaying tactics in the face of a legal mandate because of his embeddedness in the local community. The lesson here is that more attention must be paid to the processes through which key staff members form their orientations toward movement-related policies.

We also should pay more attention to how organizational members reach out to use the law and public agencies, and how appeals are made to outside authorities for help inside organizations. Members or potential members of organizations make claims with external authorities and agencies to push for organizational change. Many of these cases can be treated as "private" disputes that would seem to have little impact on broader, more "public" issues, discourses, and practices. By contrast, we argue that more attention needs to be paid to the "signaling" value of these external and public claims. When they are high profile, they carry obvious consequences for change far beyond the immediate case, as staff and officers of similarly situated organizations ponder the implications for their own practices. However, even without high profiles, such cases can provide strategies and legitimacy that course through both informal networks of activists and professional networks of lawyers.

Executive and Professional Networks and Transformation

Lounsbury, Hirsch, and Ventresca's (1998) work on the environmental movement is exemplary in drawing our attention to how professional change impacts organizational change consonant with movement goals. In the environmental case, the movement has come to represent an opportunity for the realization of professional projects. At the same time, it enhances the implementation in organizations of movement objectives. Hoffman's (2001) analysis of field-organization relationships emphasized that movement-related issues can have varying impacts on different functional/task structures and groupings in organizations (e.g., accounting, human resources, marketing, research and development, production, etc.). While it is important to emphasize the professional and middle management linkages to movements, it also is important to remember that middle managerial and professional commitments and linkages can be significantly framed and influenced by top management and its commitments. On that topic the literature is sparse.

Conclusion

Social movements bring about a great deal of social change via their impact on organizational policies and practices. As obvious as the statement is, the literature on the impact and outcomes of social movements has largely ignored it. A recent major edited collection dealing with movement outcomes (Giugni, McAdam, and Tilly 1999), for instance, did not raise the issue. Much of the literature on outcomes or impact asks how movements contribute to the enactment of legislation or changes in state policy, rather than exploring the impact of movements on organizations. This may be a bit overstated, for many scholars of particular movements have asked how that particular movement has fared in the context of a particular organization or a population of organizations. Yet the focus on particular movements does not problematize movement impact with respect to organizations, thus leading to the under-theorization of how variation in movements and organizations interacts to shape social change. By drawing on a number of different theoretical perspectives found in social movement theory, neoinstitutional organizational analysis, implementation theory, the literature on legal mobilization, the literature on culture change, and a view of organizations as open polities, we have provided the beginnings of a framework to help explain the extent to which movement goals, in all their complexity, are enacted or resisted in organizational policy, symbolism, and practice.

This chapter has tended to focus upon "progressive" movements and ignores movements of the right. But does that change the argument? It doesn't change the argument in terms of the analytic categories and processes one uses, but there well may be differences in the kinds of organizational changes that are sought by "progressive" and "conservative" movements and there also may be differences in the moral legitimacy that organizational elites attach to movement claims and rhetoric.

An important difference may well be that progressive movements seek to impose constraints on corporations and markets whereas "conservative" movements from the right aim to roll back laws constraining corporations. So the study of how progressive movements get inside organizations devolves into a study of compliance, whereas the analysis of how conservative movements penetrate organizations shades into an understanding of the dis-adoption of past acts of compliance.

However, the use of the terms "progressive" and "conservative" has a Left-Right connotation that obscures the moral, rhetorical, and emotional dimensions of movement claims, regardless of whether they are progressive or conservative. Amy Binder (2002) demonstrated that even though school authorities resisted both Afro-centrist and creationist demands for curricular reform, they granted much more legitimacy to the backers of Afro-centrism than to the backers of creationism, and manifested this difference in the way they responded to claimants.

Yet another question could be raised with respect to the types of movements we have analyzed. The claims made by the vast majority of movements (whether from the Right or Left) considered in this chapter issue from moral or social justice agendas. At the same time as organizations respond to challenges from these types of movements, they also confront movements that espouse technical and/or managerial agendas. Earlier in the chapter we briefly alluded to movements with such agendas (e.g., T-groups and the quality movement). What is unclear is how the environmental pressures and response sets differ for such movements, especially when they may not be strongly connected at all to legal or governmental regulatory structures.

Moreover, such movements certainly can cause controversy in organizations, but can they galvanize opposition groups in the same way as moral-and/or justice-charged agendas can?

In light of these concerns, an important task for future research is to delineate the boundary conditions under which organizations respond to different types of movement demands and implementation regimes, and when they are able to create their own environments and influence the design of implementation regimes. Whether it involves the design of pollution standards, the content of CAFE (Corporate Average Fuel Economy) legislation, organizations have relied on collective strategies to shape their institutional environments. So more work needs to be done on how organizations deter and divert movements, thwart the enactment of laws, undermine regulations, and shape their environments.

Another important task is to nest the study of movement impact on organizations in the larger topic of institutional and organizational change. That larger topic focuses upon economic, technological, and institutional factors external to organizations, and the way those external processes facilitate the pace, institutional stability, and interpretive underpinnings of change (Bartunek 1984; Lawrence, Winn, and Jennings 2001; Tushman and Romanelli 1985; Van de Ven and Hargrave 2004). It is especially important to join research on movement impact with previous work on organizational change because much of that literature (especially related to strategy) treats change as a planned or, at the very least, "planful" managerial action. Social movement agendas certainly can become a part of managerial strategy, but often they initially present themselves outside the parameters of anticipated organizational policy. As a result, managers are often in the position of reacting to unanticipated agendas and collective action. Several questions could be posed here, including: How are social movement agendas incorporated into managerial strategies? How do accounts offered by management for such incorporations affect both the premises and implementation of strategy?

Our analysis has predominantly emphasized the structural rather than the cultural dimensions of movement impact. We reiterate that social movements contribute to the formation of new understandings, new theories, and new categories, and in turn, these understandings and categories can become constitutive of organizational life (Rochon 1997; Skrentny 2002). By the same token, organizations also can counteract and influence categorizations. The efforts of antitobacco activists to classify cigarettes as drug delivery systems with a view to bringing them under the ambit of the FDA, and the endeavors of the tobacco industry to thwart such classification, underscore how politics and culture constitute each other. Thus, the study of movement impacts should be seen as another bridge across the chasm that has tended to separate the study of culture and organizations from the study of politics.

10

Organizational Change as an Orchestrated Social Movement

RECRUITMENT TO A CORPORATE
QUALITY INITIATIVE

David Strang and Dong-Il Jung

Understandings of organizational change, like organizations themselves, are informed by assumptions of rationality, authority, and functional integration (Meyer and Rowan 1977). The focus is on formal adoption of new procedures and their subsequent implementation. New rules are promulgated, organizational units or formal roles are created, and incentive systems are modified. The process may be messy and contested in practice – organization members may resist and strategies backfire – but these are problems to be sorted out through redoubled authoritative intervention.

Many efforts at organizational change are better understood as social movements. In these contexts, a logic of mobilization replaces a logic of authority. Activists seek to recruit adherents and broadcast success. Normative appeals to individual or collective benefits substitute for material resources. The guiding principle is not that leaders will enforce change, but that unmanaged positive feedback can permit new behaviors to diffuse and become self-sustaining.

Zald and Berger (1978) made this argument forcefully, pointing out that formal organizations are simply another type of polity within which social movements can arise. They suggest parallels between the overthrow of organizational leaders and coups d'état, whistle blowing and bureaucratic insurgency, and prison riots and mass movements. Scully and Segal (2002) and Scully and Creed (this volume) extended and subverted this

This research was supported by a grant from the Citigroup Behavioral Sciences Research Council. We thank Amy Binder, Jerry Davis, Sid Tarrow, Mayer Zald, and the participants at the Social Movement and Organizations conference for their helpful comments.

line of analysis to discuss the personal experience and strategies of "internal activists," detailing how efforts to challenge structured inequality are sustained within organizations.

This chapter examines the quality initiative of a multinational bank, here named Global Financial, to illustrate and extend the idea of an intraorganizational social movement. Of course, no one would mistake this sort of a program for a prison riot. With some effort, it could be more plausibly treated as a bureaucratic insurgency, where enlightened corporate leaders attack antique notions of command and control and seek to empower those who do the work. Quality advocates often talk this way: for example, Deming (1982) blamed executives for corporate failure and argued for eliminating barriers that rob people of the pride of workmanship. Ishikawa contended that "an organization whose members are not happy and cannot be happy does not deserve to exist" (1985: 27).

We see Total Quality Management (TQM) as a reform movement led from above, rather than a revolutionary one led from below. Quality initiatives are launched by organizational elites. The goal is performance improvement and cost containment, not personal liberation or corporate anarchy (these more outrageous ambitions are traditionally left to management gurus). We describe Global Financial's program as an "orchestrated social movement" to emphasize both the formal staging involved and its top-down character.

A note on usage. The term "social movement" combines two ideas: a processual component that refers to mobilization of groups outside institutional channels, and a substantive component indicating that the mobilized lack routine access and are willing to challenge the status quo. The substantive component often carries the weight: for example, Tilly (1984: 306) defined a social movement as a "series of interactions between power holders and persons successfully claiming to speak on behalf of a constituency lacking formal representation . . . " We put the stress on process instead, preferring "orchestrated social movements" to awkward labels such as "elite-sponsored activist-led mobilization efforts with reformist goals."

While the initiative examined here was led from the top, middle managers, professionals, and front-line workers were not pawns shifted about in a display of organizational theater (see Aguirre 1984). To the contrary: they were the actors whom elites hoped to mobilize. By structuring a change program as a social movement, organizational leaders adopt a role akin to that of studio executives promoting a film. They can advertise, shape the product to appeal to key markets, court opinion leaders, and even lower prices – but they cannot force people to watch the movie or recommend it to their friends.

Our aim is not to elaborate definitions, however, but to see what is gained by treating an organizational change program as a social movement. The first section of this chapter describes the symbolic framing and organizational structure of Global Financial's TQM program.[1] The second and main section examines the mobilization of support among Globalbankers, focusing on the role of individual values, personal involvement, prior experience, social networks, and expectations of program durability. The third section considers the implications of who was recruited, and who was not, for the fate of Global Financial's quality initiative.

To set the scene, we should note that the program studied here arose within a larger extraorganizational movement. Japan's competitive success in the 1970s and 1980s led to widespread efforts among American firms to adopt a "new quality model" (Cole 1999) grounded in customer satisfaction, continuous improvement, and small group problem solving.[2] Quality initiatives were legion within the financial services industry in the 1990s (McCabe et al. 1998), and Global Financial's program shares much with efforts elsewhere. We are struck, for example, by how closely the bank's quality initiative mirrors Hackman and Wageman's (1995) depiction of characteristic TQM programs.

The voluminous literature on TQM focuses mainly on its impact on corporate performance (Conference Board 1991; Easton and Jarrell 1998; Powell 1995) and on correlates of adoption (Gittleman, Horrigan, and Joyce 1998; Lawler, Mohrman, and Ledford 1995; Osterman 1994), with some studies doing both (Westphal, Gulati, and Shortell 1997). There is much less attention to the logic underlying TQM programs, to social dynamics that emerge within these programs, and to how employee responses affect

---

[1] We use "total quality" and TQM interchangeably through the text. Global Financial referred to its program as the "Corporate Quality Initiative" and avoided the term "total quality management" since it had been largely discredited in managerial circles by the late 1990s. The program we study is generally indistinguishable from TQM as discussed in the academic literature.

[2] While the quality movement exhibits considerable longevity, in Zald, Morrill, and Rao's language (this volume) it should be coded as generating *low* external pressure. There are no legal or regulatory requirements for firms to implement total quality, and interorganizational coercion affected small suppliers of manufacturers such as Ford but not elite banks like Global Financial. By the period studied here (the late 1990s), even informal normative expectations had become ambiguous at best.

program durability. A social movement perspective is well positioned to address these issues, opening up the black box of program adoption, impact, and abandonment to ask what happens in between.

Global Financial's Quality Initiative

Global Financial's Corporate Quality Initiative began in the first quarter of 1997. It was not the first total quality effort mounted by the elite multinational – most notably, there had been a substantial quality program in its credit card business in the early 1990s. Quality departments were also well institutionalized within Global Financial, most prominently in the Consumer Bank, and these departments played established roles. But the Quality Initiative stood out as the bank's first corporation-wide quality program and the first total quality effort that had the personal support of the bank's chief executive officer (CEO).

Global Financial's quality initiative was announced as a vehicle for profound organizational change. The organization's internal newsletter portrayed it as "the bank's breakout strategy . . . " Its CEO introduced the initiative in a taped interview distributed to all employees. In response to the question "The quality initiative – why now?" he said, "We must distinguish our presence. It's demanded by the world, will deliver services in a framework that's never existed. This program will touch every Global banker, all 92,000. We're living in a world where we must energize everybody in the company, and historically we haven't done that."

Quality was framed as offering something for everyone. For the bank, the aim was to reduce errors in customer interactions and speed up operations: "Let's improve by a factor of ten. So if it takes six months, let's do it in six days. If it takes six hours, let's do it in six minutes." For employees, a vision of new opportunities was offered:

The hierarchical management structure will have to give way to some collective activities that will improve our effectiveness in the marketplace. Decisions won't flow from a management level to people on the line who are expected to implement those decisions. . . .

We're telling everyone, choose a process, figure out what and where the problems are, work together to come up with solutions, and then put your solutions to work."

The CEO's last sentence introduces a principle of autonomous action. Employees are not informed that a new management system has been established; they are invited to "choose a process," "work together," and "put your solutions to work."

Of course, action requires perceptions of reward. The bank's CEO thus describes how the initiative would enhance life at Global Financial:

> This is going to be a much better place to come to work for every Global-banker.... We all spend a lot of our time fixing mistakes or overcoming problems. It's not only time consuming; it's frustrating and stressful.... Dealing with our customers on matters of substance, rather than on problems that originate somewhere else, will automatically make us feel far more empowered.

But it was not expected that the initiative could be fueled by its intrinsic appeal alone. The CEO added long-run personal advantage to the list: "The best people in the company are going to surface. Its going to change a lot of career paths."

These career opportunities were not built into the bank's evaluation and compensation structure, however. They depended instead on the initiative of individual managers. Managers who "got on board" might well set up major projects under the quality umbrella and reward team leaders and participants who identified productivity improvements. But managers who saw total quality as limited or ineffective would not.

For a symbolically central program, Global Financial's Quality Initiative possessed minimal organizational infrastructure. A Corporate Quality Office was formed under the directorship of one of the firm's twelve executive vice presidents, a long-standing corporate leader who had established the quality program in Credit Cards while directing that unit. A total of sixteen quality professionals made up the staff of the Corporate Quality Office. They were aided by an executive on loan from Motorola, whose Six Sigma™ methodology and cross-functional process improvement approach the bank built its program around.

The Corporate Quality Office did not act alone, of course. It worked in partnership with the bank's quality control departments, whose personnel within the United States alone numbered some 674 officers and 211 nonofficer employees. But the Corporate Quality Office lacked line authority over these much larger units, whose directors reported to business heads within their divisions.

Early in the initiative, outsiders to Global Financial were central to getting the program up and running. These included Motorola staff who instructed bank employees in statistical methodologies and crossfunctional process improvement techniques, as well as independent management consultants. For example, one of us observed a training session led by a quality professional from Global Financial's Consumer Bank, a senior trainer from a management consultancy specializing in corporate culture, and an independent consultant. As Global Financial personnel became experienced and formally licensed in the (proprietary) quality methodologies adopted by the bank, the proportion of in-house trainers and facilitators grew.

The idea was that quality was "everyone's job." Expansion of the bank's quality personnel and the formation of a powerful corporate office with line authority were avoided as fostering a quality bureaucracy. When asked who was responsible for the initiative, the CEO replied "each of us. This is how we are going to work. . . . I'm going to have a few projects on my personal quality."

Operationally, the quality initiative involved three main activities. First, all bank employees were to receive formal *quality training*. This training was organized to cascade through the organization, with executives and top managers participating in a first wave of training, followed by their direct reports, and on down through front-line workers. Quality training involved two broad components: a statistical language for describing and analyzing organizational problems, and a behavioral focus on team building, cooperation, and organizational values.

Second, operational units were asked to report their performance on a series of *quality metrics*, which counted "defects" in customer interaction such as delays in account openings and credit decisions. The Corporate Quality Office maintained a database of scores across business units, whose participation was voluntary. In keeping with the central office's lack of line authority, business units were permitted to redefine metrics to fit local circumstances.

Third, managers could form *cross-functional performance improvement (CFPI, or quality) teams* to address business challenges. Team sponsors identified a "critical business problem" and recruited participants, while quality personnel provided facilitation and support. The average project lasted about a year, with participants adding project tasks to their regular responsibilities.

Each of these activities was substantial in scope. While we lack a count of how many employees received quality training, the survey reported below suggests a figure of 82 percent among U.S. employees. Two quarters after the initiative began, thirty-six of the bank's forty-six major business units were reporting scores on quality metrics. Over twelve hundred quality teams were formed across Global Financial.

Employee Attitudes

In April 2000 we conducted a random sample survey of Global Financial employees working in the United States. Names were selected from a May 1999 employment roster, with the sampling frame defined as regular employees working thirty-five hours per week or more who had been hired before July 1998. Although 750 surveys were mailed, we later received personnel data indicating that only 649 sampled individuals were still with Global Financial in December 1999 (i.e., 101 of the sampled employees had left the bank in the last seven months of 1999). Altogether 245 completed surveys were received, for a response rate of 37.8 percent (under the implausible but conservative assumption of no additional turnover between January and April 2000).

The quality initiative was thus more than two years old when our survey was mailed. This meant that the early resource constraints and growing pains of the initiative had been overcome, but it also meant that the bloom was off the rose. The great majority of quality initiative activities that would ever occur at Global Financial had already taken place, and this fact was apparent to many of our potential respondents. We think all of this is strategic, because employees were well positioned to offer mature assessments and because the larger context did not promote forced enthusiasm for a new program.

A comparison of background characteristics shows modest differences between survey respondents and non-respondents: 53 percent of respondents and 52 percent of nonrespondents were men. The average respondent was forty-one years of age, had been with Global Financial 10.6 years, and received a salary of $69,991; nonrespondents were on average also forty-one years old, had been with the firm 11.1 years, and received a salary of $67,832. However, managers and professionals were less likely to respond to our survey than were front-line workers: 74 percent of respondents but 82 percent of nonrespondents held supervisory, professional, or administrative positions.

While research on social movements often studies participation in specific events (such as marching in a demonstration), we examine attitudes instead. An organizational change initiative is much less of a public phenomenon: it involves not collective action but many small-scale activities occurring in different parts of the organization. In addition, employee behavior cannot be treated as chosen in the sense that participation in protest movements can, since quality activities may be assigned to the employee by his or her supervisor. We thus use employee attitudes to index successful or unsuccessful mobilization, and relate these to the employee's experience and organizational location.

We found that Globalbankers held strong views on the bank's quality program and on total quality more generally. One Globalbanker we surveyed told us, "I think the focus on customer satisfaction is key to our long-term success." Other respondents took a dimmer view. Overestimating our clout within the bank, one commented, "Please don't make me go to other quality classes!"

We asked respondents for their opinion of the effectiveness of quality initiatives across five contexts, ranging from the most immediate ("this quality initiative ... applied to the work you do") to the most general ("quality initiatives in general ... applied to firms of all types"). While all responses were positively correlated, a factor analysis suggested two components: *local endorsement* (combining perceptions of the effectiveness of Global Financial's quality initiative for the respondent's work and for the respondent's department or division) and *generalized endorsement* (of total quality for firms in financial services and for firms of all types).[3]

A third common attitude expressed frustration. Many at Global Financial described the bank's quality initiative as "the flavor of the month." This characterization could refer to the intrinsic superficiality of TQM, or it could imply a critique of Global Financial. In one employee's words, "I have never thought that Global Financial is committed to quality. To me quality, if it is to be effective within a corporation, has to be as important as the bottom line. . . . To me, Global Financial's quality efforts are more "show" (for the public, press, and share-holders)." We measure *frustration* through responses to the statement "For me personally, Global Financial's Quality Initiative has led to frustration with 'flavor of the month' programs" (1 = Strongly Disagree, 5 = Strongly Agree). While measures of endorsement provide an index to recruitment to a total quality agenda, frustration captures the potential "demobilization" of Global Financial's workforce.

Figure 10.1 indicates that Globalbankers express a mix of all three attitudes. When considering one's own work and one's own department, respondents are lukewarm at best towards the quality initiative, with

---

[3] We also asked about the effectiveness of the quality initiative for Global Financial as a whole. Responses here stood between and were correlated with views of both local and generalized effectiveness. We do not include this term in the factor scales in order to develop a stronger contrast between the two.

288

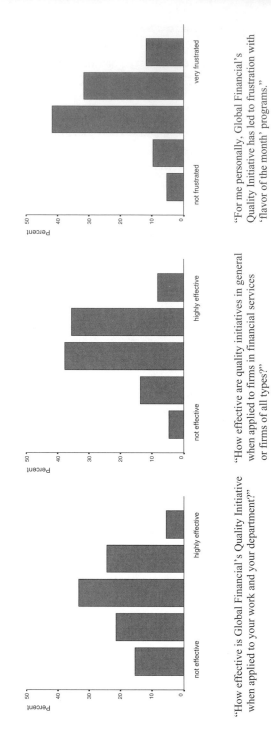

"How effective is Global Financial's Quality Initiative when applied to your work and your department?"

"How effective are quality initiatives in general when applied to firms in financial services or firms of all types?"

"For me personally, Global Financial's Quality Initiative has led to frustration with 'flavor of the month' programs."

Figure 10.1 Attitudes Toward the Quality Initiative. *Left,* Local Endorsement; *Middle,* Generalized Endorsement; *Right,* Frustration

15 percent describing it as "not effective" and only 6 percent as "highly effective." Somewhat higher levels of generalized endorsement are stated, with less direct skepticism and a stronger tendency to view quality initiatives as very effective. There is also a real sense of frustration, with many critiquing the initiative as simply the flavor of the month.

While one might expect endorsement and frustration to be inversely related, there is no correlation between either form of endorsement and our measure of frustration. Once we control for generalized endorsement, however, the relationship between frustration and local effectiveness turns modestly negative. Two years into the initiative, we see a tendency to critique Global Financial's program coupled with a more positive stance towards total quality in the abstract.

Sources of Employee Attitudes

We consider how attitudes towards Global Financial's quality initiative are rooted in individual values, concrete forms of involvement, experience with related programs, expectations about the program's future, and the views of co-workers. We then examine how attitudes vary across occupational positions within the bank, comparing managers, supervisors, professionals, and front-line workers.

With the exception of occupational position, each of these factors has a long pedigree in explaining recruitment into social movements. Much social movement research focuses on the impact of individual values, prior or concurrent protest experience, network connections to movement supporters, and calculations of the probable efficacy of action in selecting participants from this pool. For example, McAdam (1988a; McAdam and Paulsen 1993) considered the impact of attitudes, relations to other participants, and membership in related organizations in explaining recruitment to the civil rights movement.

Individual Values   Some employees may be drawn to total quality because its underlying philosophy is compatible with their own. Total quality involves a vision of organizational change that is at once scientific (decision making as statistical problem solving), social (organizations as collections of teams), personal (individual commitment and skill development), and political (empowerment within top-down leadership). Drawing on academic reviews (i.e., Hackman and Wageman 1995), practitioner discussions (i.e.,

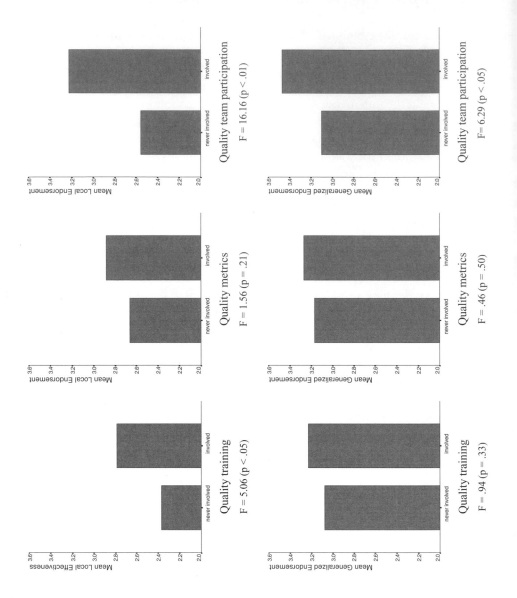

290

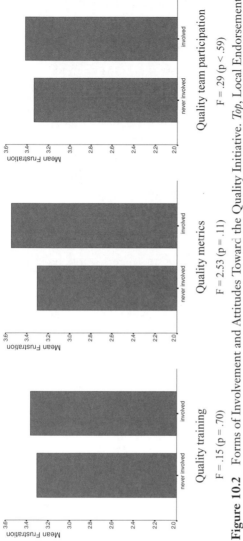

Figure 10.2 Forms of Involvement and Attitudes Toward the Quality Initiative. *Top*, Local Endorsement; *Middle*, Generalized Endorsement; *Bottom*, Frustration

291

Garvin 1988; Juran 1979), and Global Financial's quality training documents, we asked Globalbankers to evaluate eight "TQM principles."[4]

Factor analysis indicated that evaluations of all eight items load on a single factor, distinguishing those who endorse TQM principles from those who do not. This composite index of support for TQM as an idea is tied to both local and generalized endorsement of quality initiatives. The link to local assessments is modest ($r = .12$, $p = .07$) while that to generalized endorsement of quality initiatives is somewhat stronger ($r = .28$, $p < .01$). There is no relationship to our measure of frustration.

It may seem surprising that these relationships are not stronger, since we are correlating responses to two sets of questions about the effectiveness of TQM: one as an abstract set of principles and the other as a concrete program. But the modest correlation between the two, particularly when the focus is on the respondent's own workplace, echoes much social movement research. Individual values often turn out to be necessary but distant sources of recruitment, identifying a pool of potential supporters whose behavioral choices are shaped by more proximate factors (Klandermans and Oegama 1987). Here, the weak linkage may also reflect the ambiguity of the total quality framework and the potential slippage between TQM's rhetoric and programmatic realities (Zbaracki 1998).

Forms of Involvement   Formal program activities sought to directly involve employees. Quality training included instruction in statistical methods and methods of group decision making, role-playing scenarios designed to promote cooperation rather than competition, and discussion of the bank's corporate culture. Developing and implementing quality metrics drew attention to customer interactions and needs. Participation on cross-functional process improvement teams gave participants an extended and meaningful experience of team-based problem solving. We asked whether Globalbankers had been involved in the initiative in each of these ways.

Figure 10.2 shows that employees who received quality training and participated on quality teams are more likely to endorse quality activities

---

[4] These principles are "focus on customer satisfaction," "focus on cross-functional processes," "group effort rather than individual effort," "openness to experimentation and change," "development of interpersonal skills," "empowered to directly implement change," "roles based on expertise, not status," and "structured problem-solving techniques and statistical tools."

within their workplace. Participation on quality teams also spills over to boost endorsement of quality initiatives in general. By contrast, work with quality metrics has scant influence on employee attitudes.

These effects echo social movement research that emphasizes the role of personal experience in building commitment. The most intensive and demanding form of involvement (quality team participation) has the largest effect, while the most distant and impersonal (quality metrics) has a negligible impact. Our own observation of quality training showed us that Globalbankers could be strongly engaged when questions of individual commitment and personal authenticity were raised within a small group setting.

These results are also consistent with Sine and Strang's (2001) cross-national analysis of quality teams. Team participants across eleven countries expressed substantially stronger endorsement of the quality program than the average respondent in the random sample survey reported in this chapter, with variation in attitudes linked to group dynamics within the team as well as cultural orientations. Sine and Strang (2001) and Strang (2003) documented the reciprocal relationship between individual attitudes and the spread of quality team activities, with the strongest causal effects running from activities to attitudes.

Experience with Related Programs   In evaluating efforts at organizational change, Globalbankers were neither naïve nor inexperienced. Many had been involved in other quality programs, both within and outside Global Financial. Total quality has much in common with other organizational change efforts, such as business process reengineering (whose approach to process improvement is almost indistinguishable from quality's CFPI projects) and corporate culture programs (whose attempts to build commitment and trust parallel attention to the "human dimensions" of quality). We consider three kinds of experience: with other quality efforts at Global Financial, past involvement in related programs,[5] and current involvement in related programs. To simplify a complex picture, we distinguish between those who have had no experience of each sort of program, one program experience, or two or more program experiences.

Figure 10.3 indicates that prior or concurrent program experience generally boosts support for the quality initiative, as does experience with related

---

[5] These eight programs are quality circles, problem-solving groups other than quality circles, reengineering projects, self-managing work teams, culture change initiatives, flextime, telecommuting, and gainsharing/group incentive pay.

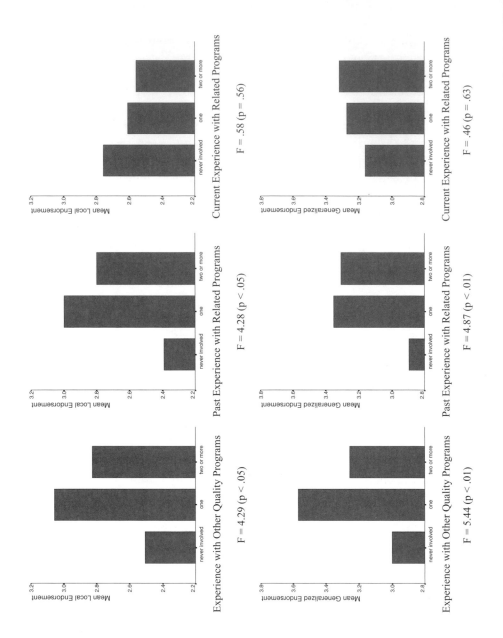

294

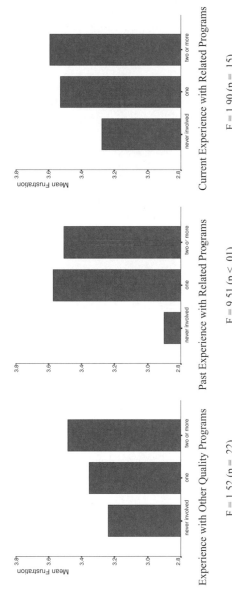

Figure 10.3 Experience with Other Quality Programs and Attitudes Toward the Quality Initiative. *Top*, Local Endorsement; *Middle*, Generalized Endorsement; *Bottom*, Frustration

programs. But there are signs of sharply diminishing returns. In most cases, experience with one program produces stronger endorsement than does experience with two or more programs. This is true of other quality programs at Global Financial and of past involvement in related programs. Current involvement has more consistent though more muted effects, tending to raise generalized endorsement while lowering local endorsement (perhaps through competition for employee attention and energy).

Frustration tends to grow with repeated exposure. It rises most sharply with past involvement in related programs, where those with any amount of involvement are significantly more likely to see the quality initiative as simply the "flavor of the month." Frustration also increases steadily with quality program experience and current involvement in related programs.[6]

These results speak to the long-term viability of the quality movement. If prior experience with quality and related programs produces commitment, the broader quality movement might win the war despite losing most of the battles. But if exposure leads to cynicism or resignation, past programs will undermine new initiatives. Our results suggest both positive feedback (through a generalized sense of the effectiveness of total quality) and negative feedback (through frustration with "flavor of the month" programs). Globalbankers are apparently becoming more convinced by TQM in principle, and less moved by it in practice.

Figure 10.4 explicates how attitudes appear to be evolving through a crosstabulation of local endorsement and frustration. Interestingly, numbers of the two "pure" types (those who endorse and are not frustrated, and those who do not endorse and are frustrated) shift little with past program experience. Instead, the main impact of past program experience seems to be to turn contented skeptics (those who do not endorse and are not frustrated) into skeptical advocates (who endorse total quality but are also frustrated by it)!

Perceptions of Program Trajectory   As the previous section makes clear, Globalbankers were well aware that change programs often have little staying power. We also found them wary about boarding a sinking ship. To do so meant, at minimum, a waste of valuable time and resources. It also

---

[6] We also examined the impact of experience with quality programs at firms outside Global Financial, which tends to depress local endorsement but has little relation to generalized endorsement or frustration.

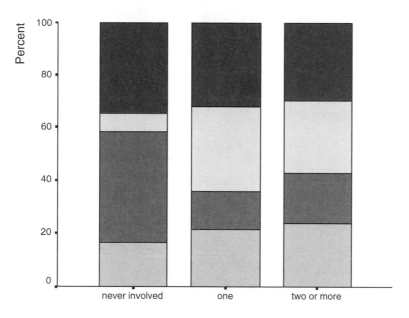

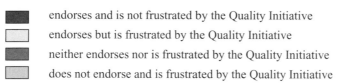

- endorses and is not frustrated by the Quality Initiative
- endorses but is frustrated by the Quality Initiative
- neither endorses nor is frustrated by the Quality Initiative
- does not endorse and is frustrated by the Quality Initiative

Figure 10.4 Past Program Experience and Mixes of Endorsement and Frustration

might lead to political damage (for example, if ambitious efforts at change antagonized "process owners").

We asked respondents about the trajectory of the quality initiative in four contexts: change over the last year within their department, change over the last year within Global Financial, expected change over the coming year within their department, and expected change over the coming year within Global Financial. These were scored on a five point scale, where 1 = Discontinued, 3 = Same Level of Activity, and 5 = Greatly Increased Activity. All four perceptions were strongly related (the lowest correlation between them is .65). Bankers seem to have used recent experience to estimate where the program was going, and generalized from the quality activities of their unit to those of the larger organization.

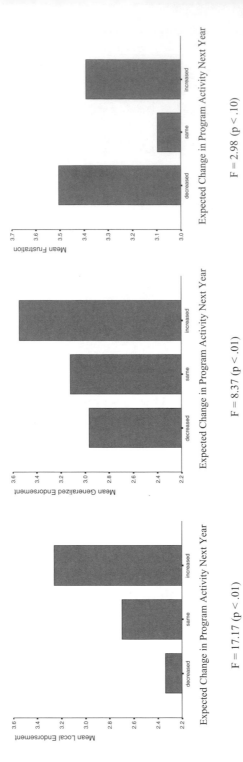

Figure 10.5 Expected Program Trajectory and Attitudes Toward the Quality Initiative. *Left*, Local Endorsement; *Middle*, Generalized Endorsement; *Right*, Frustration

298

Table 10.1. *Correlation Coefficients Between the Views of Co-workers and Attitudes Toward the Quality Initiative*

Views of Co-Workers	Local Endorsement	Generalized Endorsement	Frustration
Direct reports	.59***	.45***	−.03
Peers	.67***	.52***	−.06
Supervisor	.61***	.46***	−.05

*** p < .01 (two-tailed)

Figure 10.5 shows how expected change in the quality initiative over the next year is related to assessments of total quality. The first two panels indicate that Globalbankers who anticipate that the program will decline also evaluate quality initiatives less positively, while those who anticipate an increase in activity view quality as more effective. A more complex pattern emerges when we examine employee frustration. While those who expect program activity to decline are more frustrated than those who expect it to increase, both groups are more frustrated than those who see the program as stable. Big increases in activity may suggest that the program is the "flavor of this month" just as big decreases make it clear that the program was the "flavor of last month."

Social Networks   Relationships to other participants are one of the strongest conduits of social movement mobilization (Snow, Zurcher, and Ekland-Olsen 1980). We asked how the quality initiative was viewed by three reference groups: the respondent's direct reports, the respondent's peers, and the respondent's supervisor. Questions took the form: "To the extent you can judge, how does . . . view Global Financial's quality initiative?" (responses on a five point scale: 1 = Not Important, 5 = Critically Important).

Table 10.1 indicates that respondent attitudes are strongly related to perceptions of what supervisors, peers, and direct reports think. Globalbankers are much more likely to view the quality initiative in their workplace as effective if supervisors, peers, and direct reports see the program as important. But more than a practical local assessment is involved. Endorsement by peers and supervisors also translates into perceptions that total quality initiatives generally work. Frustration, by contrast, is uncorrelated with the views of co-workers.

Organizational Position   Finally, we consider the employee's occupational position. Work roles speak to key aspects of individual identity, orientation towards the firm, and the costs and benefits of the quality model.

TQM's advocates contend that it makes work more fulfilling. According to Joseph Juran, "the human being exhibits an instinctive drive for precision, beauty, and perfection." Adler (1993) argued that team-based opportunities to redesign work processes turn Taylorism into a "learning bureaucracy." This implies that while all sorts of employees will benefit from total quality, the benefits should be greatest for front-line workers, whose position furnishes the least scope for individual autonomy.

Critics view total quality as intensifying managerial surveillance while offering the pretense of solidarity (McCabe et al. 1998; Parker and Slaughter 1993; Sewell 1998). While some workers may be "bewitched" by these promises, the majority are likely to be "bewildered" by its apparent appeal for others, or "bothered" by its impact on the organization (Knights and McCabe 2000). Managers and supervisors should be more supportive of TQM as a powerful system of control.

A third argument is that quality is something the top gets the bottom to do to the middle. Supervisory authority is undercut by the expanded role of front-line workers, who are empowered to make policy proposals directly to higher managers. Managers and workers gain power while foremen and supervisory managers lose it. This argument often is buttressed by a cultural analysis of supervisors as ill-prepared to practice the sort of participatory, enabling style of leadership required by an empowered workplace.

We identify four occupational groups: managers, supervisors, professionals, and front-line workers. These categories are derived from responses to the survey questions "Do you supervise the work of others?" and "If yes, do individuals who you supervise themselves supervise others?" Respondents are coded as managers if they replied "yes" to both questions and as supervisors if they responded "yes" to just the first question. Among those who cite no supervisory responsibilities, we distinguish professionals from front-line workers on the basis of their occupational classification (professionals are those designated for equal employment opportunity purposes as managers, professionals, or salespersons; front-line workers those designated as technicians, operatives and office and clerical, or craft workers).

Figure 10.6 indicates modest but consistent differentials in attitudes across the four occupational groups. Front-line workers endorse total quality most strongly (a statistically significant differential when we compare

300

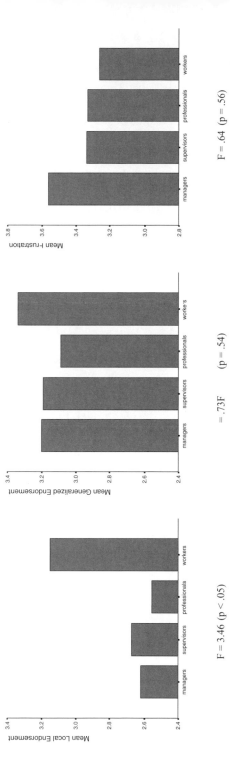

Figure 10.6 Occupational Positions and Attitudes Toward the Quality Initiative. *Left,* Local Endorsement; *Middle,* Generalized Endorsement; *Right,* Frustration

301

these workers to all other groups). Professionals are least likely to endorse the initiative, although the gap between their views and those of managerial and supervisory personnel is small.[7] Frustration toward the quality initiative is not as clearly linked to organizational position, although managers express this sentiment with the greatest force.

Absent a strong argument for false consciousness, these results are more compatible with the position of advocates that TQM empowers than with the view that it tightens the bars of the iron cage. In addition, it seems telling that the gap between front-line workers and the other occupational groups widens as the issue shifts from "firms in general" to the employee's own work situation. We pursue some of the sources of these differentials below.

Multivariate Analyses   The bivariate relationships discussed above may conceal substantial interdependencies. For example, employees whose values are aligned with total quality may be more likely to participate on quality teams, and employees with more extensive experience with total quality may have more current involvement as well. We examine multivariate models that focus on a reduced set of factors that capture the major relationships discussed above. Since network influences provide by far the largest single source of employee attitudes, we consider models that first exclude and then include supervisor and peer support for the initiative.

Table 10.2 shows that multivariate relationships are largely consistent with the bivariate relationships discussed at length above. Individual values, personal contact with the initiative, experience with related programs, and expectations that the initiative is on an upward trajectory all lead to endorsement of quality initiatives. Support for TQM principles boosts generalized endorsement of total quality. Front-line workers are more positive toward the quality initiative within their unit than managers, supervisors, and professionals are.

Table 10.2 also underlines the way employee frustration flows from positive evaluations of TQM rather than negative ones. Respondents sympathetic to TQM principles are more frustrated, not less, as are employees with extensive prior involvement in related programs. Belief that the quality program was gaining steam tended to counter these frustrations, though perhaps not for long.

---

[7] Zeitz (1996) came to similar conclusions in a study of TQM in a government office, arguing that total quality celebrates the competence of those closest to the task.

Table 10.2. *Unstandardized Coefficients from Ordinary Least Squares Regressions on Attitudes Toward the Quality Initiative*

Variable	Local Endorsement		Generalized Endorsement		Frustration	
	1	2	1	2	1	2
Constant	1.87***	.50*	1.89***	.92***	2.39***	2.66***
	(.30)	(.29)	(.29)	(.31)	(.32)	(.37)
Supports TQM principles	.15**	.05	.28***	.23***	.15**	.21***
	(.70)	(.06)	(.07)	(.07)	(.07)	(.08)
Quality program experience						
Received quality training	.38**	.33**	.06	.00	−.12	−.05
	(.18)	(.14)	(.17)	(.16)	(.19)	(.19)
On CFPI team	.68***	.44***	.25*	.10	−.24	−.22
	(.16)	(.13)	(.15)	(.14)	(.17)	(.17)
Prior quality experience	.20	.12	.18	.11	.10	.09
	(.14)	(.12)	(.14)	(.13)	(.15)	(.15)
Related program experience						
Past involvement	.35**	.26*	.44***	.38***	.47***	.46**
	(.16)	(.13)	(.15)	(.15)	(.17)	(.18)
Current involvement	−.30*	−.37***	.01	−.06	.16	.20
	(.16)	(.13)	(.15)	(.14)	(.16)	(.17)
Expected program trajectory						
Increase	.50***	.13	.27	.09	.13	.15
	(.18)	(.15)	(.17)	(.17)	(.19)	(.20)
Decrease	−.66***	−.16	−.36**	.04	.45***	.34*
	(.16)	(.14)	(.15)	(.15)	(.16)	(.18)
Occupational position						
Manager	−.42	−.16	−.09	.20	.07	−.10
	(.26)	(.22)	(.25)	(.24)	(.27)	(.29)
Supervisor	−.35*	−.17	−.22	−.04	−.02	−.08
	(.20)	(.17)	(.19)	(.18)	(.21)	(.22)
Professional	−.39**	−.20	−.23	−.01	−.03	−.14
	(.19)	(.16)	(.18)	(.18)	(.20)	(.22)
Network influences						
Supervisor's view		.24***		.19**		−.06
		(.07)		(.08)		(.09)
Peers' view		.37***		.21***		−.08
		(.07)		(.08)		(.09)
N	197	185	196	184	195	183
R^2	.36	.60	.25	.39	.12	.15

***p < .01; **p < .05 ; *p < .1

Table 10.3. *Perceptions of the Importance of the Quality Initiative from Different Vantage Points*

Occupational Positions	View from Above	View from Peers	View from Below
Managers	–	2.33	2.98
Supervisors	2.35	2.63	3.64
Professionals	2.39	2.50	–
Front–line workers	2.50	2.89	–

Peer and supervisor support for the initiative markedly boosts assessments of total quality, especially within the respondent's workplace. Network effects also interact with a number of the relationships noted above. The impact of expectations about program durability diminishes sharply and loses statistical significance when peer and supervisor support are added as explanatory factors. So do differences across occupational positions.

The relationship between social network effects and anticipated program trajectory seems transparent. Departments where co-workers and supervisors see the initiative as important are also likely to be departments where quality program activities are maintained or are increasing. And expectations of the program's future trajectory in the bank are strongly connected to observation of one's own department in the recent past.

More puzzling is the relationship between social network effects and occupational position. Why are differentials across occupational positions connected to the influence of supervisors and peers? While we cannot offer conclusive evidence, further investigation suggests that a key factor may involve structures of misperception.

Table 10.3 shows how perceptions are organized within Global Financial. The data give mean levels of local endorsement (1 indicates that the program is judged as not effective, 5 that it is highly effective). The rows indicate whose views are perceived; the columns, who is doing the perceiving. For example, the value of 2.98 in the last column of the first row indicates how respondents whom we code as supervisors rate the views of those they report to (who, if they were included in the survey sample, would be coded as managers).

Table 10.3 indicates widespread and systematic misperception of what others thought about the quality initiative. Occupational groups are consistently seen as more supportive from "below" than they are from "above." For example, front-line workers describe supervisors as rather supportive of the quality initiative (an average score of 3.64) while managers see supervisors as more skeptical (an average score of 2.35). These differences are probably tied to role-based presentations of self – bosses may feel obliged to boost corporate programs within their units, and subordinates to offer some resistance. Peers, who are perhaps in the best position to judge, rate each group's support for the initiative at levels between the (over)estimates of subordinates and the (under)estimates of superordinates.

The net result is that lower-level employees receive more positive messages about the quality program than do higher-level employees. At the extremes of the organizational hierarchy, the CEO receives only negatively slanted impressions while front-line workers receive only positively slanted impressions. The tendency of front-line workers to endorse the initiative thus seems bound up by where they stand in a system of (mis)communication.

The Impact of Partial Recruitment

At best, the corporate quality initiative failed to win the hearts and minds of Global Financial's workforce. Our survey, conducted well after the bloom was off the rose, found modest to low support and much frustration with the quality initiative. More bankers saw the quality initiative as ineffective than rated it as highly effective. About half of all respondents reported frustration with "flavor of the month" programs.

Even more consequential than average levels of endorsement and frustration may be the way these attitudes are distributed across occupational positions. The most favorable assessments come from workers on the line (actually, phone lines), while managers, supervisors, and professionals are significantly more skeptical. This is bad news politically, since executives, managers, and professionals count for much more in determining the fate of an organizational program than the organizational rank and file does.

In fact, Global Financial's quality initiative was brought to an end approximately eight months after our survey was conducted. The director of the Corporate Quality Office and a number of quality professionals left the bank, and the office itself was given a narrowed mandate within Global Financial's Consumer Bank. The quality initiative had had a short (although not uncharacteristically short) run of a little more than three years.

The proximate cause of the corporate quality initiative's demise was a change in bank leadership. The CEO whose "personal conversion" had helped launch the initiative left the bank, while the new CEO viewed total quality with unabashed skepticism. A highly favorable political opportunity structure (Tarrow 1998) had been replaced by a distinctly unfavorable one.

We would argue, however, that partial recruitment had made the quality initiative vulnerable. The new CEO's criticism was astute precisely because the program was neither taken for granted nor normatively legitimated within the bank. The fact that front-line workers rather than top managers formed its strongest constituency further reduced the quality program's political viability, making its elimination a nice way to symbolize change in bank leadership.

The long-term implications of the attitude formation process described here are also of interest. Global Financial's quality initiative was just one chapter in a long list of programs stressing cross-functional processes, participation, empowerment, and teamwork. Just as the experience of prior quality and related programs influenced recruitment to the quality program studied here, it in turn will presumably impact how Globalbankers respond to future organizational change efforts.

There are signs that the quality initiative generated some pockets of commitment that may promote future efforts. The strongest endorsement of total quality comes from those with the most extensive involvement in the initiative – bankers who participated on quality teams and whose departments maintained high and increasing levels of quality activity. These departments might continue to use quality techniques despite the demise of the larger corporate initiative.

The more typical experience, however, is frustration with the gap between what was promised and what was delivered. The most strongly voiced sentiments in our survey were those of employees who felt that the bank had failed to carry through. One Globalbanker described "A lot of lip service but no senior manager commitment," while another said, "it has turned into a 'flash in the pan' program. No data is given to us, no follow-up information or training programs have been implemented."

These expressions of betrayal felt by employees provide a strong signal that the corporate quality initiative may have undercut future programs. It is telling that employees with extensive prior experience were less impressed by TQM in practice than were Globalbankers who had been involved in a single program. And frustration increases with prior experience. This trajectory is familiar from the study of social movements, where cycles of protest wind down from exhaustion as well as from adverse shifts in political opportunity.

306

Discussion

Students of organizations generally invoke the notion of a social movement to describe extraorganizational institution building and political action. Davis and Thompson (1994) developed this sort of argument to dissect the rise of shareholder activism. Robert Cole employed the same imagery to describe the diffusion of total quality within the American business community: "In the course of responding to the Japanese challenge, a social movement developed, filled with zealots, nonbelievers, inspirational leaders, opportunists, and institutional builders" (1999: 231). The activists in the quality movement, thus understood, are individuals such as W. Edwards Deming and organizations like SEMATECH and Goal/QPC.

We think a social movement framework has utility for understanding mobilizing efforts inside as well as across organizations. This follows the logic of Global Financial's quality director, who spoke to us of "skeptics" and "converts" and of strategies for moving Globalbankers from the former category to the latter. We see the director as orchestrating a social movement rather than implementing a program, and have sought to explicate some of the mechanisms underlying recruitment (or more fashionably, "micro-mobilization").

Recruitment to Global Financial's quality initiative has much in common with recruitment into social movement protest and activity. First, support for the change program is strongly connected to the immediate personal experience of involvement. McAdam (1988a) detailed how the collective experience of Freedom Summer's orientation camps had a defining influence on idealistic middle-class youth. Similarly, if less dramatically, Globalbankers who had participated on quality teams and who had been involved in a variety of organizational change efforts were more likely to endorse total quality than Globalbankers lacking those experiences.

Second, endorsement of total quality is strongly conditioned by location within social networks and organizational units. The presence of ties to other participants is a robust predictor of social movement mobilization, and Global Financial is no exception. Those whose peers and supervisors supported the initiative were likely to endorse it themselves. Bankers in departments that established many quality activities held more favorable views than those who saw the initiative announced and then not carried through.

Finally, social movements seek recurrent mobilization without the aid of strong institutional supports, making exhaustion and burnout a common by-product. This is true as well at Global Financial, where higher levels of quality activity bred not only endorsement but also frustration. Frustration was sufficiently great that the program probably diminished the life chances of related future efforts.

Parallels between attitudes toward a quality initiative and participation in social protest are striking because the two contexts are so different. Social protest centers on dramatic conflict between the marginal and the privileged. Whether individuals can be mobilized for risky forms of collective action with unclear payoffs is highly problematic (for example, see Gould 1995). Stark opposition between the benefits and costs of action (whether framed as why people would put themselves in harm's way, or in paler form as a social dilemma) motivates the study of social movement recruitment.

There is less at stake in an effort at organizational reform, of course. Action is on a smaller scale, and there is no equivalent to the highly public, episodic character of social movement participation. While we see the program as social movement–like in form, we would not term it collective action. Organizational reform is structurally closer to a religious movement (Snow 1976) than to a political movement.

If we step back, what benefits does a social movement perspective offer the study of organizations and organizational change? First and foremost is its dynamic character. In our reading, most research on TQM develops contingency arguments about the technical, infrastructural, and cultural conditions that facilitate or block success. For example, Sitkin, Sutcliffe, and Schroeder (1994) contended that total quality is most effectively applied where the relationship between means and ends is well understood. MacDuffie (1995) documented the multiplier effects of complementary human resource practices. Douglas and Judge (2001) examined the impact of structural control systems and information flow on TQM implementation.

While contingency arguments are of central importance, they provide explanatory accounts driven by relatively fixed exogenous conditions. A social movement approach buttresses comparative statics through close attention to the way programs gain or lose momentum. Attention to the process by which support is won or lost explicates mechanisms through which structural effects operate and points to causal factors – such as network effects – that arise within mobilization efforts themselves.

Second, a social movement framework adds a political dimension to the cognitive emphasis of much work on organizational change. For example, Robert Cole's *Managing Quality Fads* (1999) probes the difficulties of organizational learning, detailing how Hewlett-Packard first underestimated and then misunderstood the total quality approach. To questions such as "What is this program?" and "What evidence is there that it works?" a social movement analysis adds "Who supports the program?" "How were they mobilized?" and "How much influence do they have?"

Third, a social movement perspective diminishes the "manager-centrism" of most discussions of organizational change. There is a strong tendency in the business literature to treat top management commitment as the holy grail that ensures program success and durability. But while CEOs can start and stop programs (as they did at Global Financial), they cannot control whether social movements flourish or fizzle. Our analysis suggests that the commitment of many actors – the CEO, top executives, middle and supervisory managers, change agents, professionals, technicians, and front-line workers – forms an evolving and interdependent system.

Finally, we should note that further development of a social movement perspective would reintroduce the extra-organizational movement neglected in this chapter. Zald, Morrill, and Rao (this volume) argue that low external pressure leads to symbolic or low-cost compliance, an insight that explains much about the fragility of TQM and related change efforts. A promising research direction is to marry the study of movements within organizations to that of movements across organizations.

11

Subverting Our Stories of Subversion

Maureen A. Scully and W. E. Douglas Creed

Three themes have gained attention in the emerging literature at the intersection of social movements, institutions, and organizations. We have drawn upon and contributed to each of these three themes, showing them to be interrelated, in our empirical work on the adoption of gay-friendly policies by organizations. The three themes are 1) social identity construction and legitimation are a basis for social movement mobilization, creating agents even while mobilizing agents; 2) the diffusion of social changes among organizations involves a concomitant diffusion of invented repertoires for action; 3) symbolic resources are vital as both tools for and outcomes of social movement activism; for example, appeals to broad cultural frames such as civil rights are tools for action, and the legitimate inclusion in these frames, such as gay rights becoming regarded as a proper civil rights concern, can be an end. Together, these three themes begin to build a new narrative of how social movements are carried forward by grassroots organizational members. In this chapter, we push on these themes in three ways, respectively: extrapolating across movements to consider concurrent social identity projects; applying a critical analysis to surface the business logics that remain taken for granted even in seemingly inventive repertoires of action; and evaluating symbolic means and ends through which a social movement achieves social change, both in analytical and political terms. Pushing harder on our own work is in the spirit of what Hirschman

We thank Jerry Davis, Mayer Zald, and the participants in the Michigan Social Movements and Organizations conference for thoughtful comments and stimulating discussion that shaped this chapter. We thank our coauthors in our research projects – John Austin, Erica Foldy, Jeff Langstraat, Brenda Lautsch, Sandy Rothenberg, and Amy Segal – for valuable collaborations and insights. We are very grateful to the participants in our studies for their candor and courage.

(1995:1) called "the propensity to self-subversion," which he described as "questioning, modifying, qualifying, and in general complicating some of my earlier propositions about social change and development." We think it is fitting and necessary that theorizing about the subversion of the status quo – even about the fairly subtle subversions of activists in the workplace – should take this reflexively subversive approach.

The focus on proactive agents, adaptive repertoires of action, and innovative appeal to symbolic resources in the organizational environment is a pendulum swing away from earlier accounts of institutional forces and structural constraints. These earlier accounts emphasized that agents talked of innovation but were startlingly alike in their approaches and outcomes, as they relied on received blueprints for behavior and imported discourses from the environment without adaptation. In this chapter, we consider whether the corrective swing of the pendulum may have gone too far and whether some useful concepts have been left behind. Perhaps the story of innovative agents has moved too far away from accounts of constraint and unintended reproduction of the status quo. Our subversions sometimes look back to elements of institutional theory that are useful and sometimes look elsewhere to ideas about power and social change from critical theory.

For each of the three themes, we open with an explanation of that theme from the literature and our own empirical work (the basis for which is laid out in the Appendix to this chapter), then we offer our subversion, and then the implications for both theory building and practical action. Our aim is to return to the data and experiences of the social activists and organizational settings that we studied to reconsider our findings from fresh angles and to suggest implications for theory and practice. Our concern is that too pat a story line has developed about agents crafting social identities, inventing and diffusing repertoires of action, and turning to discourse and meaning making for both resources and outcomes. This story line tips theory too strongly in the direction of agents who are not just proactive but efficacious in their aims, and it may not best capture or guide important dilemmas for activists.

If our work is partly about action as well as about theory, we also need to ask what concepts and developments in the literature might help us understand some of the dilemmas that arise with each of these subversions. Why have we not seen many alliances happen across social identity movements, when they seem to be natural allies in the quest for social justice and inclusion? What does it mean that the language of business practices has come to dominate micro-mobilization? Why has there been so little redistribution – evident in the growing inequality – despite the myriad of social movement activity described in the literature? These are questions for both theorists and practitioners.

"But Enough About Me": The Pitfalls of Identity as the Basis for Mobilization

Theme 1: *Social identity construction and legitimation are a basis for social movement mobilization, creating agents even while mobilizing agents.*

All three themes that we consider share a concern for reinstating the role of agents in accounts of social action, but in a situated role that does not discount structural resources or constraints. The emerging depiction of agency suggests that it entails reinterpreting and applying established cultural schemas across contexts in order to mobilize both people and cultural resources in new and different ways (Emirbayer and Mische 1998; Seo and Creed 2002). The construction of social identity is critical to a range of social movements: "Actors 'produce' collective action because they are able to define themselves and their relationship with the environment" through a contested, iterative process of identity construction (Melucci 1995: 43). The social construction of a collective identity involves defining the field of action that the actors inhabit, as well as their interests, ends, and means. This project is facilitated by networks of relationships, organizational structures, models of leadership, and technologies of communication (Melucci 1995). Agents make moves that are brave and risky in exposing their affiliation with identities and issues that challenge the status quo (Scully and Segal 2002). These constructionist notions have emerged as a critical focus of theories of institutional change. Fligstein (1997b: 398) proposed that identity construction is a key feature of institutional entrepreneurship and that "institutional entrepreneurs" are actors who have the ability to motivate cooperation by providing and maintaining the collective identities that make undertaking and justifying strategic action possible.

Our own work has contributed to this picture. We explore the microlevel mechanisms whereby workplace activists construct and legitimate a collective identity. In "Songs of Ourselves: Employees' Deployment of Social Identity in Workplace Encounters," we focused on how gay, lesbian, bisexual, and transgender (GLBT) employee activists use their stigmatized identities as the basis for micro-mobilization (Creed and Scully 2000). Micro-mobilization refers to the social psychological processes by which people are transformed into agents able to challenge the status quo (Gamson 1992) and the local tactics that contribute to the aims of broader social movements (McAdam 1988). Building on Collins's (1981) call for microtranslation of macrolevel phenomena, Gamson, Fireman, and Rytina (1982) explore how face-to-face encounters shaped political consciousness and mediated the capacity for long-term mobilization. They detailed the challenges of micro-mobilization. In workplace settings, some of these challenges can be surmounted, because the workplace provides a ready and familiar space for everyday encounters. The very prosaic nature of these encounters sometimes enables large shifts in attitudes built on small moments of connection.

We identified three distinctive and reinforcing ways in which GLBT activists deployed their identities in everyday encounters. A "claiming encounter" involves mundane chats about everyday activities, such as a woman employee saying, "Nancy and I painted the living room this weekend." The speaker names a lesbian partnership, but as an aside to the idea that she does household things just like the straight employees who are chatting. It is brave and trivial all at once. Employees often appeal to other identities – such as corporate insider, veteran employee, licensed professional, parent, grandparent, or member of the community – in conjunction with their GLBT identity. Making the GLBT identity less "othered" is at once an accomplishment and a deployable resource.

An "educative encounter" sets the stage for mutual inquiry and reciprocal respect about experiences of prejudice, fairness, and identity. For example, a lesbian accountant who formed a GLBT employee group made an appointment to have lunch with the senior vice president of Human Resources of a large financial services company after he firmly denied their request for domestic partner benefits (DPBs). She said, "Ask me anything." He had questions of curiosity: Had she always liked girls? Did she ever like boys? He confessed he had never had a chance to talk candidly about these questions, and in return he spoke openly of his boyhood in an inner-city neighborhood that was macho and homophobic. Proudford (2002) explained how "asking difficult questions" makes room for differences in the workplace. Ultimately, this company adopted DPBs, but the pathway toward this policy change was quite personal.

Finally, an "advocacy encounter" most directly attempts to win support for policy initiatives. For example, several employees told the "Dolores" story, in the company where it happened and even in nearby companies. This story of inequity in family sick leave policy was told to prompt listeners to feel how wrong it was that Bob was not allowed to take days off when his partner, Bill, had heart surgery but Dolores was allowed to stay home when her husband had a mere cold.

In each type of encounter, GLBT employee activists purposefully bring the "life world" of the victims of discrimination into face-to-face encounters in the workplace. They politicize the personal and challenge "the penumbra of social expectations" (Gamson, Fireman, and Rytina 1982: 15) that holds sexual orientation to be a private matter and silences workplace discourse on discrimination on the basis of sexual orientation (Woods 1994). The retelling of what was nicknamed "the Dolores story" allowed GLBT employees to give a short, memorable example of how heterosexist assumptions behind even the "soft" benefits such as family sick leave made their workplace experience an unfair and more challenging one.

By telling personal stories, GLBT employees both further their own legitimacy and help potential allies understand the issues on a more immediate and emotional level. The GLBT speakers paint a picture of what is distinctive about their identity, what is alike about it (vis-à-vis straight colleagues), and sometimes a tension between comforting alikeness and radical difference (Bernstein 1997). They delve deeply into the identity, to own it and to find ways to speak about it. Their presentations of self appear to be most effective when they are personally authentic (Meyerson 2001) and when they achieve a narrative fidelity that moves their audience to feel justified in joining forces to subvert the existing social arrangements (Gamson, Fireman, and Rytina 1982).

This form of political agency happens in an arena of identity projects, or an "identity field" (Hunt, Benford, and Snow 1994), where this legitimation project is highly contested (Scully, Creed, and Ventresca 1999). The field is populated by actors declaring their right to be recognized and by others (adversaries, allies, and third parties) who will or will not grant them recognition and standing (Melucci 1995). In the "subversion" that follows, we address both the intensity of the experience of constructing a legitimate social identity and the audience for that project.

Our Subversion: Extrapolating Across Multiple Social Identity–Based Movements Social identity construction is a powerful force when considering any single movement. Our first self-subversion involves extrapolating from a single social identity–based movement to the question of what might be effective for multiple, simultaneous social identity–based movements. These movements separately – and potentially collectively – work for social justice. Extrapolation is different from generalization. The

314

question is not whether the findings apply across movements; the literature has relied on the portability of analytical tools and lessons across a wide range of movements on issues from civil rights to nuclear energy to war to drunk driving. Instead, our question is whether, when we move up a level of analysis and think of a field of social movements, the social identity proclamations and dynamics that we have identified as effective actually aid or impede cross-movement alliances and goals.

Particularly regarding diversity and civil rights, there are multiple groups making related social justice claims. As discussed above, social identity as a basis for mobilization relies on an intensity of identification. What does that intensity imply for movements that, at the very least, coexist in the same social justice arena and, more fully, seek attention from the same audiences and policymakers, employ the same rhetorics of justification, and may even share overlapping memberships? The very title of our 2000 paper, "Songs of Ourselves," provokes an interesting self-subversion. How can activists learn to sing "Songs of Others" as well (Scully 2003)?

To create an identity-based set of claims strong enough to mobilize action is an intensive endeavor. An unintended consequence is that these strong identities are fostered within narrow boundaries drawn around a group. These narrow boundaries may diminish the prospects for cross-group understanding if activists are so focused on making claims for their own group that the claims of other marginalized groups are drowned out. They may thereby diminish the prospects for alliance building among potential allies for social justice.

Social movement theory and practice suggest it is advantageous for a social movement to identify the "we" who will be the agents of change as broadly as possible, while not making the "we" so broad that collective mobilization becomes too difficult. In addition, social movements define that "we" in opposition to a distinct "they." However, Gamson (1995) suggested that if "we" and "they" are too abstract, *collective* action becomes unlikely. Our subversion examines whether too strong a sense of "we" creates too insular a sense of in-group identity, impeding collective action in several ways.

The term "imaginative empathy" has been used to describe how activists connect to the people who have greater power and privilege on the social identity dimension that they represent (e.g., for GLBT activists, thinking about messages that will make sense to straight listeners), in essence to bring the "they" into the "we." Activists have to be "bicultural" (Bell 1990) and inhabit the conditions and norms of both their own and the privileged group to do their work. Allies have to be open to listening and learning and cannot use their privileges to gain stature within the movement (Chesler 1996). Alliances have been built between oppressed and privileged groups, such as mobilizing whites to do antiracist work (Thompson 2001), men to understand gender dynamics (Collinson and Hearn 1996), straight people to be GLBT allies, and, most recently, wealthy people to reduce class inequality (Rothenberg and Scully 2001).

Building alliances with the powerful is one direction of alliance. The other direction is creating alliances laterally with other marginalized groups. The development of imaginative empathy for other oppressed groups has been given much less attention. If anything, it is simple to assume that someone who has experienced oppression thereby understands oppression more generally. In our research, we did sometimes observe this connection. For example, a prominent black male senior vice president at a large firm paved the way for the GLBT employees' group, explaining that he understood the challenges of this movement, which he felt was where the black civil rights movement had been twenty years earlier (Foldy and Creed 1999). However, we also observed the process whereby employee groups that might have been natural allies did not want to be joined under a diversity umbrella, fearing that these associations would taint or water down their own claims (Scully 1997). As some examples, some religious black employees were not comfortable with gay activism. Some active straight members of the women's group were always worried about being seen as lesbians. Some GLBT groups were focused on professionals and ignored workers' concerns in order to emphasize the "we fit here as professionals" aspect of identity. Some people of color thought white women turned the issue of workplace diversity into the too easily embraced domain of work and family balance at the expense of more challenging work on racism. In short, the members of oppressed groups did not easily achieve imaginative empathy. Natural alliances are not so natural.

If politicizing the personal in "songs of ourselves" represents a good set of micro-mobilizing tactics, how well does its application extrapolate across the social movement field? Is it a good tactic for any one group considered alone, but a limited tactic when we consider all potentially aligned groups at once? It seems to be good for any one group to reframe, legitimate, and lobby hard for their concerns. But at the aggregate level, it may create cacophony, not polyphony, making shared agendas and joint wins difficult to pursue.

316

Identity politics have been celebrated recently as the domain in which activism has happened in an otherwise apolitical era. But identity politics have a troubled history. Employers used the creation of strong ethnic group identities among immigrants in the late nineteenth century to subvert collective action for better working conditions. The "divide and conquer" strategy is well known as an employer tactic for defeating unionization. The strong ethnic identities that were forged in neighborhoods were a source of stability, resources, and belonging for their members, but came with political costs in terms of a larger arena of power.

Implications for Theory and Practice   Theoretical work may need to proceed at the level of fields of social movements if we are to detect the conditions that impede or further alliances across movements or joint realization of gains. Activists may find ideas for alliance building in nascent work on a theory of listening. Listening may be the necessary counterpart to the intensity of voice that accompanies social identity construction. The literature is ripe with treatments of voice (Ashford 1998; Harquail 1996), stemming from Hirschman's (1970) provocative juxtaposition of voice and exit. In recent work, the counterpart of voice is thought to be either silence (Creed 2003; Morrison and Milliken 2000) or the conversion of exit into voice opportunities (Scully, Segal, and Lautsch 1998). However, listening may be the counterpart of voice that merits exploration.

A project on "building alliances across differences" at the Center for Gender in Organizations (CGO) at the Simmons School of Management is laying the foundations for a theory of listening and of engaging in conversations that could lead to alliances. The project draws on case studies of alliances, including Israeli and Palestinian joint peace initiatives, Hutu and Tutsi women's connections to grieve and rebuild villages together after civil war, and the surprise alliance of churches with the gay rights struggle for same-sex marriage in Vermont. One element of this theory is the importance of listening from the dual stance of oppression and privilege. When social activists are asked to view their social identities along multiple axes, most can report on experiencing a mix of privilege and oppression (e.g., upper-middle-class white gay men, straight women, etc.). In identity politics, social activists largely speak from the perspective of oppression. Rather than turning their imaginative empathy as institutional entrepreneurs toward those who are privileged vis-à-vis their own dimension of oppression, as Fligstein (1997b) discussed, activists can engage empathetically with other kinds of oppression. Proudford (2002) noted how difficult it is to "sit with one's privilege" and listen to how, "actively or passively, you may be contributing to what others experience as being silenced, being marginalized, being discounted, being oppressed."

This type of listening and empathy may require what this project calls a new "stance." "By stance, we do not mean a position, but an orientation, like the initial posture a dancer or martial artist assumes; poised, focused, with a readiness. [W]e explore two aspects of stance: the commitment to connecting with others and an appreciation for the simultaneity of identity" (Holvino and Creed 2002). This stance is contrasted to how the literature paints interest-based bargains, wherein parties to an alliance are best off if they arrive with a clear sense of their own group's interests and do not get coopted, swayed, distracted, or deterred (Kolb, personal communication, quoted in Holvino and Creed 2002). Respect for interests remains important for gauging who benefits from social changes, but paradoxically, it may be a willingness to take an open stance and let go of interest positions in a dialogue that can yield alliances that ultimately better realize more interests. This work is exploratory and invites empirical investigation.

The CGO project also emphasizes understanding the simultaneity of identities as a way to move beyond the "one at a time" or "additive" way of treating identities such as race, gender, class, and sexual orientation. The simultaneity of identity adds complexity to the concept of collective identity construction, pointing to the problem of relying upon simple oppositions such as black-white, worker-manager, women-men, and gay-straight (Holvino 2001). People who live at the "borderlands" of these identities may be translators of cross-group interests (Piore 1995) and natural ambassadors among groups. In our research, however, we found that such people more often felt marooned than multiply welcomed. For example, a black lesbian explained how time-consuming it was to attend three employee group meetings (the African American, women's, and GLBT groups) and never to quite feel her concerns taken up by any of them. The problem of narrowly drawing a "we," discussed above, gives these groups energy and identity but at the risk of leaving out precisely those of their own members who might bring special perspectives and structural locations to advance change.

The theory of listening, stance, and simultaneity as painted thus far sounds very attuned to individual and interpersonal skills, but it also attends to structural locations. Cross-group alliances must attend to the historical legacies that produced the injustices about which – and from which position – social identity groups are speaking. Empirical work toward a theory of listening might examine whether there are particular historical or structural moments that are propitious for listening. Listening will bring new elements from across social identity movements, and "the more new elements diffuse from elsewhere, become part of the available repertoire, and are translated into the bricolage, the more revolutionary and less evolutionary change becomes" (Campbell, this volume).

Let's Have a Meeting: What Really Needs to Happen During Micro-mobilization

Theme 2: *The diffusion of social changes among organizations involves a concomitant diffusion of invented repertoires for action.*

Almost fifteen years ago, DiMaggio argued that agents and agency were at best "smuggled into institutional arguments rather than theorized explicitly," leaving us with a picture of "disembodied forces" inexorably creating and maintaining institutions (1988: 9). Scholars attended to the diffusion of practices across a field until isomorphism resulted, but paid little attention to where those practices originated or to the helping hand of agents in their diffusion. We looked at a range of roles for agents – from monitors to shapers of the environment for diffusion – in our paper "More Than Switchpersons on the Tracks of History: Situated Agency and Contested Legitimacy During the Diffusion of Domestic Partner Benefits" (Scully, Creed, and Ventresca 1999).

We started out tracking the diffusion of DPBs among twenty-four organizations in a geographic field. In the middle of the ongoing diffusion process, when we conducted extensive interviews, there were nine adopters. Usually, in research on diffusion, nonadoption versus adoption is the dichotomous outcome measure. We did observe additional organizations tip from zero to one, the moment of interest in event history analyses. But what was more interesting was a parallel diffusion process, whereby not just DPBs but tactics for winning DPBs diffused across organizations. These tactics involved expanding the discourse about heterosexism in the workplace and held the potential for changes even deeper than the adoption of DPBs. In fact, some of the early adopters of DPBs contributed the least to the creation and spread of innovative tactics. They won DPBs more easily and with less of a fight, often because they had a high-level champion. They did not need to develop multipronged tactics. After winning DPBs, their GLBT employee groups were left wondering, "now what?" Meanwhile, at some nonadopter organizations, there was a flurry of activity. These organizations would be coded zero in a macrolevel view of diffusion, but were crucial at another level to the diffusion of social change tactics. By having to be always at the ready to seize opportunistic moments for advocacy, they invented a variety of tactics. For example, at one bank, a group set up a booth at a gay pride event and brought back an impressive number of new customers to show a business case for goodwill with the GLBT community.

One set of tactics we labeled "stealth legitimation." Agents carefully advanced their social change projects so as to minimize the risk of backlash that could undermine the adoption of controversial policies. They attempted to make the cases for their proposals "just enough and in just the right quarters" so that changes could be put into practice without fanfare and without inviting resistance. They spoke of moments such as "elevator chats" during which they subtly inserted their perspective. While activists felt that DPBs represented a large victory, they enhanced the legitimacy of such a policy change by painting them as a minor adjustment to the human resources benefits manual that would not cost much.

Stealth legitimation is in large part about overcoming opposition during a contested change effort. The tactics were immediately oriented toward policy changes such as DPBs but more broadly geared toward opening up pockets of safety in the workplace where conversation about people's experiences could occur. When they worked, these tactics triggered reciprocal empathetic engagement. Stealth legitimation adds another set of mechanisms to existing theories of micro-mobilization, which focus on how bystanders come to adopt injustice frames and become transformed into challengers of unjust authorities (Gamson, Fireman, and Rytina 1982). The mechanisms, not just the conditions (Strang and Meyer 1993), for diffusion are illuminated when organizational and social movement concerns are integrated (Campbell, this volume).

Actors seemed to learn and refine stealth legitimation through the sorts of workplace encounters we described above. Diffusion across organizations happened as they told stories at meetings of interorganizational networks (such as the Minnesota WorkPlace Alliance) and national organizations (such as the National Gay and Lesbian Task Force). They effectively constructed the "best practices" for the workplace aspect of a larger social movement.

What was striking was that actors diffused the spirit of these tactics, but each group remained attuned to how to adapt such tactics to their particular organizations. Stealth legitimation is in part about knowing how to fit in and read the local code. For example, one large health care organization had as its mission statement the desire to be the "premier provider of culturally sensitive and culturally competent health care." While those who penned the mission statement did not have GLBT concerns in mind, activists soon pointed out that to fulfill the mission statement, the organization should train doctors regarding the special concerns of GLBT patients and provide equitable benefits to GLBT employees. The organization adopted DPBs. The activists' tactics that won DPBs were at once patterned and novel. The diffusion of tactics might look like a received blueprint for action, but much more interpretive and translation work was involved on the part of agents.

Our Subversion: A Critical Analysis of Business as Usual "Bringing agents back in" was a needed corrective. However, the pendulum can swing too far toward an account of agents inventing completely new repertoires. Even after the claims we make above about tailored tactics, our self-subversion involves taking a closer look to discover there is some mundane scriptedness in activists' emancipatory efforts. Their basic modes of operation, if not the customized content, are quite patterned across organizations. The original insights of institutional theory remain relevant.

What institutional theory does not supply is a critical or power-based view of what kinds of activities predominate and whose interests they preserve. Specifically, when we subvert our own celebration of activists' innovations, we see activists engaged in very conventionally businesslike activities: they wear suits, hold meetings, use flip charts, create an e-mail distribution list, write up a mission statement, pursue subgoals, form subcommittees, prepare PowerPoint presentations with bullet points, court senior allies, sponsor networking events, define benchmarks, name and frame "best practices," and so on. Thus, activists use well-worn scripts, but not any old scripts. They are the repertoires of action of modern capitalist businesses, repertoires that have systematically favored privileged groups.

On the one hand, the very genius of these activists is that they make their efforts locally sensible and legitimate for business settings. As "idea merchants," they enable change by framing new ideas in terms of existing higher-order logics (Czarniawska and Joerges 1996: 36). They sell gay-friendly policies as good for business, as recruitment and retention tools, as outreach to new customer niches, and as basic employment fairness.

On the other hand, the hegemony of a business language, logic, and modus operandi clearly puts limits on how strongly activists can state a social justice agenda and how far they can push radical change. The challenge of navigating between too sedate and too radical a strategy has been considered in work on "tempered radicals," change agents who work from inside organizations by rocking the boat just enough but not too much (Meyerson 2001; Meyerson and Scully 1995). The risk in using institutionalized business logics for making change is that the change effort can be coopted.

What do businesslike repertoires of action really enable agents to accomplish? Many GLBT employees attempt to mobilize support for their proposals without challenging the authority structure. They often expressly demonstrate loyalty to the system and eschew unauthorized collective action. In a sense, it is as if they are attempting laser surgery. In many cases, they succeeded in getting human resource policy changes such as DPBs.

We found that in some instances, GLBT advocacy waned in the wake of the adoption of benefits. Changes in benefits offerings became ends in themselves, rather than a stepping-stone in a larger movement. In some other organizations, advocates engaged in self-reflection and saw their movement as having succeeded in making the corporate headquarters safe for "guppies" (gay urban professionals), but as having done little to make more rural facilities or factory floors safe for GLBT employees. In effect, their actions had generated some changes, but it was unclear how much the larger system had changed. What remained unimaginable or unimagined was a workplace free of homophobia and danger.

Institutionalized routines stabilize social arrangements, making some practices taken for granted and others unimaginable. From a constructionist perspective, the enactment of established routines reproduces the existing arrangements while departures from the routines – departures for which Jepperson (1991) argued we should reserve the term "action" – can lead to the reconstruction of social arrangements.

This self-subversion finds both action and reconstruction in agents' new repertoires of action. Moreover, we urge an emphasis on power, for example, pointing to where larger systems remain unchanged and thereby continue to redound to the benefit of the powerful. Thus, it is not just that agents' tactics retain a certain scriptedness. We are making a finer point than saying that theorists should not overendow agents with efficacy in response to the corrective urged by DiMaggio (1988) and others. We are saying more strongly that when we see scripted behavior, certain scripts are generally the ones that prevail, and they serve the particular interests of business. Organizational theorists might be prompted more often to make this critical point by importing social movement ideas.

A more radical challenge to the underlying system of business-based, private health benefits would ask why DPBs should even be relevant. The United States is the only industrial nation where health care is tied to an employer (and getting health care therefore requires being tied to an individual who is employed) rather than being a right of citizenship or residence. A national health care system would make DPBs a moot point. Thus, all the tactics deployed toward their adoption are in some ways distractions from another level of challenge to the power of large insurance companies in the entrenched system. Perhaps the adoption of DPBs permits activists to let off steam. Interestingly, large insurance companies with conservative images have been among the first adopters of DPBs and have taken pride in departing from their conservative images, but from the standpoint of our critical subversion, perhaps this move is not as surprising as it seems at first.

Implications for Theory and Practice   The study of the diffusion of repertoires of action tends to focus on instrumental practices. Micromobilization may be most successful when businesslike instrumental practices are used (Alinsky 1989). In addition, activists might experiment with a wider range of practices to subvert and suggest alternatives to businesslike ways of being. Specifically with respect to the issues of diversity and inclusion, creating a wider range of legitimate "presentations of self" at work could be a goal.

Instrumental practices tend to obscure the importance of an alternative set of practices, which might be called "relational practices" (Fletcher 1999; Miller 1976). Examples of relational practices would include those described above in terms of listening, stance, empathy, and learning from simultaneity of identities. Relational practices mean not just building networks, but knowing how to make connections via network channels. Before an endowment of resources becomes of use to groups that challenge systems, they may need to work on organizational development, including such relational practices as building loyalty, deciding together about action logistics, and dealing with internal conflict (Gamson, Fireman, and Rytina 1982).

Researchers and activists alike might take a look at this often invisible (Fletcher 1999) and underappreciated type of work that might undergird a social movement. But perhaps more powerfully in terms of social change, they might look at how such work will get imported into the business-as-usual logics that hold sway at work. Social movements about diversity are ultimately about winning space and respect for different ways of being and doing at work. This end is sometimes lost in the more policy-oriented means that employee activist groups pursue (implementing DPBs, working flexible hours, getting a member of a particular social identity group onto the board of directors, establishing promotion review boards, etc.).

The relational work accomplished in organizations is typically done by women and is underrewarded, but is nonetheless vital to team and organizational functioning, as Fletcher (1999) documented. Successful diversity activism might surface and value such work. Specifically, a hope for GLBT activism is that it might help to "unstick" some of the mechanisms that reproduce the gendering – and thereby differential valuing – of particular types and styles of work. The GLBT movement might articulate alternative views of what is masculine, what is feminine, and why this distinction should not even matter so much. Activists might make more headway by experimenting with a wider range of relational practices that subvert businesslike ways of being.

However, this broader repertoire of actions recedes from view in theory and practice. A promising direction for both theory and practice would be to look more critically at what fundamental aspects of systems really need changing, whether activist efforts are accidentally bolstering – or at least uncritically accepting – some elements of the system, and whether such fundamental changes to modern capitalist businesses are being accomplished when the work of social activism is enacted inside the workplace. The next section takes up this challenge.

Back to the Barricades Again: The Tough Issue of Redistribution

Theme 3: *Symbolic resources are vital as both tools for and outcomes of social movement activism.*

The recent emphasis on symbolic resources, such as discourse and cultural accounts, as critical tools in institutional change processes hinges on the idea that institutional reproduction is complex and uncertain, because the social world is made up of multiple conflicting systems of meaning (Friedland and Alford 1991). Agency involves exploiting these contradictions in the process of meaning-making (Sewell 1992). The focus on meaning – and on the contest to control the meaning of broadly legitimated ideals such as civil rights – becomes central to social movements. Social scientists increasingly train their lens on meaning-making projects. Methodological advances in areas such as frame analysis have made it more possible to access and understand symbolic resources such as discourse, social identity affinity, and legitimacy. Moreover, not only are symbolic tools for action considered, but symbolic outcomes become the relevant ends of social movement activism or at least the ones that receive both scholarly and media attention. Symbolic ends include more inclusive language and a sense of legitimate "standing" in civic deliberations.

We explored the relationship between cultural accounts, or institutionalized logics of action, and local legitimating accounts in our paper "Clothes Make the Person: The Tailoring of Legitimating Accounts and the Social Construction of Identity" (Creed, Scully, and Austin 2002). Our focus on accounts revealed how agents use discourse to name experiences, expose contradictions, and legitimate both social identities and social change projects. A number of studies have identified various other types of symbolic action in the workplace, where employees covertly undermine authority structures (Morrill, Zald, and Rao 2003). We examined how employees import symbolic resources to try to court authority structures and speak overtly to them in legitimate terms. We began by examining the language from the societal domain that was available to them. We found that both proponents and opponents of banning employment discrimination on the basis of sexual orientation tried to cast their approach as the one consistent with American history and the ideal of civil rights. Proponents framed those people whose support they hoped to mobilize as "right-thinking Americans" taking their place in the historical struggle for civil rights. Opponents framed the protagonists as economically powerful sodomites, their supporters as good-willed people misled by homosexuals' use of the rhetoric of civil rights, and opponents as the defenders of biblically based morality and freedom.

Access to shared historic, civic, and religious frames is a kind of symbolic resource – and coming to be seen as legitimate users of these frames is a symbolic outcome. Local actors, like employees in workplace settings, adapt and shape these texts. The result can be concrete policy changes, but as often as not, the desired result is new meaning-making, such as new language and metaphors, greater diversity of participants invited into civic debates, or greater tolerance.

Our Subversion: Assess the Extent of Fundamental Change We question whether the focus on symbolic resources and outcomes obscures the material basis of inequality and of redistribution as a remedy. Material resources, not just ideological commitment, are vital to get a social movement under way (McAdam, McCarthy, and Zald 1988). Symbolic resources, particularly when convertible back to material resources, have been added to the mix and given more attention. But the material basis of both resources and outcomes should not be lost. Our self-subversion reminds us that there is much at stake: whether changes, particularly of benefit to those least powerful and well off, are made in systems that resist changing.

Symbolic resources have the special property – which Hirschman (1995) ascribed to "moral resources" – that they are increased through use, rather than depleted through use (and in fact, they are depleted when not used – such as, for example, social capital or civic involvement). Symbolic resources are neither partitive nor scarce (Elster 1992). They can be tapped by multiple parties. The parties may compete vigorously over who has the legitimate use of them – as when proponents and opponents of gay-friendly legislation each claim the right to appeal to the civil rights frame – but this contest does not have the zero sum quality of contests over material resources. Symbolic resources are thereby different from the resources that pose the sharpest distributive dilemmas – resources that are nonpartitive and scarce, such as organs for transplant candidates, which require us to confront difficult allocative decisions (Scully and Lautsch 1999).

The literature and the practice of social movements, in their shift toward identity politics, may be losing sight of material interests and of the hard-boiled economic resources that pose distributive dilemmas. In the shift away from class, labor, or economically based politics toward identity politics, redistributive issues can be lost (Laraña, Johnston, and Gusfield 1994). There seems to be less willingness in social identity–based politics to tackle the redistributive issues that are often at the heart of social justice and the most difficult public policy debates.

A focus on social identity often seeks to enhance inclusion and belonging – moral resources that are not finite and that can be expansively applied to all in a way that enriches social life for all. But where is the concern about the growing wage gap or about poverty? Identity politics will have more power when more of the marginalized identity groups that might be mobilized– for example, former welfare recipients who have lost jobs – are enabled, by naming and speaking their identity, to advance material interests, not just to be heard and accepted. A true study of subversion should not shy away from thorny issues of redistribution.

Identity-based social movements are contrasted to movements that arise around shared interests or issues, such as peace, the environment, antinuclear, prochoice or prolife, welfare rights, or labor movements. These movements certainly use symbolic resources – indeed, the study of them has advanced the literature on discourses and frame analysis (e.g., Creed, Langstraat, and Scully 2002; Gamson and Lasch 1983). However, they also have concrete agendas about what is to be changed. Early identity politics movements also had concrete demands – such as voting rights, housing fairness, or equal pay for equal work. But there is a sense that there are fewer concrete agendas – perhaps ironically because some of the easier and more tangible wins have been achieved. For example, one workplace activist for racial equality in the workplace observed that it felt good for his group when they had some tangible agenda items, such as getting a black member for the board of directors, but once those were achieved, a vague sense of incompleteness took over. The workplace was still not friendly to blacks on an everyday basis. The nature of the next battle to pick was not clear. Saying that their interest was in something like "inclusion" or "climate" felt unsatisfying (Scully and Segal 2002). In essence, the "small wins" (Meyerson 2001) still felt small.

Researcher and activist E. J. Graff (2002: 34–5) discussed the unexpected wins of the GLBT movement while the Right held sway in the 1990s, what she calls a "cultural victory" of moving from shame, exclusion, and few legal protections to celebration, inclusion, and some significant (although still too few) legislative victories. We quote at length, because her assessment of symbolic outcomes such as freedom in contrast to redistributive outcomes is at the heart of this subversion, and because she raises her concerns from inside the movement – in the spirit of constructive self-subversion:

Unfortunately, there's very little that other progressive causes can learn from this cultural victory. "Freedom" is the consumer culture's watchword, an idea propagandized constantly: the freedom to choose one's work and one's love and to enjoy (or suffer) the consequences of one's choices. Cultural acceptance of lesbians and gay men perfectly fits that American social theology, that bedrock belief in liberty and the pursuit of happiness. But that freedom is literally priceless: It requires no new taxes. Tolerance asks for nothing from the public purse and threatens no industry; it requires no changes in hiring practices (except perhaps the rapidly spreading corporate habit of offering domestic-partnership benefits – which, not coincidentally, costs almost nothing). In fact, many companies quickly figured out that an entirely new market segment – middle-class lesbians and gay men – were actually grateful to be winked at in Volkswagen or IKEA or Miller Lite commercials. "Not only does cultural acceptance cost nothing," says Sue Hyde, New England regional organizer for the National Gay and Lesbian Task Force, "but it actually makes the rich richer."

Compare that with anything else on a progressive's wish list: universal health care, a livable minimum wage, progressive taxation, racial equality, environmental preservation, comparable worth, subsidized child care, public housing. These ask

Americans not for freedom from one another but responsibility for one another – responsibilities that are most costly for those mostly likely to vote. "To what extent is the gay and lesbian movement overall a progressive movement?" . . . While most self-identified lesbians and gay men are Democrats and many work actively on other progressive issues, there's a reason gay Republicans feel no contradiction between their two group memberships: Liberty and justice based on sexual orientation would redistribute not a penny.

Social identity–based campaigns need not be linked to reproduction of the status quo. In fact, attention to social identity can be an important part of a campaign for redistribution; issue-based movements ignore social identity politics at their peril (Holvino 2001). But the identity and redistributive aspects each must be explicitly evoked. For example, the mobilization of "living wage" campaigns draws on diverse constituencies in low-paying jobs. The successful effort at Columbia University was able to make links across race, class, gender, and nationality among the workers (Kurtz 2002).

Holding onto redistribution as an important aim may appear at first look to be in tension with the call above for activist groups to enhance their empathy and capacity to listen through adopting a more open, reflexive, and inquiring stance toward one another and toward each others' preferred change agendas. A dilemma for both theorists and practitioners to address is how activists can be respectful and adaptive regarding a diversity of interests while remaining steadfast and unyielding about the importance of redressing fundamental inequalities.

Implications for Theory and Practice This last subversion directs attention back to the ultimate ends of social movement activism: redistribution of power and resources to create a more just, peaceful, and sustainable society. Without this reflexive and critical subversion, we might risk misusing the concept of a social movement as merely a metaphor for any mobilization of collective action rather than as the process driving fundamental social change. Dick Scott said it best when, as discussant at an Academy of Management symposium in 2001 entitled "To the Barricades" – which had papers applying concepts from social movement theory to the rise and spread of workplace diversity, recycling, shareholder initiatives, and nouvelle cuisine – he quipped, "To the barricades! How do we keep the meaning of this phrase? What's at stake: We have nothing to lose but our sauces?" (our paraphrase). Scott was both warning against the trivializing of the social movement framing and issuing a call to live up to the imagery of "to the barricades" with the risky bold action and high stakes it implies. Future research should retain the distinction between "collective action" – people working concertedly toward some goal, which could include French chefs overturning traditional cuisine – and social movements, a term that should be reserved for radical mobilizations that fundamentally contest the distribution of resources and power.

Applying social movement theory to phenomena in organizational settings could move in two directions. One direction is toward enriching our understanding of organizations as places where the aims of larger social movements are realized (McAdam and Scott, this volume; Scully and Segal 2002; Zald, Morrill, and Rao, this volume). Because organizational life is subject to greater authority and fewer rights than the political and civic domain, the activism there may be particularly revealing about how to change powerful structures, even when the subversions seem small. The other direction is toward using social movement concepts to explain phenomena that, by their very location in business organizations, are fairly mundane and uncontestedly part of business as usual. In this case, social movements must be understood to be a metaphor and the tools for their analysis a usefully portable set of tools. Thus, Hackman and Wageman (1995) described the rapid spread of Total Quality Management by committed proselytizers as "like" a social movement, but certainly it is not, in fact, a social movement in the sense we endorse. It is important to be clear when the organizational phenomenon is a cell in the social movement and when it is analogized to some of the dynamics of a social movement.

What should not be lost is the spirit of social movement theory and its central project: to explain large-scale, fundamental, system-level, and even cataclysmic changes. Researchers use the powerful and colorful language of social movements in describing social change, such as "to the barricades." Interestingly, workplace activists also borrow such evocative phrases from the history of social movements ("the peasants are having an insurrection here," "the grassroots," "the raised fist in a black glove," or "picketing the CEO's office") – but they do so explicitly by way of contrast to say what they are *not* able to do at work and how far they would like to go but dare *not* (Scully and Segal 2002). Perhaps researchers should use a similar caveat in invoking social movement language and concepts. The use of this literature and these concepts may reflect a wish to see large-scale social changes afoot. But objects in this mirror actually may be smaller than they appear. Just because we are using the tools for studying large-scale social change does not mean that we have identified large-scale social change. We might be using social movement theory to celebrate changes that are not significant or fundamental. Instead, social movement theory may prove to be particularly useful, not just in the tools it gives us for excavating and explaining many types of social change, but in its call to evaluate social change projects with a tougher standard.

In short, we propose that the final question should always be, "So, has anything changed?" We closed our paper on the tailoring of legitimating accounts (Creed, Scully, and Austin 2002) with the observation that conditions in the world are more malleable than institutional accounts initially held. Discourses can be challenged by appeal to the contradictions contained within them. But the flip side of saying that things are more changeable than a theory of institutional rigidity allows is acknowledging that change is nonetheless difficult and apparent changes may be small, recirculated into reproduction, or retracted. In the spirit of self-subversion, we need to push harder on the questions about what actually changes, how we can know what changes, and whose definition and understanding of changes should be our gauge.

Conclusion

The three themes we address have been tackled to different degrees by both theorists and activists. From the first to the third subversions, we pose challenges that are increasingly radical for both theory and practice. The first subversion, on social identity construction as a movement foundation, has probably been given the most critical attention in the literature (e.g., Laraña, Johnston, and Gusfield 1994; Piore 1995). Activists' efforts at outreach to members of other identity groups appear to be beginning within their respective movements, as an appreciation of diversity within an identity group (Holvino 2001). Thus, for example, the National Gay and Lesbian Task Force has launched a major initiative to reach out to gay people across race and class lines. The second subversion addresses an issue that is, by its very nature and definition, harder to see – the taken-for-granted reasonableness of a businesslike approach to activism that domesticates change agendas. Both researchers and activists have given this issue less attention. Our third subversion is the most speculative, as it reaches toward the limit of where theorists committed to practice and activists committed to reflection have gone: the thorny question of redistribution and the disruption that a true social movement could cause. Are we really ready to go to the barricades?

This chapter points to a challenge for social movements: to find a way to have concerns about fundamental social change on which activists are unyielding and cannot be distracted or coopted, but to do so in a way that listens to many voices and continually reshapes the particulars of redistribution. The challenge for researchers using social movement theories is therefore twofold. First, we need to widen our lenses to see different kinds of change movements and to continue to be critical about both the movements and our ways of describing them. Second, and more subversively, we need to realize that we engage in praxis as well as theorizing when we study social movements. If our emerging story from the literature, as summarized in the introduction, is a paean to the social construction of identity, the circulation of micro-mobilization tactics, and the use of symbolic resources, we end up, intentionally or unintentionally, in an advocacy role for certain approaches to social movement activism. This chapter has shown that these approaches might be limiting. We need to continue to be self-subverting in our stories of subversion so that we refine our concepts in ways that both explain and also subtly direct the ways that social movements lead to fundamental social change. Instead, activists may be more successful by situating social identity constructions more broadly among many social identities, experimenting with a wider range of relational practices beyond the instrumental modes of business, and constantly coming back to the bottom line of change even amid celebrations of hard-won symbolic victories.

Appendix: Background on Our Empirical Work

Our research began as an inquiry into the dynamics of contested institutional change. In 1996, with the goal of understanding better the microlevel dynamics behind the diffusion of domestic partner benefits, we approached a network of GLBT employees, the Minnesota WorkPlace Alliance (the Alliance), which was at that time the most advanced GLBT "group of groups" in America according to the Human Rights Campaign, America's largest GLBT political organization. The Alliance provided a list of contact people at twenty-four Twin Cities employers (ranging from private foundations to Fortune 100 companies). Most were the leaders of GLBT employee groups within their organizations, while some were lone voices in workplaces that lacked formal GLBT employee groups. Through the use of two common convenience sampling strategies – snowballing (i.e., obtaining names from a contact) and recruiting (i.e., letting the contact find willing informants before divulging names to us) – our sample grew to sixty-six GLBT employee advocates, their allies, and the targets of their advocacy. Convenience sampling has clear limitations, but is generally acceptable for a qualitative study that has as its goal discovering the details of lived experience rather than generalization. In addition, it is characteristic of research on GLBT workplace issues because of the twin difficulties of gaining access to and building trust with populations whose members may be put at risk by being identified (Croteau 1996). Our sample taps the experiences of employees in several organizations and industries.

With this sample, we conducted semistructured interviews ranging in length from one to three hours. At the start of each interview, informants were told that the interviews were designed to gain insights into five broad areas of concern: 1) the history and current status of GLBT workplace concerns at each organization; 2) the nature and role of the GLBT employee group at each of the sample organizations, including their efforts, successes, and failures in advocating GLBT workplace issues; 3) the role of key organizational advocates, opponents, or idea champions in the advocacy process; 4) the references (or lack thereof) to practices and norms in other organizations in the geographic, industry, or other interorganizational field; and 5) the nature of the discourses used to advocate for inclusive policies and to explain and justify the organizational stance on domestic partner benefits. These interviews were transcribed and the content analyzed.

Conclusion

12

Social Change, Social Theory,
and the Convergence of Movements
and Organizations

Gerald F. Davis and Mayer N. Zald

The essays in this volume have brought together two fields of inquiry, the study of social movements and the study of organizations, that have shown substantial convergence in core concepts and modes of analysis (McAdam and Scott, Chap. 1; Campbell, Chap. 2). Social movements are often represented by formal organizations, and organizations respond to social movements and have movement-like processes within themselves. Thus, scholars from both areas of study are finding it useful to borrow or bridge across the boundaries. This is not an entirely new development; indeed, it has a long, if fitful, history. We will not review that history here, although Elisabeth Clemens, in the next chapter, helps us to understand why that history has been so fitful. Instead, we want to give a partial answer to the question, Why now? Why is this bridging even more relevant today than it has been in the past? What events and processes "out there" almost force us to bridge and blend these two areas?

In this era of rapid social change, organizations increasingly resemble episodic movements rather than ongoing bounded actors, and organizations and movements are changing their strategies and routines in response to similar social and technological changes. Moreover, one of the most visible social movements of our time, aimed at reining in "globalization from above," is explicitly oriented toward contemporary economic and organizational arrangements. We are not attempting a full history of the fields of study, nor of the development and intersection of movements and

We thank Chris Marquis, Tim Vogus, Klaus Weber, and Mina Yoo for research assistance and Dick Scott for extensive editorial comments on this chapter. Our arguments benefited from discussion at the first Michigan Conference on Social Movements and Organizations in May 2001.

organizations in the last several decades: thus our answer to the "why now" question is partial. The main body of this chapter focuses upon two cases, the ouster of Erap Estrada as president of the Philippines and antiglobalization protests in Washington, which we use to illustrate some of the trends toward convergence in movements and organizations.

Even though there is a history of mutual borrowing between organization studies and the study of social movements, the pace has quickened in recent years. Many years ago Zald and Berger (1978) noted the analogy between political change processes in organizations and social movements in society. They argued that the methods of challengers at the societal level – insurgencies, coups d'état, and even mass movements – had their parallels within large organizations. Few took up their argument. More recently a handful of researchers from each school has begun to draw on work from the other, using social movement theory to make sense of shareholder activism (Davis and Thompson 1994) and the organization of the biotechnology industry (Koput, Powell, and Smith-Doerr 1997), or using ecological concepts of organizations to explain the growth of feminist social movement organizations (Minkoff 1997b) or concepts from neoinstitutionalism to explain the spread of organizational repertoires among women's political organizations (Clemens 1993). In each case the concepts, mechanisms, and hypotheses from one theoretical tradition illuminated processes studied in the other.

The impetus for greater crossover comes from events in the world as well as from academic concerns. As corporations have become increasingly multinational and encompassing, they have taken on the character of polities whose "citizens" may engage in collective action to challenge policies with which they disagree (Zald and Berger 1978). For instance, Creed and Scully (1998) looked at social movements *within* and *across* organizations in their study of the spread of the policy of providing domestic partner benefits for gay and lesbian employees. Within organizations, activists had the difficult task of locating and organizing the support of employees that may have preferred anonymity. Across organizations, activists formed networks with their counterparts to share tactics and provide support, thus providing a mechanism for the diffusion of policies through interorganizational networks from below. Analogous processes characterize the spread of movement tactics *across nations*, where networks of labor, consumer, and human rights advocates seek to shape the agendas of corporations and states as the rules of the new global economy are worked out (Evans 2000). On a single day in February 2003, more than six million protesters around the world marched in dozens of cities on six continents behind the slogan "the world says no to war" in response to the anticipated U.S. invasion of Iraq, demonstrating the emergence of a vast and rapidly self-organized movement out of thin air. And *within* nations, protest movements have arisen to respond to IMF-induced policies in South Korea, U.S.-backed privatization in Puerto Rico, cross-border hostile takeovers in Germany, and the process of globalization itself in Seattle at the meetings of the World Trade Organization in 1999. In a globalizing economy, organizations are the context for, the actors in, and the objects of social movements.

We argue that processes of economic globalization, changing forms of production, the spread of information and communication technologies, and changing poles of power from states to corporations generate pressures for convergence in the processes of movements and organizations. Yet the underlying mechanisms of collective action remain the same for both organizations and movements (see Campbell, this volume). We illustrate some recent changes with brief discussions of the "popular" ouster of Erap Estrada in the Philippines and the organization of the antiglobalization protests after Seattle. We then derive some implications from these cases and suggest themes appropriate for future research.

Social Change and Convergence in Processes of Collective Action

Economic globalization – the increasing cross-border flow of capital, goods, and labor – is the master trend currently generating many of the pressures for change in movements and organizations. During the 1990s, world trade finally re-attained the levels reached prior to the first World War (about $25 billion per day in 1997), while financial flows achieved astounding levels, with foreign exchange trading at roughly $1.5 trillion per day (Gilpin 2000: 22). Portfolio investment in low-income "emerging" markets via rich-nation institutional investors increased from nearly zero in the early 1980s to $130 billion in 1996, creating an implicit competition among states to attract financial investors in local companies. At the same time, foreign direct investment by multinationals grew even more dramatically. A relative handful of global corporations controls a major part of the world's economic assets and directly or indirectly employs a substantial fraction of the global labor force. Mobile capital and global companies have become increasingly powerful instruments of economic development at the presumed expense of nation-states.

337

The countless tomes written about economic globalization hardly have achieved consensus about its implications. Some see a triumph of market-based, American-style capitalist democracy around the world (e.g., Friedman 1999), while others see predictable signs of a hegemonic crisis that will end "more or less catastrophically" for the current great powers (Arrighi and Silver 1999: 259). Skeptics see the current round of economic globalization as simply an extension of prior trends, while true believers argue that "the current world economy has no parallels in earlier times. In the new global electronic economy, fund managers, banks, corporations, as well as millions of individual investors, can transfer vast amounts of capital from one side of the world to another at the click of a mouse. As they do so, they can destabilize what might have seemed rock-solid economies – as happened in the events in Asia" (Giddens 2000: 27). What is at stake? Just as corporations compete for consumers and investors, states compete to provide the labor and investment opportunities sought by multinational investors and firms. Both in their structures and their strategies, corporations and states come to be more similar.

One outcome of this process is that sovereign boundaries begin to lose significance. James C. Scott (1997) described the ideology of "high modernism" in which clearly demarcated and centrally controlled nation-states could improve the human condition of their inhabitants with rational planning. Such schemes made the most sense when bounded economic units, such as households and firms, were contained within bounded nation-states. But in a world of transnational businesses, states do not contain firms, and their power to regulate them is limited in certain important respects. When business is mobile, states become vendors of laws and regulations, competing with other states to attract corporate buyers. Firms in turn are able to fine-tune their jurisdictions to find the right combination of corporate, securities, tax, and labor laws. To take a baroque example, in 2001 the Tommy Hilfiger Corporation, purveyor of "classic American clothing," had its corporate headquarters in Hong Kong, was legally incorporated in the British Virgin Islands, listed its shares on the New York Stock Exchange, held its annual meeting in Barbados, and contracted to have its products manufactured primarily in Mexico and Asia. Meaningful boundaries – for both firms and states – become increasingly ambiguous under these circumstances. As boundaries around nations and organizations become more permeable and old legal and regulatory structures break down, both firms and citizens are moved to mobilize.

Within the general process of economic globalization, three broad trends influence what organizations and movements do (their "productions"), how they do it (how collective action is accomplished), and to whom they do it (their targets). The first is the rise of postindustrial production and the increasing importance of service and knowledge work. Within the United States, the proportion of jobs in the service sector has long since eclipsed employment in manufacturing and agriculture. A hallmark of the service sector is that what is produced is often perceptual, emotional, symbolic, or cultural – in the extreme case, the production of spectacle. Harvey (1990) and Jameson (1991) argued for the intrinsic link between the postmodernist esthetic of ephemerality and spectacle and changes in underlying processes of production and accumulation. For businesses, "branding" and "impression management" become central managerial tasks for conveying desirable images to consumers and investors. For social movements, similarly, it is the production of impressions and emotions that are foregrounded.

The production of spectacles, as well as more conventional production, follows different patterns due to the widespread use of information and communication technologies (ICTs). The prospects for coordinated action are greatly enhanced by cell phones, the Internet, and other enabling technologies. Organized action can be more expansive, flexible, and diffuse, from how businesses organize their supply chain to the means of bringing about street protests. Organization theorists might describe this in terms of the changing transaction costs of collective action (e.g., Williamson 1994). Among businesses this shift has prompted a more industrially focused approach to the boundaries of firms, or "deverticalization" in the ungainly phrase of the corporate world, along with a network or "coalitional" approach to production (Piore and Sabel 1984; see Powell, Koput, and Smith-Doerr 1996). Thus, just as movement "productions" are often brought about by temporary coalitions of activist organizations, product lines are often produced by temporary networks of firms. This is not to say that organizations are disappearing due to advances in ICTs (cf. Brown and Duguid 2000), but that how they are collectively organized has shifted in a direction that highlights their analogy with social movements (Davis and McAdam 2000).

Finally, just as the move toward the nation-state system generated waves of contention (Tilly 1993), the growth of a global economic system has shifted the poles of power – and thus to some extent the objects of contention – from nation-states to transnational corporations and multilateral agencies and associations. We have already described how the mobility of capital compels states to act as "vendors" of laws – states do not simply regulate the entities that happen to be housed within them, but compete with other states to attract jurisdictional residents, thus subjecting themselves to the whim of the corporate and capital markets. But just as states come to look more like businesses, so do organizations come to look more like states. Building on the early insights of Selznick (1969), Edelman and colleagues (1999) described how employees came to be "citizens" of the corporate polity where they worked, with attendant rights and legalistic grievance procedures. Laws often end up creating analogs of state agencies within firms, as Dobbin et al. (1993) found in the wake of equal employment opportunity legislation. Following Zald and Berger (1978), Scully and Creed (1999) found social movements among disenfranchised gay and lesbian employees seeking equal treatment with respect to the benefits they and their families received. Moreover, consumers as well as employees treat corporations as analogous to states, and thus as appropriate objects of contention: a McDonald's in France is more likely to be the site of protests than an American embassy (see Klein 1999 on the "no-brand movement"). Through their global power and visibility, transnational corporations become salient sites of protest from within and without.

Yet while we have highlighted how changes in the global economy, information and communication technologies, and the organization of production alter the fields of action of organizations and movements, we also must emphasize what remains the same. Both movements and organizations are, at bottom, forms of organized action and as such are susceptible to similar tools of analysis (see the chapters by Campbell and by McAdam and Scott). Organizers must recruit and retain participants and provide a common orientation through training or other means, whether the form of collective action is explicitly temporary or long-term (Scott 2003). For example, both telephone call centers and high-risk actions such as Freedom Summer recruit through networks among current and prospective participants (Fernandez et al. 2000; McAdam 1986). By the same token, practices diffuse among activist organizations and firms through networks. Processes of organizational change are analogous across movements and organizations. At a fundamental level, the project of mobilizing and sustaining collective action remains the same across contexts and over time (see Campbell, this volume).

We next turn to two illustrative examples of how the study of movements and organizations might benefit from greater crossover.

The Eighteenth Brumaire of Joseph Estrada?

Karl Marx famously opened *The 18th Brumaire of Louis Bonaparte* with the quip "Hegel remarks somewhere that all facts and personages of great importance in world history occur, as it were, twice. He forgot to add: the first time as tragedy, the second as farce." The street protests that ultimately led to the ouster of Philippine President Joseph "Erap" Estrada in January 2001 followed the tracks laid down by similar events fifteen years before, when the autocratic Ferdinand Marcos was ousted by the "people power" movement. After seven years of democratic rule, Marcos had declared martial law in 1972 and continued to hold power for fourteen more years in the face of increasingly vocal domestic and foreign opposition. The assassination of Marcos's exiled rival Benigno Aquino upon his return to the Philippines in August 1983 catalyzed opposition among business and religious leaders, and in February 1986 mass street demonstrations, coupled with the defection of his top military leaders, drove Marcos into exile in Hawaii. The Manila demonstrations, centered on Epifania de los Santos Avenue (EDSA), were both nonviolent and dramatic – at one point, praying nuns faced down tanks in the street. The bloodless ouster of Marcos and the subsequent restoration of democracy came to be known as the "yellow revolution" (see McAdam et al. 2001: 107 ff. for a brief description).

If Ferdinand Marcos's ouster was tragedy, then Joseph Estrada's forced resignation when confronted by People Power II (as it was labeled) was farce. "Erap" Estrada, a popular actor, was elected by a landslide in May 1998 and was especially popular among the poor and working class. But a series of corruption scandals led to an impeachment hearing in late 2000, and foreign direct investment plummeted in the face of concerns about Estrada's management of the economy. Directors of the five largest Philippine business groups met in October to consider a response to help reassure foreign investors – who are critical for the vibrancy of the Philippine economy – and generated a plan to induce Estrada's resignation. The group revived the anti-Marcos Kompil coalition, with business executives playing a central role. Actions included mass walkouts from the stock exchange by traders wearing black armbands, and a free catered "People Power Lunch" to bring laborers and the rural poor into Manila's business district and thus increase the perceived inclusiveness of the anti-Estrada coalition. Yet Estrada remained popular with the mass of low-income Filipinos, and protests continued to be held primarily in the business districts.

Estrada's impeachment trial continued through January 2001, but when a crucial vote to prevent the release of potentially incriminating evidence went Estrada's way in the Senate, opposition rapidly crystallized in the streets as 700,000 demonstrators marched on EDSA – site of the massive anti-Marcos rallies fifteen years before. The remarkably rapid response by demonstrators to the Senate vote was enabled by two factors. First, they had been here before: the seven years of anti-Marcos activities, and particularly the actions of early 1986, created a template for collective action aimed at ousting rulers and a canonical place – EDSA – to do so. Second, word of the gathering was sent out to anti-Estrada forces via text messages sent to cell phones and pagers. "Go to EDSA" and "wear black to mourn the death of democracy" were among the several million messages transmitted in what came to be called the "pager revolution." Filipino telecommunications companies obliged their customers by moving mobile cell sites to EDSA in order to accommodate the increased traffic. The street gathering lasted for four days, with key military leaders joining the opposition (and showing support with combat troops and jet fighter flights over the presidential palace). After the Supreme Court declared that "the people have spoken" on the morning of January 20, Estrada ceded power to Vice President Gloria Macapagal Arroyo, who was supported by opposition and military leaders.

Both the why and the how of Estrada's ouster exemplify the global shifts affecting organizations and movements. First, mass movements aimed at leadership changes have often followed increases in inequality or impoverishment. But the idea that declines in foreign direct investment and loss of favor in the international capital markets should drive popular protest and nonconstitutional changes in elected leaders is new. *The Economist* commented in a 1999 article on global financial architecture that "a domestic court can fire a bankrupt firm's management.... But even the most ardent globalist is unlikely to recommend that an international bankruptcy court should be able to fire a country's government." Yet the elite-sponsored movement against Estrada in the Philippines, with cooperation from (primarily American) corporate interests, comes close to this scenario. Military coups are not historically uncommon (even those with foreign business involvement), but what distinguished Estrada's ouster is that, in a fragile democracy, perceptions of popular legitimacy behind regime changes are essential: a social movement with mass street protests conveys a sense of "the people's will" in a way that threatening moves by the military cannot.

Moreover, Philippine business elites had not misread the influence of foreign investor sentiment on the Philippine economy, as a subsequent episode demonstrates. The California Public Employees Retirement System (CalPERS), a huge and influential institutional investor, announced in February 2002 that it would no longer invest in emerging markets that failed to meet its political and financial standards and included the Philippines on its "not investment worthy" list, occasioning a 3.2 percent decline in the Manila Stock Exchange over the next three days. After lobbying by the Philippine financial secretary, CalPERS discovered that its negative rating of the Philippines was based on a clerical error, and in May restored the Philippines to the approved list. As journalists noted at the time of Estrada's ouster, foreign investment is the lifeblood of the Philippine economy, which puts political leaders in a position directly analogous to corporate leaders with respect to their investors.

Second, information and communication technologies greatly enhanced both the speed and the reach of the movement. Revolutionary literature is centuries old, and tapes of Ayatollah Khomeini's speeches circulated illicitly in pre-revolutionary Iran in what was called the "cassette revolution." But the "pager revolution" of instant text messages allowed rapid, synchronous, decentralized movement activity. No prior technology enabled news events to cascade via person-to-person communication into a street gathering of several hundred thousand people within a few hours, as happened in Manila. Moreover, participation in the "movement" was not limited by geography. A website called eLagda.com sponsored an e-mail petition against Estrada and sought to gather one million "signatures" in the form of e-mail addresses, which were gathered from Filipinos around the world who logged on to the site. Both locals and expatriates were able to follow events on the Web, using local and international media. The "imagined community" (Anderson 1983) of Filipinos had achieved a global catchment area, allowing expatriates to "participate" virtually in the movement. We anticipate that the Philippine experience of 2001 will preview similar struggles in years to come.

The A16 Protests and the Antiglobalization Movement

The Philippine movement that led to President Estrada's ouster used new technologies to achieve a traditional purpose – a change in national leadership – spurred by global economic integration. In contrast, the movement against corporate-led globalization is aimed at international economic arrangements themselves. Both in its objects and in its organizational structure, it differs from prior social movements in intriguing ways. We illustrate this with a brief description of the A16 (April 16, 2000) "Break the Bank"

343

demonstration aimed at meetings among finance ministers, the International Monetary Fund (IMF), and the World Bank in Washington, D.C.

The global justice movement made itself vividly known during the November 1999 protest against the World Trade Organization (WTO) during its meetings in Seattle. A multinational entity for regulating global trade, the WTO was accustomed to working in relative obscurity. The Seattle meeting signaled that the institutions governing global trade and global finance, and their perceived corporate beneficiaries, were obscure no more, and subsequent meetings of the representatives of global economic power (at least those held in democracies) came to expect street protests. After the "battle in Seattle," a template for mobilization for such meetings evolved in which information and communication technology – particularly cell phones and the World Wide Web – was essential infrastructure. Activists start by putting out a call on e-mail listservs (e-mail mailing lists organized around particular shared interests) with defining principles and directions to a Web site with further information about the mobilization. (The A16 mobilization site's address was www.a16.org.) Because e-mails are readily forwarded to large groups by recipients, compelling calls for action can spread widely at essentially no cost. The next step, along with recruiting participants, is to build a coalition of organizational sponsors, with a large and diverse sponsorship base a sensible goal. Because the global justice movement's ethos is one of participation and nonviolence, participants are trained both in tactics of protest and in consensus-based decision making. Analogs to corporate consulting firms have arisen to provide specialized training in advanced tactics. The Ruckus Society in Oakland, California, for instance, holds training camps and publishes manuals for activists. Its mission states: "The Ruckus Society provides environmental and human rights organizers with the tools, training, and support needed to achieve their goals. Working with a broad range of communities, organizations, and movements – from high school students to professional organizations – Ruckus facilitates the sharing of information and expertise that strengthens the capacity to change our relationship with the environment and each other" (Ruckus Society Web site).

To create more concrete infrastructure, organizers set up a "convergence center" to act as a hub, typically in an unused warehouse. The convergence center provides a location both for assembling materials for the event (e.g., giant puppets) and for getting out news from the event that can bypass traditional media (e.g., streaming video on the Web). Finally, ICTs – including cell phones and wireless e-mail communicators – enable highly flexible tactics on the ground. Strategically sited monitors with cell phones can keep organizers abreast of shifting circumstances, such as the locations and actions of police.

The A16 "mobile festival of resistance" in Washington, D.C., illustrates this template in action. The mobilization did not look or sound like a traditional protest march because of its conscious plan to convey spectacle and fun. Live music, drumming circles, dancing, and giant puppets appeared at several points in the rally. The list of co-sponsors was itself part of the spectacle, and included the AFL-CIO, the National Lawyers Guild, the Rainforest Action Network, the Green Party, the D.C. Lesbian Avengers, the Action Committee on Women's Rights in Iran, and dozens of others. The speed with which the demonstration and its sponsors were assembled was perhaps unprecedented. As Chuck Kaufman of the Alliance for Global Justice put it, "It would have been impossible to organize this demonstration so close on the heels of Seattle without the Internet" (Montgomery and Santana 2000). The Internet and computer technology were essential prior to, during, and after the demonstration. As events unfolded, freelancers with digital video cameras brought back footage of the events to the media center, where it was downloaded to computers, edited, and broadcast over the Web, providing an alternative source of information to the traditional media – almost instantaneously. Later edits were recorded onto videos made available shortly thereafter by the Independent Media Center. A16 was followed within a few months by similar rallies in Quebec and Prague.

The mobilizations for global justice, as illustrated by A16, highlight several themes that are new to contemporary movements and organizations. The factors that have prompted and enabled new forms of work and new ways to organize production in the corporate world have had a similar impact on movements. First, the "production" of the protest is explicitly spectacle and fun, rather than a straightforward expression of anger or grim determination. The A16 demonstration was itself intended to avoid the "commodified experience" that was the object of some of the protestors – ironically, since branding and spectacle are much on the minds of those running the corporations singled out by antiglobalization activists (see Klein 1999). In this sense, the postmodern esthetic washes over movements and organizations alike.

Second, for A16 ICTs were essential for enabling the mobilization and permeated its organization. Participants were recruited via the Internet, and sympathizers could make donations by credit card over the Web. Websites announced meeting times and places, distributed news and images, and provided a durable organizational infrastructure: when the D.C. police closed down the convergence center, the electronic underpinnings were simply accessed and operated from a new location. As might be anticipated by transaction cost economists (see, e.g., Williamson 1994), the Internet was a parameter shift in the transaction costs of collective action that allowed a few committed people to organize thousands of others at great speed with trivial out-of-pocket expenses. These lowered transaction costs further enabled a new and more flexible repertoire of on-the-ground actions and, not incidentally, enabled more decentralized and consensual decision making. Moreover, the means of integration among participants was primarily cultural rather than structural.

Third, the large and diverse group of sponsors for A16, as with similar demonstrations, highlights the fact that productions are not the output of a single more-or-less bounded actor but of temporary coalitions. The movement is not a property of a particular organization, or even a small number of SMOs (in contrast with the American civil rights movement, for instance). Rather, it is better characterized as a network or field, with any particular actions arising out of a particular subnetwork – a description exactly analogous to recent discussion of so-called network forms of organizations (e.g., Miles and Snow 1994; Powell 1990). Ironically, then, both global corporations and the movements that seek to influence or constrain them must address a contemporary sensibility of spectacle (Harvey 1990) and do so using a repertoire of organizational tactics and forms enabled by the same set of information technologies.

Some Common Themes

Times of upheaval can be fruitful, not only for the creation of new organizational forms and movement processes, but for the creation of new social theory. We argue that the social changes associated with our current era provide ample reason to reconsider the traditional separation of the study of social movements and of organizations. The shifting balance of power among states and transnational corporations has in some sense put them on a similar ground: both states and firms have to manage the perceptions of "consumers" and "investors," and both are objects of contention by social movements. States, such as the Philippines, become subject to economic vagaries dictated by the sentiments (and clerical errors) of distant investors. By the same token, transnational corporations are increasingly "stateless" in the sense that their activities are rarely contained within particular nations, and their decision makers are in effect consumers of institutional structures offered by states. But by their very prominence firms have become subject to the kinds of activism previously experienced primarily by states: Shell, Monsanto, and Nike were all targets of global campaigns intended to alter what they did and how they did it. As polities, corporations are subject to challenges both from within (by the "citizens" who work for them) and from without (by activists and consumers).

There is a further irony: just as corporations have come to be perceived as global centers of power populated by citizens demanding rights, on a par with nation-states, they turn out (on some accounts) to be mere legal fictions with the character of quicksilver. From a high modernist conception of the organization as a boundary-maintaining actor, we have arrived at a view of the firm as a shifting network, organizing production through webs of contracts but with "no body to kick, no soul to damn." The declining transaction costs of contracting out production and other nonessential activities, enabled in part by new information and communication technologies, put organizations on a par with movements, assembling networks of participants for relatively short-lived productions.

ICTs do not merely lower the transaction costs of established forms of collective action, however; they also enable new repertoires of contention for movements and organizations. This is well known in business, even after the electronic commerce bubble burst: few aspects of how business gets done in the West have *not* been affected by ICTs. But the speed, flexibility, global reach, and customization made possible for business are equally true of social movements. As the Philippine case illustrates, text messaging can be a powerful mobilizing device, and the World Wide Web enables a global catchment area for participation and activism. A16 shows how Web sites, cell phones, and a few observers in tall buildings can articulate shifting local terrain for marchers on the ground. And in each case the prospects for widespread engagement are enabled on a scale previously unknown. Indeed, simultaneous protests against the imminent U.S. invasion of Iraq on February 15, 2003, took place across North and South America, Europe, Asia, Africa, and Australia, involving upward of six million participants. This unprecedented global antiwar movement is impossible to imagine without contemporary information and communication technologies; the *New York Times* saw this as a manifestation of the world's second superpower – global public opinion. The prospects for genuinely global, synchronized social movements had finally been realized.

Finally, for much of the type of postindustrial collective action we have observed in recent times, the "output" of the action is image, perception, emotion. For prior movements representing clear collective interests, the intended perception is one of WUNC: we're worthy, unified, numerous, and committed. Production was aimed at enhancing power holders' assessments of each of these four dimensions. For the global justice movement represented by A16, on the other hand, participation in itself is the point. Spectacle may not be relevant for demonstrating WUNC, but it makes for a much more engaging movement, in which participation is its own reward. That is, it is perhaps engagement per se, rather than its consequences, which is valued by participants. Contests are ceremonial; victories are virtual. This idea has its counterpart in the corporate world, where brand management and investor relations (professions oriented toward shaping the perceptions of consumers and investors, respectively) are among the ascendant professions of recent years. Naomi Klein (1999: 4) summarized: pioneers such as Nike and Tommy Hilfiger "make the bold claim that producing goods was only an incidental part of their operations, and that thanks to recent victories in trade liberalization and labor-law reform, they were able to have their products made for them by contractors, many of them overseas. What these companies produced primarily were not things, they said, but *images* of their brands. Their real work lay not in manufacturing but in marketing." "The culture of the simulacrum comes to life in a society where exchange value has been generalized to the point at which the very memory of use value is effaced, a society of which Guy Debord has observed...that in it 'the image has become the final form of commodity reification'" (Jameson 1991: 18).

Implications

We have argued that what organizations and movements do, and how they do it, have rotated on the same axis, and that the greater integration of the global economy has helped shift the objects of contention from states to corporations and multinational agencies. But what is to be done in theory? What difference does all this make for research? The preceding chapters of this book provide both theoretical and empirical answers to this question. We here highlight some broad implications for research practice that are taken up in more detail elsewhere in the book: the utility of taking a *field-level perspective* on organizations and movements, and the centrality of *social mechanisms* to the types of theoretical explanations that are produced.

348

First, when social systems are not meaningfully organized into bounded, countable collective actors, as we have argued is true for much of the contemporary organizational world, it makes sense to take a field-level approach. Scholars of social movements have long recognized the value of viewing social movements not as singular "actors" but as fields made up of congeries of actors; there was no organization that was contiguous with the American civil rights movement. By the same token, understanding the evolving structures of areas of activity in economic life, such as health care provision, requires a perspective that transcends "organization" and "industry" to take into account the broader system of governance and contestation. McAdam and Scott (this volume) proposed that a field-level approach to organizations and movements highlights how a common set of questions can fruitfully guide inquiry into both realms. Institutional theorists such as DiMaggio and Powell (1983) and Scott and Meyer (1983) have argued for the value of a field-level approach to organizational life, but McAdam and Scott find that a thoroughgoing field-level analysis is more broadly applicable and illustrate it with findings from detailed studies of historical change in which the boundaries of fields, the identities of actors, and the rules of play changed substantially over time.

Second, as we have hinted previously, the basic dynamics of collective action are common across movements and organizations, and both confront similar "human resource challenges" such as recruitment, retention, socialization, coordination, and so on. But to recognize what is common requires working at the level of social mechanisms – "a set of interacting parts – an assembly of elements producing an effect not inherent in any one of them. A mechanism is not so much about 'nuts and bolts' as about 'cogs and wheels' . . . – the wheelwork or agency by which an effect is produced" (Hernes 1998: 74). Mechanisms, according to Hedstrom and Swedberg (1998b), provide "an intermediary level of analysis in-between pure description and story-telling, on the one hand, and universal social laws, on the other." As such, they are well suited to the types of "collective action by ambiguously-bounded actors" that we have described in contemporary movements and organizations. McAdam and colleagues accorded central place to the study of mechanisms in their recent effort to reorient social movement theory (McAdam, Tarrow, and Tilly 2001), and in this volume Campbell explores processes and mechanisms common to both organization theory and social movement theory.

This book seeks to show concrete research consequences exemplifying the kind of crossover for which we have argued. One purpose of the book has been to show how concepts developed in one of the domains (organization theory or social movement theory) are useful for the other. For example, theorists of organizations have contemplated alternative structures for organizations with many subunits that are geographically dispersed, and when and why they work as they do. Chapters on social movement "franchising" (by McCarthy) and on transnational social movement organizations (by Smith) document how these concepts help illuminate relatively new organizational forms in the social movement sector. Conversely, social movement scholars have described movement/countermovement dynamics during struggles over policy, which provides an enlightening framework for analyzing the struggles among the shareholder rights movement and more-or-less organized corporate elites over state-level corporate law (in the chapter by Vogus and Davis).

These chapters build on a long and fitful tradition picked up on in the article by Zald and Berger (1978) on movements within organizations. But the years since this paper was published have seen great advances in theory and methods in both organizational studies and social movement studies. Social network analysis and dynamic statistical methods, for instance, have greatly expanded the empirical sophistication and rigor of both areas and have enabled more subtle (and testable) cross-level theorizing. Thus, although we have argued that the current period is especially characterized by examples of crossover, the theory and research we present are useful to explain phenomena from earlier times (see Schneiberg and Soule, this volume). The authors of the chapters have been particularly attentive to highlighting the added value of the combined approach. We believe that the conjunction is especially useful for the analysis of movements that are global in character, but also useful for organizational change movements. For instance, those leading innovation efforts in organizations may draw implicitly or explicitly on social movement–like processes and management styles (Strang and Jung, this volume) in promoting innovations and change. We hope that other researchers are inspired by these examples to study and build theory from the new round of social movements in and around organizations that we are witnessing today.

13

Two Kinds of Stuff

THE CURRENT ENCOUNTER
OF SOCIAL MOVEMENTS
AND ORGANIZATIONS

Elisabeth S. Clemens

The warning comes from Leviticus: "You shall keep my statutes. You shall not let your cattle breed with a different kind; you shall not sow your field with two kinds of seed; nor shall there come upon you a garment of cloth made of two kinds of stuff" (cited in Douglas 1966: 53). Given these commandments, one might suspect that it is also dangerous to mix literatures of different kinds. When tie-dyed activists and poor people's marches are central to the imagery of a theory, can that theory be transposed to corporate boardrooms and back offices without doing fundamental violence to our understanding of both phenomena? When formal authority and control over resources infuse the theoretical imagination of one literature, can that body of work truly inform the analysis of resistance to authority?

As befits a volume informed by studies of protest, the contributors ignore authority and break commandments. Yet there are signs that these literatures do not mesh seamlessly. Tensions appear at the margins of arguments; hybrid models suggest possibilities of innovation but also of problematic mutations or simply sterility. Viewed in a longer perspective, however, the current effort at cross-fertilization is only the most recent in a series of encounters between two sociological lineages that seem to both attract and repel one another. Each successive encounter has been fueled by distinctive concerns and offers diverging opportunities (or obstacles) to a more fruitful engagement. Yet unlike many previous engagements, the current encounter draws inspiration largely from the organizations side of the field.

I am grateful to David Waugh-Breiger for his thought-provoking remarks at his bar-mitzvah.

This distinctive motivation illuminates how and why this encounter between literatures differs from the earlier conversations and cross-fertilizations. In the present moment, it appears, the imagery of the centralized, rational bureaucracy is increasingly unable to capture the empirical world confronted by organizational analysts. Firms are not in control of their own strategies but members of strategic alliances; traditional hierarchical relationships may be cross-cut by matrix forms of organization or overlapping "team" arrangements; companies pursue reinvention not only by seeking to recreate corporate cultures and brands, but by dismembering and reassembling themselves through spin-offs and acquisitions. Faced with fluid alliances, unclear lines of authority, and recombinant parts, organizational analysts have rifled through the social sciences in search of new theoretical images or tools – drawn from network methods, cultural theory, politics, artificial intelligence – that will help to explain this strange new world.

As organizational researchers have foraged more broadly in search of analytic tools to understand the world of corporations, the intermittent conversation of organizational analysis with social movement theory has been rejoined. For both literatures, the encounter has reinforced an appreciation of the varieties of organizational form; organizational research has been further enriched by attention to mobilization, conflict, and process. But, as is too often the case with happy couples, the match also reinforces mutual weaknesses, in this case a problematic and conflicted relationship to the core imagery of formal organization. For all the potency of new forms of mobilization and innovative strategies, modern societies are pervaded by deeply entrenched structures of formal power which set the terms upon which social movements encounter corporations, or members of corporations behave like activists.

An Uneasy Alliance

The effort to link the study and practice of organizing movements and formal organizations is far from new. But, to date, the mixing has occurred more extensively on the social movements side of the equation. For these scholars and activists, there often has been a deep discomfort with the very concept of organization. Understood as systems of order and authority, organization seems incompatible with projects of social change. In his classic study of the German Social Democratic Party, Robert Michels (1962 [1911]) equated organization with oligarchy, tracking the moderation of radical political impulses by the routinized political engagement central to electoral competition and legislative participation. As social movement research developed as a major area of sociological research, early contributors battled over the claim that formal organization necessarily undercuts effective mobilization (Cloward and Piven 1984; Gamson and Schmeidler 1984).

One of the great contributions of feminist analyses of social movement organizations has been to explore these tensions. In the nineteenth century, Spiritualists advocated "no-organizationism" and suffragist Lucy Stone compared organizations to Chinese footbinding, declaring that she "had had enough of thumb-screws and soul screws never to wish to be placed under them again" (quoted in Clemens 1997: 187). For contemporary feminists, the classic text was provided by Jo Freeman's analysis of "the tyranny of structurelessness" (1972; see also Alter 1998; Bordt 1997). These arguments suggest a deep tension between the efficacy of movement organization and participants' (as well as analysts') expectations for particular meanings of equality, styles of involvement, and qualities of authenticity.

But despite this strain of suspicion toward formal organization, second wave feminism produced a rich array of novel organizational forms, "the harvest of the new women's movement" (Ferree and Martin 1995). These experiments in form challenged the automatic equation of "organization" with "formal, bureaucratic hierarchy." Studies of feminism – both first and second wave – documented how projects of mobilizing without creating entrenched leadership could generate political advantages (Clemens 1993) as well as chronic instabilities and conflicts (Whittier 1995). Comparative research demonstrated that the structured salience of gender for national polities is shaped by the prevalence of such antiorganizational feminist organizations as opposed to the dominance of more centralized and hierarchical political organizations such as electoral parties (Ferree et al. 2002: 72–5). Discussions of "organization" – generic, undifferentiated, implicitly hierarchical – were replaced by analysis of "organizational forms," understood as plural and diverse.

Whereas certain strands of feminism, in particular, have understood formal organization as antithetical to authentic participation, other activists at other times have celebrated organization as the key to success. In 1914, Wisconsin's social democratic unionists declared:

The ancient Greeks used the word "organization" and defined it as an instrument, engine, machine or tool for making or moving anything. To us as organized workers, organization means or is our instrument for enforcing just dealings, shorter hours of labor, better pay, safe and decent and sanitary conditions of labor. . . . This tool – organization – will yet pry the locks from firetrap factories and even force the courts to a sense of social responsibility. (Wisconsin State Federation of Labor 1914)

A line of too-often-forgotten studies in the "old institutionalism" argued that the success of mobilization could often be traced to distinctive organizational technologies and strategies (Ostrander 1957; Ullman 1955). Recent work has renewed this interest. Across movements or episodes of mobilization, organizational form appears crucial for movement success, particularly by the relatively powerless: disenfranchised women adopted "business methods" to gain the right to vote and help to deprive men of the right to drink (Clemens 1997); Mexican-American activists drew on exemplars of revolutionary solidarity and religious confraternity to organize agricultural workers when the AFL-CIO (American Federation of Labor and Congress of Industrial Organizations) and Teamsters had failed (Ganz 2000). These organizational analyses of movement development fit poorly with studies of social movements that equate mobilization exclusively with protest, defining organizations that engaged in forms of routine politics as beyond the scope of movement studies (on the price of this analytic move, see Goldstone 2003) and overlooking the extent to which "movement organizations" may strategically adopt organizational forms or alternate between protest in the streets and lobbying in legislatures (Clemens 1996).

Fed by diverse streams of work – feminism, the old institutionalism, among others – this growing attention to variation in organizational form represented a partial break from the core imagery of resource mobilization theory. Long the major point of conjuncture between organizational and social movement research, resource mobilization theory built on assumptions that contrasted sharply with "no-organizationism" and the "iron rule of oligarchy." Like the case studies of the older institutionalist tradition just discussed, proponents of resource mobilization theory (McCarthy and Zald 1977) portrayed formal organization as an asset that enhanced collective action and protected against the evanescent character of many protest efforts. In contrast to the vision attributed to Michels, in which organizations master their members, organizations were understood as resources to be deployed by activists.

For all their disagreements, however, a particular image of organization is shared by the feminist no-organizationists, the old institutionalists, and scholars in the resource mobilization tradition. In each case, the oppressiveness or the efficacy of formal organization was attributed to traits such as centralization and hierarchy.[1] These traits, after all, informed classics of organizational analysis such as Weber's essay on bureaucracy and classical management theory just as they were enacted by the practices of scientific management (Morgan 1997; Scott 2003). But, in recent decades, organizations scholars themselves have questioned this basic theoretical imagery. Organizations have come to be seen as relatively open to their environments, both constituted by and embedded in networks of relationships that are not ordered hierarchically. Consequently, core questions of organization theory have increasingly raised issues about mobilization and coordination in contexts lacking the centralized hierarchies of rational bureaucracy.

These developments within organizational theory have contributed to a reengagement with social movement research through at least two different channels. First, as organizational theorists moved away from the rational model of hierarchical bureaucracy, they have looked for other imageries of social ordering. To the extent that work on social movements has been infused by the spirit of no-organizationism, this was a mutually agreeable encounter. Second, from the opposite direction, a growing number of scholars within political sociology and social movement research have drawn on advances in organization theory without activating the older debates and antipathies (for a review, see Clemens and Minkoff 2004). This friendly borrowing is possible, at least in part, because organization theory has become more expansive, conceptualizing organizations as "rational, natural, and open systems" (see McAdam and Scott, this volume). This organizationally inclined social movements literature has grown steadily, producing a flurry of major new studies that pay attention to organizational models as forms of culture and matrices of practice (Armstrong 2002; Clemens 1997; Lichterman 1996; Polletta 2002; Stevens 2001; Warren 2001). The world also has provided relevant cases; many newer movements explicitly foreground nonhierarchical models of organization, and the alliance structures and consensus-based decision making that are emblematic of many environmental and global movements (Polletta 2002; Davis and Zald, this volume). Consequently, once organizational scholars came calling, a congenial reception was likely.

---

[1] As Ferree and Mueller (2004) argued, resource mobilization theory "guided social movement thinking in the United States toward theorizing the hierarchical, centralized, formalized organization as the normative 'SMO.'"

A New Conversation?

Given this history of episodic encounters, what is distinctive about the current conversation between social movement scholars and organizational analysts? Above all, this renewed engagement is marked by its origins in the latter camp. Whereas theories of mobilization and protest have a complex and conflicted relationship with the concept of formal organization, much of the literature on formal organization has developed in blithe ignorance of social movement theory. The disconnect was, perhaps, clearest in studies that treated organizations as both rational and closed systems. As McAdam and Scott (this volume) explain, shifts toward "natural" or "open" models of organizations invited a more political view of organizations that addressed both contention within the organization and relations across the boundary between organization and environment (Davis and Powell 1992).

This blurring of the boundary around the firm allowed two distinct moves that shape the current engagement of social movement and organization theory. First, the relevance of relationships was no longer defined by the formal organization chart; forms of coordination grounded in personal networks as well as nonauthoritative projects of mobilization were made visible, as were influences that transgressed the official boundaries of an organization. Captured in the image of organizations as "open systems" (Scott 2003), this shift highlighted the importance of "politics" in contexts usually bereft of recognizable political mechanisms (elections to factory councils would be an exception). In the absence of the institutional framework that sustains core political activities such as "voting" and "representation," the imagery of social movements has proved to be a powerful tool for understanding the dynamics of mobilization and conflict that cross-cut formal relationships of authority within firms or agencies. As Strang and Jung (this volume) recognize in their study of "orchestrated mobilization," even managers may sometimes choose to work outside the lattice of formal authority in order to harness the "voluntary" contributions of their subordinates. More typical of this move, however, have been studies that explore how subordinates within organizations engage in politics despite the lack of any of the formal rights of citizenship – the vote, the petition, assembly – that structure conflict and competition in the realm of institutional politics. Although "organizations as politics" has been a standard lens within organization theory (Morgan 1997), the shift from "politics" to "social movements" highlights patterns of mobilization distinct from both the lines of formal authority and the personal ties evoked by "informal organization." Mobilization may – and frequently does – run along lines of personal relationships and friendship, but the imagery of social movement theory implies conscious and strategic coordination of action that does not rely on – indeed, typically opposes – coordination that is based on legitimate authority.

Conceivably, nonauthoritative coordination might be effected solely by means of relationships and resources internal to an organization. Close analyses of organizational politics, however, reveal many instances in which broader cultural and political shifts trigger and structure conflict within a firm or agency. Grievances within a firm may be linked to symbols, technologies, and identities grounded in domains outside of work (see Scully and Creed, this volume); the outcomes of such mobilization, in turn, may be shaped by shifts in formal authority (Raeburn 2001; Thornton and Ocasio 1999). As Zald, Morrill, and Rao (this volume) elaborate, the outcomes of struggles in open organizational polities are jointly shaped by pressures exerted by internal actors aligned with broader social movements and the will and capacity of organizational authorities to resist.

For all the distance between these arguments and the classic imagery of formal organizational authority, however, a focus on particular organizations continues to structure these investigations. While open systems imagery requires a shift from bounded organizational case studies to analyses of "focal" organizations embedded in relations or buffeted by movements, the shift to address nonauthoritative modes of coordinated action does not in itself require systematic attention to entire populations of organizations or fields of interaction. But the current engagement of social movement theory and organizational analysis is structured by the combination of a shift to field-level analysis with attention to nonauthoritative coordination.

Following the norms of social science, the encounter may be captured in a two-by-two table. Both social movement and organizational analysis have, traditionally, been at home in studies of focal organizations. If the classical bureaucracy is the exemplary image for organization theorists, the case study of a movement represents the core genre of social movement research. Image and genre might be combined – as in Selznick's *Organizational Weapon* (1952) – but movement studies tended to focus on nonauthoritative, nonhierarchical relationships such as recruitment.

Whereas "social movements and organizations" evokes a Venn diagram of two overlapping literatures that define a single domain for cooperation between scholars from the two initial specialties, the chapters suggest that the mixing of kinds produces a more complex terrain (Figure 13.1).

	Focal Organization	Organizational Field
Authoritative coordination: yes	Bureaucratic authority within the firm or public agency Organization as weapon; organization as oligarchy	Studies of competition within populations of firms (e.g., Carroll & Hannan 2000; Hannan & Freeman 1989) or social movement organizations (Minkoff 1999) Studies of populations of public entities (e.g., Scott and Meyer 1994) or social movements (e.g., McCarthy, this volume) in multi-tier systems or federations. Organizations viewed as embedded informal, authoritative relations with other organizations.
Authoritative coordination: no	Mobilization into membership or activity Focal-organization analysis of the impact of social movements (Scully and Creed; Zald, Morrill, and Rao, both this volume) or "orchestrated mobilization" (Strang and Jung, this volume)	"Social Movements" but explicitly not the focal-organization, single movement style of study (e.g., Armstrong; Smith; Schneiberg and Soule, all this volume) Firms and formally organized political actors (e.g., unions) engaged in collective action or coalition politics (e.g., Vogus and Davis, this volume)

Figure 13.1 Social Movements and Organizations: A Taxonomy of Research Frames

The contributors, it seems, are brought together by relations of structural equivalence, and by their common rejection of an imagery of organizations as delimited entities defined by centralized, hierarchical authority. This rejection, however, is profoundly asymmetrical across the two literatures.

Within social movement theory, the imagery of hierarchical organization has been particularly fraught. For the past three decades, formal organization has been either denounced as the enemy of significant protest (for a slice of this debate, see Cloward and Piven 1984; Gamson and Schmeidler 1984) or "black-boxed" as a resource for activists. This aversion to treating social movement organizations as formal organizations runs deep; even in the contributions to this volume, the chapters most concerned with social movement organizations address relations *among* organizations rather than reviving the once-heated debates over forms of authority *within* movement organizations. This interorganizational focus is one of the most distinctive contributions of McCarthy's analysis of the franchise form and federation as well as Smith's survey of transnational movement organizations. By illuminating the franchise and federation, McCarthy provides an important caveat to the tendency of organizational analysts to equate social movements with nonauthoritative forms of coordination. Many of the movements now recognized as historically consequential were structured by highly elaborated divisions of labor and rules of deference between (relatively) subordinate locals and their regional or national counterparts (Skocpol 1999b: 47–9). In her study of transnational social movements, Smith adds nuance to this point, recognizing variation in the form of relationships among member organizations in multinational alliances.

Within organizational research, however, the turn to social movement imagery is linked with claims of change, innovation, and flexibility. Consequently, when juxtaposed to one another, the analyses of organizational conflict within firms envisioned as open polities under pressure from social movements seem hardly to belong to the same conversation as these studies of formal relationships among discrete social movement organizations. By extending the analysis of formal ties to a broader organizational field, McCarthy and Smith seem rather more aligned with the institutional analyses of John Meyer and his many colleagues, which track the adoption of policies or organizational forms across a world polity in which nations are linked to one another by formal ties of treaty or membership (e.g., Strang 1990) as well as across organizational populations subject to a single legal regime (e.g., Dobbin et al. 1993; Edelman 1990).[2] Whereas the "open polity" analyses of organizational conflict reveal the complex dynamics within organizations, these interorganizational studies attend to formal ties that structure broader fields of influence and coordination.

Either of these moves represents a considerable advance beyond the automatic assumption of the rational, bureaucratic firm as the appropriate template for research and theorizing. Yet the promise of the current engagement of organizational analysis and social movement theory lies in the efforts to sustain both moves at once. Recognizing that social organization rests on multiple forms of coordination – authoritative rules and relationships, symbolic resonance, embedding in personal ties, alignment of interests – a growing body of studies insists on an expansive delineation of their inquiry. Frequently motivated by an interest in institutional change, this approach insists on recognizing heterogeneity in both the forms of coordination and the character of organizations. This dual agenda does not produce a neat taxonomy in which movement organizations rely on one form of coordination while firms rely on another. Instead, the intuition common to these projects is that any given organization may be structured around or penetrated by multiple modes of collective action at the same time that it exists in diverse relationships – of ownership, alliance, emulation, resistance – with a heterogeneous field of other organizational actors.

At this point, social movement scholars might well sit back and congratulate themselves for developing a model of collective action now recognized by the privileged researchers in business schools. But, in time, the paranoia of those who challenge authority will reassert itself. "A field of other organizations?" Drawing on the presumptions of their many informants, movement theorists might well wonder what has happened to that other really big organizational actor: the state. In the current encounter, the flurry of alliances and mobilization and coalitions obscures the formal institutions of rule.

Two, Four, Six, Eight – It's Time to Think About the State

Throughout these chapters, the iconic images of contemporary protest involve clashes between social movements and the transnational development

---

[2] Another variant addresses populations of clearly bounded organizations in relationships of imitation and competition (e.g., Carroll and Hannan 2000; Hannan and Freeman 1989). Debra Minkoff (1999) has been the leading proponent of applying this lens of population ecology to the study of social movement organizations.

of capitalist enterprises. In the streets of Seattle, Washington, D.C., Prague, and Quebec City, activists have mobilized to denounce and dramatize the transformation of economic regimes that facilitate trade while threatening the legal protections for labor, the environment, and national sovereignty itself. Yet to address these moments as encounters between social movements and corporations (or even corporations acting like or penetrated by social movements) misses a key feature. These clashes occur at locales defined by gatherings of government representatives engaged in formal renegotiations of the rules for international trade and development. Activism, both in the streets and in corridors filled with lobbyists, is directed at institutional politics.

For a project linking research on social movements and organizations, these highlights of contemporary protest contain both substantive and theoretical lessons. If the agenda is to integrate the empirical study of social movements with the empirical study of formal organizations, the lack of attention to formal political institutions is problematic. Many critical struggles are *about* the rules of the game rather than *within* those rules. Here, bringing the state back in facilitates a better understanding of processes of institutional change as well as awareness of institutional change as a goal of contending parties. In more theoretical terms, the mobilizations against globalization underscore the relevance of institutional theory for this dialogue between social movement research and organizational analysis. If rules and legitimate models are consequential, then we should expect there to be contestation over the character of these rules and models. Yet, it remains surprisingly easy to decouple institutional politics from discussions of mobilization and protest.[3]

Institutional politics, however, provides an exceptionally rich terrain for the integration of social movement research and organizational analysis. To take advantage of this opportunity, we need to interrogate key boundary claims embedded in both dominant frameworks for social movement research and studies of institutional change. The divide between scholarship on social movements and formal politics is multiply embedded in the social sciences. The former belongs to sociology, the latter largely to political science. Within sociology, a few eccentrics do address formal political institutions, but they are organized through a distinct section and

---

[3] In this regard, the "state-free" character of the market theory lurking in the shadows of much organizational analysis may reinforce this de-coupling of mobilization/protest from institutional politics.

reproduced through separate graduate seminars and reading lists. What exemplars of and assumptions about politics inform this widely accepted division of labor?

Three sources for this persistent abyss between literatures suggest themselves. First, the divide between contentious and institutional politics has enormous plausibility for key cases in the development of social movement theory: the closed or, at best, partially open polities of nineteenth-century Europe and the pre–civil rights American South. To the extent that these cases were critical sites for theoretical development (as they were in classic works too numerous to list), this divide is embedded in theory and research designs which may then be transposed to other topics where the divide is more problematic. Second, the ideology of the great protest wave of the 1960s and 1970s championed a rejection of "politics as usual" even as activist strategies and careers bridged these domains (think only of the McGovern campaign, or the careers of Senator Kerry of Massachusetts and Joschka Fischer of the German Green Party). Finally, the advancement of protest event analysis as a central methodology in social movement research has indirectly reinforced this divide by circumscribing a particular set of events reported in the news in particular ways. Unintentionally, this extremely productive methodology may truncate our view of the strategies and tactics employed by activists and corporations alike.

The uncritical acceptance of this divide presents an obstacle to the conversation between social movement theory and organizational analysis advanced by this volume. To the extent that challenging movements and large corporations are the central exemplars for these theoretical literatures, this divide curtails appreciation of the range of actions and strategies deployed by challengers. As I have documented in work on turn-of-the-century movements (Clemens 1997), activists were quite conscious of moving between quiet lobbying or "the still hunt," electoral mobilization, the cultivation of solidarity, and protest. For corporations, a focus on protest makes still less sense. For large firms and trade associations, mobilization takes place through fundraising, advertising, public relations, and other activities far removed from the streets; this claim also holds for movement organizations (Goldstone 2003). For both challengers and corporations, formal political institutions are a central terrain for these strategies. At a more theoretical level, attention to multiple forms and objects of mobilization restores attention to agency and strategic innovation on the part of activists and entrepreneurs alike.

Once formal political institutions are reestablished as objects of mobilization, the conversation between social movement research and organizational analysis promises to advance our understanding of institutional origins and processes of institutional change with respect to the organization of political governance and economic regimes (Bartley 2003; Schneiberg and Soule, this volume). These have been difficult topics insofar as various institutionalisms have begun with strong imageries of institutions as deeply embedded in history and resources (e.g., the historical institutionalism of Steinmo, Thelen, and Longstreth 1992) or as "taken-for-granted" and therefore durable models structuring social life (e.g., Powell and DiMaggio 1991).

But by taking institutions as potential objects of contestation, these strong imageries can be displaced by a sense of "institutional" as a quality that varies. Contenders – whether mobilized protestors or corporate lobbyists – may strive to undermine the taken-for-grantedness of arrangements through campaigns of critical consciousness raising or to embed a model in highly publicized studies flowing from think tanks (e.g., Murray's *Losing Ground*) and volumes of highly technical regulations. Models or mechanisms may be enhanced through new resources (e.g., the funding of faith-based organizations) or hobbled as resources are restricted (e.g., the defunding of and class action constraints on legal services). Embedding and disembedding, knitting together and pulling apart, appear as crucial projects for challenge and mobilization (Clemens and Cook 1999).

Viewed through an expanded definition of the forms of mobilization and with attention to institutions as objects of contention, the state appears as a hub of activism. Whereas public policies effectively served as the repositories of the successful mobilizations of the past – social security for the Townsend movement, the National Labor Relations Board for organized labor – movements to transform or undermine these policy achievements also can be understood as projects of mobilization and challenge. As Vogus and Davis document, threatened firms and unions joined forces *to secure legislation*. In other settings, these actors face each other in direct conflict. Privatization and contracting out move employment – a key resource – out of the unionized domains secured by AFSCME and the teachers' unions and into labor markets where large corporations have greater advantage. Similarly, provisions within NAFTA move environmental and labor standards disputes into jurisdictions less subject to national political mobilizations. Such struggles over transformations of jurisdiction and structures of access are not limited to the United States; the consolidation of the

European Union, for example, has been shot through with similar struggles over the rules of the game. Protest is an important part of the repertoire of contention – whether the parade of turtles and Teamsters or attacks on McDonald's in France – but only one part. Particularly if we are to understand the role of corporations in these struggles, attention must be paid to other paths of mobilization and levers of power. By bringing the state back in again, the stakes and opportunities in confrontations between corporations and social movements become clearer.

Coordination Without Clear Authority

The call to remember the importance of formal politics, however, does not imply that the encounter of organizations and social movements can be conveniently subsumed under conventional political sociology. Rather, by remembering the existence of formal institutions of authoritative coordination and conflict resolution, we can recognize some of what is distinctive in large-scale collaborations and conflicts that take place without resort to political institutions. Leviticus notwithstanding, the danger in the current conversation is less the combination of two kinds of stuff than the ease with which this combination permits a vision of coordination and conflict in which there are two and only two kinds of stuff. In such a restricted combination, power, domination, authoritative decision making are obscured. For all that a renewed acquaintanceship between literatures is most welcome, it should not come at a high price of forgetting.

The renewed conversation between organizational scholars and social movement theorists, however, underscores the extent to which nonauthoritative coordination pervades social organization, ordering, and conflict. Just as what happens in corporations may be shaped by systems of relationships unimagined by formal organizational charts, a wide range of inter-organizational and political conflicts also may be structured by mobilizations that resemble (or clearly are) social movements,[4] a point familiar

---

[4] In this respect, organizational research should avoid replicating the focus on the left which has tended to characterize the literature on social movements. In addition to tracking the influence of employee mobilizations for domestic partner benefits (e.g., Scully and Creed, this volume; Raeburn 2001), new research should address the impact of conservative mobilizations among both corporate elites (e.g., through the funding of think tanks and lobbying organizations) and the sort of grassroots effort represented by the success of the prolife movement leveraging Warren Buffet's acquisition of Berkshire Hathaway into a major revision in the firm's corporate giving program, which had included considerable support of Planned Parenthood by Buffet himself.

from both conspiracy theories and studies of power elites. In their effort to comprehend the variety of ways of organizing or organizational forms, the joint project of social movement theory and organizational analysis represents a model for a renewed appreciation of the many ways of creating and exerting power.

References

A. M. Best Company. 1906–40. *Best's Insurance Reports: Fire and Marine Edition.* New York: A. M. Best Company.

Abbott, Andrew. 1988. *The System of Professions: An Essay on the Division of Expert Labor.* Chicago: University of Chicago Press.

Abrahamson, Eric, and Gregory Fairchild. 1999. "Management Fashion: Lifecycles, Triggers, and Collective Learning Processes." *Administrative Science Quarterly* 44:708–40.

Abrahamson, Eric, and Lori Rosenkopf. 1993. "Institutional and Competitive Bandwagons." *Academy of Management Review* 18:487–517.

Adam, Barry D. 1987. The *Rise of a Gay and Lesbian Movement.* Boston: Twayne Publishers.

Adler, Paul S. 1993. "The 'Learning Bureaucracy': New United Motors Manufacturing Incorporated." In *Research in Organizational Behavior,* vol. 15, edited by B. M. Staw and L. L. Cummings. Greenwich, CT: JAI Press, 111–94.

Advocate. 1971. Editorials.

Aguirre, B. E. 1984. "The Conventionalization of Collective Behavior in Cuba." *American Journal of Sociology* 90:541–66.

Aldrich, Howard E. 1979. *Organizations and Environments.* Englewood Cliffs, NJ: Prentice-Hall.

Aldrich, Howard E. 1999. *Organizations Evolving.* Thousand Oaks, CA: Sage.

Aldrich, Howard E., and C. Marlene Fiol. 1994. "Fools Rush In? The Institutional Context of Industry Construction." *Academy of Management Review* 19: 645–70.

Alford, Robert R. 1975. *Health Care Politics: Ideological and Interest Group Barriers to Reform.* Chicago: University of Chicago Press.

Alinsky, S. 1989. *Rules for Radicals: A Practical Primer for Realistic Radicals.* New York: Vintage Books.

Allison, Paul D. 1984. *Event History Analysis: Regression for Longitudinal Event Data.* Beverly Hills: Sage.

Allison, Paul D. 1995. *Survival Analysis Using the SAS System.* Cary, NC: SAS Institute.

References

Alter, Catherine. 1998. "Bureaucracy and Democracy in Organizations: Revisiting Feminist Organizations." In *Private Action and the Public Good*, edited by W. W. Powell and E. S. Clemens. New Haven: Yale University Press.

Altman, Dennis. 1982. "The Gay Movement Ten Years Later." *The Nation*: 494–6.

Altman, Dennis. 1993. *Homosexual Oppression and Liberation*. New York and London: New York University Press.

Amenta, Edwin, Bruce G. Carruthers, and Yvonne Zylan. 1992. "A Hero for the Aged? The Townsend Movement, the Political Mediation Model, and US Old-Age Policy, 1934–1950." *American Journal of Sociology* 98:308–39.

Anderson, Benedict. 1983. *Imagined Communities: Reflections on the Origin and Spread of Nationalism*. London: Verso.

Andrews, Kenneth T. 2001. "Social Movements and Policy Implementation: The Mississippi Civil Rights Movement and the War on Poverty, 1965–1971." *American Sociological Review* 66:71–95.

Anglin, Robert A. 1949. "A Sociological Analysis of a Pressure Group." Ph.D. dissertation, Department of Sociology, University of Indiana.

Armstrong, Elizabeth A. 1998. "Multiplying Identities: Identity Elaboration in San Francisco's Lesbian/Gay Organizations, 1964–1994." Ph.D. dissertation, Department of Sociology, University of California, Berkeley.

Armstrong, Elizabeth A. 2002a. "Crisis, Collective Creativity, and the Generation of New Organizational Forms: The Transformation of Lesbian/Gay Organizations in San Francisco." In *Research in the Sociology of Organizations*, vol. 19, edited by Michael Lounsbury and Marc Ventresca. Oxford: JAI Press, 361–95.

Armstrong, Elizabeth A. 2002b. *Forging Gay Identities: Organizing Sexuality in San Francisco, 1950–1994*. Chicago: University of Chicago Press.

Arrighi, Giovanni, and Beverly J. Silver, 1999. "Hegemonic Transitions: Past and Present." *Political Power and Social Theory* 13:239–75.

Arthur, W. Brian. 1994. *Increasing Returns and Path Dependence in the Economy*. Ann Arbor: University of Michigan Press.

Ashford, S. J. 1998. "Championing Charged Issues: The Case of Gender Equity Within Organizations." In *Power and Influence in Organizations*, edited by R. M. Kramer and M. A. Neale. Thousand Oaks, CA: Sage, 349–80.

Atkinson, Michael M., and William D. Coleman. 1985. "Corporatism and Industrial Policy." In *Organized Interests and the State*, edited by Alan Cawson. London: Sage, 23–44.

Baggett, Jerome P. 2001. *Habitat for Humanity: Building Private Homes, Building Public Religion*. Philadelphia: Temple University Press.

Balkin, J. M. 1998. *Cultural Software: A Theory of Ideology*. New Haven: Yale University Press.

Balser, Deborah B. 1997. "The Impact of Environmental Factors on Factionalism and Schism in Social Movement Organizations." *Social Forces* 76:199–228.

Bandy, Joe, and Jackie Smith. 2005. "Conclusions: What Have We Learned?" In *Coalitions Across Borders: Transnational Protest and the Neoliberal Order.*" Boulder, CO: Rowman and Littlefield.

368

References

Barley, Stephen M. 1986. "Technology as an Occasion for Structuring: Evidence from Observations of CT Scanners and the Social Order of Radiology Departments." *Administrative Science Quarterly* 31:78–108.

Baron, James N., Frank Dobbin, and P. Devereaux Jennings. 1986. "War and Peace: The Evolution of Modern Personnel Administration in U.S. Industry." *American Journal of Sociology* 92:250–83.

Bartley, Timothy. 2003. "Certifying Forests and Factories: The Emergence of Private Systems for Regulating Labor and Environmental Conditions." Ph.D dissertation, Department of Sociology, University of Arizona.

Bartley, Timothy, and Marc Schneiberg. 2002. "Rationality and Institutional Contingency: The Varying Politics of Economic Regulation in the Fire Insurance Industry." *Sociological Perspectives* 45:47–79.

Bartunek, Jean. 1984. "Changing Interpretive Schemes and Organizational Restructuring: The Example of a Religious Order." *Administrative Science Quarterly* 29:355–72.

Baucus, D. A., and M. S. Baucus. 1996. "Consensus in Franchise Organizations: A Cooperative Arrangement Among Entrepreneurs." *Journal of Business Venturing* 11:359–78.

Baum, Joel A. C., and Christine Oliver. 1992. "Institutional Embeddedness and the Dynamics of Organizational Populations." *American Sociological Review* 4:540–59.

Baum, Joel A. C., and Walter W. Powell. 1995. "Cultivating an Institutional Ecology of Organizations: Comment on Hannan, Carroll, Dundon, and Torres." *American Sociological Review* 60:529–38.

Baum, Joel A. C., and Jintendra V. Singh, eds. 1994. *Evolutionary Dynamics of Organizations*. New York: Oxford University Press.

Baumgartner, Frank R., and Bryan D. Jones. 1993. *Agendas and Instability in American Politics*. Chicago: University of Chicago Press.

Baumgartner, Frank R., and Beth L. Leech. 1998. *Basic Interests: The Importance of Groups in Politics and in Political Science*. Princeton: Princeton University Press.

Becker, Theodore, and Malcolm M. Feeley. 1973. *The Impact of Supreme Court Decisions: Empirical Studies*. New York: Oxford University Press.

Bell, E. L. 1990. "The Bi-Cultural Life Experiences of Career Oriented Black Women." *Journal of Organizational Behavior* 11:459–77.

Benford, Robert D., and David A. Snow. 2000. "Framing Processes and Social Movements: An Overview and Assessment." *Annual Review of Sociology* 26:611–39.

Berger, Peter, and Thomas Luckmann. 1967. *The Social Construction of Reality*. New York: Anchor Books.

Berk, Gerald. 1994. *Alternative Tracks: The Constitution of American Industrial Order, 1865–1917*. Baltimore: Johns Hopkins University Press.

Berle, Adolph, Jr., and Gardiner C. Means. 1932. *The Modern Corporation and Private Property*. New York: Macmillan.

Bernstein, Mary. 1997. "Celebration and Suppression: The Strategic Uses of Identity by the Lesbian and Gay Movement." *American Journal of Sociology* 103:531–65.

Bernstein, Mary. 2002. "Identities and Politics: Toward an Historical Understanding of the Lesbian and Gay Movement." *Social Science History* 26:531–81.

Besset, A. E., and W. Bunch. 1989. "The Promise of Recycling." In *Rush to Burn: Solving America's Garbage Crisis?* by *Newsday* staff. Washington, DC: Island Press, 217–39.

Best, Michael. 1990. *The New Competition: Institutions of Industrial Restructuring.* Cambridge: Harvard University Press.

Binder, Amy J. 2002. *Contentious Curricula: Afro-centrism and Creationism in American Public Schools.* Princeton: Princeton University Press.

Blasius, Mark, and Shane Phelan, eds. 1997. *We Are Everywhere: A Historical Sourcebook of Gay and Lesbian Politics.* New York: Routledge.

Blau, Peter M. 1955. *The Dynamics of Bureaucracy.* Chicago: University of Chicago Press.

Blossfeld, H., and Rohwer, G. 1995. *Techniques of Event History Modeling.* Mahwah, NJ: Lawrence Erlbaum.

Blumberg, L., and Gottlieb, R. 1989. *War on Waste.* Washington, DC: Island Press.

Boli, John, and George M. Thomas. 1997. "World Culture in the World Polity: A Century of International Non-Governmental Organization." *American Sociological Review* 62:171–90.

Boli, John, and George M. Thomas. 1999. "INGOs and the Organization of World Culture." In *Constructing World Culture: International Nongovernmental Organizations Since 1865*, edited by J. Boli and G. M. Thomas. Stanford: Stanford University Press, 13–48.

Bordt, Rebecca L. 1997. *The Structure of Women's Nonprofit Organizations.* Bloomington: Indiana University Press.

Bourdieu, Pierre. 1977. *Outline of a Theory of Practice.* Cambridge: Cambridge University Press.

Bowen, William G., and Derek K. Bok. 1999. *The Shape of the River: Long Term Consequences of Considering Race in College and University Admissions.* Princeton: Princeton University Press.

Boyer, Robert, and J. Rogers Hollingsworth. 1997. "From National Embeddedness to Spatial and Institutional Nestedness." In *Contemporary Capitalism: The Embeddedness of Institutions*, edited by J. Rogers Hollingsworth, Robert Boyer, Peter Lange, Robert H. Bates, Ellen Comisso, Peter Hall, Joel Migdal, and Hellen Milner. Cambridge: Cambridge University Press, 433–84.

Bradach, Jeffrey L. 1998. *Franchise Organizations.* Boston: Harvard Business School Press.

Brearley, Harry Chase. 1916. *The History of the National Board of Fire Underwriters.* New York: Frederick Stokes Company.

Breines, Wini. 1989. *Community and Organization in the New Left, 1962–1968: The Great Refusal.* New Brunswick and London: Rutgers University Press.

Brickley, James A., and Frederick H. Dark. 1987. "The Choice of Organizational Form: The Case of Franchising." *Journal of Financial Economics* 18:401–20.

Brint, Steven, and Jerome Karabel. 1991. "Institutional Origins and Transformations: The Case of American Community Colleges." In *The New Institutionalism in Organizational Analysis*, edited by Walter W. Powell and Paul DiMaggio. Chicago: University of Chicago Press, 337–60.

References

Broshears, Ray. 1971. "S.I.R., the Society for Individual Rights, Conducts Fantastic 'Work-In' at Federal Building." *Gay Activists Alliance Lifeline*:1.

Brown, John Seely, and Paul Duguid. 2000. *The Social Life of Information*. Boston: Harvard Business School Press.

Brown, Lawrence D, 1983. *Politics and Health Care Organizations: HMO's as Federal Policy*. Washington, DC: Brookings Institution.

Brown, Lawrence D., and Jonathan A. Fox. 1998. "Accountability Within Transnational Coalitions." In *The Struggle for Accountability: The World Bank, NGOs, and Grassroots Movements*, edited by J. A. Fox and L. D. Brown. Cambridge: MIT Press, 439–84.

Brown, W. O. 1998. "Transaction Costs, Corporate Hierarchies, and the Theory of Franchising." *Journal of Economic Behavior and Organization* 36:319–29.

Brulle, Robert J. 2000. *Agency, Democracy and Nature: The U.S. Environmental Movement from a Critical Theory Perspective*. Cambridge: MIT Press.

Brysk, Alison. 1996. "Turning Weakness into Strength: The Internationalization of Indian Rights." *Latin American Perspectives* 23:38–58.

Brysk, Alison. 2000. *From Tribal Village to Global Village: Indigenous Peoples' Struggles in Latin America*. Stanford: Stanford University Press.

Buck, Solon. 1913. *The Granger Movement*. Cambridge: Harvard University Press.

Burstein, Paul. 1991. "Legal Mobilization as a Social Movement Tactic: The Struggle for Equal Employment Opportunity." *American Journal of Sociology* 96:1201–25.

Burt, Ronald S. 1992. *Structural Holes*. Cambridge: Harvard University Press.

Burt, Ronald S. 1993. "The Social Structure of Competition." In *Explorations in Economic Sociology*, edited by Richard Swedberg. New York: Russell Sage Foundation, 65–103.

Burton, M. G., and J. Higley. 1987. "Elite Settlements." *American Sociological Review* 52:295–307.

Buthe, Tim. 2002. "Taking Temporality Seriously: Modeling History and the Use of Narratives as Evidence." *American Political Science Review* 96:481–93.

Calavita, Kitty, Henry N. Pontell, and Robert H. Tillman. 1996. *Big Money Crime: Fraud and Politics in the Savings and Loan Crisis*. Berkeley: University of California Press.

Campbell, John L. 1988. *Collapse of an Industry: Nuclear Power and the Contradictions of U.S. Policy*. Ithaca: Cornell University Press.

Campbell, John L. 1997. "Mechanisms of Evolutionary Change in Economic Governance: Interaction, Interpretation, and Bricolage." In *Evolutionary Economics and Path Dependence*, edited by Lars Magnusson and Jan Ottosson. Cheltenham, UK: Edward Elgar, 10–31.

Campbell, John L. 1998. "Institutional Analysis and the Role of Ideas in Political Economy." *Theory and Society* 27:377–409.

Campbell, John L. 2001. "Convergence or Divergence? Globalization, Neoliberalism and Fiscal Policy in Postcommunist Europe." In *Globalization and the European Political Economy*, edited by Steven Weber. New York: Columbia University Press, 107–39.

Campbell, John L. 2004. "The Problem of Change." In J. L. Campbell, *Institutional Change and Globalization*. Princeton: Princeton University Press.

Campbell, John L., J. Rogers Hollingsworth, and Leon N. Lindberg, eds. 1991. *Governance of the American Economy*. Cambridge: Cambridge University Press.

Campbell, John L., and Leon N. Lindberg. 1990. "Property Rights and the Organization of Economic Activity by the State." *American Sociological Review* 55, 634–47.

Campbell, John L., and Leon N. Lindberg. 1991. "The Evolution of Governance Regimes." In *Governance of the American Economy*, edited by John L. Campbell, J. Rogers Hollingsworth, and Leon N. Lindberg. Cambridge: Cambridge University Press, 319–55.

Campbell, John L., and Ove K. Pedersen. 1996. "The Evolutionary Nature of Revolutionary Change." In *Legacies of Change: Transformations of Postcommunist European Economies*, edited by John L. Campbell and Ove K. Pedersen. New York: Aldine de Gruyter, 207–50.

Campbell, John L., and Ove K. Pedersen. 2001. "The Second Movement in Institutional Analysis." In *The Rise of Neoliberalism and Institutional Analysis*, edited by John L. Campbell and Ove K. Pedersen. Princeton: Princeton University Press, 249–82.

Carroll, Glenn R., and Michael T. Hannan. 2000. *The Demography of Corporations and Industries*. Princeton: Princeton University Press.

Carroll, Glenn R., and Anand Swaminathan. 2000. "Why the Microbrewery Movement? Organizational Dynamics of Resource Partitioning." *American Journal of Sociology* 106:715–62.

Carruthers, Bruce G., and Sarah Babb. 1996. "The Color of Money and the Nature of Value: Greenbacks and Gold in Postbellum America." *American Journal of Sociology* 101:1556–91.

Carson, Rachel. 1962. *Silent Spring*. Boston: Houghton Mifflin.

Chalmers, David Mark. 1987. *Hooded Americanism: The History of the Ku Klux Klan*, 3rd ed. Durham, NC: Duke University Press.

Chandler, Alfred D., Jr. 1977. *The Visible Hand: The Managerial Revolution in American Business*. Cambridge: Harvard University Press.

Chandler, Alfred D., Jr., and Herman Daems, eds. 1980. *Managerial Hierarchies: Comparative Perspectives on the Rise of the Modern Industrial Enterprise*. Cambridge: Harvard University Press.

Chesler, Mark. 1996. "White Men's Roles in Multicultural Coalitions." In *Impacts of Racism on White Americans*, 2nd ed., edited by B. Bowser and R. Hunt. Thousand Oaks, CA: Sage Publications, 202–29.

Clegg, Stewart R., and D. Dunkerley. 1977. *Critical Issues in Organizations*. London: Routledge and Kegan Paul.

Clegg, Stewart R., and D. Dunkerley. 1980. *Organization, Class and Control*. London: Routledge and Kegan Paul.

Clemens, Elisabeth S. 1993. "Organizational Repertoires and Institutional Change: Womens' Groups and the Transformation of U.S. Politics, 1890–1920." *American Journal of Sociology* 98:755–98.

References

Clemens, Elisabeth S. 1996. "Organizational Form as Frame: Collective Identity and Political Strategy in the American Labor Movement." In *Comparative Perspectives on Social Movements: Opportunities, Mobilizing Structures, and Cultural Framings*, edited by D. McAdam, J. McCarthy, and M. Zald. New York: Cambridge University Press, 205–26.

Clemens, Elisabeth S. 1997. *The People's Lobby: Organizational Innovation and the Rise of Interest Group Politics in the United States, 1890–1925*. Chicago: University of Chicago Press.

Clemens, Elisabeth S. 1999. "Continuity and Coherence: Periodization and the Problem of Institutional Change." In *Social Time and Social Change: Perspectives on Sociology and History*, edited by F. Engelstad and R. Kalleberg. Oslo: Scandinavian University Press, 62–83.

Clemens, Elisabeth S. 2002. "Invention, Innovation, Proliferation: Explaining Organizational Growth and Change." *Research in the Sociology of Organizations*, vol. 19. Oxford: JAI Press, 397–411.

Clemens, Elisabeth S., and James Cook. 1999. "Politics and Institutionalism: Explaining Durability and Change." *Annual Review of Sociology* 25:441–66.

Clemens, Elisabeth S., and Debra C. Minkoff. 2004. "Beyond the Iron Law: Rethinking the Place of Organizations in Social Movement Research." In *The Blackwell Companion to Social Movements*, edited by D. A. Snow, S. A. Soule, and H. Kriesi. Malden, MA: Blackwell, 155–70.

Cloward, Richard A., and Frances Fox Piven. 1984. "Disruption and Organization: A Rejoinder." *Theory and Society* 13:587–99.

Cole, Robert E. 1999. *Managing Quality Fads: How American Business Learned to Play the Quality Game*. Oxford: Oxford University Press.

Cole, Robert E., and W. Richard Scott, eds. 2000. *The Quality Movement and Organization Theory*. Thousand Oaks, CA: Sage.

Collins, Randall. 1975. *Conflict Sociology: Toward an Explanatory Science*. New York: Academic Press.

Collins, Randall. 1981. "On the Microfoundations of Macrosociology." *American Journal of Sociology* 86:984–1013.

Collinson, D. J., and J. Hearn, eds. 1996. *Men as Managers, Managers as Men: Critical Perspectives on Men, Masculinities, and Management*. London: Sage.

Conference Board. 1991. *Employee Buy-In to Total Quality*. New York: Conference Board.

Crane, Frederick G. 1962. *Automobile Insurance Rate Regulation*. Columbus: Ohio State University Press.

Crane, Frederick G. 1972. "Rate Regulation: The Reason Why." *Journal of Risk and Insurance* 39:511–34.

Creed, W. E. Douglas. 2003. "Voice Lessons: Tempered Radicalism and the Use of Voice and Silence." *Journal of Management Studies* 40:1503–36.

Creed, W. E. Douglas, J. Langstraat, and Maureen A. Scully. 2002. "A Picture of the Frame: Frame Analysis as Technique and as Politics." *Organizational Research Methods* 5:34–55.

Creed, W. E. Douglas, and Maureen A. Scully. 1998. "Switchpersons on the Tracks of History: Situated Agency and Contested Legitimacy in the Diffusion of

Domestic Partner Benefits." Paper presented at the annual meeting of the Academy of Management, San Diego, CA.

Creed, W. E. Douglas, and Maureen A. Scully. 2000. "Songs of Ourselves: Employees' Deployment of Social Identity in Workplace Encounters." *Journal of Management Inquiry* 9:391–412.

Creed, W. E. Douglas, Maureen A. Scully, and John R. Austin. 2002. "Clothes Make the Person: The Tailoring of Legitimating Accounts and the Social Construction of Identity." *Organization Science* 13:475–96.

Crenson, M. A. 1971. *The Un-Politics of Air Pollution.* Baltimore: Johns Hopkins Press.

Cress, Daniel M. 1997. "Nonprofit Incorporation Among Movements of the Poor: Pathways and Consequences for Homeless Social Movement Organizations." *The Sociological Quarterly* 38:343–60.

Croteau, J. M. 1996. "Research on the Work Experiences of Lesbian, Gay, and Bisexual People: An Integrative Review of Methodology and Findings." *Journal of Vocational Behavior* 48:195–209.

Cullen, Pauline. 2003. "European NGOs and EU-Level Mobilization for Social Rights." Ph.D. dissertation, State University of New York at Stony Brook.

Cutler, Marvin. 1956. *Homosexuals Today: A Handbook of Organizations and Publications.* Los Angeles: ONE.

Cyert, Richard M., and James G. March. 1963. *A Behavioral Theory of the Firm.* Englewood Cliffs, NJ: Prentice-Hall.

Czarniawska, Barbara, and B. Joerges. 1996. "Travel of Ideas." In *Translating Organizational Change,* edited by Barbara Czarniawska and Guje Sevon. New York: Walter de Gruyter, 13–48.

Czarniawska, Barbara, and Guje Sevon. 1996. "Introduction." In *Translating Organizational Change,* edited by Barbara Czarniawska and Guje Sevon. New York: Walter de Gruyter, 1–12.

Dalton, M. 1959. *Men Who Manage.* New York: John Wiley.

Daly, Herman. 2002. "Globalization Versus Internationalization, and Four Economic Arguments for Why Internationalization Is a Better Model for World Community." Paper presented at the Conference on Globalization and Social Change, College Park, MD.

D'Aunno, Thomas, Robert Sutton, and Richard Price. 1991. "Isomorphism and External Support in Conflicting Institutional Environments: A Study of Drug Abuse Treatment Units." *Academy of Management Journal* 3:636–61.

David, Paul A. 1985. "Clio and the Economics of QWERTY." *American Economic Review* 75:332–7.

Davis, Flora. 1999. *Moving a Mountain: The Women's Movement in America Since the 1960s.* Urbana-Champaign: University of Illinois Press.

Davis, Gerald F. 1991. "Agents Without Principles? The Spread of the Poison Pill Through the Intercorporate Network." *Administrative Science Quarterly* 36:583–613.

Davis, Gerald F., Kristina Diekmann, and Catherine Tinsley. 1994. "The Decline and Fall of the Conglomerate Firm in the 1980s: The De-institutionalization of an Organizational Form." *American Sociological Review* 59:547–70.

References

Davis, Gerald F., and Henrich Greve. 1997. "Corporate Elite Networks and Governance Changes in the 1980s." *American Journal of Sociology* 103:1–37.

Davis, Gerald F., and Doug McAdam. 2000. "Corporations, Classes, and Social Movements." In *Research in Organizational Behavior*, vol. 22, edited by Barry Staw and Robert I. Sutton. Oxford: Elsevier Science, 195–238.

Davis, Gerald F., and Walter W. Powell. 1992. "Organization-Environment Relations." In *Handbook of Industrial and Organizational Psychology*, vol. 3 (2nd edition), edited by M. Dunnette. Palo Alto, CA: Consulting Psychologist Press.

Davis, Gerald F., and Gregory E. Robbins. 2005. "The Fate of the Conglomerate Firm in the United States." In *How Institutions Change*, edited by W. W. Powell and D. L. Jones. Chicago: University of Chicago Press.

Davis, Gerald F., and Suzanne K. Stout. 1992. "Organization Theory and the Market for Corporate Control: A Dynamic Analysis of Large Takeover Targets." *Administrative Science Quarterly* 37:605–33.

Davis, Gerald F., and Tracy A. Thompson. 1994. "A Social Movement Perspective on Corporate Control." *Administrative Science Quarterly* 39:141–73

Davis, Gerald F., and Michael Useem. 2002. "Top Management, Company Directors, and Corporate Control." In *Handbook of Strategy and Management*, edited by Andrew Pettigrew, Howard Thomas, and Richard Whittington. London: Sage, 233–59.

Delacroix, Jacques, and Hayagreeva Rao. 1994. "Externalities and Ecological Theory: Unbundling Density Dependence." In *Evolutionary Dynamics of Organizations*, edited by Joel A. C. Baum and Jitendra Singh. New York: Oxford University Press, 255–68.

Delgado, Gary. 1986. *Organizing the Movement: The Roots and Growth of ACORN*. Philadelphia: Temple University Press.

Della Porta, Donatella. 1996. "Social Movements and the State: Thoughts on the Policing of Protest." In *Comparative Perspectives on Social Movements*, edited by Doug McAdam, John D. McCarthy, and Mayer N. Zald. New York: Cambridge University Press, 62–92.

Della Porta, Donatella, and D. Rucht. 2002. "The Dynamics of Environmental Campaigns." *Mobilization* 7:1–14.

D'Emilio, John. 1983. *Sexual Politics, Sexual Communities: The Making of a Homosexual Minority in the United States, 1940–1970*. Chicago: University of Chicago Press.

D'Emilio, John. 1992 [1972]. "Foreword." In *Out of the Closets: Voices of Gay Liberation*, edited by Karla Jay and Allen Young. New York and London: New York University Press, xi–xxix.

D'Emilio, John. 1992a. "After Stonewall." In *Making Trouble: Essays on Gay History, Politics, and the University*, edited by John D'Emilio. New York: Routledge, 234–74.

D'Emilio, John, ed. 1992b. *Making Trouble: Essays on Gay History, Politics, and the University*. New York: Routledge.

Deming, W. Edwards. 1982. *Out of the Crisis*. Cambridge: MIT Center for Advanced Engineering Study.

Derthick, Martha, and Paul J. Quirk. 1985. *The Politics of Deregulation*. Washington, DC: Brookings Institution.

Dezalay, Yves, and Byant G. Garth. 1996. *Dealing in Virtue: International Commercial Arbitration and the Construction of a Transnational Legal Order*. Chicago: University of Chicago Press.

Diani, Mario. 2003. "The Terrestrial Emporium of Contentious Knowledge." *Mobilization* 8:109–12.

DiMaggio, Paul J. 1983. "State Expansion and Organizational Fields." In *Organizational Theory and Public Policy*, edited by Richard H. Hall and Robert E. Quinn. Beverly Hills: Sage, 147–61.

DiMaggio, Paul J. 1988. "Interest and Agency in Institutional Theory." In *Institutional Patterns and Organizations: Culture and Environment*, edited by Lynne Zucker. Cambridge: Ballinger, 3–22.

DiMaggio, Paul J. 1991. "Constructing an Organizational Field as a Professional Project: U.S. Art Museums, 1920–1940." In *The New Institutionalism in Organizational Analysis*, edited by Walter W. Powell and Paul J. DiMaggio. Chicago: University of Chicago Press, 267–92.

DiMaggio, Paul J. 1994a. "Meaning and Measurement in the Sociology of Culture." *Poetics* 22:263–372.

DiMaggio, Paul J. 1994b. "Culture and Economy." In *Handbook of Economic Sociology*, edited by Neil J. Smelser and Richard M. Swedberg. Princeton: Princeton University Press, 27–57.

DiMaggio, Paul J. 1997. "Culture and Cognition." *Annual Review of Sociology* 23:263–87.

DiMaggio, Paul J., and Walter W. Powell. 1983. "The Iron Cage Revisited: Institutional Isomorphism and Collective Rationality in Organizational Fields." *American Sociological Review* 48:147–60.

DiMaggio, Paul J., and Walter W. Powell. 1991. "Introduction." In *The New Institutionalism in Organizational Analysis*, edited by Walter W. Powell and Paul J. DiMaggio. Chicago: University of Chicago Press, 1–40.

Djelic, Marie-Laure. 1998. *Exporting the American Model: The Postwar Transformation of European Business*. New York: Oxford University Press.

Djelic, Marie-Laure, and Sigrid Quack. 2003. "Introduction." In *Globalization and Institutions: Redefining the Rules of the Economic Game*, edited by Marie-Laure Djelic and Sigrid Quack. New York: Edward Elgar.

Dobbin, Frank. 1992. "The Origins of Private Social Insurance: Public Policy and Fringe Benefits in America, 1920–1950." *American Journal of Sociology* 97:1416–50.

Dobbin, Frank. 1994. *Forging Industrial Policy: The United States, Britain, and France in the Railway Age*. New York: Cambridge University Press.

Dobbin, Frank, and Timothy Dowd. 2000. "The Market That Anti-Trust Built." *American Sociological Review* 65:631–57.

Dobbin, Frank, and John R. Sutton. 1998. "The Strength of a Weak State: The Rights Revolution and the Rise of Human Resource Management Divisions." *American Journal of Sociology* 2:441–76.

References

Dobbin, Frank, John R. Sutton, John W. Meyer, and W. Richard Scott. 1993. "Equal Opportunity Law and the Construction of Internal Labor Markets." *American Journal of Sociology* 99:396–427.

Domhoff, William G. 1998. *Who Rules America? Power and Politics in the Year 2000*. Mountain View, CA: Mayfield Publishing Company.

Dong, Arthur. 1995. *The Question of Equality: Part One, Out Rage '69*. New York: A Production of Testing the Limits for the Independent Television Service.

Doremus, Paul N., William W. Keller, Louis W. Pauly, and Simon Reich. 1998. *The Myth of the Global Corporation*. Princeton: Princeton University Press.

Douglas, Mary. 1966 . *Purity and Danger: An Analysis of the Concepts of Pollution and Taboo*. Boston: Routledge and Kegan Paul.

Douglas, Mary. 1986. *How Institutions Think*. Syracuse, NY: Syracuse University Press.

Douglas, Thomas J., and William Q. Judge, Jr. 2001. "Total Quality Management Implementation and Competitive Advantage: The Role of Structural Control and Exploration." *Academy of Management Journal* 44:158–69.

Dowell, Glen, Anand Swaminathan, and James Wade. 2002. "Pretty Pictures and Ugly Scenes: Political and Technological Maneuvers in High Definition Television." Presented at the Conference on Social Movements and Organizations Theory, University of Michigan, Ann Arbor.

Duberman, Martin. 1993. *Stonewall*. New York: Penguin Books.

Dudziak, Mary L. 1988. "Desegragation as a Cold War Imperative." *Stanford Law Review* 41:61–120.

Dudziak, Mary L. 2000. *Cold War Civil Rights*. Princeton: Princeton University Press.

Easterbrook, F. H., and D. R. Fischel. 1991. *The Economic Structure of Corporate Law*. Cambridge: Harvard University Press.

Easton, George S., and Sherry L. Jarrell. 1998. "The Effects of Total Quality Management on Corporate Performance: An Empirical Investigation." *Journal of Business* 71:253–307.

Echols, Alice. 1989. *Daring to Be BAD: Radical Feminism in America, 1967–1975*. Minneapolis: University of Minnesota Press.

Echols, Alice. 1992. "'We Gotta Get Out of This Place:' Notes Toward a Remapping of the Sixties." *Socialist Review* 22:9–33.

Edelman, Lauren B. 1990. "Legal Environments and Organizational Governance: The Expansion of Due Process in the American Workplace." *American Journal of Sociology* 95:1401–40, 1531–76.

Edelman, Lauren B. 1992. "Legal Ambiguity and Symbolic Structures: Organizational Mediation of Civil Rights Law," *American Journal of Sociology* 97:1531–76, 1401–40.

Edelman, Lauren B. 2003. "Constructed Legalities: The Endogeneity of Law." In *How Institutions Change*, edited by W. Powell and D. Jones. Chicago: University of Chicago Press.

Edelman, Lauren B., Susan E. Abraham, and Howard S. Erlanger. 1992. "Professional Construction of Law: The Inflated Threat of Wrongful Discharge." *Law and Society Review* 26:47–83.

Edelman, Lauren B., Susan E. Petterson, Elisabeth Chambliss, and Howard S. Erlanger. 1991. "Legal Ambiguity and the Politics of Compliance: Affirmative Action Officers' Dilemma." *Law and Policy* 13:73–97.

Edelman, Lauren B., and Robin Stryker. Forthcoming. "A Sociological Approach to Law and the Economy." In *Handbook of Economic Sociology*, 2nd ed., edited by Neil Smelser and Richard Swedberg. Princeton: Princeton University Press.

Edelman, Lauren B., and Mark C. Suchman. 1997. "The Legal Environment of Organizations." *Annual Review of Sociology* 23:479–515.

Edelman, Lauren B., Christopher Uggen, and Howard S. Erlanger. 1999. "The Endogeneity of Legal Regulation: Grievance Procedures as Rational Myth." *American Journal of Sociology* 105:406–54.

Edmunds, Margaret, Richard Frank, Michael Hogan, Dennis McCarty, Rhonda Robinson-Beale, and Constance Weisner, eds. 1997. *Managing Managed Care: Quality Improvement in Behavioral Health*. Washington, DC: National Academy Press.

Edwards, Bob, and Kenneth T. Andrews. 2002. "Methodological Strategies for Examining Populations of Social Movement Organizations." Paper presented at the annual meetings of the American Sociological Association, Chicago.

Edwards, Bob, and Michael Foley. 2002. "Social Movements Beyond the Beltway: The Diversity of Social Movement Organizations in an Era of Devolution and Deregulation." Unpublished manuscript.

Einwohner, Rachel L. 1999. "Practices, Opportunity, and Protest Effectiveness: Illustrations from Four Animal Rights Campaigns." *Social Problems* 46: 169–86.

Elliot, K. A., and R. B. Freeman. 2000. "White Hats or Don Quixotes? Human Rights Vigilantes in the Global Economy." *National Bureau of Economic Research Conference on Emerging Labor Market Institutions* (www.nber.org/-confer/2000/si2000/elliot.pdf).

Elster, Jon. 1989. *Nuts and Bolts for the Social Sciences*. New York: Cambridge University Press.

Elster, Jon. 1992. *Local Justice: How Institutions Allocate Scarce Goods and Necessary Burdens*. New York: Russell Sage Foundation.

Elster, Jon. 1998. "A Plea for Mechanisms." In *Social Mechanisms: An Analytical Approach to Social Theory*, edited by Peter Hedström and Richard Swedberg. New York: Cambridge University Press, 45–73.

Emirbayer, Mustafa, and A. Mische. 1998. "What Is Agency?" *American Journal of Sociology* 103:962–1023.

Epstein, Steven. 1987. "Gay Politics, Ethnic Identity: The Limits of Social Constructionism." *Socialist Review* 17:10–54.

Epstein, Steven. 1999. "Gay and Lesbian Movements in the United States: Dilemmas of Identity, Diversity, and Political Strategy." In *The Global Emergence of Gay and Lesbian Politics*, edited by Barry D. Adam, Jan Willem Duyvendak, and Andre Krouwel. Philadelphia: Temple University Press, 30–90.

References

Escoffier, Jeffrey. 1985. "Sexual Revolution and the Politics of Gay Identity." *Socialist Review* July-October:119–53.

Espeland, Wendy Nelson. 1998. *The Struggle for Water: Politics, Rationality, and Identity in the American Southwest*. Chicago: University of Chicago Press.

Evans, Peter. 2000. "Fighting Marginalization with Transnational Networks: Counter-Hegemonic Globalization." *Contemporary Sociology* 29:230–41.

Ewick, Patricia, and Susan S. Silbey. 1998. *The Common Place of Law: Stories from Everyday Life*. Chicago: University of Chicago Press.

Eyestone, Robert. 1977. "Confusion, Diffusion, and Innovation." *American Political Science Review* 71:441–47.

Fama, Eugene, and Michael C. Jensen. 1983. "Separation of Ownership and Control." *Journal of Law and Economics* 26:301–25.

Fernandez, Roberto M., Emilio J. Castilla, and Paul Moore. 2000. "Social Capital at Work: Networks and Employment at a Phone Center." *American Journal of Sociology* 105:1288–356.

Ferree, Myra Marx, William Anthony Gamson, Jürgen Gerhards, and Dieter Rucht. 2002. *Shaping Abortion Discourse: Democracy and the Public Sphere in Germany and the United States*. New York: Cambridge University Press.

Ferree, Myra Marx, and Patricia Yancey Martin. 1995. *Feminist Organizations: Harvest of the New Women's Movement*. Philadelphia: Temple University Press.

Ferree, Myra Marx, and Carol Mueller. 2004. "Feminism and the Women's Movement: A Global Perspective." In *The Blackwell Companion to Social Movements*, edited by David A. Snow, Sarah A. Soule, and Hanspeter Kriesi. New York: Blackwell, 576–607.

Fisher, Julie. 1993. *The Road from Rio: Sustainable Development and the Nongovernmental Movement in the Third World*. Westport, CT: Praeger.

FitzGerald, Frances. 1986 [1981]. *Cities on a Hill: A Journey Through Contemporary American Cultures*. New York: Simon and Schuster.

Fletcher, J. K. 1999. *Disappearing Acts: Gender, Power and Relational Practice at Work*. Cambridge: MIT Press.

Fligstein, Neil. 1990. *The Transformation of Corporate Control*. Cambridge: Harvard University Press.

Fligstein, Neil. 1996. "Markets as Politics: A Political-Cultural Approach to Market Institutions." *American Sociological Review* 61:656–73.

Fligstein, Neil. 1997a. "Fields, Power, and Social Skill: A Critical Analysis of the New Institutionalisms." Unpublished manuscript. Department of Sociology, University of California, Berkeley.

Fligstein, Neil. 1997b. "Social Skill and Institutional Theory." *American Behavioral Scientist* 40:397–505.

Fligstein, Neil. 2001a. *The Architecture of Markets: An Economic Sociology of Twenty-First Century Capitalist Societies*. Princeton: Princeton University Press.

Fligstein, Neil. 2001b. "Social Skill and the Theory of Fields." *Sociological Theory* 19(2):105–25.

Fligstein, Neil, and Doug McAdam. 1995. "A Political-Cultural Approach to the Problem of Strategic Action." Unpublished paper. Department of Sociology, University of California, Berkeley.

Fligstein, Neil, and Iona Mara-Drita. 1996. "How to Make a Market: Reflections on the Attempt to Create a Single Market in the European Union." *American Journal of Sociology* 102:1–32.

Foldy, Erica G., and W. E. Douglas Creed. 1999. "Action Learning, Fragmentation, and the Interaction of Single, Double, and Triple Loop Change: A Case of Gay and Lesbian Workplace Advocacy." *Journal of Applied Behaviorial Science* 35(2):207–27.

Fox, Jonathan. 2002. "Assessing Binational Civil Society Coalitions: Lessons from the Mexico-U.S. Experience." In *Cross-Border Dialogues: U.S.-Mexico Social Movement Networking*, edited by D. Brooks and J. Fox. La Jolla: Center for U.S.-Mexican Studies, University of California-San Diego, 341–417.

Fox, Jonathan, and L. David Brown. 1998. *The Struggle for Accountability: The World Bank, NGOs, and Grassroots Movements*. Cambridge: MIT Press.

Fox, Stephen. 1981. *John Muir and His Legacy*. Boston: Little, Brown.

Frank, David John, John W. Meyer, and David Miyahara. 1995. "The Individualist Polity and the Prevalence of Professionalized Psychology: A Cross National Study." *American Sociological Review* 60:360–77.

Frank, R. 2000. "Herd on the Street: For Corporate Leaders in Manila, Economy Can't Survive Estrada – President's Scandals Compel Businessmen to Adopt a Risky Activist Stance – For the Poor, Only Deja Vu." *Wall Street Journal*, December 6, 2000, A.1.

Frank, Thomas. 2001. *One Market, Under God: Extreme Capitalism, Market Populism, and the End of Economic Democracy*. New York: Doubleday.

Freeman, Jo. 1972. "The Tyranny of Structurelessness." *The Second Wave* 2 (1). Reprinted in *Women in Politics*, edited by Jane Jaquette. New York: Wiley, 1974.

Freidson, Eliot. 1970a. *Profession of Medicine: A Study of the Sociology of Applied Knowledge*. New York: Dodd, Mead.

Freidson, Eliot. 1970b. *Professional Dominance: The Social Structure of Medical Care*. Chicago: Aldine.

Friedland, Roger. 2002. "Money, Sex, and God: The Erotic Logic of Religious Nationalism." *Sociological Theory* 20:381–425.

Friedland, Roger, and Robert Alford. 1991. "Bringing Society Back In: Symbols, Practices and Institutional Contradictions." In *The New Institutionalism in Organizational Analysis*, edited by Walter W. Powell and Paul J. DiMaggio. Chicago: University of Chicago Press, 232–63.

Friedman, Thomas L. 1999. *The Lexus and the Olive Tree: Understanding Globalization*. New York: Farrar, Strauss, Giroux.

Fuchs, Victor. 1974. *Who Shall Live? Health, Economics and Social Choice*. New York: Basic Books.

Fuller, Sally R., Lauren B. Edelman, and Sharon F. Matusik. 2000. "Legal Readings: Employee Interpretation and Mobilization of Law." *Academy of Management Review* 25:200–16.

Gaffney, Edward M. 1984. *Ascending Liability in Religious and Other Nonprofit Organizations*. Macon, GA: Mercer University Press.

References

Galaskiewicz, Joseph, and Stanley Wasserman. 1989. "Mimetic Processes Within an Interorganizational Field: An Empirical Test." *Administrative Science Quarterly* 34:454–79.

Gamson, Joshua. 1998. "Must Identity Movements Self-Destruct? A Queer Dilemma." In *Social Perspectives in Lesbian and Gay Studies: A Reader*, edited by Peter M. Nardi and Beth E. Schneider. London: Routledge:589–604.

Gamson, William A. 1968. *Power and Discontent*. Homewood, IL: Dorsey.

Gamson, William A. 1975. *The Strategy of Social Protest*. Homewood, IL: Dorsey.

Gamson, William A. 1990. *The Strategy of Social Protest*, 2nd ed. Belmont, CA: Wadsworth.

Gamson, William A. 1992. "The Social Psychology of Collective Action." In *Frontiers in Social Movement Theory*, edited by Aldon D. Morris, and Carol M. Mueller. New Haven: Yale University Press, 53–76.

Gamson, William A. 1995. "Hiroshima, the Holocaust, and the Politics of Exclusion: 1994 Presidential Address to the American Sociological Association." *American Sociological Review* 60:1–20.

Gamson, William A., Bruce Fireman, and Steven Rytina. 1982. *Encounters with Unjust Authority*. Homewood, IL: Dorsey.

Gamson, William A., and K. E. Lasch. 1983. "The Political Culture of Social Welfare Policy." In *Evaluating the Welfare State: Social and Political Perspective*, edited by Shimon E. Spiro and Ephraim Yuchtman-Yaar. New York: Academic Press, 397–415.

Gamson, William A., and David S. Meyer. 1996. "Framing Political Opportunity." In *Comparative Perspectives on Social Movements*, edited by Doug McAdam, John D. McCarthy and Mayer N. Zald. New York: Cambridge University Press, 275–90.

Gamson, William A., and Emilie Schmeidler. 1984. "Organizing the Poor." *Theory and Society* 13:567–84.

Ganz, Marshall. 2000. "Resources and Resourcefulness: Strategic Capacity in the Unionization of California Agriculture, 1959–1966." *American Journal of Sociology* 105:1003–62.

Garvin, David. 1988. *Managing Quality*. New York: Free Press.

Gerlach, L., and V. Hine. 1970. *People, Power, Change*. New York: Bobbs-Merrill.

Giddens, Anthony. 2000. *Runaway World: How Globalization Is Reshaping Our Lives*. New York: Routledge.

Gilpin, Robert. 2000. *The Challenge of Global Capitalism: The World Economy in the 21st Century*. Princeton: Princeton University Press.

Gitlin, Todd. 1987. *The Sixties: Years of Hope, Days of Rage*. New York: Bantam Books.

Gittleman, Maury, Michael Horrigan, and Mary Joyce. 1998. "'Flexible' Workplace Practices: Evidence from a Nationally Representative Survey." *Industrial and Labor Relations Review* 52:99–115.

Giugni, Marco, Doug McAdam, and Charles Tilly, eds. 1999. *How Social Movements Matter*. Minneapolis: University of Minnesota Press.

Goffman, Erving. 1974. *Frame Analysis*. New York: Harper Colophon.

Goldstone, Jack A. 1980. "The Weakness of Organization: A New Look at Gamson's the Strategy of Social Protest." *American Journal of Sociology* 85:1017–42.

Goldstone, Jack A. 2003. "Introduction: Bridging Institutionalized and Noninstitutionalized Politics." In *States, Parties and Social Movements: Protest and the Dynamics of Institutional Change*, edited by J. A. Goldstone. New York: Cambridge University Press, 1–25.

Goldstone, Jack A., and Charles Tilly. 2001. "Threat (and Opportunity): Popular Action and State Response in the Dynamics of Contentious Action." In *Silence and Voice in the Study of Contentious Politics*, edited by R. R. Aminzade. Cambridge: Cambridge University Press, 179–94.

Goodwin, Jeff, James Jasper, and Francesca Polletta, eds. 2001. *Passionate Politics: Emotions in Social Movements*. Chicago: University of Chicago Press.

Goodwyn, Lawrence. 1978. *The Populist Moment: A Short History of the Agrarian Revolt in America*. Oxford: Oxford University Press.

Gould, Kenneth A., Allan Schnaiberg, and Adam S. Weinberg. 1996. *Local Environmental Struggles*. New York: Cambridge University Press.

Gould, Roger V. 1993. "Trade Cohesion, Class Unity, and Urban Insurrection: Artisanal Activism in the Paris Commune." *American Journal of Sociology* 98:721–54.

Gould, Roger V. 1995. *Insurgent Identities: Class, Community, and Protest in Paris from 1848 to the Commune*. Chicago: University of Chicago Press.

Gouldner, Alvin. 1954. *Patterns of Industrial Bureaucracy*. Glencoe, IL: Free Press.

Graff, E. J. 2002. "How the Culture War Was Won: Lesbians and Gay Men Defeated the Right in the 1990s, but Tougher Battles Lie Ahead." *The American Prospect* October 21:33–36.

Granovetter, Mark. 1974. *Getting a Job: A Study of Contacts and Careers*. Chicago: University of Chicago Press.

Granovetter, Mark. 1985. "Economic Action and Social Structure: The Problem of Embeddedness." *American Journal of Sociology* 91:481–510.

Granovetter, Mark. 2000. "The Economic Sociology of Firms and Entrepreneurs." In *Entrepreneurship: The Social Science View*, edited by Richard Swedberg. New York: Oxford University Press, 244–76.

Grant, H. Roger. 1979. *Insurance Reform: Consumer Action in the Progressive Era*. Ames: University of Iowa Press.

Gray, Andrew. 1998. "Development Policy, Development Protest: The World Bank, Indigenous Peoples, and NGOs." In *The Struggle for Accountability: The World Bank, NGOs, and Grassroots Movements*, edited by J. A. Fox and L. D. Brown. Cambridge: MIT Press, 267–301.

Gray, Virginia, and David Lowery. 1996. *The Population Ecology of Interest Representation*. Ann Arbor: University of Michigan Press.

Greenwood, Royston, and C. R. Hinings. 1993. "Understanding Strategic Change: The Contribution of Archetypes." *Academy of Management Journal* 36:1052–81.

Greenwood, Royston, Roy Suddaby, and C. R. Hinings. 2002. "Theorizing Change: The Role of Professional Associations in the Transformation of Institutionalized Fields." *Academy of Management Journal* 45:58–80.

Greve, Henrich. 1995. "Jumping Ship: The Diffusion of Strategy Abandonment." *Administrative Science Quarterly* 40:444–73.

References

Greve, Henrich, David Strang, and Nancy Brandon Tuma. 1995. "Specification and Estimation of Heterogeneous Diffusion Processes." *Sociological Methodology* 25:377–420.

Gronbjerg, Kirsten A. 1992. "Developing a Universe of Nonprofit Organizations: Methodological Considerations." *Nonprofit and Voluntary Sector Quarterly* 18:63–80.

Guillén, Mauro. 1994. *Models of Management.* Chicago: University of Chicago Press.

Guillén, Mauro. 2001. *The Limits of Convergence.* Princeton: Princeton University Press.

Gulati, Ranjay, and Martin Gargiulo. 1999. "Where Do Interorganizational Networks Come From?" *American Journal of Sociology* 104:1439–93.

Gurr, Ted R. 1971. *Why Men Rebel.* Princeton: Princeton University Press.

Guthrie, Doug. 1999. *Dragon in a Three-Piece Suit: The Emergence of Capitalism in China.* Princeton: Princeton University Press.

Hackman, J. Richard, and Ruth Wageman. 1995. "Total Quality Management: Empirical, Conceptual, and Practical Issues." *Administrative Science Quarterly* 40: 309–42.

Haines, Herbert H. 1984. "Black Radicalization and the Funding of Civil Rights: 1957–1970." *Social Problems* 32:31–43.

Haines, Herbert H. 1988. *Black Radicals and the Civil Rights Mainstream, 1954–1970.* Knoxville: University of Tennessee Press.

Hall, Mitchell K. 1990. *Because of Their Faith: CACCAV and Religious Opposition to the Vietnam War.* New York: Columbia University Press.

Hamilton, Gary G., and Nicole Woolsey Biggart. 1988. "Market, Culture and Authority: A Comparative Analysis of Management and Organization in the Far East." *American Journal of Sociology* 94:S52–S94.

Handler, Joel F. 1978. *Social Movements and the Legal System: A Theory of Law Reform and Social Change.* New York: Academic Press.

Handy, Daniel. 1916. "Anti-Compact Laws." In *The History of the National Board of Fire Underwriters*, edited by Harry Brearley. New York: Frederick A. Stokes Company, 282–96.

Hannan, Michael T., and Glenn R. Carroll. 1992. *Dynamics of Organizational Populations: Density, Legitimation and Competition.* New York: Oxford University Press.

Hannan, Michael T., and John Freeman. 1977. "The Population Ecology of Organizations." *American Journal of Sociology* 82:929–64.

Hannan, Michael T., and John Freeman. 1989. *Organizational Ecology.* Cambridge: Harvard University Press.

Hanson, Jon S., Robert E. Dineen, and Michael B. Johnson. 1974. *Monitoring Competition: A Means of Regulating the Property and Liability Insurance Business.* Milwaukee, WI: National Association of Insurance Commissioners.

Hanson, P. 1972. *Recycling Programs in the U.S.* Washington, DC: U.S. Environmental Protection Agency.

Harquail, Cecilia V. 1996. "When One Speaks for Many: The Influence of Social Identification on Group Advocacy in Organizations." Ph.D. dissertation, University of Michigan, Ann Arbor.

Harrington, Scott. 1984. "The Impact of Rate Regulation on Prices and Underwriting Results in the Property-Liability Insurance Industry: A Survey." *Journal of Risk and Insurance* 51:577–623.

Harvey, David J. 1990. *The Condition of Postmodernity*. Oxford: Blackwell.

Haunschild, Pamela. 1993. "Interorganizational Imitation: The Impact of Interlocks on Corporate Acquisition Activity." *Administrative Science Quarterly* 38:564–92.

Haunschild, Pamela. 1994. "How Much Is That Company Worth? Interorganizational Relationships, Uncertainty and Acquisition Premiums." *Administrative Science Quarterly* 39:391–411.

Haunschild, Pamela, and Ann Miner. 1997. "Modes of Interorganizational Imitation: The Effects of Outcome Salience and Uncertainty." *Administrative Science Quarterly* 42:472–500.

Haveman, Heather A. 1993. "Follow the Leader: Mimetic Isomorphism and Entry into New Markets." *Administrative Science Quarterly* 38:593–627.

Haveman, Heather A. 2000. "The Future of Organizational Sociology: Forging Ties Among Paradigms." *Contemporary Sociology* 29:476–86.

Haveman, Heather A., and Hayagreeva Rao. 1997. "Structuring a Theory of Moral Sentiments: Institutional and Organizational Coevolution in the Early Thrift Industry." *American Journal of Sociology* 102:1606–51.

Haveman, Heather A., and Hayagreeva Rao. Forthcoming. "Hybrid Forms and Institution/Organization Co-Evolution in the Early California Thrift Industry." In *How Institutions Change*, edited by Walter W. Powell and Daniel L. Jones. Chicago: University of Chicago Press.

Haydu, Jeffrey. 1998. "Making Use of the Past: Time Periods as Cases to Compare and as Sequences of Problem Solving." *American Journal of Sociology* 104:339–71.

Hedström, Peter, and Richard Swedberg, eds. 1998a. *Social Mechanisms: An Analytical Approach to Social Theory*. Cambridge: Cambridge University Press.

Hedström, Peter, and Richard Swedberg. 1998b. "Social Mechanisms: An Introductory Essay." In *Social Mechanisms: An Analytical Approach to Social Theory*, edited by Peter Hedström and Richard Swedberg. New York: Cambridge University Press, 1–31.

Heimer, Carol. 1985. *Reactive Risk and Rational Action: Managing Moral Hazards in Insurance Contracts*. Berkeley: University of California Press.

Heimer, Carol. 1999. "Competing Institutions: Law, Medicine, and Family in Neonatal Intensive Care." *Law and Society Review* 33:17–66.

Hernes, Gudmund. 1998. "Real Virtuality." In *Social Mechanisms: An Analytical Approach to Social Theory*, edited by Peter Hedström and Richard Swedberg. Cambridge: Cambridge University Press.

Herrigel, G. 1994. "Industry as a Form of Order: A Comparison of the Historical Development of Machine Tool Industries in the United States and Germany." In *Governing Capitalist Economies*, edited by J. R. Hollingsworth, P. C. Schmitter, and W. Streeck. Oxford: Oxford University Press, 97–128.

Herrigel, Gary. 1996. *Industrial Constructions: The Source of German Industrial Power*. New York: Cambridge University Press.

References

Hill, Heather C. 2000. "Implementation Networks: Non-State Resources for Getting Policy Done." Ph.D. dissertation, Department of Political Science, University of Michigan, Ann Arbor.

Hirsch, Paul M. 1986. "From Ambushes to Golden Parachutes: Corporate Takeovers as an Instance of Cultural Framing and Institutional Integration." *American Journal of Sociology* 91:800–37.

Hirsch, Paul M. 1997. "Sociology Without Social Structure: Neoinstitutional Theory Meets Brave New World." *American Journal of Sociology* 102:1702–23.

Hirsch, Paul M., and Michael Lounsbury. 1997. "Ending the Family Quarrel: Toward a Reconciliation of 'Old' and 'New' Institutionalism." *American Behavioral Scientist* 40:406–18.

Hirschman, Albert O. 1970. *Exit, Voice, and Loyalty*. Cambridge: Harvard University Press.

Hirschman, Albert O. 1995. *The Propensity to Self-Subversion*. Cambridge: Harvard University Press.

Hobbs, Clarence W. 1925. "State Regulation of Insurance Rates." *Proceedings of the Casualty Actuarial Society* 11 (June):218–75.

Hobbs, Clarence W. 1941–2. "State Regulation of Insurance Rates, Part II: Regulation of Rates and Rating Organizations." *Proceedings of the Casualty Actuarial Society* 28 (May):344–460.

Hoffman, Andrew J. 1999. "Institutional Evolution and Change: Environmentalism and the US Chemical Industry." *Academy of Management Journal* 42:351–74.

Hoffman, Andrew J. 2001 [1997]. *From Heresy to Dogma: An Institutional History of Corporate Environmentalism*. Stanford: Stanford Business Books. (Originally published in 1997 by Lexington Books.)

Hoffman, Andrew J. 2001. "Linking Organizational and Field-Level Analysis: The Diffusion of Corporate Environmental Practice." *Organization and Environment* 14:133–56.

Hoffman, Andrew J., and Marc J. Ventresca, eds. 2002. *Organizations, Policy, and the Natural Environment: Institutional and Strategic Perspectives*. Stanford: Stanford University Press.

Hollingsworth, J. Rogers. 1991. "The Logic of Coordinating American Manufacturing Sectors." In *Governance of the American Economy*, edited by John L. Campbell, J. Rogers Hollingsworth, and Leon N. Lindberg. New York: Cambridge University Press, 35–73.

Hollingsworth, J. Rogers. 1997. "Continuities and Changes in Social Systems of Production: The Cases of Japan, Germany and the United States." In *Contemporary Capitalism: The Embeddedness of Institutions*. Cambridge: Cambridge University Press, 265–310.

Holvino, E. 2001. "Complicating Gender: The Simultaneity of Race, Gender, and Class in Organizational Change(ing)." Center for Gender in Organizations Working Paper No. 14, Simmons School of Management, Boston.

Holvino, E., and W. E. Douglas Creed. 2002. Briefing paper on Working Across Differences Project. Center for Gender in Organizations, Simmons School of Management, Boston.

Humphreys, Laud. 1972. *Out of the Closets: The Sociology of Homosexual Liberation*. Englewood Cliffs, NJ: Prentice-Hall.

Hunt, S. A., R. D. Benford, and D. A. Snow. 1994. "Identity Fields: Framing Processes and the Social Construction of Movement Identities." In *New Social Movements: From Ideology to Identity*, edited by E. Laraña, H. Johnston, and R. Gusfield. Philadelphia: Temple University Press, 185–208.

Irkin, Michael Francis. 1969. "The Homosexual Liberation Movement: What Direction?" *San Francisco Free Press*:8–9.

Ishikawa, Kaoru. 1985. *What Is Total Quality Control? The Japanese Way*. Englewood Cliffs, NJ: Prentice-Hall.

Jacobs, David, Michael Useem, and Mayer N. Zald. 1991. "Firms, Industries and Politics." In *Research in Political Sociology*, vol. 5, edited by P. Washburn. Greenwich, CT: JAI Press, 141–67.

Jacobs, Ronald N. 1996. "Civil Society and Crisis: Culture, Discourse, and the Rodney King Beating." *American Journal of Sociology* 101:1238–72.

Jacoby, Sanford. 1985. *Employing Bureaucracy*. New York: Columbia University Press.

James, Scott C. 1999. "Prelude to Progressivism: Party Decay, Populism and the Doctrine of 'Free and Unrestricted Competition' in American Antitrust Policy." *Studies in American Political Development* 12:288–336.

Jameson, Fredric. 1991. *Postmodernism, or, the Cultural Logic of Late Capitalism*. Durham, NC: Duke University Press.

Jang, Yong Suk. 2000. "The Worldwide Founding of Ministries of Science and Technology, 1950–1990." *Sociological Perspectives* 43:247–72.

Jasper, James, and Dorothy Nelkin. 1991. *The Animal Rights Crusade: The Growth of a Moral Protest*. New York: Free Press.

Jay, Karla, and Allen Young, eds. 1992 [1972]. *Out of the Closets: Voices of Gay Liberation*. New York and London: New York University Press.

Jenkins, J. Craig. 1985a. "Foundation Funding of Progressive Social Movements." In *The Grant Seekers Guide*, edited by Jill Shellow. Nyack, NY: Glenmeade, 7–17.

Jenkins, J. Craig. 1985b. *The Politics of Insurgency: The Farm Worker Movement in the 1960s*. New York: Columbia University Press.

Jenkins, J. Craig. 1987. "Nonprofit Organizations and Policy Advocacy." In *The Nonprofit Sector*, edited by W. W. Powell. New Haven: Yale University Press, 296–318.

Jenkins, J. Craig, and Craig M. Ekert. 1986. "Channeling Black Insurgency: Elite Patronage and Professional Social Movement Organizations in the Development of the Black Movement." *American Sociological Review* 51:812–29.

Jensen, Michael C. 1988. "Takeovers: Their Causes and Consequences." *Journal of Economic Perspectives* 2:21–48.

Jepperson, Ronald L. 1991. "Institutions, Institutional Effects, and Institutionalism." In *The New Institutionalism in Organizational Analysis*, edited by Walter W. Powell and Paul J. DiMaggio. Chicago: University of Chicago Press, 143–63.

Jepperson, Ronald L., and John Meyer. 1991. "The Public Order and the Construction of Formal Organizations." In *The New Institutionalism in Organizational*

References

Analysis, edited by Walter W. Powell and Paul J. DiMaggio. Chicago: University of Chicago Press, 204–31.

Johnston, Hank, and Bert Klandermans, eds. 1995. *Social Movements and Culture*. Minneapolis: University of Minnesota Press.

Joskow, Paul. 1973. "Cartels, Competition and Regulation in the Property and Liability Insurance Industry." *Bell Journal of Economic and Management Science* 4:375–427.

Juran, Joseph M. 1974. *Quality Control Handbook*. New York: McGraw-Hill.

Katz, Milton S. 1986. *Ban the Bomb: A History of SANE, the Committee for a Sane Nuclear Policy, 1857–1985*. Westport, CT: Greenwood Press.

Katzenstein, Mary F. 1998. *Faithful and Fearless: Moving Feminist Protest Inside the Church and the Military*. Princeton: Princeton University Press.

Kaufmann, P. J., R. M. Gordon, and J. E. Owens. 2000. "Alternative Profitability Measures and Marketing Channel Structure: The Franchise Decision." *Journal of Business Research* 50:217–24.

Keck, Margaret, and Kathryn Sikkink. 1998. *Activists Beyond Borders: Transnational Advocacy Networks in International Politics*. Ithaca, NY: Cornell University Press.

Keller, Morton. 1981. "The Pluralist State: American Economic Regulation in Comparative Perspective, 1900–1930." In *Regulation in Perspective*, edited by Thomas McCraw. Cambridge: Harvard Business School Press, 56–94.

Keller, Morton. 1990. *Regulating a New Economy: Public Policy and Economic Change in America, 1900–1933*. Cambridge: Harvard University Press.

Kelly, Erin, and Frank Dobbin. 1999. "Civil Rights Law at Work: Sex Discrimination and the Rise of Maternity Leave Policies." *American Journal of Sociology* 105:455–92.

Kempton, Willett, Dorothy C. Holland, Katherine Bunting-Howarth Erin Hannan, and Christopher Payne. 2001. "Local Environmental Groups: A Systematic Enumeration in Two Geographical Areas." *Rural Sociology* 66:557–78.

Kentucky. 1912. *Annual Report of Insurance Commissioner of the State of Kentucky for the Year Ending December 31st 1912; Part I: Fire, Marine and Inland Insurance*. Frankfort: Kentucky State Journal Publishing Co.

Kentucky. 1913. *Annual Report of Insurance Commissioner of the State of Kentucky for the Year Ending December 31st 1913; Part I: Fire, Marine and Inland Insurance*. Louisville: George G. Fetter.

Kentucky. 1914. *Annual Report of Insurance Commissioner of the State of Kentucky for the Year Ending December 31st 1914; Part I: Fire, Marine and Inland Insurance*. Louisville: George G. Fetter.

Kentucky. 1916. *Annual Report of Insurance Commissioner of the State of Kentucky for the Year Ending December 31st 1916; Part I: Fire, Marine and Inland Insurance*. Louisville: George G. Fetter.

Kentucky. 1917. *Annual Report of Insurance Commissioner of the State of Kentucky for the Year Ending December 31st 1917; Part I: Fire, Marine and Inland Insurance*. Louisville: George G. Fetter.

Kerr, K. Austin. 1985. *Organized for Prohibition: A New History of the Anti-Saloon League*. New Haven: Yale University Press.

Khagram, Sanjeev, James V. Riker, and Kathryn Sikkink. 2002. *Restructuring World Politics: Transnational Social Movements, Networks, and Norms*. Minneapolis: University of Minnesota Press.

Kimball, D. 1992. *Recycling in America*. Santa Barbara, CA: ABC-CLIO.

Kimball, Spencer. 1960. *Insurance and Public Policy*. Madison: University of Wisconsin Press.

Kissack, Terence. 1995. "Freaking Fag Revolutionaries: New York's Gay Liberation Front, 1969–1971." *Radical History Review* 62:104–34.

Kitschelt, Herbert. 1986. "Political Opportunity Structures and Political Protest: Anti-Nuclear Movements in Four Democracies." *British Journal of Political Science* 16:57–85.

Kitschelt, Herbert, Peter Lange, Gary Marks, and John D. Stephens. 1999. "Convergence and Divergence in Advanced Capitalist Democracies." In *Continuity and Change in Contemporary Capitalism*, edited by Herbert Kitschelt, Peter Lange, Gary Marks, and John D. Stephens. New York: Cambridge University Press, 427–60.

Kjaer, Peter, and Ove K. Pedersen. 2001. "Translating Liberalization: Neoliberalism in the Danish Negotiated Economy." In *The Rise of Neoliberalism and Institutional Analysis*, edited by John L. Campbell and Ove K. Pedersen. Princeton: Princeton University Press, 219–48.

Klandermans, Bert. 1997. *The Social Psychology of Protest*. Cambridge, MA: Blackwell.

Klandermans, Bert, and Dirk Oegama. 1987. "Potentials, Networks, Motivations, and Barriers: Steps Toward Participation in Social Movements." *American Sociological Review* 52:519–31.

Klein, Janice A. 1991. "A Reexamination of Autonomy in Light of New Manufacturing Practices." *Human Relations* 44:21–38.

Klein, Naomi. 1999. *No Logo*. New York: Picador.

Kleiner, Art. 1996. *The Age of the Heretics: Heroes, Outlaws, and Forerunners of Corporate Change*. New York: Doubleday.

Klienman, Daniel, and Steven Vallas. 2001. "Science, Capitalism and the Rise of the 'Knowledge Worker': The Changing Structure of Knowledge Production in the US." *Theory and Society* 30:451–92.

Knights, David, and Darren McCabe. 2000. "Bewitched, Bothered and Bewildered: The Meaning and Experience of Teamworking for Employees in an Automotive Company." *Human Relations* 53:1481–517.

Koput, Kenneth W., Walter W. Powell, and Lauren Smith-Doerr. 1997. "Interorganizational Relations and Elite Sponsorship: Mobilizing Resources in Biotechnology." Unpublished manuscript, University of Arizona.

Kraatz, Matthew S., and Edward J. Zajac. 1996. "Causes and Consequences of Illegitimate Organizational Change." *American Sociological Review* 61:812–36.

Kriesi, Hanspeter. 1996. "The Organizational Structure of New Social Movements in a Political Context." In *Comparative Perspectives on Social Movements*, edited by Doug McAdam, John D. McCarthy, and Mayer N. Zald. New York: Cambridge University Press, 152–84.

References

Kriesi, Hanspeter, R. Koopmans, J. W. Duyvendak, and M. G. Giugni. 1995. *The Politics of New Social Movements in Western Europe: A Comparative Analysis*. Minneapolis: University of Minnesota Press.

Kurtz, S. 2002. *Workplace Justice: Organizing Multi-Identity Movements*. Minneapolis: University of Minnesota Press.

Kurzman, Charles. 1998. "Organizational Opportunity and Social Movement Mobilization: A Comparative Analysis of Four Religious Movements." *Mobilization* 3:23–49.

Lamoreaux, Naomi R. 1985. *The Great Merger Movement in American Business, 1895–1904*. Cambridge: Cambridge University Press.

Lant, Theresa K., and Joel A. C. Baum. 1995. "Cognitive Sources of Socially Constructed Competitive Groups: Examples from the Manhattan Hotel Industry." In *The Institutional Construction of Organizations: International and Longitudinal Studies*, edited by W. R. Scott and S. Christensen. Thousand Oaks, CA: Sage, 15–38.

LaNuez, Danny, and James M. Jermier. 1994. "Sabotage by Managers and Technocrats: Neglected Patterns of Resistance at Work." In *Resistance and Power in Organizations*, edited by James M. Jermier, David Knights, and William R. Nord. London: Routledge, 219–51.

Laraña, E., H. Johnston, and R. Gusfield. 1994. *New Social Movements: From Ideology to Identity*. Philadelphia: Temple University Press.

Lawler, Edward III, Susan Mohrman, and Gerald Ledford, Jr. 1995. *Creating High Performance Organizations*. San Francisco: Jossey-Bass.

Lawrence, Paul R., and Jay Lorsch. 1967. *Organization and Environment: Managing Differentiation and Integration*. Boston: Graduate School of Business Administration, Harvard University.

Lawrence, T., M. Winn, and P. D. Jennings. 2001. "Power and the Temporal Dynamics of Institutional Change." *Academy of Management Review* 26(4):624–44.

Layton, Azza Salama. 2000. *International Politics and Civil Rights Policies in the United States, 1941–1960*. Cambridge: Cambridge University Press.

Leblebici, Huseyin, Gerald R. Salancik, Anne Copay, and Thomas King. 1991. "Institutional Change and the Transformation of Interorganizational Fields: An Organizational History of the U.S. Radio Broadcasting Industry." *Administrative Science Quarterly* 36:333–63.

Lenin, V. I. 1969 [1902]. *What Is to Be Done?* New York: International Publishers.

Levi-Strauss, Claude. 1966. *The Savage Mind*. Chicago: University of Chicago Press.

Lewis, Tammy L. 2002. "Transnational Conservation Movement Organizations: Shaping the Protected Area Systems of Less Developed Countries." In *Globalization and Resistance: Transnational Dimensions of Social Movements*, edited by J. Smith and H. Johnston. Boulder, CO: Rowman and Littlefield, 65–84.

Licata, Salvatore J. 1981. "The Homosexual Rights Movement in the United States: A Traditionally Overlooked Area in American History." *Journal of Homosexuality* 6:161–89.

Lichterman, Paul. 1996. *The Search for Political Community: American Activists Reinventing Commitment*. New York: Cambridge University Press.

Lie, John. 1992. "The Concept of Mode of Exchange." *American Sociological Review* 57:506–34.

Lilly, Claude C. 1976. "A History of Insurance Regulation in the United States." *Chartered Property and Casualty Underwriters Annals* 29 (June):99–115.

Lin, Ann Chih. 2000. *Reform in the Making: The Implementation of Social Policy in Prison.* Princeton: Princeton University Press.

Lindberg, Leon N., and John L. Campbell. 1991. "The State and the Organization of Economic Activity." In *Governance of the American Economy*, edited by John L. Campbell, J. Rogers Hollingsworth, and Leon N. Lindberg. New York: Cambridge University Press, 356–442.

Locke, Richard M., and Kathleen Thelen. 1995. "Apples and Oranges Revisited: Contextualized Comparisons and the Study of Comparative Labor Politics." *Politics and Society* 23:337–67.

Lofland, John, and Michael Jamison. 1985. "Social Movement Locals: Modal Movement Structures." In *Protest: Studies of Collective Behavior and Social Movements*, edited by John Lofland. New Brunswick, NJ: Transaction, 201–18.

Long, J. S. 1997. *Regression Models for Categorical and Limited Dependent Variables.* Thousand Oaks, CA: Sage.

Louisville Board of Trade. 1912. *Report of the Special Fire Insurance Committee.* Louisville, KY: George H. Holt.

Lounsbury, Michael. 2001. "Institutional Sources of Practice Variation: Staffing College and University Recycling Programs." *Administrative Science Quarterly* 46:29–56.

Lounsbury, Michael. 2002. "Institutional Transformation and Status Mobility: The Professionalization of the Field of Finance." *Academy of Management Journal* 45:255–66.

Lounsbury, Michael, Paul M. Hirsch, and Marc J. Ventresca. 1998. "An Institutional Process Perspective on the Coevolution of Recycling in the Solid Waste Field, 1963–95." Working Paper 98–17, Institute for Policy Research, Northwestern University.

Lounsbury, Michael, and Bill Kaghan. 2001. "Organizations, Occupations and the Structuration of Work." *Research in the Sociology of Work* 10:25–51.

Lounsbury, Michael, and Marc J. Ventresca. 2002. "Social Structure and Organizations Revisited." *Research in the Sociology of Organizations*, vol. 19. New York: JAI/Elsevier, 1–36.

Lounsbury, Michael, Marc J. Ventresca, and Paul M. Hirsch. 2003. "Social Movements, Field Frames and Industry Emergence: A Cultural-Political Perspective of U.S. Recycling." *Socio-Economic Review* 1:71–104.

MacDuffie, John P. 1995. "Human Resource Bundles and Manufacturing Performance: Organizational Logic and Flexible Production Systems in the World Auto Industry." *Industrial and Labor Relations Review* 48:197–221.

Manne, Henry G. 1965. "Mergers and the Market for Corporate Control." *Journal of Political Economy* 73:110–20.

Mansbridge, Jane. 1986. *Why We Lost the ERA.* Chicago: University of Chicago Press.

References

March, James G. 1962. "The Business Firm as a Political Coalition." *Journal of Politics* 24:662–78.

March, James G., and Johan P. Olsen. 1976. *Ambiguity and Choice in Organizations*. Bergen, Norway: Universitetsforlaget.

March, James G., and Johan P. Olsen. 1984. "The New Institutionalism: Organizational Factors in Political Life." *American Political Science Review* 78:734–49.

March, James G., and Johan P. Olsen. 1989. *Rediscovering Institutions*. New York: Free Press.

March, James G., and Herbert A. Simon. 1958. *Organizations*. New York: Wiley.

"Marching in the Pride Parade? Here's How to Find Your Contingent..." 1995. *San Francisco Bay Times*:8.

Marchington, Mick, Adrian Wilkinson, Peter Ackers, and John Goodman. 1994. "Understanding the Meaning of Participation: Views from the Workplace." *Human Relations* 47:865–85.

Mariolis, Peter, and Maria H. Jones. 1982. "Centrality in Corporate Interlock Networks: Reliability and Stability." *Administrative Science Quarterly* 27:571–84.

Marjoribanks, Timothy. 2000. *News Corporation, Technology and the Workplace: Global Strategies, Local Change*. New York: Cambridge University Press.

Marotta, Toby. 1981. *The Politics of Homosexuality*. Boston: Houghton Mifflin.

Martin, Del. 1970. "Del Martin: Columnist Resigns, Blasts Male Chauvinism." *Vector* (October):35–7.

Martin, Del, and Phyllis Lyon. 1991. *Lesbian/Woman*. Volcano, CA: Volcano Press.

Marullo, Sam, Ron Pagnucco, and Jackie Smith. 1996. "Frame Changes and Social Movement Contraction: U.S. Peace Movement Framing After the Cold War." *Sociological Inquiry* 66:1–28.

Marx, Gary T. 1979. "External Efforts to Damage or Facilitate Social Movements: Some Patterns, Explanations, Outcomes, and Complications." In *The Dynamics of Social Movements*, edited by Mayer N. Zald and John D. McCarthy. Cambridge, MA: Winthrop, 94–125.

Mazmanian, Daniel, and Paul Sabatier. 1989. *Implementation and Public Policy*. Lanham, MD: University Press of America.

McAdam, Doug. 1982. *Political Process and the Development of Black Insurgency, 1930–1970*. Chicago: University of Chicago Press.

McAdam, Doug. 1983. "Tactical Innovation at the Pace of Insurgency." *American Sociological Review* 48:735–53.

McAdam, Doug. 1986. "Recruitment to High-Risk Activism: The Case of Freedom Summer." *American Journal of Sociology* 92:64–90.

McAdam, Doug. 1988a. *Freedom Summer*. Oxford: Oxford University Press.

McAdam, Doug. 1988b. "Micromobilization Contexts and Recruitment to Activism." In *From Structure to Action: Comparing Social Movement Research Across Cultures*, edited by B. Klandermans, H. Kriesi, and S. Tarrow. Greenwich, CT: JAI Press, 125–54.

McAdam, Doug. 1996. "Conceptual Origins, Current Problems, Future Directions." In *Comparative Perspectives on Social Movements: Political Opportunities,*

Mobilizing Structures, and Cultural Framings, edited by Doug McAdam, John D. McCarthy, and Mayer N. Zald. Cambridge: Cambridge University Press, 23–40.

McAdam, Doug. 1998. "On the International Origins of Domestic Political Opportunities." In *Social Movements and American Political Institutions*, edited by Anne N. Constain and Andrew S. McFarland. Boulder, CO: Rowman and Littlefield, 251–67.

McAdam, Doug. 1999a. "Introduction to the Second Edition." In *Political Process and the Development of Black Insurgency, 1930–1970*, revised ed. Chicago: University of Chicago Press, vii–xlii.

McAdam, Doug. 1999b. *Political Process and the Development of Black Insurgency, 1930–1970*, revised ed. Chicago: University of Chicago Press.

McAdam, Doug, John D. McCarthy, and Mayer N. Zald. 1988. "Social Movements." In *Handbook of Sociology*, edited by Neil J. Smelser. Newbury Park, CA: Sage, 695–737.

McAdam, Doug, John D. McCarthy, and Mayer N. Zald, eds. 1996a. *Comparative Perspectives on Social Movements*. New York: Cambridge University Press.

McAdam, Doug, John D. McCarthy, and Mayer N. Zald. 1996b. "Introduction: Opportunities, Mobilizing Structures, and Framing Processes – Toward a Synthetic, Comparative Perspective on Social Movements." In *Comparative Perspectives on Social Movements*, edited by Doug McAdam, John D. McCarthy, and Mayer N. Zald. New York: Cambridge University Press, 1–20.

McAdam, Doug, and Ronnelle Paulson. 1993. "Specifying the Relationship Between Social Ties and Activism." *American Journal of Sociology* 99:640–67.

McAdam, Doug, and William H. Sewell, Jr. 2001. "It's About Time: Temporality in the Study of Social Movements and Revolutions." In *Silence and Voice in the Study of Contentious Politics*, edited by Ronald R. Aminzade, Jack A. Goldstone, Doug McAdam, Elizabeth J. Perry, William H. Sewell, Jr., Sidney Tarrow, and Charles Tilly. Cambridge: Cambridge University Press, 89–125.

McAdam, Doug, Sidney Tarrow, and Charles Tilly. 1999. "Toward an Integrated Perspective on Social Movements and Revolutions." In *Comparative Politics: Rationality, Culture, and Structure*, edited by Mark Lichbach and Alan Zuckerman. New York: Cambridge University Press, 142–73.

McAdam, Doug, Sidney Tarrow, and Charles Tilly. 2001. *Dynamics of Contention*. New York: Cambridge University Press.

McCabe, Darren, David Knights, Deborah Kerfoot, Glenn Moran, and Hugh Willmott. 1998. "Making Sense of Quality? Towards a Review and Critique of Quality Initiatives in Financial Services." *Human Relations* 51:389–412.

McCammon, Holly J. 2002. "Stirring up Suffrage Sentiment: The Formation of the State Women Suffrage Organizations, 1966–1914." *Social Forces* 80:449–80.

McCammon, Holly J., Karen E. Campbell, Ellen M. Granberg, and Christine Mowery. 2001. "How Movements Win: Gendered Opportunity Structures and U.S. Women's Suffrage Movements, 1866–1919." *American Sociological Review* 66:49–70.

McCann, Michael W. 1994. *Rights at Work: Pay Equity and the Politics of Legal Mobilization*. Chicago: University of Chicago Press.

References

McCann, Michael W. 1998. "How Does Law Matter for Social Movements." In *How Does Law Matter*, edited by Bryant G. Garth and Austin Sarat. Evanston, IL: Northwestern University Press, 76–108.

McCarthy, John D. 1987. "Pro-Life and Pro-Choice Mobilization: Infrastructure Deficits and New Technologies." In *Social Movements in an Organizational Society*, edited by Mayer N. Zald and John D. McCarthy. New Brunswick, NJ: Transaction Publishers, 49–66.

McCarthy, John D. 1996. "Mobilizing Structures: Constraints and Opportunities in Adopting, Adapting and Inventing." In *Comparative Perspectives on Social Movements: Political Opportunities, Mobilizing Structures and Cultural Framings*, edited by Douglas McAdam, John D. McCarthy, and Mayer N. Zald. Cambridge: Cambridge University Press.

McCarthy, John D., David W. Britt, and Mark Wolfson. 1991. "The Institutional Channeling of Social Movements in the Modern State." *Research in Social Movements, Conflict and Change* 13:45–76.

McCarthy, John D., and Jim Castelli. 1994. *Working for Justice: The Campaign for Human Development and Poor Empowerment Groups.* Washington, DC: Life Cycle Institute, Catholic University of America.

McCarthy, John D., Jackie Smith, and Mayer N. Zald. 1996a. "Accessing Public, Media, Electoral, and Governmental Agendas." In *Comparative Perspectives on Social Movements: Political Opportunities, Mobilizing Structures, and Cultural Framings*, edited by Doug McAdam, John D. McCarthy, and Mayer N. Zald. Cambridge: Cambridge University Press, 291–311.

McCarthy, John D., Jackie Smith, and Mayer N. Zald. 1996b. "Media Discourse, Movement Publicity, and the Generation of Collective Action Frames: Theoretical and Empirical Exercises in Meaning Construction." In *Comparative Perspectives on Social Movements: Political Opportunities, Mobilizing Structures, and Cultural Framings*, edited by Doug McAdam, John D. McCarthy, and Mayer N. Zald. Cambridge: Cambridge University Press, 312–37.

McCarthy, John D., and Mark Wolfson. 1992. "Consensus Movements, Conflict Movements, and the Cooptation of Civic and State Infrastructures." In *Frontiers in Social Movement Theory*, edited by Aldon Morris and Carol M. Mueller. New Haven: Yale University Press, 273–97.

McCarthy, John D., and Mark Wolfson. 1996. "Resource Mobilization by Local Social Movement Organizations: Agency, Strategy and Organization in the Movement Against Drinking and Driving." *American Sociological Review* 61:1070–88.

McCarthy, John D., Mark Wolfson, David P. Baker, and Elaine Mosakowski. 1988. "The Founding of Social Movement Organizations: Local Citizens' Groups Opposing Drunken Driving." In *Ecological Models of Organizations*, edited by Glenn R. Carroll. Cambridge: Ballinger, 71–84.

McCarthy, John D., Mark Wolfson, and Debra S. Harvey. 1987. *Chapter Survey Report: Project on the Citizens Movement Against Drunk Driving*. Washington, DC: Center for the Study of Youth Development, Catholic University of America.

McCarthy, John D., and Mayer N. Zald. 1973. *The Trend of Social Movements in America: Professionalization and Resource Mobilization*. Morristown, NJ: General Learning Press.

McCarthy, John D., and Mayer N. Zald. 1977. "Resource Mobilization and Social Movements: A Partial Theory." *American Journal of Sociology* 82:1212–41.

McCarthy, John D., and Mayer N. Zald. 2001. "The Enduring Vitality of the Resource Mobilization Theory of Social Movements." In *Handbook of Sociological Theory*, edited by Jonathan H. Turner. New York: Kluwer Academic/Plenum, 533–65.

McCraw, Thomas. 1984. *Prophets of Regulation*. Cambridge: Harvard University Press.

McGuire, Patrick, Mark Granovetter, and Michael Schwartz. 1993. "Thomas Edison and the Social Construction of the Early Electricity Industry in America." In *Explorations in Economic Sociology*, edited by Richard Swedberg. New York: Russell Sage Foundation, 312–46.

McGurn, Patrick S., Sharon Pamepinto, and Adam B. Spector. 1989. *State Takeover Laws*. Washington, DC: Investor Responsibility Research Center.

McNeely, Connie L. 1995. "Prescribing National Education Policies: The Role of International Organizations." *Comparative Education Review* 39:483–507.

Meier, August, and Elliot Rudwick. 1973. *CORE: A Study in the Civil Rights Movement, 1948–1968*. New York: Oxford University Press.

Meier, Kenneth. 1988. *The Political Economy of Regulation: The Case of Insurance*. Albany: State University of New York Press.

Melhado, Evan M. 1988. "Competition Versus Regulation in American Health Policy." In *Money, Power and Health Care*, edited by Evan M. Melhado, Walter Feinberg, and Harold M. Swartz. Ann Arbor, MI: Health Administration Press, 15–102.

Melucci, Alberto. 1995. "The Process of Collective Identity." In *Social Movements and Culture*, edited by Hank Johnston Hank and Bert Klandermans. Minneapolis: University of Minnesota Press.

Mendel, Peter J. 2002. "International Standardization and Global Governance: The Spread of Quality and Environmental Management Standards." In *Organizations, Policy, and the Natural Environment: Institutional and Strategic Perspectives*, edited by Andrew J. Hoffman and Marc J. Ventresca. Stanford, CA: Stanford University Press, 407–31.

Menzel, H. 1960. "Innovation, Integration, and Marginality: A Survey of Physicians." *American Sociological Review* 25:704–13.

Merritt Committee. 1909–1911. "Hearings Before the Joint Committee of the Senate and Assembly." New York Assembly Documents, No. 30. Albany: J. B. Lyon.

Merritt Committee. 1911. "Report of the Joint Committee of the Senate and Assembly of the State of New York Appointed to Investigate the Corrupt Practices in Connection with Legislation, and the Affairs of Insurance Companies Other Than Those Doing Life Insurance Business." New York Assembly Documents, No. 30. Albany: J. B. Lyon.

Merton, Robert K. 1967. "On Sociological Theories of the Middle Range." In *On Theoretical Sociology*. New York: Free Press, 39–72.

Meyer, David S., and Douglas R. Imig. 1993. "Political Opportunity and the Rise and Decline of Interest Group Sectors." *Social Science Journal* 30:253–70.

References

Meyer, David S., and S. Staggenborg. 1996. "Movements, Countermovements, and the Structure of Political Opportunity." *American Journal of Sociology* 101:1628–60.

Meyer, David S., and Sidney Tarrow. 1998. "A Movement Society: Contentious Politics for a New Century." In *The Social Movement Society: Contentious Politics for a New Century*, edited by D. S. Meyer and S. Tarrow. New York: Rowman and Littlefield, 1–28.

Meyer, John W. 1970. "The Charter: Conditions of Diffuse Socialization in Schools." In *Social Processes and Social Structure*, edited by W. Richard Scott. New York: Holt, Rinehart and Winston, 564–78.

Meyer, John W., John Boli, George Thomas, and Francisco O. Ramirez. 1997. "World Society and the Nation State." *American Journal of Sociology* 103:1444–81.

Meyer, John W., David John Frank, Ann Hironaka, Evan Schofer, and Nancy Tuma. 1997. "The Structuring of a World Environmental Regime, 1870–1990." *International Organization* 51:623–51.

Meyer, John W., and Ronald Jepperson. 2000. "The 'Actors' of Modern Society: The Cultural Construction of Social Agency." *Sociological Theory* 18:101–20.

Meyer, John W., Francisco O. Ramirez, and Yasmin Soysal. 1992. "World Expansion of Mass Education, 1870–1980." *Sociology of Educational* 65:128–49.

Meyer, John W., and Brian Rowan. 1977. "Institutionalized Organizations: Formal Structure as Myth and Ceremony." *American Journal of Sociology* 83:340–63.

Meyer, John W., and W. Richard Scott. 1983. *Organizational Environments: Ritual and Rationality*. Beverly Hills: Sage.

Meyerson, Debra E. 2001. *Tempered Radicals: How People Use Difference to Inspire Change at Work*. Boston: Harvard Business School Press.

Meyerson, Debra E., and Maureen Scully. 1995. "Tempered Radicalism and the Politics of Ambivalence and Change." *Organization Science* 6:585–600.

Mezias, Stephen J. 1990. "An Institutional Model of Organizational Practice: Financial Reporting at the Fortune 200." *Administrative Science Quarterly* 35:431–57.

Michels, Robert. 1962 [1911]. *Political Parties: A Sociological Study of the Oligarchical Tendencies of Modern Democracy*. New York: Free Press.

Miles, Raymond E., and Charles C. Snow. 1994. *Fit, Failure, and the Hall of Fame*. New York: Free Press.

Miller, J. B. 1976. *Toward a New Psychology of Women*. Boston: Beacon Press.

Minkoff, Debra C. 1993. "The Organization of Survival: Women's and Racial-Ethnic Voluntarist and Activist Organizations, 1955–1985." *Social Forces* 71:887–908.

Minkoff, Debra C. 1995. *Organizing for Equality: The Evolution of Women's and Racial-Ethnic Organizations in America, 1955–1985*. New Brunswick, NJ: Rutgers University Press.

Minkoff, Debra C. 1997a. "Producing Social Capital: National Social Movements and Civil Society." *American Behavioral Scientist* 40:606–19.

Minkoff, Debra C. 1997b. "The Sequencing of Social Movements." *American Sociological Review* 62:779–99.

Minkoff, Debra C. 1999. "Bending with the Wind: Strategic Change and Adaptation by Women's and Racial Minority Organizations." *American Journal of Sociology* 104:1666–703.

Mintz, Beth, and Donald A. Palmer. 2000. "Business and Health Care Policy Reform in the 1980s: The 50 States." *Social Problems* 47:327–59.

Mische, A., and P. Pattison. 2000. "Composing a Civic Arena: Publics, Projects, and Social Settings." *Poetics* 27:163–94.

Mizruchi, Mark S. 1989. "Similarity of Political Behavior Among Large American Corporations." *American Journal of Sociology* 95: 401–24.

Mizruchi, Mark S. 1992. *The Structure of Corporate Political Action: Interfirm Relations and Their Consequences.* Cambridge: Harvard University Press.

Mizruchi, Mark S. 1996. "What Do Interlocks Do? An Analysis, Critique, and Assessment of Research on Interlocking Directorates." *Annual Review of Sociology* 22:271–98.

Mizruchi, Mark S., and Lisa Fein. 1999. "The Social Construction of Organizational Knowledge: A Study in the Uses of Coercive, Mimetic and Normative Isomorphism." *Administrative Science Quarterly* 44:653–84.

Mohr, John. 1992. "Community, Bureaucracy and Social Relief: An Institutional Analysis of Organizational Forms in New York City, 1888–1917." Ph.D. dissertation, Department of Sociology, Yale University.

Montgomery, David, and Arthur Santana. 2000. "Rally Web Site Also Interests the Uninvited: D.C. Police Are Monitoring Information Posted Online." *Washington Post,* April 2.

Moore, Curtis, and Alan Miller. 1994. *Green Gold: Japan, Germany, the United States, and the Race for Environmental Technology.* Boston: Beacon Press.

Moore, Kelly, and N. Hala. 2002. "Organizing Identity: The Creation of *Science for the People.*" In *Research in the Sociology of Organizations,* vol. 19, edited by M. Lounsbury and M. J. Ventresca. New York: JAI Press, 309–35.

Morgan, Gareth. 1997. *Images of Organization,* 2nd ed. Thousand Oaks, CA.: Sage.

Morrill, Calvin. 1991. "Conflict Management, Honor, and Organizational Change." *American Journal of Sociology* 97:585–621.

Morrill, Calvin. 1995. *The Executive Way: Conflict Management in Corporations.* Chicago: University of Chicago Press.

Morrill, Calvin. 2003. "Institutional Change and Interstitial Emergence: The Growth of Alternative Dispute Resolution in American Law, 1965–1995." In *How Institutions Change,* edited by W. Powell and D. Jones. Chicago: University of Chicago Press.

Morrill, Calvin, Mayer N. Zald, and Hayagreeva Rao. 2003. "Covert Political Conflict in Organizations: Challenges from Below." *Annual Review of Sociology* 29: 391–415.

Morris, Aldon. 1993. "Birmingham Confrontation Reconsidered: An Analysis of the Dynamics and Tactics of Mobilization." *American Sociological Review* 58:621–36.

Morris, Aldon. 2000. "Reflections on Social Movement Theory: Criticisms and Proposals." *Contemporary Sociology* 29:445–54.

References

Morrison, Elizabeth W., and Frances J. Milliken. 2000. "Organizational Silence: A Barrier to Change and Development in a Pluralistic World." *Academy of Management Review* 25:706–25.

Mowbray, Albert. 1946. *Insurance*. New York: McGraw Hill.

Murphy, Gillian Hughs. 2002. "A Double-Edged Sword: Coalitions and the Development of the Global Environmental Movement." M.A. thesis, Department of Sociology, University of Washington, Seattle.

Murray, Charles. 1984. *Losing Ground: American Social Policy, 1950–1980*. New York: Basic Books.

Murray, Stephen O. 1996. *American Gay*. Chicago: University of Chicago Press.

Myrdal, Gunnar. 1970. "America Again at the Crossroads." In *Roots of Rebellion: The Evolution of Black Politics and Protest Since World War II*, edited by Richard P. Young. New York: Harper and Row, 13–46.

Nakamura, Robert T., and Smallwood Frank. 1980. *The Politics of Policy Implementation*. New York: St. Martin's Press.

National Center for Charitable Statistics. 1997. *State Nonprofit Almanac: Profiles of Charitable Organizations*. Washington, DC: Urban Institute Center on Nonprofits and Philanthropy.

National Convention of Insurance Commissioners (NCIC). 1915. *Proceedings of the Forty-Sixth Session of the National Convention of Insurance Commissioners, Del Monte, California*, September 21–24, 1915. (Includes adjourned meeting in New York on December 8, 1914, and meeting in Chicago on April 12, 1915.) Columbia, SC: R. L. Bryan Company.

Nelkin, Dorothy, and Michael Pollak. 1981. *The Atom Besieged: Extraparliamentary Dissent in France and Germany*. Cambridge: MIT Press.

Nelson, Richard R., and Sidney G. Winter. 1982. *An Evolutionary Theory of Economic Change*. Cambridge: Harvard University Press.

New York State Insurance Department. 1911–1932. *Annual Report of the Superintendent of Insurance of the State of New York* and *Report on Official Examinations*. New York Senate Documents, New York Assembly Documents, and New York Legislative Documents. Albany: J. B. Lyon.

New York State Joint Legislative Committee on Housing. 1922. *Intermediate Report of the Joint Legislative Committee on Housing*. New York Legislative Documents, No. 60. Albany: J. B. Lyon.

Noakes, John A. 2000. "Official Frames in Social Movement Theory: The FBI, HUAC, and the Communist Threat in Hollywood." *Sociological Quarterly* 41: 657–80.

Noll, Roger G. 1983. "The Political Foundations of Regulatory Policy." *Journal of Institutional and Theoretical Economics* 139:377–404.

North, Douglass C. 1981. *Structure and Change in Economic History*. New York: W. W. Norton.

North, Douglass C. 1990. *Institutions, Institutional Change and Economic Performance*. New York: Cambridge University Press.

Oberschall, Anthony. 1996. "Opportunities and Framing in the Eastern European Revolts of 1989." In *Comparative Perspectives on Social Movements*, edited by Doug

McAdam, John D. McCarthy, and Mayer N. Zald. New York: Cambridge University Press, 93–121.

Ocasio, William. 1997. "Towards an Attention-Based View of the Firm." *Strategic Management Journal* 18:187–206.

Oliver, Christine. "Antecedents of Deinstitutionalization." *Organization Studies* 13:563–88.

Oliver, Pamela E., and Mark Furman. 1990. "Contradictions Between National and Local Organizational Strength: The Case of the John Birch Society." *International Social Movement Research* 2:155–77.

Oliver, Pamela E., and Gerald Marwell. 1992. "Mobilizing Technologies for Collective Action." In *Frontiers in Social Movement Theory*, edited by Aldon D. Morris and Carol McClurg Mueller. New Haven: Yale University Press, 251–72.

Orfield, Gary, Susan E. Eaton, and the Harvard Project on School Desegregation. 1996. *Dismantling Desegregation: The Quiet Reversal of Brown v. Board of Education*. New York: New Press.

Orloff, Ann, and Theda Skocpol. 1984. "Why Not Equal Protection? Explaining the Politics of Public Social Spending in Britain, 1900–1911, and the United States, 1880s–1920." *American Sociological Review* 49:726–50.

Orren, Karen, and Stephen Skowronek. 1999. "Beyond the Iconography of Order: Notes for a 'New Institutionalism.'" In *The Dynamics of American Politics*, edited by Lawrence Dodd and Calvin Jillson. San Francisco: Westview Press, 311–30.

Oster, S. M. 1996. "Nonprofit Organizations and Their Local Affiliates: A Study in Organizational Forms." *Journal of Economic Behavior and Organization* 30:83–95.

Osterman, Paul. 1994. "How Common Is Workplace Transformation and Who Adopts It?" *Industrial and Labor Relations Review* 47:173–88.

Ostler, Jefferey. 1993. *Prairie Populism*. Lawrence: University of Kansas.

Ostrander, Gilman M. 1957. *The Prohibition Movement in California, 1848–1933*. University of California Publications in History, no. 57.

Packard, Vance. 1960. *The Waste Makers*. New York: D. McKay Co.

Palmer, Donald, and Brad N. Barber. 2001. "Challengers, Elites, and Owning Families: A Social Class Theory of Corporate Acquisitions in the 1960s." *Administration Science Quarterly* 46:87–120.

Palmer, Donald, P. Devereaux Jennings, and Xueguang Zhou. 1993. "Late Adoption of the Multidivisional Form by Large U.S. Corporations: Institutional, Political, and Economic Accounts." *Administrative Science Quarterly* 38:100–31.

Parker, Kent. 1965. "Ratemaking in Fire Insurance." In *Property and Liability Handbook*, edited by John Long and Davis Gregg. Homewood, IL: Richard Irwin, 169–89.

Parker, Mike, and Jane Slaughter. 1993. "Should the Labor Movement Buy TQM?" *Organizational Change Management* 6:43–57.

Parsa, Misagh. 2000. *States, Ideologies, and Social Revolutions*. New York: Cambridge University Press.

Patterson, Edwin. 1927. *The Insurance Commissioner in the United States*. Cambridge: Harvard University Press.

References

Pavalko, Eliza. 1989. "State Timing of Policy Adoption: Workmen's Compensation in the United States, 1909–1929." *American Journal of Sociology* 95:592–615.

Peoples' Global Action. 2000. "Worldwide Resistance Roundup: Newsletter 'Inspired by' Peoples' Global Action." London.

Perrow, Charles. 1986. *Complex Organizations: A Critical* Essay, 3rd ed. Glenview, IL: Scott, Foresman.

Perrow, Charles. 2000. "An Organizational Analysis of Organizational Theory." *Contemporary Sociology* 29:469–74.

Perrow, Charles. 2002. *Organizing America: Wealth, Power, and the Origins of Corporate Capitalism*. Princeton: Princeton University Press.

Pettigrew, Andrew, and Richard Whipp. 1991. *Managing Change for Competitive Success*. Oxford: Blackwell.

Pfeffer, Jeffrey. 1981. *Power in Organizations*. Marshfield, MA: Pitman.

Pfeffer, Jeffrey. 1992. *Managing with Power: Politics and Influence in Organizations*. Boston: Harvard Business School Press.

Pfeffer, Jeffrey, and Gerald Salancik. 1978. *The External Control of Organizations*. New York: Harper and Row.

Pierson, Paul. 2000a. "Not Just What, But When: Timing and Sequence in Political Processes." *Studies in American Political Development* 14 (Spring):72–92.

Pierson, Paul. 2000b. "Increasing Returns, Path Dependence, and the Study of Politics." *American Political Science Review* 94:251–67.

Piore, Michael J. 1995. *Beyond Individualism: How Social Demands of the New Identity Groups Challenge American Political and Economic Life*. Cambridge: Harvard University Press.

Piore, Michael J., and Charles F. Sabel. 1984. *The Second Industrial Divide*. New York: Basic.

Piven, Frances Fox, and Richard Cloward. 1979. *Poor People's Movements*. New York: Vintage.

Plummer, Brenda Gayle. 1996. *Rising Wind: Black Americans and U.S. Foreign Affairs, 1935–1960*. Chapel Hill: University of North Carolina Press.

Polletta, Francesca. 2002. *Freedom Is an Endless Meeting: Democracy in American Social Movements*. Chicago: University of Chicago Press.

Polletta, Francesca, and James M. Jasper. 2001. "Collective Identity and Social Movements." *Annual Review of Sociology* 27:283–305.

Powell, Thomas C. 1995. "Total Quality Management as Competitive Advantage: A Review and Empirical Study." *Strategic Management Journal* 16:15–37.

Powell, Walter W. 1990. "Neither Market nor Hierarchy: Network Forms of Organizations." In *Research in Organizational Behavior*, edited by Barry Staw and Larry L. Cummings. Greenwich, CT: JAI Press, 12:295–336.

Powell, Walter W. 1991. "Expanding the Scope of Institutional Analysis." In *The New Institutionalism in Organizational Analysis*, edited by Walter Powell and Paul DiMaggio. Chicago: University of Chicago Press, 183–203.

Powell, Walter W. 1999. "The Social Construction of an Organizational Field: The Case of Biotechnology." *International Journal of Biotechnology* 1:42–66.

Powell, Walter W., and Paul J. DiMaggio, eds. 1991. *The New Institutionalism in Organizational Analysis*. Chicago: University of Chicago Press.

Powell, Walter W., Kenneth W. Koput, and Laurel Smith-Doerr. 1996. "Interorganizational Collaboration and the Locus of Innovation: Networks of Learning in Biotechnology." *Administrative Sciences Quarterly* 41:116–45.

Powers, Patricia R. 1984. "Focused Energy: A Study of Public Interest Advocates." Ph.D. dissertation, American Studies Department, University of Maryland.

Pressman, Jeffrey, and Aaron Wildavsky. 1979. *Implementation: How Great Expectations in Washington Are Dashed in Oakland; or, Why It's Amazing That Federal Programs Work at All, This Being the Sage of the Economic Development Administration, as Told by Two Sympathetic Observers Who Seek to Build Morals on a Foundation of Ruined Hopes*. Berkeley: University of California Press.

Proudford, K. 2002. "Asking the Question: Uncovering the Assumptions That Undermine Conversations Across Race." *CGO Insights*, no. 14. Boston: Center for Gender in Organizations, Simmons School of Management.

Putnam, Robert D. 2000. *Bowling Alone: The Collapse and Revival of American Community*. New York: Simon and Schuster.

Raeburn, Nicole. 2001. "Seizing and Creating Institutional Opportunities: Mobilizing for Lesbian, Gay, and Bisexual Rights in the Workplace." Paper presented at the annual meeting of the American Sociological Association. Anaheim, Calif.

Ramirez, Francisco O., and John Boli. 1987. "The Political Construction of Mass Schooling: European Origins and Worldwide Institutionalization." *Sociology of Education* 60:2–17.

Ranney, Austin. 1976. "Parties in State Politics." In *Politics in the American States*, 3rd ed., edited by Herber Jacob and Kenneth Vines. Boston: Little, Brown and Co.

Rao, Hayagreeva. 1998. "Caveat Emptor: The Construction of Nonprofit Watchdog Organizations." *American Journal of Sociology* 103:912–61.

Rao, Hayagreeva, Phillipe Monin, and Rodolphe Durand. 2001. "Identity Movements and the Redefinition of Social Identity: Why French Chefs Abandoned Classical Cuisine for Nouvelle Cuisine." Unpublished manuscript, Roberto C. Goizueta Business School, Emory University, Atlanta.

Rao, Hayagreeva, Calvin Morrill, and Mayer N. Zald. 2000. "Power Plays: How Social Movements and Collective Action Create New Organizational Forms." *Research in Organization Behavior* 22:239–82.

Rao, Hayagreeva, and Jitendra V. Singh. 1999. "Types of Variation in Organizational Populations: The Speciation of New Organizational Forms." In *Variations in Organization Science: In Honor of Donald T. Campbell*, edited by Joel A. C. Baum and William McKelvey. Beverly Hills, CA: Sage, 63–78.

Rao, Hayagreeva, and K. Sivakumar. 1999. "Institutional Sources of Boundary-Spanning Structures: The Establishment of Investor Relations Departments in the *Fortune* 500 Industrials." *Organization Science* 10:27–42.

Reitzes, D. C., and D. C. Reitzes. 1987. *The Alinsky Legacy: Alive and Kicking*. Greenwich, CT: JAI Press.

Rettig, Richard, and Normal Levinsky, eds. 1991. *Kidney Failure and the Federal Government*. Washington, DC: National Academy Press.

Riegel, Robert. 1916. *Fire Underwriters Associations in the United States*. New York: Chronicle Co.

References

Riegel, Robert. 1917a. "Rate-Making Organizations in Fire Insurance." *Annals of the American Academy of Political and Social Science* 70(159):172–98.

Riegel, Robert. 1917b. "Problems of Fire Insurance Rate Making." *Annals of the American Academy of Political and Social Science* 70(159):199–219.

Riegel, Robert. 1927. "The Regulation of Fire Rates." *Annals of the American Academy of Political and Social Science* 219(March):114–20.

Risse, Thomas, and Kathryn Sikkink. 1999. "The Socialization of International Human Rights Norms into Domestic Practices: Introduction." In *The Power of Human Rights: International Norms and Domestic Change*, edited by Thomas Risse, Stephen C. Ropp, and Kathryn Sikkink. New York: Cambridge University Press, 1–38.

Robinson, James C. 1999. *The Corporate Practice of Medicine: Competition and Innovation in Health Care.* Berkeley: University of California Press.

Robinson, William. 1996. *Promoting Polyarchy.* New York: Cambridge University Press.

Rochon, Thomas R. 1997. *Cultural Moves: Ideas, Activism, and Changing Values.* Princeton: Princeton University Press.

Roe, Mark J. 1991. "A Political Theory of American Corporate Finance." *Columbia Law Review* 91(10):10–67.

Roe, Mark J. 1994. *Strong Managers, Weak Owners: The Political Roots of American Corporate Finance.* Princeton: Princeton University Press.

Roe, Mark J. 1996. "Chaos and Evolution in Law and Economics." *Harvard Law Review* 109(3):641–68.

Rogers, Mary Beth. 1990. *Cold Anger: A Story of Faith and Power Politics.* Denton: University of North Texas Press.

Romano, Roberta. 1992. "Rethinking Takeover Regulation." *Journal of Applied Corporate Finance* 5(3):47–57.

Romano, Roberta. 1993. *The Genius of American Corporate Law.* Washington, DC: AEI Press.

Rooney, Jim. 1995. *Organizing the South Bronx.* Albany: SUNY Press.

Rose, Michael D. 1967. "State Regulation of Property and Casualty Insurance Rates." *Ohio State Law Journal* 28:669–733.

Rosenkopf, L., A. Metiu, and V. George. 2001. "From the Bottom Up? Technical Committee Activity and Alliance Formation." *Administrative Science Quarterly* 46:748–72.

Rothenberg, Sandra, and Maureen Scully. 2001. "Mobilization of the Wealthy in the Fight Against Income Inequality." Unpublished paper.

Rothman, Franklin Daniel, and Pamela E. Oliver. 2002. "From Local to Global: The Anti-Dam Movement in Southern Brazil, 1979–1992." In *Globalization and Resistance: Transnational Dimensions of Social Movements*, edited by J. Smith and H. Johnston. Lanham, MD.: Rowman and Littlefield, 115–31.

Rothschild-Whitt, Joyce. 1979. "Conditions for Democracy." In *Communes, Coops and Collectives*, edited by J. Case and R. C. R. Taylor. New York: Pantheon, 215–44.

Roy, William G. 1997. *Socializing Capital: The Rise of the Large Industrial Corporation.* Princeton: Princeton University Press.

Rucht, Dieter. 1996. "The Impact of National Contexts on Social Movement Structures: A Cross-Movement and Cross-National Comparison." In *Comparative Perspectives on Social Movements*, edited by Doug McAdam, John D. McCarthy, and Mayer N. Zald. New York: Cambridge University Press, 185–204.

Ruckus Society, Web site, Accessed March 2003. <http://www.ruckus./org/about/mission.html>

Ruef, Martin, and W. Richard Scott. 1998. "A Multidimensional Model of Organizational Legitimacy: Hospital Survival in Changing Institutional Environments." *Administrative Science Quarterly* 43:877–904.

Rule, Sheila. 1981. "Arrest of Innis Brings More Controversy to CORE." *New York Times*, August 28:B3.

Rupp, Leila J. 1997. *Worlds of Women: The Making of an International Women's Movement*. Princeton: PrincetonUniversity Press.

Sabatier, Paul A. 1975. "Social Movements and Regulatory Agencies: Toward a More Adequate – and Less Pessimistic – 'Theory of Clientele Capture.'" *Policy Sciences* 6:301–42.

Sabatier, Paul A., and Daniel A. Mazmanian. 1983. *Can Regulation Work? The Implementation of the 1972 California Coastal Initiative*. New York: Plenum Press.

Sabel, Charles F. 1993. "Studied Trust: Building New Forms of Cooperation in a Volatile Economy." In *Explorations in Economic Sociology*, edited by Richard Swedberg. New York: Russell Sage Foundation, 104–44.

Sabel, Charles F., and Jonathan Zeitlin. 1997. "Stories, Strategies, Structures: Rethinking Historical Alternatives to Mass Production." In *Worlds of Possibility*, edited by Charles F. Sabel and Jonathan Zeitlin. Cambridge: Cambridge University Press, 1–33.

Sahlins, Marshall. 1981. *Historical Metaphors and Mythical Realities*. Ann Arbor: University of Michigan Press.

Sale, Kirkpatrick. 1973. *SDS*. New York: Random House.

Saller, C. 1998. *Working Children*. Minneapolis: Carolrhoda Books.

Sanders, Elizabeth. 1986. "Industrial Concentration, Sectional Competition and Anti-Trust Politics in America, 1880–1980." *Studies in American Political Development* 1:142–214.

Sanders, Elizabeth. 1999. *Roots of Reform: Farmers, Workers, and the American State, 1877–1917*. Chicago: University of Chicago Press.

Saxenian, Annalee. 1994. *Regional Advantage: Culture and Competition in Silicon Valley and Route 128*. Cambridge: Harvard University Press.

Schmidt, Laura Anne. Forthcoming. *The Corporate Transformation of American Health Care: A Study in Institution-Building*. Princeton: Princeton University Press.

Schnaiberg, Allan. 1973. "Politics, Participation, and Pollution: The 'Environmental Movement.'" In *Cities in Change: Studies on the Urban Condition*, edited by John Walton and Donald E. Carns. Boston: Allyn and Bacon.

Schnaiberg, Allan, and Kenneth A. Gould. 1994. *Environment and Society*. New York: St. Martin's Press.

References

Schneiberg, Marc. 1999. "Political and Institutional Conditions for Governance by Association: Private Order and Price Controls in American Fire Insurance." *Politics and Society* 27:67–103.

Schneiberg, Marc. 2002. "Organizational Heterogeneity and the Production of New Forms: Politics, Social Movements and Mutual Companies in American Fire Insurance, 1900–1930." *Research in the Sociology of Organizations*, 19:39–89.

Schneiberg, Marc, and Tim Bartley. 2001. "Regulating American Industries: Markets, Politics, and the Institutional Determinants of Fire Insurance Regulation." *American Journal of Sociology* 107:101–46.

Schneiberg, Marc, and Elisabeth Clemens. 2003. "The Typical Tools for the Job: Research Strategies in Institutional Analysis." In *How Institutions Change*, edited by W. Powell and D. Jones. Chicago: University of Chicago Press.

Schumpeter, Joseph A. 1983 [1934]. *The Theory of Economic Development*. New Brunswick, NJ: Transaction Books.

Schwartz, Michael. 1976. *Radical Protest and Social Structure: The Southern Farmers' Alliance and Cotton Tenancy, 1880–1890*. Chicago: University of Chicago Press.

Schwartz, Michael, and Shuva Paul. 1992. "Resource Mobilization Versus the Mobilization of People: Why Consensus Movements Cannot Be Instruments of Social Change." In *Frontiers in Social Movement Theory*, edited by Aldon D. Morris and Carol M. Mueller. New Haven: Yale University Press, 205–23.

Schweber, Libby. 1996. "Progressive Reformers, Unemployment, and the Transformation of Social Inquiry in Britain and the United States." In *States, Social Knowledge, and the Origins of Modern Social Policies*, edited by Dietrich Rueschemeyer and Theda Skocpol. Princeton: Princeton University Press, 163–200.

Scott, James C. 1997. *Seeing Like a State: How Certain Schemes to Improve the Human Condition Have Failed*. New Haven: Yale University Press.

Scott, W. Richard. 1987. "The Adolescence of Institutional Theory." *Administrative Science Quarterly* 32:493–11.

Scott, W. Richard. 1994a. "Conceptualizing Organizational Fields: Linking Organizations and Societal Systems." In *Systemrationalitat und Partialinteresse*, edited by Hans-Ulrich Derlien, Uta Gerhardt, and Fritz W. Scharpf. Baden-Baden: Nomos, 203–21.

Scott, W. Richard. 1994b. "Institutional Analysis: Variance and Process Theory Approaches." In *Institutional Environments and Organizations*, edited by W. Richard Scott, J. W. Meyer, and Associates. Thousand Oaks, CA: Sage, 81–99.

Scott, W. Richard. 1995. *Institutions and Organizations*. Thousand Oaks, CA: Sage.

Scott, W. Richard. 2001. *Institutions and Organizations*, 2nd ed. Thousand Oaks, CA: Sage.

Scott, W. Richard. 2003. *Organizations: Rational, Natural, and Open Systems*, 5th ed. Upper Saddle River, NJ: Prentice Hall.

Scott, W. Richard, and John W. Meyer. 1983. "The Organization of Societal Sectors." In *Organizational Environments: Ritual and Rationality*. Beverly Hills: Sage, 129–54.

Scott, W. Richard, and John W. Meyer. 1991. "The Organization of Societal Sectors: Propositions and Early Evidence." In *The New Institutionalism in Organizational*

Analysis, edited by Walter W. Powell and Paul J. DiMaggio. Chicago: University of Chicago Press, 108–40.

Scott, W. Richard, and John W. Meyer, eds. 1994. *Institutional Environments and Organizations: Structural Complexity and Individualism*. Thousand Oaks, CA: Sage.

Scott, W. Richard, Martin Ruef, Peter J. Mendel, and Carol A. Caronna. 2000. *Institutional Change and Healthcare Organization: From Professional Dominance to Managed Care*. Chicago: University of Chicago Press.

Scully, Maureen A. 1997. "A Rainbow Coalition or Different Wavelengths? Relationships Among Networks for African American, Women, and Gay and Lesbian Employees." Symposium overview presented at the annual meeting of the Academy of Management, Boston.

Scully, Maureen A. 2003. "Songs of Others: Bystanders and Allies Respond to Injustice to Other." Unpublished manuscript.

Scully, Maureen A., and W. E. Douglas Creed. 1999. "Restructured Families: Issues of Equality and Need." *The Annals of the American Academy of Political and Social Science: Special Issue on Work and Family* 562:47–65.

Scully, Maureen A., W. E. Douglas Creed, and M. Ventresca. 1999. "More Than Switchpersons on the Tracks of History: Situated Agency and Contested Legitimacy During the Diffusion of Domestic Partner Benefits." Unpublished manuscript.

Scully, Maureen A., and B. Lautsch. 1999. "Life Itself and Life Chances: Using Medical Ethics to Understand Organizational Allocations." Unpublished manuscript.

Scully, Maureen A., and A. Segal. 2002. "Passion with an Umbrella: Grassroots Activists in the Workplace." In *Research in the Sociology of Organizations*, vol. 19, edited by M. Lounsbury, and M. J. Ventresca. Oxford: JAI Press, 127–70.

Scully, Maureen A., A. Segal, and B. Lautsch. 1998. "Exit in Many Voices." Unpublished manuscript.

Seidman, Steven. 1993. "Identity and Politics in a 'Postmodern' Gay Culture: Some Historical and Conceptual Notes." In *Fear of a Queer Planet: Queer Politics and Social Theory*, edited by Michael Warner. Minneapolis: University of Minnesota Press, 105–42.

Seldman, N. 1986. "The United States Recycling Movement, 1968–1986: A Review." Unpublished manuscript, Washington, DC: Institute for Local Self-Reliance.

Seldman, N. 1995. "Recycling – History in the United States." In *Encyclopedia of Energy Technology and the Environment*, edited by A. Bisio and S. Boots. New York: Wiley, 2352–67.

Selznick, Philip. 1948. "Foundations of the Theory of Organization." *American Sociological Review* 13:25–35.

Selznick, Philip. 1949. *TVA and the Grass Roots*. Berkeley: University of California Press.

Selznick, Philip. 1952. *The Organizational Weapon*. New York: McGraw-Hill.

Selznick, Philip. 1969. *Law, Society, and Industrial Justice*. New York: Russell Sage Foundation.

References

Seo, M., and W. E. Douglas Creed. 2002. "Institutional Contradictions, Praxis, and Institutional Change: A Dialectical Perspective." *Academy of Management Review* 27:1–26.

Sewell, Graham. 1998. "The Discipline of Teams: The Control of Team-Based Industrial Work Through Electronic and Peer Surveillance." *Administrative Science Quarterly* 43:397–428.

Sewell, William H., Jr. 1992. "A Theory of Structure: Duality, Agency, and Transformation." *American Journal of Sociology* 98:1–29.

Sewell, William H., Jr. 1996. "Historical Events as Transformations of Structures: Inventing Revolution at the Bastille." *Theory and Society* 25:841–81.

Sewell, William H., Jr. 2001. "Space in Contentious Politics." In *Silence and Voice in the Study of Contentious Politics*, edited by Ronald R. Aminzade, Jack A. Goldstone, Doug McAdam, Elizabeth J. Perry, William H. Sewell, Sidney Tarrow, and Charles Tilly. Cambridge: Cambridge University Press,

Sikkink, Kathryn. 1993. "Human Rights, Principled Issue-Networks, and Sovereignty in Latin America." *International Organization* 47:411–41.

Sikkink, Kathryn, and Jackie Smith. 2002. "Infrastructures for Change: Transnational Organizations, 1953–1993." In *Restructuring World Politics: The Power of Transnational Agency and Norms*, edited by S. Khagram, J. Riker, and Kathryn Sikkink. Minneapolis: University of Minnesota Press, 24–44.

Simon, Herbert A. 1945. *Administrative Behavior: A Study of Decision-Making Processes in Administrative Organization*. New York: Macmillan Company.

Sine, Wesley D., and Robert David. 2003. "Environmental Jolts, Institutional Change and the Creation of Entrepreneurial Opportunity in the US Electrical Utility Industry." *Research Policy* 32:185–207.

Sine, Wesley D., and David Strang. 2001. "On the Road Again: Quality Teams and National Culture in a Global Bank." Paper presented at the annual meeting of the American Sociological Association, Anaheim, CA.

Sitkin, Sim B., Kathleen M. Sutcliffe, and Roger G. Schroeder. 1994. "Distinguishing Control from Learning in Total Quality Management: A Contingency Perspective." *Academy of Management Review* 19:537.

Sitkoff, Harvard. 1978. *A New Deal for Blacks*. New York: Oxford University Press.

Sklair, Leslie. 2001. *The Transnational Capitalist Class*. Cambridge: Blackwell.

Sklar, Martin J. 1988. *The Corporate Reconstruction of American Capitalism, 1890–1916: The Market, the Law, and Politics*. Cambridge: Cambridge University Press.

Skocpol, Theda. 1992. *Protecting Soldiers and Mothers: The Political Origins of Social Policy in the United States*. Cambridge: Harvard University Press.

Skocpol, Theda. 1999a. "Advocates Without Members: The Recent Transformation of American Civic Life." In *Civic Engagement in American Democracy*, edited by Theda Skocpol and Morris P. Fiorina. Washington, DC: Brookings Institution Press, 461–510.

Skocpol, Theda. 1999b. "How Americans Became Civic." In *Civic Engagement in American Democracy*, edited by Theda Skocpol and Morris P. Fiorina. Washington, DC: Brookings Institution Press.

Skocpol, Theda, and Kenneth Finegold. 1982. "State Capacity and Economic Intervention in the Early New Deal." *Political Science Quarterly* 92:255–78.

Skowronek, Stephen. 1982. *Building a New American State*. Cambridge: Cambridge University Press.

Skrentny, John David. 1996. *The Ironies of Affirmative Action*. Chicago: University of Chicago Press.

Skrentny, John David. 1998. "The Effect of the Cold War on African-American Civil Rights: American and World Audience, 1945–1968." *Theory and Society* 27:237–85.

Skrentny, John David. 2002. *The Minority Rights Revolution*. Cambridge: Harvard University Press

Skrentny, John David. Forthcoming. *The Rights Revolution*. Chicago: University of Chicago Press.

Smelser, Neil. 1962. *Theory of Collective Behavior*. New York: Free Press.

Smith, David H. 1997. "The Rest of the Nonprofit Sector: Grassroots Associations as the Dark Matter Ignored in Prevailing 'Flat Earth' Maps of the Sector." *Nonprofit and Voluntary Sector Quarterly* 26:114–31.

Smith, Jackie. 1997. "Characteristics of the Modern Transnational Social Movement Sector." In *Transnational Social Movements and World Politics: Solidarity Beyond the State*, edited by Jackie Smith, Charles Chatfield, and Ron Pagnucco. Syracuse, NY: Syracuse University Press, 42–58.

Smith, Jackie. 1998. "Global Civil Society: Transnational Social Movement Organizations and Social Capital." *American Behavioral Scientist* 42:93–107.

Smith, Jackie. 2002a. "Globalizing Resistance: The Battle of Seattle and the Future of Social Movements." In *Globalization and Resistance: Transnational Dimensions of Social Movements*, edited by Jackie Smith and H. Johnston. Lanham, MD: Rowman and Littlefield, 183–99.

Smith, Jackie. 2002b. "Bridging Global Divides? Strategic Framing and Solidarity in Transnational Social Movement Organizations." *International Sociology* 17 (4):505–28.

Smith, Jackie. 2004. "Exploring Connections Between Global Integration and Political Mobilization." *Journal of World Systems Research* 2004:255–85.

Smith, Jackie, Charles Chatfield, and Ron Pagnucco, eds. 1997. "Characteristics of the Modern Transnational Social Movement Sector." In *Transnational Social Movements and World Politics: Solidarity Beyond the State*. Syracuse, NY: Syracuse University Press.

Smith, Jackie, Ron Pagnucco, and George Lopez. 1998. "Globalizing Human Rights: Report on a Survey of Transnational Human Rights NGOs." *Human Rights Quarterly* 20:379–412.

Smith, Jackie, Ron Pagnucco, and Winnie Romeril. 1994. "Transnational Social Movement Organizations in the Global Political Arena." *Voluntas* 5:121–54.

Snow, David A. 1976. *The Nichiren Shoshu Buddhist Movement in America*. Ann Arbor, MI: University Microforms.

Snow, David A. 1992. "Master Frames and Cycles of Protest." In *Frontiers in Social Movement Theory*, edited by Aldon Morris and Carol McClurg Mueller. New Haven: Yale University Press:133–55.

Snow, David A., and Robert D. Benford. 1988. "Ideology, Frame Resonance, and Participant Mobilization." In *From Structure to Action: Social Movement*

References

Participation Across Cultures, edited by Bert Klandermans, Hanspeter Kriesi, and Sidney Tarrow. Greenwich, CT: JAI Press, 197–217.

Snow, David A., and Robert D. Benford. 1992. "Master Frames and Cycles of Protest." In *Frontiers in Social Movement Theory*, edited by Aldon Morris and Carol McClurg Mueller. New Haven: Yale University Press:133–55.

Snow, David A., E. Burke Rochfold, Jr., Steven K. Worder, and Robert D. Benford. 1986. "Frame Alignment Processes, Micromobilization, and Movement Participation." *American Sociological Review* 51:464–81.

Snow, David A., Louis A. Zurcher, and Sheldon Ekland-Olsen. 1980. "Social Networks and Social Movements: A Microstructural Approach to Differential Recruitment." *American Sociological Review* 45:797–801.

Soule, Sarah A. 1997. "The Student Divestment Movement in the United States and Tactical Diffusion: The Shantytown Protest." *Social Forces* 75:855–83.

Soule, Sarah A. 2003. "Divestment by Colleges and Universities in the United States: Institutional Pressures Toward Isomorphism." In *How Institutions Change*, edited by Walter W. Powell and Daniel L. Jones. Chicago: University of Chicago Press.

Soule, Sarah A., and Jennifer Earl. 2001. "The Enactment of State-Level Hate Crime Law in the United States: Intrastate and Interstate Factors." *Sociological Perspectives* 44:281–305.

Soule, Sarah A., and Yvonne Zylan. 1997. "Runaway Train? The Diffusion of State-Level Reforms in ADC/AFDC Eligibility Requirements, 1950–1967." *American Journal of Sociology* 3:733–62.

Soysal, Yasmin. 1994. *Limits of Citizenship: Migrants and Postnational Membership in Europe*. Chicago: University of Chicago Press.

Spectator Company. 1901–55. *Fire Insurance: Laws, Taxes, Fees*. Philadelphia: Spectator Company.

Spectator Company. 1911–24. *Fire Insurance: Laws, Taxes, Fees*. Philadelphia: Spectator Company.

Spectator Company. 1906–40. *Insurance Year Book: Fire and Marine*. Philadelphia: Spectator Company.

Stark, David. 1996. "Recombinant Property in East European Capitalism." *American Journal of Sociology* 101:993–1027.

Starr, Paul M. 1982. *The Social Transformation of American Medicine*. New York: Basic Books.

Stein, Marc. 2000. *City of Sisterly and Brotherly Loves: Lesbian and Gay Philadelphia, 1945–1972*. Chicago: University of Chicago Press.

Steinmo, Sven, Kathleen Thelen, and Frank Longstreth. 1992. *Structuring Politics: Historical Institutionalism in Comparative Analysis*. New York: Cambridge University Press.

Stevens, Mitchell L. 2001. *Kingdom of Children: Culture and Controversy in the Homeschooling Movement*. Princeton: Princeton University Press.

Stinchcombe, Arthur L. 1965. "Social Structure and Organizations." In *Handbook of Organizations*, edited by J. G. March. Chicago: Rand McNally, 142–93.

Stinchcombe, Arthur L. 1968. *Constructing Social Theories*. Chicago: University of Chicago Press.

Stinchcombe, Arthur L. 1998. "Monopolistic Competition as a Mechanism: Corporations, Universities, and Nation-States in Competitive Fields." In *Social Mechanisms: An Analytical Approach to Social Theory*, edited by Peter Hedström and Richard Swedberg. New York: Cambridge University Press, 267–305.

Stinchcombe, Arthur L. 1999. "Ending Revolutions and Building New Governments." *Annual Review of Political Science* 2:49–73.

Stoker, Robert. 1991. *Reluctant Partners: Implementing Federal Policy.* Pittsburgh: University of Pittsburgh Press.

Stone, M. M., B. Bigelow, and W. Crittenden. 1999. "Research on Strategic Management in Nonprofit Organizations – Synthesis, Analysis and Future Directions." *Administration and Society* 31:378–423.

Strang, David. 1990. "From Dependency to Sovereignty: An Event History Analysis of Decolonization, 1870–1987." *American Sociological Review* 55:846–60.

Strang, David. 2003. "The Diffusion of TQM Within a Global Bank." In *Geography and Strategy – Advances in Strategic Management*, vol. 20, edited by J. A. C. Baum and O. Sorenson. Stamford, CT: JAI Press, 275–97.

Strang, David, and Ellen M. Bradburn. 2001. "Theorizing Legitimacy or Legitimating Theory? Neoliberal Discourse and HMO Policy, 1970–1989." In *The Rise of Neoliberalism and Institutional Analysis*, edited by John L. Campbell and Ove K. Pedersen. Princeton: Princeton University Press, 129–58.

Strang, David, and Patricia Mei Yin Chang. 1993. "The International Labor Organization and the Welfare State: Institutional Effects on National Welfare Spending, 1960–80." *International Organization* 47(2):235–62.

Strang, David, and Michael W. Macy. 2001. "In Search of Excellence: Fads, Success Stories, and Adaptive Emulation." *American Journal of Sociology* 107:147–82.

Strang, David, and John W. Meyer. 1993. "Institutional Conditions for Diffusion." *Theory and Society* 22:487–511.

Strang, David, and John W. Meyer. 1994. "Institutional Conditions for Diffusion." In *Institutional Environments and Organizations*, edited by W. Richard Scott and John Meyer. Thousand Oaks, CA: Sage, 100–12.

Strang, David, and Sarah A. Soule. 1998. "Diffusion in Organizations and Social Movements: From Hybrid Corn to Poison Pills." *Annual Review of Sociology* 24:265–90.

Strang, David, and Nancy Brandon Tuma. 1993. "Spatial and Temporal Heterogeneity in Diffusion." *American Journal of Sociology* 99:614–39.

Streeck, Wolfgang. 1997. "Beneficial Constraints: On the Economic Limits of Rational Voluntarism." In *Contemporary Capitalism: The Embeddedness of Institutions*, edited by J. Rogers Hollingsworth and Robert Boyer. New York: Cambridge University Press, 197–219.

Streeck, Wolfgang, and Philippe C. Schmitter. 1985. "Community, Market, State – and Associations? The Prospective Contribution of Interest Governance to Social Order." In *Private Interest Government: Beyond Market and State*, edited by Wolfgang Streeck and Philippe C. Schmitter. Beverly Hills: Sage, 1–29.

Stryker, Robin. 1994. "Rules, Resources, and Legitimacy Processes: Some Implications for Social Conflict, Order, and Change." *American Journal of Sociology* 99:847–910.

References

Stryker, Robin. 2000. "Legitimacy Processes as Institutional Politics: Implications for Theory and Research in the Sociology of Organizations." In *Research in the Sociology of Organizations*, vol. 17, edited by S. Bacharach and E. Lawler. Greenwich, CT: JAI Press, 179–223.

Stryker, Susan, and Jim Van Buskirk. 1996. *Gay by the Bay: A History of Queer Culture in the San Francisco Bay Area*. San Francisco: Chronicle Books.

Subramanian, G. 2001. "The Influence of Antitakeover Statutes on Incorporation Choice: Evidence on the 'Race' Debate and Antitakeover Overreaching." Harvard Business School Working Paper, Harvard University, Cambridge.

Suchman, Mark C. 1995. "Managing Legitimacy: Strategic and Institutional Approaches." *Academy of Management Review* 20:571–610.

Suchman, Mark C. 1997. "On Beyond Interest: Rational, Normative and Cognitive Perspectives in the Social Scientific Study of Law." *Wisconsin Law Review* 3:475–7.

Suchman, Mark C. Forthcoming. "Constructed Ecologies: Reproduction and Structuration in Emerging Organizational Communities." In *How Institutions Change*, edited by Walter W. Powell, and Daniel L. Jones. Chicago: University of Chicago Press.

Sutton, John R., and Frank Dobbin. 1996. "The Two Faces of Governance: Responses to Legal Uncertainty in US Firms, 1955–1985." *American Sociological Review* 61:794–811.

Sutton, John R., Frank Dobbin, John W. Meyer, and W. Richard Scott. 1994. "The Legalization of the Workplace." *American Journal of Sociology* 99:944–71.

Swaminathan, Anand, and James B. Wade. 2001. "Social Movement Theory and the Evolution of New Organizational Forms." In *The Entrepreneurship Dynamic in Industry Evolution*, edited by C. B. Schoonhoven and E. Romanelli. Stanford: Stanford University Press, 286–313.

Swank, Duane, and Cathie Jo Martin. 2001. "Employers and the Welfare State: The Political Economic Organization of Firms and Social Policy in Contemporary Capitalist Democracies." *Comparative Politics* 34(8):889–923.

Swedberg, Richard. 1994. "Markets as Social Structures." In *Handbook of Economic Sociology*, edited by N. J. Smelser and Richard Swedberg. Princeton: Princeton University Press, 255–82.

Swedberg, Richard, ed. 2000. *Entrepreneurship: The Social Science View*. New York: Oxford University Press.

Swidler, Ann. 1986. "Culture in Action: Symbols and Strategies." *American Sociological Review* 51:273–86.

Swidler, Ann. 2001. *Talk of Love: How Culture Matters*. Chicago: University of Chicago Press.

Tarrow, Sidney. 1994. *Power in Movement: Social Movements, Collective Action and Politics*. New York: Cambridge University Press.

Tarrow, Sidney. 1996. "States and Opportunities: The Political Structuring of Social Movements." In *Comparative Perspectives on Social Movements*, edited by Doug McAdam, John D. McCarthy, and Mayer N. Zald. New York: Cambridge University Press, 41–61.

Tarrow, Sidney. 1998. *Power in Movement: Social Movements and Contentious Politics*, 2nd ed. Cambridge: Cambridge University Press.

Tarrow, Sidney. 2001a. "Transnational Politics: Contention and Institutions in International Politics." *Annual Review of Political Science* 4:1–20.

Tarrow, Sidney. 2001b. "Rooted Cosmopolitans: Transnational Activists in a World of States." Working Paper 2001–3, Cornell University Workshop on Transnational Contention, Ithaca, NY.

Taylor, Verta. 1989. "Social Movement Continuity: The Women's Movement in Abeyance." *American Sociological Review* 54:761–75.

Taylor, Verta. 2003. "Plus ça change, plus c'est la même chose." *Mobilization* 8:122–6.

Taylor, Verta, and Nancy E. Whittier. 1992. "Collective Identity in Social Movement Communities: Lesbian Feminist Mobilization." In *Frontiers in Social Movement Theory*, edited by Aldon Morris and Carol McClurg Mueller. New Haven: Yale University Press, 104–29.

Teal, Donn. 1995. *The Gay Militants: How Gay Liberation Began in America, 1969–1971*. New York: St. Martin's Press.

Thelen, Kathleen. 1999. "Historical Institutionalism in Comparative Politics." *Annual Review of Political Science* 2:369–404.

Thelen, Kathleen. 2000a. "Timing and Temporality in the Analysis of Institutional Evolution and Change." *Studies in American Political Development* 14 (Spring): 101–8.

Thelen, Kathleen. 2000b. "How Institutions Evolve: Insights from Comparative-Historical Analysis." Unpublished manuscript, Department of Political Science, Northwestern University.

Thom, Mary. 2000. "Promises to Keep: Beijing and Beyond." *Ford Foundation Report* 31:30–3.

Thompson, B. W. 2001. *A Promise and a Way of Life: White Antiracist Activism*. Minneapolis: University of Minnesota Press.

Thompson, Frank J. 1981. *Health Policy and the Bureaucracy*. Cambridge: MIT Press.

Thompson, James D. 1967. *Organizations in Action*. New York: McGraw Hill.

Thornton, Patricia D. 1999. "The Sociology of Entrepreneurship." *Annual Review of Sociology* 25:19–46.

Thornton, Patricia H., and William Ocasio. 1999. "Institutional Logics and the Historical Contingency of Power in Organizations: Executive Succession in the Higher Education Publishing Industry, 1958–1990." *American Journal of Sociology* 105:801–43.

Tilly, Charles. 1978. *From Mobilization to Revolution*. Reading, MA: Addison-Wesley.

Tilly, Charles. 1984. "Social Movements and National Politics." In *Statemaking and Social Movements: Essays in History and Theory*, edited by C. Bright and S. Harding. Ann Arbor: University of Michigan Press, 297–317.

Tilly, Charles. 1993. *European Revolutions, 1492–1992*. Oxford: Blackwell.

Tilly, Charles. 1998. *Durable Inequalities*. Berkeley: University of California Press.

Tilly, Charles, and James Rule. 1965. *Measuring Political Upheaval*. Princeton: Center for International Studies, Princeton University.

Tilly, Charles, Louise Tilly, and Richard Tilly. 1975. *The Rebellious Century, 1830–1930*. Cambridge: Harvard University Press.

References

Tolbert, Pamela, and Lynne G. Zucker. 1983. "Institutional Sources of Change in the Formal Structure of Organizations: The Diffusion of Civil Service Reform, 1880–1935." *Administrative Science Quarterly* 28:22–39.

Tolbert, Pamela, and Lynne G. Zucker. 1996. "The Institutionalization of Institutional Theory." In *Handbook of Organization Studies*, edited by S. Clegg, C. Hardy, and W. Nord. Thousand Oaks, CA: Sage, 175–90.

Tontz, Robert. 1964. "Membership of General Farmers' Organizations, United States, 1874–1960." *Agricultural History* 38(2):143–56.

Tuma, Nancy Brandon, and Michael T. Hannan. 1984. *Social Dynamics: Models and Methods*. Orlando: Academic Press.

Tushman, Michael L., and Elaine Romanelli. 1985. "Organizational Evolution: A Metamorphisis Model of Convergence and Reorientation." In *Research in Organizational Behavior*, edited by B. Staw and L.L. Cummings. Greenwich, CT: JAI Press, 171–222.

Udell, Gerald G. 1972. "The Franchise Agreement." *The Cornell Hotel and Resturant Administration Quarterly* 13:12–21.

Ullman, Lloyd. 1955. *The Rise of the National Trade Union: The Development and Significance of Its Structure, Governing Institutions, and Economic Policies*. Cambridge: Harvard University Press.

UNDP. 1999. *Human Development Report*. New York: Oxford University Press.

Union of International Associations. Annual. *Yearbook of International Organizations*. Brussels: Union of International Associations.

United States Bureau of the Census. 1902. *Twelfth Census of the United States: 1900*. Washington, DC: Government Printing Office.

United States Bureau of the Census. 1913. *Thirteenth Census of the United States: 1910*. Washington, DC: Government Printing Office.

United States Bureau of the Census. 1918. *Financial Statistics of States 1917*. Washington, DC: Government Printing Office.

United States Bureau of the Census. 1922. *Statistical Abstract of the United States: 1921*. Washington, DC: Government Printing Office.

United States Bureau of the Census. 1923. *Fourteenth Census of the United States: 1920*. Washington, DC: Government Printing Office.

United States Bureau of the Census. 1930. *Statistical Abstract of the United States: 1930*. Washington, DC: Government Printing Office.

United States Bureau of the Census. 1933. *Fifteenth Census of the United States: 1930*. Washington, DC: Government Printing Office.

United States Bureau of the Census. 1939. *Statistical Abstract of the United States: 1938*. Washington, DC: Government Printing Office.

United States Bureau of the Census. 1943. *Sixteenth Census of the United States: 1940*. Washington, DC: Government Printing Office.

United States Department of Commerce. 2001. *U.S. Industry and Trade Outlook*. Washington, DC: Government Printing office.

United States Senate. 1961. *The Insurance Industry Rates, Rating Organizations and State Rate Regulation*. Congressional Report 831. Washington, DC: Government Printing Office.

Useem, Michael. 1984. *The Inner Circle: Large Corporations and the Rise of Business Political Activity in the U.S. and U.K.* New York: Oxford University Press.

Useem, Michael. 1996. *Investor Capitalism.* New York: Basic Books.

Uzzi, Brian. 1996. "The Sources and Consequences of Embeddedness for the Economic Performance of Organizations: The Network Effect." *American Sociological Review* 61:674–98.

Vaid, Urvashi. 1995. *Virtual Equality: The Mainstreaming of Gay and Lesbian Liberation.* New York: Anchor Books.

Valelly, Richard. 1989. *Radicalism in the States.* Chicago: University of Chicago Press.

Van de Ven, Andrew H., and T. Hargrave. 2004. "Social, Technical and Institutional Change: A Literature Review and Synthesis." In *Handbook of Organizational Change and Innovation,* edited by Andrew Van de Ven and S. Poole. New York: Oxford University Press.

Van de Ven, Andrew H., Douglas E. Polley, Raghu Garud, and Sankaran Venkataraman. 1999. *The Innovation Journey.* New York: Oxford University Press.

Vector. 1971. Untitled article, 4.

Verba, Sidney, Kay Lehman Schlozman, and Henry E. Brady. 1995. *Voice and Equality: Civic Voluntarism in American Politics.* Cambridge: Harvard University Press.

Vogel, Steven K. 1996. *Freer Markets, More Rules: Regulatory Reform in Advanced Countries.* Ithaca, NY: Cornell University Press.

Voss, Kim. 1993. *The Making of American Exceptionalism: The Knights of Labor and Class Formation in the Nineteenth Century.* Ithaca, NY: Cornell University Press.

Voss, Kim. 1996. "The Collapse of a Social Movement: The Interplay of Mobilizing Structures, Framing and Political Opportunities in the Knights of Labor." In *Comparative Perspectives on Social Movements,* edited by Doug McAdam, John D. McCarthy, and Mayer N. Zald. Cambridge: Cambridge University Press, 227–58.

Wade, Wyn Craig. 1998. *The Fiery Cross: The Ku Klux Klan in America.* New York: Oxford University Press.

Walker, Jack L. 1969. "The Diffusion of Innovations Among the American States." *American Political Science Review* 63:880–99.

Walker, Jack L. 1983. "The Origins and Maintenance of Interest Groups in America." *American Political Science Review* 77:390–406.

Walker, Jack L. 1991. *Mobilizing Interest Groups in America: Patrons, Professions and Social Movements.* Ann Arbor: University of Michigan Press.

Wallach, Lori, and Michelle Sforza. 1999. *Whose Trade Organization? Corporate Globalization and the Erosion of Democracy.* Washington, DC: Public Citizen.

Wallis, Roy. 1977. *The Total Road to Freedom: A Sociological Analysis of Scientology.* New York: Columbia University Press.

Walsh, James P., and J. K. Seward. 1990. "On the Efficiency of Internal and External Corporate Control Mechanisms." *Academy of Management Review* 15:421–58.

Walton, John, and David Seddon. 1994. *Free Markets and Food Riots: The Politics of Global Adjustment.* Cambridge, MA: Blackwell.

References

Wandel, William Hamlin. 1935. "The Control of Competition in Fire Insurance." Lancaster, PA: Art Printing Company.

Warkentin, Craig. 2001. *Reshaping World Politics: NGOs, the Internet, and Global Civil Society*. New York: Rowman and Littlefield.

Warren, Mark R. 2001. *Dry Bones Rattling: Community Building to Revitalize American Democracy*. Princeton: Princeton University Press.

Warren, Mark R., and Richard L. Wood. 2001. *Faith-Based Organizing: The State of the Field*. Jericho, NY: Interfaith Funders.

Wasby, Stephen L. 1970. *The Impact of the United States Supreme Court: Some Perspectives*. Homewood, IL: Dorsey Press.

Wayne, D. L. 1990. "Takeovers Face New Obstacles." *New York Times*, April 19:D1.

Weber, Max. 1968 [1924]. *Economy and Society: An Interpretive Sociology*, Guenther Roth and Claus Wittich, eds. New York: Bedminister Press.

Weed, Frank J. 1991. "Organizational Mortality in the Anti-Drunk Driving Movement: Failure Among Local MADD Chapters." *Social Forces* 69:851–68.

Weir, Margaret, and Theda Skocpol. 1985. "State Structures and the Possibilities for 'Keynesian' Responses to the Great Depression in Sweden, Britain and the United States." In *Bringing the State Back In*, edited by Peter Evans, Dietrich Rueschemeyer, and Theda Skocpol. Cambridge: Cambridge University Press, 106–68.

Weiss, Linda. 1988. *Creating Capitalism: The State and Small Business Since 1945*. New York: Blackwell.

Westphal, James D., Ranjay Gulati, and Steven M. Shortell. 1997. "Customization or Conformity? An Institutional and Network Perspective on the Content and Consequences of TQM Adoption." *Administrative Science Quarterly* 42:366–94.

White, William D. 1982. "The American Hospital Industry Since 1900: A Short History." In *Advances in Health Economics and Health Services Research*, vol. 3, edited by Richrd M. Scheffler. Greenwich, CT: JAI Press, 143–70.

Whittier, Nancy. 1995. "Turning It Over: Personnel Change in the Columbus, Ohio, Women's Movement, 1969–1984." In *Feminist Organizations: Harvest of the New Women's Movement*, edited by M. F. Ferree and P. Y. Martin. Philadelphia: Temple University Press.

Wholey, Douglas R., and Susan M. Sanchez. 1991. "The Effects of Regulatory Tools on Organizational Populations." *Academy of Management Review* 16:743–67.

Wilde, Melissa J. 2004 "How Culture Mattered at Vatican II: Collegiality Trumps Authority in the Council's Social Movement Organizations." *American Sociological Review* 69:576–602.

Willetts, Peter. 1996. *The Conscience of the World: The Influence of NGOs in the United Nations System*. London: C. Hurst.

Willetts, Peter. 1999. "The Rules of the Game: The United Nations and Civil Society." In *Whose World Is It Anyway? Civil Society, the United Nations, and the Multilateral Future*, edited by J. W. Foster and A. Anand. Ottawa: United Nations Association of Canada, 274–83.

Williams, D. L. 1999. "Why Do Entrepreneurs Become Franchises? An Empirical Analysis of Organizational Choice." *Journal of Business Venturing* 14:103.

Williams, Walter, and Richard F. Elmore, eds. 1976. *Social Program Implementation*. New York: Academic Press.

Williamson, Oliver E. 1985. *The Economic Institutions of Capitalism*. New York: Free Press.

Williamson, Oliver E. 1994. "Transaction Cost Economics and Organization Theory." In *Handbook of Economic Sociology*, edited by Neil J. Smelser and Richard Swedberg: Princeton: Princeton University Press, 77–107.

Wilson, William J. 1973. *Power, Racism, and Privilege*. New York: Free Press.

Wirth, David. 1998. "Partnership Advocacy in World Bank Environmental Reform." In *The Struggle for Accountability: The World Bank, NGOs, and Grassroots Movements*, edited by J. A. Fox and L. D. Brown. Cambridge: MIT Press, 51–79.

Wisconsin State Federation of Labor. 1913. *Report of the Wisconsin Legislative Fire Insurance Investigating Committee of the Senate and Assembly*. Madison: Democrat Printing Co.

Wolfson, Mark. 2001. *The Fight Against Big Tobacco: The Movement, the State, and the Public's Health*. New York: Aldine de Gruyter.

Wolters, Raymond. 1970. *Negroes and the Great Depression*. Westport, CT: Greenwood Press.

Woods, J. D. 1994. *Corporate Closets: The Professional Lives of Gay Men in America*. New York: Free Press.

Wu, Lawrence L. 1990. "Simple Graphical Goodness-of-Fit Tests for Hazard Rate Models." In *Event History Analysis in Life Course Research*, edited by K. U. Mayer and N. B. Tuma. Madison: University of Wisconsin Press, 184–99.

Yale Law Journal. 1954. "The American Medical Association: Power, Purpose, and Politics in Organized Medicine." *Yale Law Journal* 63:938–1022.

Yamaguchi, Kazuo. 1991. *Event History Analysis*. Newbury Park, CA: Sage.

Young, Allen. 1992 [1972]. "Out of the Closets, Into the Streets." In *Out of the Closets: Voices of Gay Liberation*, edited by Karla Jay and Allen Young. New York: New York University Press, 6–30.

Young, Brigitte. 1991. "The Dairy Industry: From Yeomanry to the Institutionalization of Multilateral Governance." In *Governance of the American Economy*, edited by John L. Campbell, J. Rogers Hollingsworth, and Leon N. Lindberg. New York: Cambridge University Press, 236–58.

Young, Dennis R. 1989. "Local Autonomy in a Franchise Age: Structural Change in National Voluntary Associations." *Nonprofit and Voluntary Sector Quarterly* 18:101–17.

Young, Dennis R. 1991. "The Structural Imperatives of International Advocacy Associations." *Human Relations* 44:921–41.

Young, Dennis R., Neil Bania, and Darlyne Bailey. 1994. "The Structure of National Nonprofit Associations: Survey Results." Working paper, Washington, DC: Aspen Institute.

Zald, Mayer N. 1967. "Sociology and Community Organization Practice." In *Organizing for Community Welfare*, edited by Mayer N. Zald. Chicago: Quadrangle Books, 27–61.

References

Zald, Mayer N. 1970a. *Organizational Change: The Political Economy of the YMCA.* Chicago: University of Chicago Press.

Zald, Mayer N. 1970b. "Political Economy: A Framework for Comparative Analysis." In *Power in Organizations*, edited by Mayer N. Zald. Nashville, TN: Vanderbilt University Press, 221–61.

Zald, Mayer N. 1988. "The Future of Social Movements." In *Social Movements in an Organizational Society*, edited by Mayer N. Zald and John D. McCarthy. New Brunswick, NJ: Transaction, 319–36.

Zald, Mayer N. 1996. "Culture, Ideology, and Strategic Framing." In *Comparative Perspectives on Social Movements*, edited by Doug McAdam, John D. McCarthy, and Mayer N. Zald. New York: Cambridge University Press, 261–74.

Zald, Mayer N. 2000. "Ideologically Structured Action: An Enlarged Agenda for Social Movement Research." *Mobilization* 5:1–16.

Zald, Mayer N., and Roberta Ash. 1966. "Social Movement Organizations: Growth, Decay and Change." *Social Forces* 44:327–40.

Zald, Mayer N., and Michael A. Berger. 1978. "Social Movements in Organizations: Coup d'Etat, Insurgency, and Mass Movements." *American Journal of Sociology* 83:823–61.

Zald, Mayer N., and Patricia Denton. 1963. "From Evangelism to General Service: On the Transformation and Character of the YMCA." *Administrative Science Quarterly* 8:214–34.

Zald, Mayer N., and John D. McCarthy. 1980. "Social Movement Industries: Competition and Cooperation Among Social Movement Organizations." *Research in Social Movement, Conflict and Change* 3:1–20.

Zald, Mayer N., and John D. McCarthy. 1987. "Social Movement Industries: Competition and Conflict among SMOs." In *Social Movements in an Organizational Society: Collected Essays*, edited by Mayer N. Zald and John D. McCarthy. New Brunswick, NJ: Transaction Books, 161–80.

Zald, Mayer N., Calvin Morrill, and Hayagreeva Rao. 2002. "How Do Social Movements Penetrate Organizations? Environmental Impact and Organizational Response." Paper presented at the Conference on Organizations and Social Movements, May 10–11, University of Michigan, Ann Arbor.

Zald, Mayer N., and Bert Useem. 1987. "Movement and Countermovement Interaction: Mobilization, Tactics, and State Involvement." In *Social Movements in an Organizational Society*, edited by Mayer N. Zald and John D. McCarthy. New Brunswick, NJ: Transaction Publishers.

Zbaracki Mark J. 1998. "The Rhetoric and Reality of Total Quality Management." *Administrative Science Quarterly* 43:602–36.

Zeitlin, Maurice. 1974. "Corporate Ownership and Control: The Large Corporation and the Capitalist Class." *American Journal of Sociology* 79:1073–119.

Zeitz, Gerald. 1996. "Employee Attitudes Toward Total Quality Management in an EPA Regional Office." *Administration and Society* 28:120–43.

Zhou, Xueguang. 1993. "Occupational Power, State Capacities, and the Diffusion of Licensing in the American States: 1890 to 1950." *American Sociological Review* 58:536–52.

Zucker, Lynne G. 1977. "The Role of Institutionalization in Cultural Persistence." *American Sociological Review* 42:726–43.

Zysman, John. 1994. "How Institutions Create Historically Rooted Trajectories of Growth." *Industrial and Corporate Change* 3:243–83.

Author Index

Author Index

Author Index

Author Index

Subject Index